AF893729

Filip Geerardyn

FREUD'S PROJECT:

ON THE ROOTS OF PSYCHOANALYSIS

Foreword by
Julien Quackelbeen

Translation by
Philippe Vandendaele

REBUS PRESS LTD

First Published
by Rebus Press Ltd.
76 Haverstock Hill
London NW3 2BE

Originally published in Dutch as *Freuds psychologie van het oordeel, Over het begin van de psychoanalyse*, by Idesça, Ghent, 1993. Copyright © 1993 by Idesça

English translation copyright © 1997 by Philippe Vandendaele

All rights reserved. No part of this book may be reprinted or reproduced or utilized in any form or by any electronic, mechanical, or other means, now known or hereafter invented, including photocopying and recording, or in any information storage or retrieval system, without permission in writing from the publishers.

ISBN 1900877090

CONTENTS

FOREWORD

How 'pre-analytical' are some of Freud's texts?

All too often, one embarks upon the examination of a genius' work with the analysis of his first masterpiece, while previous writings are considered as a mere prelude, to be viewed with a hint of nostalgic pity. This was precisely the case with the study of Freud, which usually begins with *The Interpretation of Dreams*, or less abruptly, with the *Studies on Hysteria*. When other (or older) documents were first published, they served primarily as an illustration to his biography — even for analysts. They were later interpreted as a preamble to the actual development of a new discipline. By adopting this approach, one simply confirms one's expectations; one reads with no sense of surprise what one knew all along. At best, the early writings of the great master of Vienna are brought to bear on the later canonical texts and are thus granted little autonomy.

Filip Geerardyn has chosen an interpretation that is at right angles to such reductive readings. He has approached the impact of Bernheim, Charcot and Breuer through a rather novel reading of the early writings. In a similar way, and with an uninhibited sense of wonder, he has read *On Aphasia* and translated the *Project for a Scientific Psychology* into Dutch.

I do not wish to suggest that we are dealing with a reading that is totally at odds with the tradition, with a completely independent or objective interpretation of Freud's work. Certainly not. We recognise that any interpretation of Freud reveals how one classifies psychoanalysis; that any approach ultimately contains an idea of what is intended with the course of treatment; and that for the attentive reader any piece of writing exposes the angle from which the author proceeds. However, recognising this does not alter the fact that one can opt for an approach that is not purely reductive, and that from the outset one can direct one's attention to Freud's irreducible uniqueness, at least when comparing him to the numerous authors who also proceed from the active unconscious as demonstrated by Charcot. Hence, nothing diverts Geerardyn's attention from the element of wonder in Freud. This is especially obvious when he is faced with some of the epistemological hinge points in Freud's early texts.

Prominent philosophers from various schools of thought have tackled problems which emerge from psychoanalysis, such as those pertaining to its scientific nature (falsifiability, e.g. Popper), its objectivity (the constitution of the object of psychoanalysis, e.g. Petitot), its explanation and causality (e.g. Wittgenstein, Habermas), and its interpretation (e.g. Ricoeur). Nevertheless, the majority of the difficulties they emphasised remain as yet unresolved. This is most probably due to the dogmatic and almost systematically negative attitude adopted by some. It is odd to witness how hastily and inaccurately many philosophers and epistemologists seem to operate. This contrasts with the meticulousness which, according to Granger, is specific to any serious epistemological analysis.

Consequently, analysts who are concerned with epistemological questions often come back empty-handed and none the wiser after having consulted these works, which display a rather perfunctory attitude to issues of epistemological foundation. The epistemological analyses developed from within psychoanalysis, and more particularly from within the Lacanian tradition, are all too often tainted with an unacceptable bias: both Freud's early and later texts are frequently 'understood' and 'explained' on the basis of what Lacan had to say about them in his own terminology.

By following the non-reductive disposition mentioned above, the author of the present book arrives at an entirely different and original understanding of the problem of psychoanalytical epistemology.

Going back to the roots of psychoanalysis, he argues in a convincing, critical and detailed manner that the essence of Freud's field of interest already finds expression in his so-called pre-analytical writings. Every work under discussion in this book bears witness to the fact that Freud did not shirk from the necessities he encountered during therapy, which was after all the very object of his theorising. Geerardyn pays especial attention to the psychological and metapsychological models informing this thinking. The core of Freud's interest consists of psychological mechanisms and patterns as well as their accompanying treatment.

The analysis of the *Project* also brings to light the wealth and coherence of Freud's progression in an enthusiastic way. This text is regarded as Freud's most systematic and comprehensive answer to the epistemological problems of 'understanding' and 'explaining', which emanate from the psychological apparatus. Undoubtedly one of the great virtues of the author is to have shown that the pre-analytical/analytical division — also in respect to the *Project* — cannot possibly hold, despite the neurological terminology and the quantitative introduction which has puzzled many a commentator.

Finally, I wish to draw attention to the fact that, by combining epistemology, history and analytical theory, the author succeeds in linking together a number of themes and questions which have traditionally remained disparate. The place that the judgement occupies here is paramount. It is the main thread throughout the entire work which, together with Jerusalem (from the point of view of philosophy) and the *Project* (from a clinical angle), ensures the unity and coherence of the Freudian voyage of discovery.

This is not to say that all questions are answered. It is interesting, for instance, to see how Geerardyn describes Freud's mixing of two classes, that of generality and that of particularity, as he developed his theory of judgement. While neither the epistemological status of this mélange nor the theory's explanatory claims are self-evident, the thesis advocated by the author is often intriguing and inviting.

The epistemological consequences of this for the relation of theory to practice remain as yet obscure. A further merit of the author is to have illustrated how Freud came to be confronted with certain necessities which seemingly presented themselves to others (like Lacan) in exactly the same way.

In this book, Filip Geerardyn opens up a series of avenues, which not only render certain aspects of the existing epistemological analyses untenable, but which are also relevant to the psychoanalytical theory Freud later explicitly formulated. Yet again, one observes that a historical approach offers insights into the status of psychoanalytical theory and to its central categories, thus eliciting the problematic relation of the generality of theory to the particularity of the course of treatment.

Julien Quackelbeen

PREFACE

> "Historia abscondita — Every great man has a retroactive impact: all of history is weighed again for his sake, and a thousand secrets from the past crawl out from under their stones — into his lustre. Surely it cannot be imagined, what is yet to be history. In essence the past is probably still undiscovered! Still so many retroactive forces are needed!"
>
> *Nietzsche*

This book is written with students of clinical psychology in mind. It invites them to turn their attention to the period in which clinical psychology as such came into existence. In other words, it commences by presenting fundamental epistemological questions: what is, what can and what does clinical psychology have to be? I will not draw the answer to these questions from what is at present portrayed in the literature as being clinical psychology. Not only might this yield a dry overview of the proliferation of theories and therapeutical techniques, it would also mislead students into thinking that the choice of a praxis and the concomitant theory merely boils down to a question of preference. Rather, I aim at the commitment to truth presupposed in each and every single one of them, because there is only one psyche whose laws can indeed be discovered.

The method employed in my investigation into the origin of clinical psychology is a historiographical one. I therefore almost automatically come in contact with the itinerary covered by Sigmund Freud, an itinerary that brought him from neurology to psychology. Who will deny that the founder of psychoanalysis was also the first person systematically to explore the psyche from a clinical-psychological vantage point? Who will deny that he was also the first person who attempted to shape the development of clinical psychology? And who will deny that any form of psychotherapy is somehow

tributary to the discovery of the unconscious?
Most importantly, I have also chosen not to proceed too hastily. An epistemological approach, by its very nature, demands an unhurried and meticulous reading of the original texts in which a discipline is rooted. I have thus focused on one of Freud's early manuscripts, namely the *Project for a Scientific Psychology*.

Over the years Freud's *Project* has acquired a particular significance for me. I first became acquainted with this posthumously published manuscript in Lacan's seminar on *The Ethics of Psychoanalysis* in which he alludes to it.[1] I admit to not having understood much of this unusual work at the time. This was probably due to the numerous allusions to frames of reference which were unfamiliar to me. In spite of this, Freud's manuscript somehow intrigued me, as it displays a particularly linear construction and it also contains several passages in which important theoretical insights, appertaining to the later psychoanalytical theory, are either expressed for the first time or are prefigured.
A cartel on the *Project*, composed of Peter Dyck, Olivier Neirynck, Julien Quackelbeen, Gertrudis Van de Vijver and myself, took the initiative to provide an annotated translation of Freud's manuscript.[2] The lengthy deliberations and the careful considerations involved in the translation of a major work into one's own mother tongue was also a lesson in discipline. Our admiration for the manuscript and our conviction that we were face to face with the foundation of psychoanalytical epistemology merely strengthened us in our undertaking.
Gertrudis Van de Vijver is no stranger to the aforementioned discipline. As a philosopher and epistemologist, her publications have always borne witness to her aversion towards any form of dogmatism arising from the theoretical corpus of psychoanalysis.[3] It is in a similar spirit that I have undertaken my own examination.
I have purposely confined my exploration to my own field, i.e. clinical psychology. Unlike the numerous existing analyses of Freud's *Project* — most of which lay stress either on the allusions to it in Freud's later works or on Lacan's reading of it — I started out with an idea put forward by Julien Quackelbeen. In his book, *Zeven avonden met Jacques Lacan*, he suggests a reading of the *Project* commencing with the necessities from which Freud himself started.[4]

I tackle this question at two distinct levels:
In the first part of the book, I examine Freud's clinical itinerary prior to his writing of the *Project* in 1895. In this way, the text, serving as an answer to a clinic of the excessively intense idea, qualifies as a clinical psychological one. Four texts function as points of reference during the course of this itinerary: 1. Charcot's *Clinical Lectures on the Diseases of the Nervous System*; 2. Bernheim's *Suggestive Therapeutics*; 3. Freud and Breuer's *Studies on Hysteria*; 4. Freud's *On Aphasia.*
In the second part of this book, I question the epistemological necessity of Freud's premise in the *Project*, i.e. quantity Q and neurone N. Wilhelm Jerusalem's book on *Die Urteilsfunction* (*The Function of Judgement*) helps me to shed more light on Freud's peculiar epistemological operation. This operation involves subjecting his object of analysis, the psyche, to a judgement, as defined by Jerusalem. I summarise Freud's 'primary judgement' as the condition for the constitution of his scientific object, the unconscious.
I would like to express my gratitude to the second year students of the academic year 1991-1992 who collaborated with me for a part of this book. I also wish to thank both my former and present colleagues at the Department of Psychoanalysis and Clinical Consulting at the University of Ghent. I wish to extend a special credit to Katrien Libbrecht and Ann Van Neygen both of whom advised and assisted me in the process of making this text intelligible and fit to be read.
I am grateful to Gertrudis Van de Vijver for her enriching collaboration.
Finally, I am indebted to Professor Julien Quackelbeen who made this project possible.

Filip Geerardyn

PART I

THE CLINIC OF THE EXCESSIVELY INTENSE IDEA

INTRODUCTION

From the beginning of the *Project*, Freud makes it plain that the idea of conceiving of psychical processes as "quantitatively determined states of specifiable material particles" was a direct result of his clinic.[1] Thus, his psychology for neurologists can be interpreted as an attempt to find an answer to the clinical-psychological problems he was confronted with.[2] Later, in the second part of the *Project*, Freud further examines this clinic. Quoting from a case study, he demonstrates that the status of a symptom is on a par with that of the "excessively intense idea", and that, as such, it is also determined by the psychical mechanism of repression. Such an "excessively intense idea" disappears or is dissolved when the repression of underlying ideas is eliminated by expressing memories associatively intertwined with the symptom.[3]
In the *Project*, Freud thus aims to construct a theory for these elementary empirical observations. In this respect, his construction fully deserves to be classified as 'psychological'. Firstly, it explores the determining influence of the *psychical elements* (ideas) which exert a pathogenic effect after having been shut off from consciousness by the *psychical mechanism* of repression. In addition, Freud sets himself the task of explaining *psychical treatment* or psychotherapy. Finally, the text endeavours to shed more light on normal psychological processes from the vantage point of clinical psychology.[4]
Such a perspective on the *Project*, i.e. as a direct answer to the clinic of the excessively intense idea, raises questions about the factors which led to its creation: for instance, where and when did Freud first experience the need to provide a psychological explanation of clinical empirical phenomena?

From a historical and scientific point of view, this question goes far beyond the strictly psychoanalytical field. It deals with one of the first and most developed attempts at writing a usable psychology which is directly related to the clinic. The origin of psychoanalysis thus coalesces with that of clinical psychology in general.

Answering the aforementioned question forces me to digress from the *Project*, as it faces me with the task of mapping the entire trajectory covered by Freud prior to his writing of this key text. I also set myself the target of gathering evidence enabling me to legitimise statements about the epistemology of the *Project*.[5]

In the first part of my examination, I discuss four discernible themes in Freud's work anterior to his writing of the *Project*. These are as follows: 1. Freud's confrontation with the psychical influencing of patients by Jean-Martin Charcot; 2. the hypnotic suggestion as described and applied by Hippolyte Bernheim; 3. Freud's collaboration with Breuer; 4. Freud's study *On Aphasia*.

These four themes relate to the period from October 1885 (when Freud spent several months in the Salpêtrière)[6] to May 1895 (when the *Studies on Hysteria* were published).[7] On the basis of these themes, I wish to account for the trajectory covered by Freud from the moment he effectively started treating neurotics in his private practice.

This, however, does not mean that I employ a linear and progressive model in order to understand the development of Freud's theory. Mannoni, for one, rightly points out that one must make a distinction between the knowledge Freud acquires from Charcot and what he learns from Breuer.[8]

However, I drew inspiration from an essential and unmistakable characteristic of Freud's work for the formulation of my premise. One observes time and time again that the construction of his theory, his frequent reformulations and the new orientations he adopted in his work, were the result of his referral to the clinic, and the problems that he encountered there. The reading of the *Project* as an answer to the clinic of the excessively intense idea presupposes that similar characteristics can be attributed to Freud's so-called pre-analytical texts. If this can be demonstrated, then one of the reasons for making the pre-analytical/analytical distinction disappears.

The idea of an epistemological breach functions as a second key point, once again dissuading the reader from adopting the perspective of a linear development. Freud's psychology neither ensues logically from scientific frames of reference familiar to him nor from what he could learn from Meynert, Charcot, Bernheim or Breuer about neurological and psychological theory. Rather, his theory results from his adoption of a new epistemological viewpoint. Once Freud had well and truly subscribed to the viewpoint on the operation of a psychical mechanism, it became possible to speak of a logical development of his theory, that is to say, one which sprang logically from the dialectic with the clinic.

From all that is mentioned above, it is understandable why I have focused on what presented itself to Freud as a clinic in the first part of this book. For each of the four themes I have alluded to, I will focus on the analysis of one particular book.

CHAPTER 1

Clinical Lectures on the Diseases of the Nervous System

"I have already formed myself a favourable impression of Paris and I could turn very poetical and compare it to a gigantic, beautifully adorned sphinx which devours all strangers that are unable to unravel its mystery (...)"

Sigmund Freud[1]

"Gentlemen, — It is now nearly twelve years ago that in recommencing within these walls a course of instruction, which had already existed for four years, I ventured to hope that this great asylum of human miseries, where so many leaders of French medicine had achieved distinction, would become one day a properly organised centre for the teaching and investigation of diseases of the nervous system."

Jean-Martin Charcot[2]

Freud was very much put out in early December 1885. He had expected a lot from his stay with Charcot at the Salpêtrière where he was to further develop his neuroanatomical expertise. He felt that the French school had a lot of new things to offer, both in its mode of working and its exploration of new subjects in the field of neuropathology which were not dealt with in Germany or Austria. The conditions in the Parisian laboratories were, however, not equipped to welcome foreign researchers. Hence Freud decided to give up his research in the laboratory and even toyed with the idea of returning to Vienna.[3] The only alternative left open to him was to attend Charcot's lectures and clinical demonstrations. Although Freud's admiration for his master may well have been boundless, he regretted the fact that Charcot did not devote more attention to him than to the other numerous attendants.

In the same week, however, Freud came up with the idea of offering Charcot his services as a translator for the third volume of his *Leçons sur les maladies du système nerveux* (*Clinical Lectures on the Diseases of the Nervous System*). Helped by a lady friend, Freud sent a missive to Charcot in which he stressed that, as far as his French was concerned, he suffered only slightly from "motor aphasia and not from sensory aphasia".[4] Charcot promptly accepted this offer and Freud set to work at full tilt. So much so that the German translation appeared in as early as July 1886, well before the French edition.[5]

The aforementioned volume gives one a better idea than any other source of Charcot's influence on Freud. For not only do the *Lectures* translated by Freud retain Charcot's own peculiar style, but they also contain a number of lectures Freud actually attended during his rather short stay at the Salpêtrière. One can easily trace the different themes which Freud would later describe as those which he was introduced to for the first time that winter: the anatomo-clinical method, hysteria in both sexes, traumatic hysteria and "le grand hypnotisme" (Major hypnotism), etc.

Considering that Freud only stayed four and a half months at the Salpêtrière, one can legitimately suppose that it was precisely his translation of the *Lectures* that enabled him fully to apprehend the sense or direction of Charcot's progression. Freud also emphasises the profound impression the lectures of the master had on him. Although some may well have been dismissive of Charcot's dramatic teaching style, the fact remains that his lectures were extremely well prepared and solidly structured.[6] The lectures collected in the volume translated by Freud give an excellent overview of Charcot's progression in the field of hysteria, which brought him from neurology to psychology. There can be no doubt as to the meaning of this progression. As Freud writes at the end of his article about the comparison of organic and hysterical paralyses: "Charcot was the first to teach us that to explain the hysterical neurosis we must apply to psychology."[7]

Anatomo-clinical method

In Paris, Freud was confronted with an approach to the diseases of the nervous system that differed radically from what he was used to. Between 1882 and 1885, when Freud was under the supervision of Nothnagel and

Meynert, he revealed himself as an expert at making neuroanatomical diagnoses. Basically, he departed from clinically observable symptoms of the syndrome and then put forward a number of hypotheses about the causes of the disorder. These hypotheses were the product of a thorough knowledge of the anatomy of the nervous system. Neuroanatomical knowledge about the structure and functioning of the nervous system had, in turn, largely reaped the fruits of advanced neuropathological research. Autopsies on patients were therefore the ultimate criterion neuroanatomists adhered to for the acquisition of knowledge in their field. However, these methodical approaches soon attained their explanatory potential. In about 1885, the triumph of cerebral localisation had already attained its peak. Neuropathology had not been able to live up to its promise.[8]

From the second half of last century onwards, a new discipline began to emerge. It went beyond the level of anatomy and pushed back the frontiers of neuroanatomy. Indeed, physiology in general and electrophysiology in particular were to become the field in which the functioning and disfunctioning of the nervous system (mental disorders) would have to be studied. This was the orientation explicitly advocated by Meynert. It became known as the 'anatomo-physiological' method as opposed to Charcot's 'anatomo-clinical' method.

Nevertheless, Charcot placed great expectations upon physiology: "In this respect, gentlemen, I must be allowed to declare my firm belief that the wide intervention of the anatomical and physiological sciences in the affairs of medicine is an essential condition to progress; a statement which, by frequent repetition, has verily by this time become almost a platitude."[9]

This, however, did not mean to Charcot that the clinical picture of the different diseases of the nervous system was no longer to occupy a central position in neuropathological knowledge: "But the point that I wish especially to insist on is this; in order that the intervention of these sciences may be legitimate, and really fruitful, it should take place under conditions that should never be forgotten. Allow me to recall to your minds the opinion which that most illustrious physiologist thus expressed: 'Pathology,' he said, 'should not be subordinated to physiology. Quite the reverse. Set up first the medical problem which arises from the observation of a malady, and afterwards seek for a physiological explanation. To act otherwise would be to risk overlooking the patient, and distorting the malady.' These are excellent words, which I have ventured to quote verbatim, because they are absolutely significant. They enable us to clearly understand that the whole domain of pathology appertains strictly to the physiologist who, systematically confined within the precincts of his laboratory, disdains the teaching of the hospital ward."[10]

To Charcot, knowledge about nervous diseases depended on *nosography*, i.e. the precise description of separate syndromes. Consequently, neuroanatomy and neurophysiology acquired the status of auxiliary disciplines supporting nosography: it furnishes to nosography more fixed, more material characters than appertain to the symptoms alone. The distinction between organic and hysterical paralysis offers a good illustration of this position. Unlike any approach based on the mere observation of visible symptoms, anatomy made possible a clearer distinction between both syndromes.[11]

Freud found that the central place assigned to nosography was reflected in the lay-out of the Salpêtrière. In contrast to the disposition in the Viennese "Allgemeine Krankenhaus" where the psychiatric patients were randomly dispersed throughout the clinic, every block in the Salpêtrière corresponded to a particular syndrome. That Charcot's acknowledgement of the autonomy of hysteria can be traced back to this principle is well illustrated by the fact that patients suffering from hysteria were already grouped together, quite some time before any systematic examination of the disease was undertaken. In 1870, quite by chance, Charcot became the head of the ward where so-called 'non-alienated' were housed. This came about because the building where they had been accommodated was in urgent need of restoration. The administration of the Salpêtrière made a virtue of a necessity and separated the 'alienated' from the 'non-alienated'. The latter could be divided into two subgroups each of which displayed a similar symptomatology; 'épilepsie simple' and hysteria. This classification was based on the occurrence of generalised convulsive crises in both neuroses and the absence of any organic lesion of the cortex.[12]

This undoubtedly represented a turning point in Charcot's career. In 1870 he abandoned the field of organic diseases of the nervous system which he was so familiar with. From now on, even in the absence of lesions, patients were subjected to the same anatomo-clinical method: hysteria would at all costs become a disease like any other. It would be allotted its place within science.[13]

Charcot commenced by systematically observing and describing the symptomatology of hysteria, apparently with success. As early as 1874, he dedicated three lectures to the convulsive paroxysmal crises (the most neurological manifestation of hysteria), as well as to its most common syndromes, such as paralysis, anaesthesia and contractions. The construction of the picture of hysteria would gradually be completed on the basis of this symptomatology.[14]

Hysteria

Charcot deserves praise for having made 'hysterical neurosis' a subject worthy of study by positing its clinical unity. In his 1893 obituary, Freud may well have overestimated Charcot's influence, as Jones believes, yet Charcot's progression in the study of hysteria was undoubtedly a source of inspiration for Freud.[15]

In 1882, when the very first Chair of Neurology in the world was created at the Salpêtrière, Charcot had already begun developing a clinical tableau of hysteria.[16] The symptomatology had been recorded and major hysterical attacks ("grande hystérie") no longer held any secrets for Charcot. The most difficult part of the task incumbent on him, however, was still to come. For the hypothesis that hysteria was caused by a functional or dynamic lesion was not enough to provide a solid anatomical (neurological) foundation which would definitively establish hysteria as a legitimate object of research. Charcot hoped to advance his research by employing a method which was new to the field of medicine; namely the experiment.[17] In this way, he systematically compared the hysterical manifestations of known organic diseases of the nervous system.

His empirical attitude is evident from the very way in which he turned this "great asylum of human miseries", in a rather short time, into a "living pathological museum" (i.e. the Salpêtrière).[18] Charcot, who described himself as "un visuel", never failed to make the newest technologies available to the Salpêtrière in an effort to portray hysteria. The pride with which Charcot enumerated his new acquisitions resonated at the inaugural lecture for the Chair of Neurology. "Thus, to the Infirmary is added an Out-patient department, and to this, hospital wards (limited to the reception of diseases of the nervous system). All forms a complete whole, of which the different parts are intimately connected, and which now supplement our different means of teaching and research. We possess a *Pathological Museum*, to which is attached a studio for *moulding* and *photography*; a well-fitted Laboratory of pathological *anatomy* and *physiology*, which is in strange contrast with the narrow, badly-lighted room, that was the only resort where I and my pupils worked, and which we defined by the name of 'laboratory', for nearly fifteen years; an *Ophthalmological room*, necessary complement to a neuropathological laboratory; and the *Lecture Hall*, in which I have the honour to receive you today, and which is provided, as you see, with all the modern apparatus for demonstration. We possess, moreover, a service richly endowed with all the apparatus necessary for the practice of *electro-diagnosis* and *electro-therapy*; and here numerous patients come, three times a week, to receive the treatment appropriate to their condition."[19]

Alongside this battery of the newest devices, two structural changes were also of importance. I already mentioned one, namely Charcot's appointment as head of the new ward. The second structural change had to do with Charcot's effort to create a ward which would meet his own research plans in a way that the "living pathological museum" could not.

In 1870, the Salpêtrière housed about 5,000 patients, the majority of whom were incurable and thus admitted for life. All ages and a wide variety of diseases (especially neurological ones) were represented. This institution was thus an exceptional research centre, since there were several specimens available for each clinical type. This is one of the reasons Freud reported for having chosen the Salpêtrière as the destination of his study tour.[20]

A drawback, however, was that traditionally only the severest cases and incurables were admitted, whereas patients suffering from latent forms of the disease were not accepted. This made research more difficult. However, under Charcot's impetus, a clinic was set up at the gates of the Salpêtrière where consultations were available and medicine was dispensed. "It was possible to remedy them by instituting, at the entrance to the Infirmary buildings, an *out-patient department*, with a dispensary attached. It was hoped that the *chronic* sufferers, who often have a difficulty in obtaining admission to the hospitals, and who even then do not invariably find the means of treatment appropriate to their state, would flock to such an institution in great numbers (...) To make this department perfect and complete, it yet required a *space* ["service"] within the Infirmary where certain of the patients, who come to us from outside, could be temporarily admitted as in-patients. (...) All the obstacles were one by one removed, and now we have wards for the temporary admission of cases. They contain eighty beds — forty for women and forty for men."[21]

I would like to make two observations in this respect.
Firstly, the importance of this 'service' in the establishment of hysteria as an autonomous clinical entity seems obvious from the numerous case studies in the volume translated by Freud. As I will show later, the endorsement of hysteria's autonomy came about by sanctioning the hysterical status of traumatic neurosis. At that time, most cases of traumatic neuroses presented by Charcot in his lectures were *men*, whereas previously men were virtually absent in the Salpêtrière. Men only became objects of study after the foundation of the out-patient department. When speaking of imminent discharges from the institute or when making a prognosis as to their chances of recovery, Charcot is referring to these cases.
Secondly, if my supposition about the special place that this new *ward* occupied in Charcot's heart is correct, it is difficult for me to overestimate the impact Charcot's teaching and demonstrations had on Freud. For it is precisely this kind of neurotic that Freud was to encounter in his private practice from 1886 onwards.

Charcot's original intention of attempting to provide a solid and, if possible, neuroanatomical or neurophysiological basis for this new clinical entity, was probably over-ambitious. Charcot himself recognised this, as the following rather prophetic statement indicates: "From what has been said it will be understood how much importance we ought to accord in our studies to the anatomo-pathological method of research. But you are aware, gentlemen, that there still exists at the present time a great number of morbid states, evidently having their seat in the nervous system, which leave in the dead body no material trace that can be discovered. Epilepsy, hysteria, even most inveterate cases, chorea[22], and many other morbid states which would take us too long to enumerate, come to us like so many sphinx, which deny the most penetrating anatomical investigations. These symptomatic combinations deprived of anatomical substratum, do not present themselves to the mind of the physician with that appearance of solidity, of objectivity, which belong to affections connected with an appreciable organic lesion."[23]
The alternative 'explanation' proposed by Charcot for the construction of these symptoms is known; they were thought to be the result of a 'functional' or 'dynamic' lesion of the nervous system. This explanation, however, added nothing to the term 'neurosis', which was coined by the Scotsman, W. Cullen in 1777.[24] It would be erroneous to proceed under the impression that

Charcot was satisfied with his explanation. His obstinate attempts to visualise and to objectify the 'nervous diseases', and his constant meticulous comparison of the hysterical symptomatology with the analogous phenomenology of diseases which can be explained by the presence of organic lesions, indicate that sooner or later Charcot envisaged submitting a more positive explanation to the panel of physicians. What is more, Freud took leave of Charcot with the well-defined assignment of elucidating the difference between hysteric and organic paralyses on the basis of his observations at the Salpêtrière.[25]

To Charcot, the fact that hysteria did not comply with the laws of anatomo-pathology was not sufficient a reason to exclude it from nosography. One therefore has to accept hysteria as it presents itself, and one should not be misled by the problems it poses. When one examines hysteria closely, one is forced to acknowledge that it follows a certain pattern. This was the most important lesson Charcot claimed to have learned from the observation of hysterical attacks: "Allow me to mention but one example, to recall to your minds the description of an attack of hysteria major ("la grande attaque hystérique"), which is reduced at the present time to a very simple formula. Four periods succeed each other in the complete attack with mechanical regularity — Ist, epileptoid; 2nd, great movements (struggling, purposeless)[26]; 3rd, passionate attitudes (purposive); 4th, terminal delirium. But the attacks may be incomplete, each of the periods may appear alone, or again one or two among them will be found wanting. We understand thus how many varieties can result from these combinations but it will always be easy to those who possess the formula to bring them under one fundamental type."[27] Hysterical crises and other manifestations of this disease are thus governed by well-defined laws. What is more, Charcot was convinced that he had conclusively shown that hysteria was not a modern disease of our civilisation, a symptom of the industrial revolution. Rather, hysteria, with its convulsions and contractions, was as old as humanity itself. For hysterical attacks take place in accordance with universal rules, "in all countries, all times, all races".[28]

The formal description of the successive stages of an hysterical attack already encapsulated the sense of the progression that Charcot was going to cover, a progression which would lead him from neurology (epilepsy) to psychology (delirium). I reread Charcot's *Lectures* keeping this 'sense' in mind, and sought to locate a psyche, a psychology.[29] This psyche must be elicited from *within* the rigid frame of this mechanistic sequence. For the patient, this entails locating that point where the crisis appears to be linked to a psychical element i.e., a *content*, an *idea* or a *representation*. The priority of the clinical entity posited by Charcot is interpreted as the condition for the emergence of the psyche.

Charcot was quick to recognise the eminently affective nature of the hysterical crisis. What this means is that it is connected with a personal tragedy that is enacted and that expresses, externalises and exposes itself. Although Charcot did not have a theory at his disposal which would enable him to classify hysteria, its emotional content was nonetheless obvious to him. Although the 'content' is lacking in the first stage (the epileptoid), a note was sometimes taken in the Salpêtrière on the link between the last stage and the life history of the patient. This happened in the presentation of the famous case Ler. This forty-eight year old woman, who had been hospitalised for over twenty years, often became prey to unusual convulsions reminiscent of the description of a possessed person. This "wild staring" and "unchained fury" shouted, screamed, and cursed imaginary people. Charcot pointed out that her delirium went back to events which had seemingly triggered the first crises. As a child she was frightened by a dog, at 16 years of age she was rooted to the spot with fear at the sight of the body of a woman who had been killed. To make matters worse, soon after that, a robber frightened her in a forest.[30]

Sexuality

There is no psyche without Eros. However, as far as Eros is concerned, history has always portrayed Charcot as the one who dispelled the obscure link between hysteria and sexuality from his theory. Despite this, Trillat observes that it was Charcot who originally (1870-1872) drew a link between certain forms of hysteria and the ovaries.[31] Amongst other things, he was intrigued by the ovarian over-sensitivity displayed by hysterical patients. It was thus tempting to make a connection between this zone and hysterical manifestations. In this respect, Charcot made a link with the past and deplored the fact that this unmistakable evidence had been lost from view. He criticised Briquet, who held the view that the ovarian pains were exclusively muscular in origin and consequently had nothing to do with the ovaries. Charcot disproved this in his demonstrations and suspected that Briquet by-passed this explanation out of prudishness. Charcot wrote the following about Briquet's essay: "This is an excellent book ... but it does perhaps display one weakness: any subject relative to the ovarium and the uterus is treated with a disposition that is highly singular for a physician, i.e. with a kind of prudishness or inexplicable sentimentalism. With respect to these questions, only one concern seems to preoccupy the author. For instance, he asserts that by wishing to link everything to the uterus, one turns hysteria into a salacious affection, a shameful illness which tends to make the hysterical patient the subject of loathing and pity. In truth, gentlemen, the problem does not lie here. For my part, I do not believe that lasciviousness always plays a role in hysteria. As a matter of fact, I believe the contrary to be true. Nor am I an exclusive adherent of the old doctrine that solely looks for the cause of hysteria in the genitals, even though I do deem that it has been sufficiently demonstrated that the ovarium does play a major part in a particular form of hysteria. I would thus like to call this form ovarian hysteria."[32]

The notion that Charcot totally dissociated hysteria from the uterus and ovaries in order to conceive of it as a disease of the nervous system is a simplification[33], firstly, because he never succeeded in rooting hysteria in the field of neurology and secondly, because Charcot never really glossed over the importance of sexuality. In his nosography, for instance, the ovaries, as well as other parts of the body, were granted the status of hysterogenic zones, i.e. a part of the body pre-eminently prone to bring on hysterical attacks when touched. Rumour also has it that during social gatherings at Charcot's house it was often said that some nervous disorders always have something to do with the genitals ("la chose génitale"), but that was better kept quiet.[34] It seems to me fairly unlikely, in the light of the above quotation, that Charcot, who was confronted with hysterical patients on a daily basis, would have scotomized the importance of sexuality in both the clinical picture and the aetiology of hysteria. Such a reasoning would surely make of Charcot a rather blind 'visuel'. The theory, propounded, amongst others, by Roudinesco, that Charcot turned a blind eye out of a theoretical exigency, does not sound at all convincing.[35] The hypothesis of the functional lesion in concurrence with the import of the hereditary factor can hardly be called a theory.[36] It strikes me that it was essentially theoretical incapacity which was responsible for the exiguous attention Charcot devoted to sexuality.[37]

Male and traumatic hysteria

The alleged clinical entity of hysteria, as conceptualised by Charcot in his nosography, was not however granted a long life. History revealed that hysterical manifestations originated from suggestion and identification. The picture of the "grande hystérie" (major hysteria) was composed from a minimal number of hysterical patients who mimicked each other's symptoms and the phenomenology that left a mark on their body.
One notion from Charcot's work certainly outlived him, namely traumatic neurosis.[38] I have already pointed out that, thanks to the creation of a ward for temporary admissions (the out-patient department), Charcot was offered the opportunity to study less serious "diseases of the nervous system" and that he also could direct his attention to *male cases of hysteria* which proved instrumental in establishing his claim on hysteria.

Let us take a closer look at these male cases of hysteria: "And here is another point worthy of mention; those adult men who are a prey to the hysterical neurosis do not always present, far from it, feminine characteristics; they are, at least in a great number of cases, robust men presenting all the attributes of the male sex; they may be soldiers or artisans, married and the fathers of families; men in whom one would be very astonished, unless forewarned, to meet with an affection considered by most as an exclusively feminine disease."[39]
It is beyond doubt that both the "grande hystérie" and the "forme fruste"[40] can occur in men. These "robust men" also displayed the known hysterical stigmata, such as sensory and sensitive hemi-anaesthesia[41], hysterogenic zones (albeit with a predilection for some of them such as the head and the side of the stomach) and hysterical paralysis. Only "the ovarian phenomenon (...) is usually wanting in the male; but in them, in some cases at any rate, pressure on the testicles, when it is retained in the canal, provokes or arrests an attack."[42]
The most important new element Charcot could glean from male hysterical patients was the understanding that the disease was apparently caused by a trauma. In the account of every single patient an etiological moment could be discerned, usually an accident, which was not necessarily serious. To cite an example:

"The patient is a man 34 years old, a blacksmith, father of four children, robust enough, and without any sign of effeminacy. I may tell you at once that we have not been able to find in him any antecedent taint of a neuropathic order, neither hereditary nor personal; no moral emotion can be ascertained as the actual cause of the complaint, and, indeed, no other cause of any sort excepting the burn. On June 26th last a boar of iron heated to white touched his forearm and left hand. The burn, though slight, took six weeks to heal, and at the present time there remains a violet-red patch of 3 or 4 centimetres [1 1/4 inches] broad, and 10 or 12 long [4 to 5 inches], occupying the lower part of the fore arm and the back of the hand. The accident does not seem to have caused much emotion, and the contracture does not seem to have followed the injury immediately; strange to say it became developed gradually. In the history of hysterical contracture due to a traumatic cause this is an exceptional circumstance. A few days after the accident, says he, his arm felt heavy, it became difficult to bend his fingers, feeling as though they were benumbed; but as for the contracture, it came on without the intervention of a fresh cause seven weeks later."[43]

How could Charcot possibly diagnose such cases of traumatic diseases of the nervous system as being hysteria? Quite simply. He observed that the symptomatology corresponded to one he could artificially induce in his hysterical patients by means of hypnosis. Take for instance, the case of the patient Le Log., who suffered from a traumatic paralysis of the lower limbs. Following the example of Trillat, whose work I consulted on numerous occasions in order to have a better idea of Charcot's influence of Freud, I will now also examine this particular case at length.[44]

The case 'Le Log.'

"The man named Le Log. was born in a little village of Brittany, and he is now twenty-nine years of age. One of his first cousins was subject to epilepsy (a falling down, calling out, biting of tongue, etc). One of his sisters, who finally died of typhoid fever, had had "nervous attacks". The patient has also suffered from typhoid fever, and after this he remained *aphonic* for several months.

He came to Paris when twelve years old, knowing but little French; at the present time he is able to read, but he can only write with difficulty. People who know him have given him a very good character. He has always been amiable, and obliging. He is a steady lad. He is not gloomy, nor is he alcoholic. By occupation he was formerly a cook's assistant; but lately, for want of better work, he went into the service of a florist in the market. His work consisted in selling in the market during the morning, and in the afternoon, every second or third day, he went to a horticulturist at St. Cloud to fetch plants. These he brought back on a little hand-barrow, which he drew, while his master's son, young Conr., helped by pushing behind.

It was on returning from St. Cloud in this fashion on October 21st, 1885, about 6 o'clock in the evening, that the accident happened which was the cause of all his troubles. On this evening, when it was nearly very dark, Le Log. was dragging his barrow along the road beside the Seine.

He had arrived at the top of the Pont des Invalides, when all of a sudden, a heavily laden laundryman's van, driven by some drunken men at railway speed, charged into him. The wheel of the hand-barrow was struck, and Le Log. was violently thrown on to the footpath, from which he was picked up absolutely unconscious. The horse of the laundryman's van *did not pass over him*. There was no apparent wound, nor was any blood discovered about his person. Le Log. was placed upon his barrow and was taken in the first place to a chemist's shop, where he remained for about twenty minutes, and was then carried, still unconscious, to the Beaujon Hospital.
The preceding details were given by young Conr., and confirmed, moreover, by a man named L., a post-office official at the Palais de l'Industrie, who was present during the collision. The account which Le Log. himself gives of the affair when he is questioned is a very different one. *He has made out a long history of the accident* in which he firmly believes, and of which the circumstances appear to him from time to time *in his dreams*. The laundryman's van came charging along with much noise; the horse fell right upon him, and struck him in the breast with the head. He fell down, struck his head violently on the ground, and finally *the heavy van passed completely over his body, across the upper part of the thighs*. Generally, when his dream arrives at this point, the patient wakes up suddenly screaming. At the Hôtel Dieu, and here also at the Salpêtrière, he has often been heard to cry out 'stop don't drive on, the horse is going to crush me.'
As a matter of fact, the patient has completely lost all recollection of what passed at the moment of the accident. It is very probable that he was affected at the time by an *intense cerebral commotion*, followed by a form of *amnesia*."[45]

Immediately after the accident, Le Log. felt as though his lower limbs were dead. In addition, he had large bruises on the hip, the right groin, and the lower abdomen. Although plagued by headaches, he could go home after a few hours, where he remained confined to bed for a week. One day, when he left his home to visit a friend, he was seized by a severe attack and lost consciousness. He was then admitted to the Hôtel Dieu for two months. During his first week, Le Log. was in a state of coma. After waking from this state he displayed all the symptoms of hysterical mutism.[46] The motor weakness of the lower limbs, imperfect at first, gradually became complete. After his admission to the Salpêtrière, the following symptoms (as well as the usual attacks) were discernible: a generalised state of sadness, tiresome dreams, dizziness in his ears, the vision of flames before his eyes, facial contortions, etc. But Charcot's attention was principally drawn to the patient's lower limbs, and in particular to their sensitivity:

"Hence, as far as concerns the paralysis, the case of Le Log. does not differ clinically in any essential particular from the case of hypnotisable hemi-anaesthetic hysterical subjects whose lower limbs have been paralysed by means of suggestion."[47]

The clinical similarity incited Charcot to draw a parallel between paralysis resulting from suggestion of the hysterical patient under hypnosis and the form of paralysis observed in the present case. How could this be explained? Charcot postulated that an identical phenomenology logically warranted the supposition that a similar mechanism underlay both forms of paralysis.

"Now, when in a somnambulic subject one *suggests* by speech *the idea* of the motor weakness of a limb, and one sees this *idea* effectively realised under the special form of paralysis which has just been described, one can hardly in the present state of science refuse to admit that it depends upon a *dynamic lesion* affecting the motor and sensory zones of the grey cortex of the brain which in a normal state presides over the functions of that limb. Consequently we are in this way led to propose as a very plausible hypothesis that *in Le Log. the production of the paralysis is due to an analogous process.*
Without doubt, the objections may be raised to this explanation that in the first place the patient had not been hypnotised, and in the second the conditions of a suggestion cannot be found in this case, — at first sight at any rate. But in reference to these two points the following circumstances may be mentioned.
It is certain that the mental state which is to be found in the somnambulic period of hypnotism does not constitute the only condition where, in consequence of the obnubilation of consciousness, of the facile dissociation of the ego, it may be possible to awake in the mind an idea or a group of associated ideas which, freed from all control, all opposition, may become developed into an autonomous condition which acquires by that very fact an enormous force, and a power of realisation which is almost without limits."[48]

Charcot stressed that it was not uncommon to observe identical paralyses in the case of intoxication (such as hash and alcohol) or in the event of a *psychical commotion.* Charcot traced all the circumstances in the history of Le Log. which were necessary to create the adequate mental state for the objective realisation of suggestions:

"It will be remembered that, thrown violently on to the pavement, Le Log. lost consciousness immediately; that he remained comatose for several hours, and afterwards he was plunged, for the two or three days which followed the accident, into a state of veritable intellectual torpor; in a word, he presented at that time the condition of physical obnubilation suitable for the efficacy of suggestions."[49]

Where is the actual suggestion to be found in Le Log.'s account? According to Charcot, not all suggestions are brought into play by means of *speech.* There are, for instance, suggestions which are the result of the perception of an odour, a taste, or the sight of a particular object; and even though suggestions are produced by another person, "nevertheless they often occur in consequence of a sensitive or sensorial modification developed either spontaneously or accidentally in the patient himself in a way that is known as *auto-suggestion*".[50]

An unmistakable shift towards psychology takes place in this statement. If one takes a closer look at the aforementioned citation, it is clear that the term 'functional or dynamic lesion' refers only to an *elliptic indication* of a psychical process, and no longer to an organic change.[51] In order to sustain this 'elliptic indication' Charcot used the idiom of psychology, speaking of an unconscious or subconscious psychical state. This state can be caused by either a physical or a psychical trauma, and is characterised by an obnubilation of consciousness and a dissociation of the ego, enabling an idea or a chain of associated ideas to be awoken in 'psychical organs' by means of suggestion or auto-suggestion. Free from all control or criticism, these ideas may develop into an autonomous condition which thus acquires an unlimited force of realisation. Hence the hysterical symptom must be viewed as the realisation of an unconscious or subconscious idea.

Charcot's progression that started with neurology, leads one to ascertain the psychogenic nature of the symptoms of hysteria. The language in which this was couched did not differ greatly from that used by Breuer and Freud. Still, was it possible in this instance to speak of a clinic of the excessively intense idea?

The "traitement psychique"

There is at least one factor pointing in the direction of such a clinic. Similar psychological hypotheses resulting from comparable experiments are mentioned elsewhere in Charcot's book. In addition, one can observe that it was the artificial induction and annihilation of hysterical symptomatology which places Charcot on the track of a psychical treatment, "un traitement psychique".

"Our two patients, Porcz. and Pin., have been subjected for some days to a regular treatment, on which I will say a few words. The treatment consists of two elements. On the one hand, it is in a sense indirect, in that it relates either to the general state or to the hysterical diathesis. Twice a day Pin. receives a general cold douche, takes a sulphur bath three times a week. Every other day both are treated with static electricity. This agent is useful, as you know, to modify perversions of sensibility. Experience has for a long time taught us that, as a consequence of an electro-static bath, sensibility in most cases of hysterical anaesthesia, reappears, at first for a time, for some hours perhaps, then according as the baths are repeated, for a longer period, for several days, for example; and finally by the continuation of treatment it becomes re-established in a definite manner. Further, at the same time that a more or less durable return of the sensibility takes place, the other hysterical phenomena, the attacks, for example, are favourably modified, or disappear.

But I wish specially to call your attention to the second part of our treatment; it is based on that idea which we have just been discussing, viz. that in our two patients the paralysis may have been caused by a mechanism analogous to that which in the 'hypnotics' determined paralysis by suggestion. The various attempts at hypnotisation which we made in these two men, and which, if they had succeed, would have singularly lightened our task, being unsuccessful, we were constrained to adopt the following means. In the first place we acted, and continued to act every day on their minds as much as possible, affirming in a positive manner a fact of which we are ourselves perfectly convinced — that their paralysis, in spite of its long duration, is not incurable, and that, on the contrary, it will certainly be cured by means of appropriate treatment, at the end possibly of some weeks, if they would only be good enough to aid us."[52]

The 'psychical treatment' of hysterical paralysis aimed, as it were, at strengthening the idea or representation of the movement that the paralysed limbs had to perform. For this purpose certain exercises were prescribed for the patient. Charcot, alluding to Maudsley and Müller, stressed the importance of a mental impression of the movement, which was proven by the 'miraculous' cure of imaginary paralysis by means of an energetic injunction:

"In these cases *the idea of movement*, the belief that it will take place, is, in the inner conscience, *the movement itself.* (...) We know that a sudden injunction sometimes determines the cure of a psychical paralysis of long standing, and which may have resisted the various agencies. Thus, for example, a patient is forcibly made to leave her bed, in which she may have long remained motionless from a paraplegia of this kind; being placed on her feet, she is told to 'walk', and forthwith she walks."[53]

Charcot warned that this energetic method might affect the doctor's authority if the desired effect failed to take place. Therefore, Charcot opted carefully to 'develop' the idea in question by means of physical exercises:

"We act *psychically*. It is well known, unless I am mistaken, that the production of an image, or of a mental representation, no matter how summary or rudimentary it may be of the movement to be executed, is an indispensable preliminary condition to the execution of that movement. But it is probable that, in the case of our two patients, the conditions which normally preside over the representation of the mental image have been so seriously affected as to render its formation impossible, or at least very difficult, in consequence of an inhibitory action exercised over the cortical motor centres by *the fixed idea* of motor weakness. It is to that circumstance that the objective realisation of the paralysis is greatly due. If this be so, we can readily conceive that the repetition of the dynamometric exercise would tend to revive in the centres the motor representation, which is a necessary preliminary to the voluntary movement; and that, as we have seen, these movements tend to become more and more energetic, according as they are repeated."[54]

This, however, does not mean that one should consider Charcot as a great healer. To him, hypnotic suggestion was first and foremost a means to show *experimentally* the similarity between traumatic and hysterical neurosis. Despite all the 'miraculous' recoveries, the Salpêtrière remained primarily a *research centre* where nosography took precedence over therapy. In his *Lectures*, his attention was accordingly directed to the description of the diverse syndromes and to phenomena like hysterical mutism, hystero-traumatic manifestations, etc. There was only one lecture entirely dedicated to the treatment of hysteria which, in Charcot's eyes, could be divided into 'psychical or moral treatment' on the one hand and 'medical treatment' on the other.[55]

The psychical or moral treatment meant that the patient had to be isolated from the environment where hysteria developed, and was not allowed any visits from parents or friends. Following a case of epidemic hysteria which affected three children from one family after a séance, Charcot prescribed that the victims had to be separated from each other.[56]
Charcot gave several examples of the usefulness of such a "traitement moral". For instance, he recounted the story of a nervous father who inquired every evening at quarter to five about his son's health. The son never failed to respond to this inquiry with convulsive attacks.[57] Even more distressing was the case of the fourteen year old girl suffering from hysterical or nervous anorexia. When the parents called upon Charcot as a last resort, he replied:

"It is unnecessary for me to come. (...) I can, without seeing the patient, give you the appropriate advice. Bring the child to Paris, place her in one of our hydrotherapeutic establishments, leave her there, or at least when you go away make her believe that you have quitted the capital, inform me of it, and I will do the rest."[58]

Six weeks later he received a message stating that all his prescriptions had been followed to the letter, but that the girl was nevertheless in mortal danger. However, Charcot remarked that the most important prescription had been disregarded: the parents had refused to leave the sickbed of their child. But now that the situation was so desperate, they finally agreed to it. After the girl had speedily recovered, she confessed to Charcot that:

"As long as papa and mama had not gone — in other words, as long as you had not triumphed (for I saw that you wished to shut me up), I was afraid that my illness was not serious, and as I had a horror of eating, I did not eat. *But when I saw that you were determined to be master, I was afraid*, and in spite of my repugnance I tried to eat, and I was able to, little by little.' I thanked the child for her confidence, which as you will understand is a lesson in itself."[59]

Needless to say, such a "traitement morale" has little connection with a psychical treatment or psychotherapy (however beneficial it may be in certain cases to isolate patients in our day and age).[60] In the case of the girl, one can say at the very most that her acknowledgement of Charcot's mastery, or her attribution of that position to Charcot, triggered a therapeutic effect. This effect was by no means a minor one, for it saved her life. But with this we have not yet touched upon her hysteria. Charcot recognised the therapeutic potential of isolating patients and of hypnotic suggestion. But to acquire a thorough understanding of both phenomena would have led him to renounce the foundation of his own research project, i.e. the development of a clinical tableau of hysteria.[61]

Charcot's influence on Freud

If one wishes to know about Charcot's influence on Freud, it seems most appropriate to allow Freud himself to speak. In July 1886, Freud had already completed the translation of the *Lectures*. He manifestly drew inspiration from this translation for the account of his stay in Paris[62] and made no secret of his enthusiasm for Charcot and his lectures. He particularly emphasised his introduction to the field of hysteria — including male hysteria. These were the two elements Freud initially pointed up as being innovative.
Immediately after returning to Vienna, he gave two lectures on hypnosis: the first on 14 May for the 'Wiener Physiologische Klub', and the second on 27 of the same month for the 'Psychiatrische Gesellschaft'. Two lectures to the 'K.K. Gesellschaft der Ärzte' on male hysteria, followed in October of the same year.[63]
Freud discerned and recognised the sense of Charcot's progression, a path that led from neurology to psychology: "Charcot was the first to teach us that to explain the hysterical neurosis we must apply to psychology."[64] But,

psychology and the concomitant psychotherapy were merely present in Charcot's work in a rudimentary form and the master was not exactly bursting with impatience to take up the challenge. "He was not a reflective man, not a thinker: he had the nature of an artist — he was, as he himself said, *a visuel*, a man who sees."[65] Moreover it is plain to see that providing a psychological explanation for hysteria represented the biggest obstacle blocking the shift from neurology to psychology. This shift could not occur in a linear fashion. Rather, it called for the adoption of an entirely new epistemological viewpoint, which would lead to the construction of a clinically usable psychology. To Freud, it was unmistakable that it was Charcot who — via hysteria — had designated the *psyche* as the continent to be mapped for this clinical psychology.

Nevertheless, Charcot's suggestion did require an 'incubation period'. It was not until 1890 that one could find the first traces of a psychology in Freud's publications. I will mention two of these publications since they refer to Charcot. In the paper 'Some Points for a Comparative Study of Organic and Hysterical Motor Paralysis', Freud evaluates the nature of hysterical motor paralysis.[66] He departs from the observation — which, as I have shown, was extensively illustrated and described at the Salpêtrière — that the symptomatology of hysterical patients matches almost perfectly that of the known organic cerebral motor paralyses. Characteristic of the latter is the fact that the location of the cerebral lesion brings about the complete paralysis of all parts of the body which are represented in the affected part of the brain. This contrasts with the periphero-spinal paralysis which, responding to the principle of a point-by-point projection, has a repercussion on, say, one single muscle.[67] Cerebral, and particularly cortical paralysis appealed to the imagination of the unsuspecting observer, be he hysterical or not. These patients were indeed the worst off, as usually one of their bodily functions was completely lost: they could no longer walk, they could not move their arm, etc. As a result, their "Mitleidwert"[68] (pity value) scored significantly higher among the hysterical patients of the Salpêtrière: the latter patients only copied the phenomenology of the global representation-paralysis.

Hysterical paralysis differs, however, from its cortical equivalent, as it is not subjected to the rules holding that the distal part of the limb is always more affected than the proximal one. It was thus very possible to induce only a paralysis of just the upper arm by means of hypnosis. As far as the isolation of the disease was concerned, Freud predictably situated hysterical paralysis

between projection paralysis (too specific) and representation paralysis (too general).[69]
A second difference has to do with the intensity of the symptoms. Freud mentions that in the case of hysterical patients the intensity of the symptoms is excessive when compared to those occurring in organic paralysis.[70]
How can one explain this peculiar phenomenon? "Since there can only be a single cerebral anatomy that is true, and since it finds expression in the clinical characteristics of the cerebral paralyses, it is clearly impossible for that anatomy to be the explanation of the distinctive features of hysterical paralysis. For that reason we must not draw conclusions on the subject of cerebral anatomy that are based on the symptomatology of those paralyses."[71]
To come to a useful explanation, Freud was compelled to *interpret* Charcot's notion of the functional or dynamic lesion. He asked the reader's permission "(...) to move on to psychological ground — which can scarcely be avoided in dealing with hysteria".[72] One can only explain the parallels between the symptomatology of hysterical paralysis — which is entirely independent from the anatomy of the nervous system — and that of cerebral organic paralysis by referring to the popular *idea* of the body. The aforementioned 'lesion' brought on an alteration of this *idea*, such as the idea of the arm. "Considered psychologically, the paralysis of the arm consists in the fact that the conception of the fact cannot enter into association with the other ideas constituting the ego of which the subject's body forms an important part. The lesion would therefore be *the abolition of the associative accessibility of the conception of the arm*. The arm behaves as though it did not exist for the play of associations."[73] Note the strong correspondence with Charcot's reasoning which I alluded to earlier.[74] What is more, Freud's description of the psychical organisation of the ego can also be found in Charcot: "Consequently the idea, or group of ideas suggested, are met with in a state of isolation, free from the control of that large collection of personal ideas long accumulated and organised, which constitute the conscience properly so-called, the *ego*."[75]
In the paper he published with Breuer, Freud expounds upon the psychical mechanism: the exclusion from the association (with other ideas) takes place because the 'unconscious' association with the memory of the trauma charges the idea in question with an "Affektbetrag" (a quota of affect) — precisely like the humorous story of the loyal servant who refused ever to wash his hand after the king touched it.[76] This marks an important difference from Charcot's formulation. What Charcot perceived as a 'powerful idea', was

conceived of by Freud as an idea charged with a quota of affect.[77] Such a quantitative conception of psychical mechanisms was eventually to lead to the formulation of the psychical mechanisms of defence and repression. The 'removal of associative accessibility' (Freud) or the 'dissociation from the ego' (Charcot) still reflected a passive process in which the agent was found in the quantity.

In his 1893 obituary of Charcot, Freud charts two epistemological positions which can be found in the *Lectures*.[78] Freud, however, seems to have ascribed the psychological position to himself, while stressing Charcot's merits for the nosographical approach and the etiological importance of heredity.

The painful expressions of affect visible in a hysterical patient can be traced back to a trauma whose memory remains sealed off from the psychical processes of the ego. As a result, the patient claims to know nothing about the recollection or representation of the trauma which determines his suffering. "No one should object that the theory of the splitting of consciousness as a solution to the riddle of hysteria is much too remote to impress an unbiased and untrained observer. For, by pronouncing possession by a demon to be the cause of hysterical phenomena, the Middle Ages in fact chose this solution; it would only have been a matter of exchanging the religious terminology of that dark and superstitious age for the scientific language of today."[79]

Despite Charcot having demonstrated that hysteria had long existed — notably via his study of witch trials — he approached it like any other neuropathological subject matter: he provided a description of the phenomenon, showed the pattern and laws and taught us to recognise the symptoms that enable us to make a diagnosis. As for aetiology, he opted for an easy formula: i.e., hysteria results from an inherited degeneration and is part of the "famille névropathique". All the other etiological factors only function as "agents provocateurs".[80]

Conclusion

The subject matter drawn so far from the *Lectures* leads me to put forward the following interpretation: Sigmund Freud's stay in Paris brought him in contact with a systematic *psychical influencing*. These experiments, conducted with the help of hypnotic suggestion, were important to Charcot in establishing hysteria as a clinical entity, and corresponded to his anatomo-clinical nosographical method. Freud, for his part, gleaned two things from this long progression: on the one hand, the conviction that neuroses and hysteria both had to be explained in psychological terms, and on the other hand, an insight into the possibility of a psychical treatment.

I have shown that both psychology and psychical treatment were explicitly prefigured in the *Lectures*. We also know that Charcot eventually realised where his progression could lead him.[81] This does not mean, however, that one has to blow such indications out of proportion. Charcot's notion of the 'powerful idea' and his description of the ego also appear in the writings of Herbart and Meynert. 'Psychology' and 'psychical treatment' were in effect grand words for what Freud could glean from Charcot. The field in which the construction of both was to take place, was certainly not ready to be explored at the Salpêtrière. Let us bear in mind for the time being that Freud primarily realised the need for a usable clinical psychology.

CHAPTER 2

Suggestive Therapeutics

> "But I can remember even then feeling a muffled hostility to this tyranny of suggestion. When a patient who showed himself unamenable was met with the shout: 'What are you doing? *Vous vous contre-suggestionnez!*', I said to myself that this was an evident injustice and an act of violence. For the man certainly had a right to counter-suggestions if people were trying to subdue him with suggestions. Later on my resistance took the direction of protesting against the view that suggestion, which explained everything, was itself to be exempt from explanation."
>
> *Sigmund Freud*[1]

It is interesting to pause for a moment and to take stock of the fact that Freud's progression towards a 'psychology for neurologists' and towards his *Project*, brought him to a number of institutions or clinics. The significance of these institutions is ambiguous. It is, nevertheless, undeniable that it was in these very institutions that he was introduced to the systematic use of psychical influencing of individuals and to the pervasive lack of a psychology. Equally undeniable, is that Freud had to distance himself or, to put it differently, to emancipate himself from the group mechanisms prevailing in these institutions.

The first institution was the Viennese "Allgemeine Krankenhaus" where Freud trained under Meynert to improve his knowledge of neuropathology with an eye to starting his own practice. As is well known, the neuroanatomy taught there consisted in formulating a hypothesis about the location of the lesion in the nervous system on the basis of the symptomatology. This discipline presupposed a thorough neuro-anatomical knowledge and Freud certainly had come to the right place, for Meynert was regarded as one of the most distinguished neuroanatomists of the time. However, the "Allgemeine Krankenhaus" was not equipped with a separate psychiatric ward. The patients deemed fit for neuropathological diagnosis and prognosis, were dispersed over the different wards of the hospital. This actuality, along with the anatomo-physiological method of approach commended by Meynert, explains why there was room neither for the psyche nor for a psychical treatment within the walls of this institute.

As I have observed previously, the conditions at the Salpêtrière were entirely different. Charcot's anatomo-clinical method, together with the relatively large groups of 'neuroses' housed in the Salpêtrière, created an ideal breeding ground facilitating the emergence of the psyche. The clinical tableau of hysteria, as Charcot thought fit to describe it, was determined by psychical group mechanisms.[2]

On his return from Paris, Freud was still a very long way from a psychological theory. What he initially retained was a reference to a 'psychology' that would function as a basis for explaining and perhaps even treating neuroses. The technique of hypnotic suggestion was the starting point which was to bring him to a third institute: Hippolyte Bernheim's clinic in Nancy. What happened there, between 1885 and 1895, can truly be qualified as unique. In this institute, classical medical practice was complemented and even replaced by the psychotherapeutic technique of hypnosis.[3]

Another translation

December 1887. Freud was completely immersed in the study of hypnosis and informed Fließ of his intention to translate Bernheim's book on suggestion.[4] His conviction that the technique of hypnosis was granted a promising future in the practice of neurology served as a catalyst. The available therapeutic means for the treatment of neuroses — Weir-Mitchell rest-cures, massage, hydro-therapy, electro-therapy — were quite insufficient. And by now Freud, who had given prominence to Charcot's views on hysteria, received neurotics who were referred to him by his colleagues. By translating Bernheim's book, Freud not only wanted to keep up with the field, he also experienced the need to advance his knowledge of the psychical treatment of neuroses.

Charcot had already introduced him to the application of hypnosis as a therapeutic means, although this subject was dealt with in a cursory manner. For at the Salpêtrière nosography was prime and hypnosis operated essentially as an experimental demonstration.

A totally different and auspicious note on the therapeutic potential of hypnosis emanates from Bernheim's book. This may explain Freud's intention of translating it. In Vienna, like in the rest of the German speaking world, a pronounced scepticism on the subject of hypnosis still subsisted. The reality of hypnotic phenomena was fiercely contested and the alleged effects were either put down to the credulity of the observer or to simulation on the part of the subject of the experiment. This dismissal is illustrated by the polemic involving Meynert and Freud. To Freud, *Suggestive Therapeutics* was a solid introduction to the study of hypnosis. He described it as particularly stimulating and inclined "to destroy the belief that the problem of hypnosis is still surrounded, as Meynert asserts, by a 'halo of absurdity'."[5] Freud sharply criticised Meynert for rejecting this new method, not on the basis of any experimental grounds, but on the basis of the authority he had acquired in other fields.[6]

"The achievement of Bernheim", according to Freud, "consists precisely in stripping the manifestations of hypnotism of their strangeness by linking them up with familiar phenomena of normal psychological life and of sleep."[7] Freud thus found Bernheim meritorious for having transferred the question of hypnosis to the field of psychology.

After Charcot, Bernheim represents a second landmark on his road to psychology and psychical treatment. Although Freud personally found it difficult to apply hypnosis in his private practice, he was to remain grateful to Bernheim, whom he considered a forerunner in the field of psychotherapy. In this chapter, I will illustrate that this was not just a gratuitous homage.

"Tout est dans la suggestion"

An unsuspecting visitor to the clinic in Nancy would have been surprised by how easily hypnosis was induced in patients and by the central place it occupied as a therapeutic method. This technique was successfully applied to the majority of the patients, regardless of disease, sex, age or temperament. Contrary to the opinion held in Paris, hypnotic phenomena were not the exclusive prerogative of one disease. In Nancy, the use of hypnotic suggestion, as a part of therapy, contributed to the standard arsenal physicians had at their disposal.

While Liébault argued that approximately one in five to one in six hypnotised people pass into a state of somnambulism (that is, a hypnotic state followed by amnesia), Bernheim rather proudly mentioned in the introduction of his book: "In our hospital service, where the physician has greater authority over the patients, and where imitation and the force of example, perhaps, form a veritable suggestive atmosphere, the proportion of somnambulists is much larger, and we sometimes succeed in putting half if not a larger proportion of our subjects into this condition."[8]

Such an artificial or hypnotic sleep does not differ at all from natural sleep. All the 'hypnotic' phenomena, such as a change in sensitivity, motility, thought and imagination, as well as in illusions and hallucinations must be summoned by the intervention of suggestion. "Hallucinations", according to Bernheim, "are only suggested dreams; dreams are only spontaneous hallucinations."[9] Similar phenomena can also be occasioned by entering 'en rapport' with a sleeping person, or indeed with someone who is awake, provided he has been adequately exercised.[10]

To Bernheim, this conclusion represented a second argument against Charcot's conception which equated hypnotic sleep with a neurosis analogous to hysteria. It is possible to arouse hysterical phenomena at will, yet they cannot be attributed to hypnosis. They are merely determined by the physician's suggestion or, in some cases involving particularly sensitive people, by auto-suggestion.

Bernheim's 'explanation' of the mechanism of suggestion is relatively simple: every psychological state is characterised by a certain degree of suggestibility. In the waking state, this feature is "then either neutralized or restrained by the faculties of reason, attention and judgement."[11] The aforementioned mental faculties are weakened and obnubilated in both natural and artificial sleep. Imagination rules unchallenged and all the sensory impressions are absorbed unchecked by the brain which turns them into actions, sensations, movements and symbols. On the one hand, the new sense of consciousness or the 'altered nature of the psyche' makes the brain more compliant, more malleable and more receptive to suggestion and, on the other hand, "more apt to react upon the functions and organs by inhibition or dynamogeny."[12]

Yet, sleep cannot be said to be the essential characteristic of hypnosis. Both Liébault and Bernheim, charted the various degrees of hypnosis which they could establish empirically. The highest degree of psychical influencing by means of hypnosis is the somnambulistic state accompanied by total amnesia.[13] Such a classification based on the phenomenology is to some extent arbitrary and appears to be utterly irrelevant as regards therapy.

Suggestion is also effective without any form of sleep being induced. Bernheim therefore proposed to define hypnosis differently, namely as "the induction of a peculiar psychical condition which increases the susceptibility to suggestion."[14] It is of course correct to argue that induced sleep — when and if it can be induced — underpins suggestibility, but it is not a *conditio sine qua non.* The essence of hypnosis is suggestion. A further advantage of this definition, still according to Bernheim, is that other phenomena can also be placed under the heading of hypnosis and be examined as such. Take for example the fascination some people have for shiny objects or for the eyes.[15]

The status of Bernheim's explanation

Bernheim's position is unambiguously psychological: the effective foundation of hypnotic phenomena lies in the *psychical mechanism* of suggestion. This does not necessarily mean that one comes across an elaborate theory in Bernheim. In fact, he does not go beyond the stage of observation, as Freud put it in connection to *Studies on Hysteria.*[16] The following excerpt bears witness to this:

"I proceed to hypnotize in the following manner. I begin by saying to the patient that I believe benefit is to be derived from the use of suggestive therapeutics, that it is possible to cure or to relieve him by hypnotism; that there is nothing either hurtful or strange about it; that it is an ordinary sleep or torpor which can be induced in everyone, and that this quiet, beneficial condition restores the equilibrium of the nervous system, etc. If necessary, I hypnotize one or two subjects in his presence, in order to show him that there is nothing painful in this condition and that it is not accompanied with any unusual sensation. When I have thus banished from his mind the idea of magnetism and the somewhat mysterious fear that attaches to that unknown condition, above all when he has seen patients cured or benefited by the means in question, he is no longer suspicious, but gives himself up, then I say, "Look at me and think of nothing but sleep. Your eyelids begin to feel heavy, your eyes tired. They begin to wink, they are getting moist, you cannot see distinctly. They are closed." Some patients close their eyes and are asleep immediately. With others, I have to repeat, lay more stress on what I say, and even make gestures. (...) I use the word sleep, in order to obtain as far as possible over the patients, a suggestive influence which shall bring about sleep or a state closely approaching it. (...) It is sleep by suggestion, — a type of sleep which I insinuate into the brain."[17]

When he states that he "insinuates" an idea "into the brain" by means of suggestion, Bernheim does not deny the fact that other elemental factors, such as telepathy and medication, which critics associated with his method, lack any sort of reality. Were these phenomena effectively to exist, they would be part of another field and not that of suggestion. As far as he is concerned, Bernheim only deals with "verbal suggestion and its application to therapeutics".[18]

The procedure described here brings about the above mentioned weakening and annihilation of the superior mental faculties in the patient. Everything fits perfectly into place: we are apparently dealing with *suggested suggestibility*. Whether one can grant the status of explanation to the postulate of a psychical mechanism, namely the "introduction into the brain" of a psychical element (an idea), is an entirely different question. This does not seem to concern Bernheim, for, he is mostly intent on either demonstrating the force that springs from the physician's *authority* or the therapeutic efficiency of his method. In Nancy, trying to cure, was traditionally high on the agenda; it was just as important as nosography was at the Salpêtrière.

At this juncture, however, a problem emerges. Bernheim rightly criticises the clinical tableau of hysteria as postulated by Charcot, because, if based on suggestion, it must be devoid of any reality. Yet, Bernheim sees no problem whatsoever with the idea of the suggested suggestibility. This is also apparent from the second part of the book which discusses the therapeutic effects of suggestion. These effects are confined to the elimination of the symptoms. The question as to the durability of the effects after the patients have left the climate of suggestibility is never raised.

Authority

I already pointed out when discussing Charcot's *Clinical Lectures*, that the demonstrations with the help of hypnosis made a great impression on Freud. While one cannot credit Freud with being particularly suggestible, it appears that this impression was further accentuated by his reading of Bernheim's book. As I observed, Charcot's importance to Freud was to point at the psyche. On the other hand, I believe that Bernheim's specific importance lay in having aroused and described a whole series of intriguing psychical phenomena.

In Bernheim's book, Freud encountered numerous phenomena which he had been introduced to elsewhere, such as hysterical paralysis (Charcot).[19] Other phenomena were new to him and it would take him years before he could actually grasp the notion of resistance and place it in a coherent theory.

An important difference from Charcot's *Clinical Lectures*, is that Bernheim conceived of the hypnotic phenomena he experimentally conjured up in his demonstrations as *an sich* — i.e., free from any syndrome. This is an attitude one will encounter in Freud's *Studies on Hysteria*. In these studies, he will come to the conclusion that the psychical mechanism of resistance and the operation of the psycho-cathartic method are not merely limited to hysteria. This signified a definitive emancipation from the influence of both Charcot and Breuer.[20]

A second difference is that Bernheim does not systematically make use of his method of treatment as a research instrument for probing into the psyche. As regards his experiments, they seemed to be geared more towards showing the scope and influence of his authority. On this particular subject, Freud was to opt for an approach closer to that of Charcot's. For Charcot, unlike Bernheim, unmistakably aimed at constructing a science.

In the climate of the clinic, which was auspicious to his experiments, Bernheim displayed impressive ingenuity, sometimes drawing inspiration from the literature he had at his disposal.[21] I will now move on to a discussion of some of Bernheim's conclusions which one will later encounter in Freud's work.

False connections

The 'false connection' is the first phenomenon worthy of especial attention. When Freud is confronted with this while treating hysterical patients, he recalls having found it described by Bernheim and refers to the experiments relating to it in Nancy.

"On another occasion when my colleague, M. Charpentier, was present I suggested to him [a patient] when he first fell asleep that as soon as he waked, he should take my colleague's umbrella, which was lying on the bed, open it, and walk twice up and down the piazza on which the room opened. It was some time afterward when I waked him. Before his eyes were open, we went quickly out of the room so that the suggestion might not be recalled by our presence. We

> soon saw him coming with umbrella in his hand, but not open (in spite of the suggestion). He walked twice up and down the corridor. I said to him, "What are you doing ?" He answered, "I am taking the air." — "Why, are you warm?" — "No, it is only my idea; I occasionally walk up and down here." — "What is the umbrella for ? It belongs to Mr. Charpentier." — "What! I thought it was mine, it looks something like mine; I shall take it back to the place I took it from." Sometimes the subject tires himself out in trying to find a reason for the ideas in his brain. One day I suggested to the same subject that as soon as he waked, he should go to a certain patient in the same room and ask how he was. He did so as soon as he awoke, and when I asked him why he did it, and whether he was especially interested in that patient, he replied, "No, it was just an idea." Then after thinking a moment, added "He would not let us sleep last night." Thus he tried to explain the idea to himself by the wish to know, whether the sick patient would allow them to sleep that night or not."[22]

Freud also comes across this *post-facto* reasoning in the explanations and illustrations given by his patients on their anxieties, dreams and corresponding ideas.[23]
A good example of the elucidation of such a 'false connection' can be found in the case description of Emmy von N. Freud treats this 40 year old, but still young looking woman, who suffers from anxiety accompanied by self-reproach. Upon his question as to the cause of her state, she answers that she is worried about the safety of her two daughters, who she had finally allowed to use the lift of the Pension where they resided. She did so because the eldest daughter had trouble from her right ovaries and pains in her right leg. Emmy, however, had heard that the lift might not have been dependable and hence reproached herself for having given them permission to use it. Freud, who knew the Pension, disbelieved the explanation for her anxiety and set himself the task of finding out the real reason via hypnosis.

The elucidation of this 'false connection' occurs in three stages. Freud did not hypnotise his patient right away. He started instead with a massage session, which he resumed on the same day after an interval of several weeks. In the course of this session, Emmy recounted some loosely connected recollections which seemed to be connected with her mood of discomfort. For instance, she spoke about a toad found in a cellar, an eccentric mother nursing her idiotic son in an odd fashion, and a woman shut up in an asylum because she suffered from melancholia. After having told these gruesome stories she reassumed her cheerful air and then launched into a digression on her relationship with prominent men from Austria or abroad. Freud admitted having difficulties reconciling such an active life with the image he had of this severely neurotic woman.

During the second stage of this elucidation, Emmy was hypnotised and thus less reserved on the subject of her anxiety and self-reproach. The reason for her ill-humour in the mornings simply had to do with her apprehension about menstruating which would interfere with the massage session which she seemingly enjoyed.[24]

In a long footnote, in which he examines a second example of 'false connection' in Emmy's case, Freud comes up with an interpretation of identical phenomena: a rational and unintelligible motivation in a patient's account always represents suspicion of the physician and an unwillingness to know the actual cause.

If one looks again at the above-mentioned example, it appears that the two conditions for the 'false connection' coalesce into a single one, that is the eroticized transference of the rather young widow on to the physician.[25] The discrepancy between Bernheim's mere observation and description of 'false connection' and Freud's analysis of it, speaks for itself. What is more, Freud did not confine himself merely to analyzing particular instances. In his *Project*, the 'false connection' and the speech of 'hysterical patients' developed into paradigms for his psychical treatment and, at same time, became the starting point for his psychology.

Resistance

The automatic obedience Bernheim managed to trigger in his patients was, however, not unlimited. For instance, when he suggested stealing an object, the suggestion was not always heeded by the patient: "The desire to carry out the act no doubt is more or less imperative, but they resist to it to a certain extent."[26] Moreover, Bernheim was familiar with the resistance phenomenon that could already take place when attempting to put the patient in a hypnotic state. While, for some, a mild suggestion sufficed, "(...) with others quiet suggestion has no effect. With these, it is better to be abrupt, to restrain with an authoritative voice the inclination to laugh, or the weak and involuntary resistance which this manoeuvre may provoke."[27]

Since hypnotic sleep depends on suggestion itself, it is clear that not every patient can be hypnotised. Indeed, Bernheim recognised the importance of the resistance factor when intending to use suggestion as a therapeutic means.

Although the book principally reports on successful treatments, it also indicates that patients can cause the therapy to fail. The volition in hypnotic sleep need not have completely disappeared, it may very well be that the person refuses to heed the suggestion or that s/he withdraws from its influence.

Bernheim experienced such a resistance in the case of certain nervous diseases: "There are hysterical patients who, as you say, are difficult to hypnotize. Among cases of neuropathy there are also refractory subjects. The insane, cases of melancholia, and of hypochondriasis, and people of mobile imagination, who do not know how to concentrate their attention, those who are entirely absorbed by emotion, whose minds are preoccupied by various ideas, — all these oppose a conscious or unconscious moral resistance to suggestion."[28] And he goes on to write: "Melancholic, hypochondriac, and certain neuropathic cases, often rebel against hypnotic sleep; they do not allow themselves to be influenced. What is told them makes no impression; or if the hypnotic suggestion succeeds with some, the therapeutic suggestion remains inefficacious."[29]

Let us take a closer look at the way in which Bernheim dealt with resistance. To Bernheim, suggestion involved 'introducing' an idea into the brain of another person. This introduction is facilitated when one manages to enhance suggestibility, or, in other words, when the 'resistance' against suggestion is curbed.[30] The ideal situation occurs when the patient has reached the stage of hypnotic sleep.

In the event of a failed suggestion, Bernheim never raised the question as to why it failed or as to the reason for this resistance. He merely observed the resistance mechanism and circumvented any explanation by putting forward the following consideration: however enhanced it may be, suggestibility never enables one to turn the hypnotised patient into a complete automaton entirely given up into the physician's hands. "[Hypnosis] increases the cerebral docility; it makes the automatic activity preponderate over the will. But the latter persists to a certain degree, the subject thinks, reasons, discusses, accepts more readily than in the waking condition, but does not always accept, especially in the light degrees of sleep."[31]

Bernheim further attributed the resistance he experiences to the patients' (especially hysterical patients) malicious satisfaction in resisting the physician's efforts. Likewise, the influence of the patient's surroundings can also be designated as a source for the evoked resistance: "Other people laugh at them, make fun of "magnetism"[32], say that it only affects simple-minded people, and can do no good."[33]

While the resistance against the hypnosis was to prompt Freud to modify his therapeutical technique — notably by focusing the patient's attention on his/her own ideas or representations — Bernheim reacted inversely.[34] When his efforts were in vain, he too abandoned the hypnosis of recalcitrant hysterical patients. But he did so precisely because in such cases suggestion "(...) only helps to direct the patient's attention upon himself and indirectly invokes auto-suggestion."[35] Bernheim displayed no interest at all in 'auto-suggestion', that is to say, for the patient's own ideas or thoughts.[36]

Instead, he attempted to enhance his influence in various ways, for instance, by repeating the suggestion or by wielding more authority.[37] His clinic too can be qualified as one of the 'excessively intense' idea in which the intensity of the suggested idea battles with the strength of the resistance or, with the intensity of the 'counter-suggestion'.[38]

Scene

Driven by his curiosity to determine the scope of suggestion, Bernheim stages very dramatic scenes featuring his patients. He once told one of them that he had been insulted by an imaginary person standing at the door of the ward.

"I gave him an imaginary dagger (a paper-cutter) and ordered him to kill the man. He hastened forward and ran the dagger resolutely into the door, and then stood staring with haggard eyes and trembling all over. "What have you done, unhappy man?" I said. "He is dead, he is bleeding, the police are coming." He stood terrified. He was led before an imaginary magistrate (my interne). "Why did you murder this man?" "He insulted me." "We do not kill the man who insults us. You must be complained of to the police. Did any one tell you to kill him ?" He answers, "M. Bernheim did." I say to him, "You are to be taken before the justice. You killed this man. I said nothing to you, you act as your own master."

He was taken before my *chef de clinic*, who played the part of magistrate. "Why did you kill this man ?" "He insulted me." "That is curious; one does not answer an insult by a dagger thrust. Where you in full possession of your faculties ? They say that your mind is sometimes affected." "No, sir." "They say you are subject to attacks of somnambulism. Perhaps you had to obey some strange impulse under the influence of some one who could have forced you to act ?" "No, sir, I acted from my own impulse because he insulted me." "Think, sir; it is a question of your life. Speak frankly in your own interest. How is it ? Before the magistrate, you stated that the idea of killing this man was suggested to you by M. Bernheim." "No, sir, I acted entirely upon my own free will." "You know M. Bernheim well, you go to him at the hospital to be hypnotized." "I only know M. Bernheim, because I go to the hospital for treatment and he gives me electricity to cure my nervous trouble, but aside from this, I do not know him. I cannot tell you that he told me to kill this man because he has not told me anything." And the magistrate could not get the truth from him, because for him the truth was my last suggestion, — that he acted of his own free will. The significance of this experiment deserves thorough consideration from a psychological and medico-legal point of view."[39]

The patient retained no memory about the staged act after awaking from hypnosis. Bernheim opines that the terrifying emotions experienced by the patient left no traces on his brain. The patient in question was exceptionally suitable for such psychodramas, as it was quite easy to metamorphose him into the most diverse figures. He could assume identities ranging from a young child to a general leading his troops, or from a timid girl to a pious pilgrim. "'You are a dog.' He gets down on all fours, barks, pretends to bite, and does not change his position, until I restore his own personality, or that of some one else, to him."[40]

Suchlike scenes also present themselves in yet a different format. Patients are sometimes encouraged to re-enact scenes from their past. S., a 39 year old former non-commissioned officer, is a case in point. He is an excellent subject for hypnotism and executes all the orders with the painful meticulousness and prompt obedience typical of former soldiers.

"I say: "You are now in the year 1870, a sergeant at the head of your company; you are at the battle of Gravelotte." - He thinks a minute, as if to arouse memories. They come back to him, form pictures in his mind, and force themselves upon him with striking vividness. He gets up, calls his men, commands them, marches, and places them for action. The enemy is at hand! He lies down, puts his gun to his shoulder, and shoots several times consecutively. Some of his men fall; he encourages the others. "Shelter yourselves behind this bush; we must retreat!" And he goes through all the movements of the struggle with the men, as memory revives them.
I make him imagine himself at the battle of Patay, where he was wounded. He falls, does not speak, puts his hand to his head, does not move. Then he comes to himself again, asks for a doctor, imagines himself being carried into an ambulance, calls a nurse to dress his wound, etc."[41]

In this way, Bernheim has his patients featuring in their own lives. He observed that S. knew that he himself was next to him during the enactment. But at the same time, S. labours under the impression that he was actually on a battle field and forcefully gave expression to the dreams Bernheim had induced him to experience. Bernheim invokes a split in personality to account for this phenomenon. Alluding to Maudsley, he makes a comparison with what can be perceived in dreams. In dreams one is simultaneously oneself and someone else, precisely like the above mentioned case of the somnambulistic patient who, while thinking he is a dog, still answers the questions put to him. In dreams one imagines oneself back in one's youth. Memories deeply embedded in one's brain are aroused and take the shape of a symbol. Ghosts materialise and one talks to them, yet one's consciousness of the present has not evaporated. One's dreams are often so vivid that one has to convince oneself that "It is only a dream".[42]

Rapport and automation

An element that remains obscure in Bernheim's book is the famous *rapport*. What such a 'relation' presupposes and what enables it to operate on a therapeutic plane, is not expounded upon. In some cases there is enough *rapport* for all sorts of experiments, but not enough for therapy. Take the case of the young hysterical girl who had very vivid dreams in a state of hypnotic sleep.[43] When she was dreaming about her mother, Bernheim would promptly play the part of the mother and let the girl help him with the domestic chores. After she had completed these chores, he took her out for a walk and a swim, etc. Bernheim managed to get her to do anything, but failed to achieve any therapeutic effect. A singularity of this patient was that she did not have the slightest consciousness of reality, hence, according to Bernheim, the impossibility of generating a *rapport*. This implies that a prerequisite for this *rapport*, as conceived of by Bernheim, is the awareness of being under influence.

The *rapport*, just like suggestion, is ascribed the status of an instrument. However, Bernheim does not have a theory at his disposal to chart both elements. I would like to add another point, namely that the phenomenon goes far beyond the hypnotic situation. When a patient has been hypnotised either once or several times, in other words, when a *rapport* has been established, it continues to operate in the waking state. Then, all the hypnotic phenomena can also be invoked without any form of artificial sleep.[44] They do not result from a magnetic fluid or from any other emanation transferred from one organism to another. Rather, they rest solely on suggestion, that is, "(...) in the

influence exerted by an idea which has been suggested to, and received by the mind."[45]
The psychological state in which someone simply accepts another person's suggestion, is what Bernheim called 'credulity'. Everyone has a certain degree of credulity, as it forms one of the necessary conditions for education, tradition, making agreements, social order and, of course, suggestion. When the belief in or the attribution of authority fails, the impression of suggestion will be too feeble to "(...) make the mind carry it out automatically, without first estimating its expediency."[46]

At first sight, such an automatic reaction seems unnatural. On a closer inspection it becomes plain that there is no real difference between the hypnotic state and the so-called normal state of consciousness. A large number of processes in the human organism invariably take place automatically, with no assistance from our will or consciousness. The complex vegetative phenomena and the reflexive operation of the spinal cord are carried out automatically and 'unconsciously'. To back this claim up, Bernheim alludes to what one can observe in a new born baby. Any sort of voluntary activity is thence excluded. This ties in perfectly with that which anatomy teaches us, i.e. the nervous system of the new born is as yet not sufficiently developed[47]: "The child is impulsive, it acts from instinct, that is to say, it is entirely given over to its automatism. It jumps, laughs, screams, makes faces, cries, according to the impressions it receives. It sings, when a familiar air awakens in it the idea of song."[48] Automatisms of this sort are still present in adults who would be all too happy to abandon themselves to them, "(...) if the condition of mind developed by education, the reserve imposed by custom, and our introspection, did not intervene as moderating and regulating influences, to impose a check to the cerebral automatism awakened by sensorial suggestion."[49]

The psychical organ: inhibition and facilitation

In his explanation of the mechanism of suggestion, Bernheim describes the brain as a *psychical organ* having as its most important functions both to check the reflexive processes and to intervene to correct, complete or explain perceptions. These perceptions spring from two sources. They either come to us from the outside world via sensory perception — and consequently belong

to the realm of suggestion, or alternatively, they are the result of recollected images aroused by memory. Because of the imperfect nature of our conscious ego and our sensory perception, we are constantly exposed to the most diverse illusions and suggestions. This is clearly illustrated in the case of dreams, in which our lethargic consciousness ceases to check the ideas that come up. In dreams, the most impossible things are regarded as objective reality. One is accordingly highly credulous, because one lacks the possibility of *judging*.[50] Also, as soon as one's *attention* is distracted from one's occupation — the reading of a book for example — one's mind falls into the hands of images created by the imagination, until consciousness reasserts itself and dispels these dream images, destroying the deceit and prowling of the mind and restoring reality.[51]
It ensues from this conception, that the psychical cannot simply be equated with consciousness. As well as the conscious or voluntary cerebral activity, Bernheim also distinguishes the automatic one. Moreover, the entanglement of the functions of attention, reality-testing and judgement is a subject that will feature prominently in Freud's conception of the operation of the psychical apparatus.[52] Bernheim, for his part, is not overly interested in the other psychical processes occurring when consciousness is lacking. He simply uses the break-down of consciousness and of the concomitant mechanisms in order to propose an explanation for the impact of suggestion. "Our errors, illusions, and hallucinations are not all spontaneous or consecutive to an imperfect sensorial impression; they may be suggested to our minds by others, and they are sometimes accepted without being challenged."[53]

To Bernheim, hypnosis is ultimately characterised by an altered partitioning of the excitation of the nervous system. Under hypnosis, i.e. in the case of suggestion, an "(...) increase of the reflex ideo-motor, ideo-sensitive, and ideo-sensorial excitability" is achieved.[54] In other words, under hypnosis, the suggested ideas, circumventing the will, are turned into movement or sensation.
The regulation of the partitioning of excitation occurs through the intervention of two opposing mechanisms: *inhibition* and *facilitation*.[55] The withdrawal of inhibition by consciousness facilitates the reflexive mechanisms. Consequently, hypnosis could just as well be described as a clash of various inhibition and facilitation effects, and the nervous system could accordingly be conceived of as containing quantitatively changing "nervous energy".[56]

Facilitation, however, is not merely described negatively as the withdrawal of inhibition mechanisms, it is also explicated as the result of frequent repetitions of one similar phenomenon. This, as a matter of fact, is how Bernheim explains why some patients who frequently partook in sessions of hypnotism, remained prone to developing hypnotic phenomena in a waking state. In other words, the degree of facilitation is determined by the repetition of the suggestion.

Forgetting and remembering

Another important observation is that post-hypnotic amnesia is not as absolute as one may originally suppose.[57] Bernheim is of the opinion that there is nothing easier than arousing memories of impressions that acted on the somnambular patient during sleep. It suffices to say to them: "You will now remember everything that you did during sleep and what happened to you", for this to actually happen. And if necessary, Bernheim places his hand on the patient's head "to concentrate his attention", a technique, as we know, which Freud was also to employ.[58] After a while, the latent[59] memories emerge. Freud was to refer to such an experiment by Bernheim to justify why he no longer used hypnosis to explore the life history of his patients.[60]

The waking and the sleeping states are characterised by activity and the primacy of respectively "the thinking part of the brain or the higher function" and "the lower function". Bernheim does not have an accurate anatomical relation in mind, but he names two different states of consciousness which can easily merge. In essence, he argues that, in full waking state, cerebral activity is located 'elsewhere' than in the sleeping state. When one passes from one state to another, only the centre of gravity of the cerebral activity shifts. On awaking from natural or hypnotic sleep the attention is again directed at the outside world and thought is restored. Passing over from one state to another thus involves a 'forgetting' linked to the attention of the individual person.

I should like to point out that Bernheim, like Breuer, reasons in terms of different states of consciousness.[61] However, Breuer's explanation of hysteria as being determined by hypnoid states of consciousness takes root in the difficulty — the impossibility even — of passing over between different states. It is, in other terms, based on the *impossibility of remembering*. This, according to Breuer, can only be cancelled out by inducing a pathogenic state in the patient by means of hypnosis.[62] It was Freud who — proving Bernheim to be right — was to demonstrate that forgetting was out of the question and that remembering could also take place without the hypnotic technique.

Therapeutic effects

The entire second part of the book is a description of 105 observations of the therapeutic effects of suggestion.[63] Bernheim clearly aimed at convincing the reader by the sheer accumulation of cases. The cases discussed cover a wide spectrum, ranging from pure organic disorders to various pains and neuralgia, as well as cases of hysteria, neuropathies and other neuroses. The subdivision of the different categories is fairly sloppy and the criteria used for this subdivision are not specified. When dealing with the subject of the psychical influencing of organic diseases, Bernheim stresses that he does not claim to be able to wholly or conclusively treat such diseases via the psyche. This being said, it has long been known in medical circles that someone who knows he is loved, recovers more speedily than someone who does not. Can one therefore deny a loved one, who is waiting to be operated on, such an aid to recovery? The systematic application of suggestion and the recognition of its serviceability in the daily medical praxis, was the only new element found in Nancy.[64]

The case studies themselves offer no substantial gain, surplus or any form of quest. They respond to a stereotypical pattern recording the date of the patient's admission, the symptoms he or she displays, the degree of suggestibility, the duration of the treatment and finally, the frequently successful outcome. What stands out in these case studies is Bernheim's exclusive attention to symptoms and his dedication to cure. It is furthermore plain to see that he is not concerned at all with explaining or further developing theoretical insights relating to the psyche. It suffices to cite one single example to form an idea of the *modus operandi* in use in the Nancy clinic.

Observation number XXIII[65] records the admission in March 1884 of a 17 year old girl who had suffered from a number of physical ailments for the previous two months: pains in the limbs, palpitations, tingling sensation, headaches and vertigo, loss of appetite accompanied by a feeling of constriction in the throat after meals, coughing without phlegm, ... The history of this patient only teaches us that she had never had a hysterical attack and that she had left home two months previously due to a disagreement. The medical examination of her heart and respiratory tract

revealed nothing abnormal. Her left arm was insensitive up to the pectoral arch. Other than that her senses functioned normally. Bernheim diagnosed this as neuropathy.
The first examination focused on the aforementioned anaesthesia: a coin attached to her arm brought back the sensitivity within three minutes without transference[66] taking place. Since then sensitivity has remained intact.
At the end of May, the patient complained of shoulder pains. She was easy to put into hypnotic sleep and Bernheim caused the pains to disappear by means of suggestion whenever this symptom reoccurred, suggestion was simply repeated until the pains had completely gone after about one week.
However, during the same month an eczematous eruption of syphilis was observed. After treatment with mercury the rash disappeared. Bernheim decided to turn his patient into a decent girl with the help of hypnosis. His hope of succeeding in this undertaking was founded on the fact that she was easily put into a somnambular state. Thus during hypnotic sleep he had her perform chores such as sweeping the ward, carrying trays and doing the laundry. She performed all these chores with her eyes closed and remembered nothing of it upon waking.
However, at a later stage, she displayed a new symptom: she showed an unsurmountable dislike for meat. Eliminating the complaint by direct use of suggestion produced no results and Bernheim resorted to changing her personality in order to make the girl eat meat. This had a positive outcome: when assuming the personality of her aunt, she would devour big chunks of meat.
Moralising suggestions were on the other hand less successful. When she was under hypnosis, Bernheim made her promise to continue working on the ward as a nurse and not to take any lovers, but to become a decent religious girl. She agreed to all of this and her unpredictable and somewhat common personality disappeared for a while. But this was to no avail. Later, she suddenly left the hospital and the very same day she was seen in town in the company of vagrants. Bernheim concluded the case with these words: "She becomes more than ever a *puella publica*. She was susceptible to suggestion of every kind."

A typical feature of Bernheim's case description, is that he does not raise questions about the aetiology of the symptom or the meaning of it at any moment whatever. The rendition of the case fails to grasp the ambivalent nature of the patient's 'dislike for meat'. The pivotal part of his psychical treatment resides in his wielding of authority in order to impose ideas on the patient's mind. When suggestion fails, only one explanation is deemed possible, i.e. the presence in the patient of a resistance that takes the shape of auto- or counter-suggestion. Therapy is thence viewed as some sort of battle against the purely 'mechanistic' intervention of the physician and of his authority. And when the most persistent attempts fail, Bernheim argues that with "(...) this sort of patient, auto-suggestion is stronger than a suggestion from sone one else. They listen to their inner feelings, they call them up, they are in relationship only with themselves; they are *auto-suggestionists*."[67]

What is more, Bernheim is not interested in the life history of his patients. There is no room in his psychical treatment for the speech of his patients. At most, one learns how a particular syndrome appeared in the patient. There are, in this instance, very few allusions to the patient's family situation.[68]

Bernheim's influence on Freud: Emmy von N.

Freud always emphasised that from the moment he turned to the technique of hypnosis he adopted a different mode of operation from Bernheim's. One explanation for this is that, from the outset, Freud investigated the cause or the aetiology of hysterical symptoms.

One could argue that Freud learned from Breuer's treatment of Anna O., that in hysteria there exists a connection between the symptom and the ideational life of the patient. As a result, one could claim that the idea and its concurring affect can be identified as being the pathogenic element. When the patient manages to put these excessively intense ideas into words during the course of the talking cure, the symptoms vanish. The most important guideline one can glean from this outline of a psychical treatment, is the attention paid — not so much to the symptom — but to the ideas and recollections intertwined in it.

Herein lies the radical difference with Bernheim who, as we have seen, avoided at all costs grafting his psychological influence to what he called the auto-suggestion of his patients. Instead, his psychical treatment required the *diversion* of the patient's attention away from his own ideas by focusing wholly on the physician's suggestions. As such, he tried to avoid, as much as possible, arousing the patient's resistance. Consequently, it was better to avoid awakening the patient's ideas. If he succeeded in all this, Bernheim would enter *en rapport* with his patients, or put differently, his patients would confer on him the authority needed to complete the suggestion successfully. For what is authority after all, if not *delegated* authority? In the Nancy institute it was allegedly very easy for Bernheim to acquire such authority, albeit on a collective scale.

This information throws a different light on Freud's evaluation of himself as a mediocre hypnotiser. That he, unlike Bernheim, could not boast of something resembling authority in his praxis — if one is to presume that he desired such a thing — can at least partially be put down to his position, which did not enable him to exploit the group element. Furthermore, Freud's persistent focus on his patients' ideas as they came up in their accounts, explains why he had to face to the phenomenon of resistance more frequently and intensely.

So, does all this mean that Bernheim's influence on Freud is hardly worth mentioning? By no means. Freud himself always pointed out that hypnotic therapy was adumbrative of the psychoanalytic treatment. For even when one subverts something the allusion to it still remains effective — albeit in a specific way. The case history of Emmy von N. offers an outstanding example of this subversion.

One also has to bear in mind that the idea of conceiving of dreams as "Normalvorbild" of the psychopathological process, was, as it were, there for the taking and it may well be this healer's most enriching contribution. Finally, let me point out that *Suggestive Therapeutics* contains numerous allusions to various authors — such as Maury, Maudsley and Delboeuf — who will reappear later in Freud's work.[69]

A reading of the case of Emmy von N. enables one to find an answer to the 'how and why' of Freud's emancipation from the hypnotic technique. Freud started the treatment of this 40 year old woman on 1 May 1888, that is to say 3 months prior to the publication of his translation of the first part of Bernheim's book.[70] Hence, one ought not to be surprised to find references to this translation in his discussion of the case history.

Emmy suffered from a number of hypnotic symptoms: anxiety, self-reproach and ill-humour. However, she could be put into the highest form of hypnotic sleep with the greatest ease. Freud, who took an interest both in this woman's symptoms and in her personality, decided to start therapy in accordance with Breuer's method, i.e. the application of hypnosis in order to provoke the catharsis of affects and ideas. At least, this is what he writes in the introduction to the case when preparing his report for publication.

Yet the notes he took in the course of the first three weeks of treatment give another impression. He seems only to have borrowed the formal characteristics of Breuer's treatment of Anna O. For instance, on his suggestion, she was admitted into a nursing home where he was at leisure to pay her a visit *twice a day* — just like Breuer did with Anna O. A second characteristic, i.e. the hypnoid state Breuer's patient reached spontaneously, had, in Emmy's case, to be conjured up by means of hypnosis.

As far as speech is concerned, Freud's reporting on the first session reminds one more of Bernheim's book than of Breuer's case description. Freud is enthralled by his expectations about the efficiency of direct suggestion and starts off by using conventional invocations. When Emmy suffers from gastric pains he makes them disappear by means of suggestion and when she is unable to sleep, he instils the idea of sleep into her mind.

A particular circumstance, however, changed the course of treatment almost from the start. As Emmy's condition had temporarily improved, a few years previously due to a course of massage combined with hydro-therapy, Freud decided to prescribe the same treatment now. Freud massaged her whole body twice a day, prior to each hypnotic session. In the course of this massage session Emmy started to speak spontaneously. What she said during these sessions attracted Freud's attention and it was this that he would gradually get his, as yet direct suggestions, to tie in with.

One morning she related a series of gruesome stories about animals to Freud. She had read one of them in the *Frankfurter Zeitung*. The story was about how a boy had died of fright after he had been tied up and a white mouse had been put into his mouth. As she told the story, Emmy displayed signs of horror and at a certain moment declaimed a sort of formula to protect herself from the horrifying images of mice and rats: "Keep still! — Don't say anything! — Don't touch me!" Freud dispersed these animal hallucinations during the hypnosis and read the paper to verify her story. There was no mention at all of either mice or rats. Emmy had introduced these herself "from her delirium". In the evening, Freud checked whether his suggestion had any effect at all and, to his satisfaction, he observed that she had no recollection whatsoever of the animals.

To use Freud's own terms, his interventions mainly consist in 'expunging', 'wiping out', 'mitigating', 'extracting', 'resolving', 'prohibiting', and 'regulating' the symptoms and ideas that emerge in the course of the treatment. His general attitude is that of the 'soothing', 'calming' and 'learned' physician 'ensuring' a prompt recovery, 'promising' a regular menstrual cycle, but who at times resorts to a 'white lie'. Freud repeatedly verified the effects of either his suggestive influence or of his authority and took note, in this instance, of the success of his intervention.

Emmy's attitude to Freud was by no means one of obedient submission, comparable to that which Bernheim was in a position to arouse in his clinic. Freud invoked two reasons to account for this. Firstly, Emmy had long been profoundly critical of the interventions of physicians in general and, secondly Freud realised that suggestion was a notably ineffective tool to probe into memories. One cannot simply 'wipe out' a memory. Take, for instance, Emmy's animal hallucinations. The elimination of these by means of suggestion turned out to be short-lived. Freud reproached himself for not having carried through the analysis of his patient's memory systematically enough, and consequently for not having been able completely to expunge her pathogenic memories.

Indeed, he should have been able to predict Emmy's resistance from his reading of Bernheim's book. *The patient's resistance to recovery increases as the patient's attention is directed towards his own ideas.* This was what happened as Freud grafted his suggestion onto the stories she spontaneously told during the massage that preceded the actual hypnotic session.

Freud could not boast of having entered 'en rapport' with his patient. Yet one cannot say that — despite her unruliness — he left her indifferent. What then did Emmy's speech represent to Freud and what was the element bolstering and mediating it?

Emmy was, in any case, not the type of accommodating patient who would be satisfied by putting forward mere physical symptoms or conversion symptoms to be 'wiped out' by her physician. She suffered mainly from apparently unfounded ill-humour, anxieties and self-reproaches. These states of affect were rooted in her ideational life. Freud was astonished by these and took an interest in her story. But, at most, she could give poor and incomplete answers as to the cause of her anxieties and self-reproaches. Freud was unable to make any sense of what she told him. For what she said when in a waking state seemed to perturbed by 'something' which came from 'elsewhere'.

The course of treatment allowed Freud to complete Breuer's observation of the pathogenic influence of memories and at the same time corroborated it. The reminiscences and scenes conjured up by Emmy made it possible to isolate the false connection and the fragments of hysterical delirium that she herself inserted into her account. Every single state of affect in Emmy was entangled in an idea or a scene and each word, in turn, called forth an affect. When discussing the phenomenon of false connection, I demonstrated that a disruption of the hysterical speech cannot be dissociated from the eroticized transference. In other words, *the very condition of the psychical treatment calls forth the disruptive affect.* One encounters for the first time what Freud was later to call transference neurosis, i.e. neurosis as it is aroused by the transference itself.[71]

The *subversion* or inversion of psychical influencing as conceived of by Bernheim bears on the two factors that enable it. Firstly, as far as *speech* is concerned, the patient's metonymic association comes to substitute for the suggestion of ideas which were 'introduced into the brain' by the physician. This substitution results from Freud's inversion of the 'direction' of the focus of attention. Secondly, the patient's *concentration* on the physician is replaced by a 'look within', that is to say, the subject's attention is directed at the ideas that surface from within himself. This inversion means that the *rapport*, (i.e. the influence of the authority attributed to physician) is substituted for the influence of the sexual affect which reveals itself through the transference phenomenon.

At the same time, this subversion lends to the analytic device the quality of a therapeutic means and, makes it a most fitting instrument to probe into the human psyche. It would obviously take quite some time before Freud could actually chart the psyche and its mechanisms. Yet this subversion, in all its simplicity, can to be considered as *the condition for the discovery of the unconscious*. In the next chapter, I will to take a closer look at the insight which equates the status of speech under transference to that of the false connection. For that purpose, I will mainly be drawing on the remaining sections of the *Studies on Hysteria*. Only later, i.e. in the *Project*, does one come across Freud's first rigorous and systematic attempt to theorise the 'hysterical compulsion' or 'hysterical proton pseudos'.

Nancy versus Paris: hysteria revisited?

An aspect of Freud's foreword, written in 1888, can be explained by taking into account his personal experience with hypnosis as developed in the case history of Emma von N. In it a certain degree of reservation about some of Bernheim's conceptions transpires. Bernheim's book may well have been an ideal propaganda tool for mitigating the averse disposition towards psychical treatment in Vienna, yet Freud was still somewhat reluctant to embrace Bernheim's 'one-sided' theoretical viewpoint. He was quite perplexed by the status of hypnosis. He was torn between Charcot's conception holding that hypnosis is determined by a heightened excitation of the nervous system, i.e.

a *physiological* alteration, and that of Bernheim, who propounded that hypnosis was determined by suggestion, that is to say, by something of a *psychical* nature.

Suggestive Therapeutics clearly acquires a special significance in the then-prevailing polemic between the schools of Nancy and Paris. Bernheim appeared as the mouthpiece of those who maintained that all hypnotic phenomena are reducible to one point of origin. They argued that their source is without exception to be found in suggestion, i.e, "a conscious idea, which has been introduced into the brain of the hypnotised person by an external influence and has been accepted by him as though it had arisen spontaneously."[72] In this respect, all hypnotic phenomena were regarded as psychical phenomena, that is to say, as being the work of suggestions.

Opposing this conception were those adhering to the idea that some hypnotic phenomena can be put down to physiological changes, i.e. the displacement of excitation in the nervous system: hence these people spoke of physical or physiological hypnotic phenomena.

The principal subject of this dispute was Charcot's description of 'le grand hypnotisme'.

Charcot, who had acquired his knowledge of hypnotism through his experience with hysterical patients, conceived of the hypnotic state that can be induced in these patients, as a real neurosis exhibiting a succession of distinct stages, each having specific characteristics. The physician can, at will, have the subject of the experiment pass over from one stage to another by carrying out certain tricks.

The three stages in question had long been described by Charcot and in his *Lectures* he merely sums them up. "I would remind you that in the *lethargic phase* of what is called *great hypnotism*, the mental inertia is so absolute that in general it is impossible to enter into relation with the hypnotised subject or to communicate any idea to him by any process whatever."[73] The lethargic state can be induced by staring at an object or by exerting a light pressure on the pupil covered by the eyelids. In this case, there is no mention of suggestion.

"But it is not thus in the other two phases of hypnotism. Thus in *catalepsy* — I speak here only of true catalepsy, such as I have described — certain phenomena of suggestion are easily obtained, and owing to their simplicity and their small tendency to become generalised, they are relatively easy of analysis."[74] It is enough to open a 'lethargic' patient's eyelids in order to reach this stage and the patient's body will imperturbably assume and keep any position in which it is put. "Here, as in the preceding phase, there is mental inertia, but it is less profound, less absolute; it has become possible, indeed, to produce a sort of partial waking in the organ of the psychic faculties. Thus one can call into existence an idea, or a group of ideas connected together by previous associations. But this group set in action will remain strictly limited. There will be no propagation, no diffusion of the communicated movement; all the rest will remain asleep. Consequently the idea, or group of ideas suggested, are met with in a state of isolation, free from the control of that large collection of personal ideas long accumulated and organised, which constitute the conscious properly so-called, the *ego*. It is for this reason that the movements which exteriorly represent the acts of unconscious cerebration are distinguished by their automatic and purely mechanical character. Then it is truly that we see before us the *human machine* ["l'homme machine"] in all its simplicity, dreamt of by De la Mettrie."[75]

The suggestion referred to here mainly operates via the muscles. If the hands of the subject of the experiment are placed as if to blow a kiss, his face will assume a smiling expression. But if his fists are shut, as if ready to fight, one will correspondingly observe a menacing expression on his face.

By stroking the patient's head once or repeatedly, the third stage — the *somnambulic* stage — can be attained. Mental obnubilation persists, but the number of ideas that can be activated is less restricted and the induced psychical phenomena spreads. This is in accordance with the "tendency to the reconstitution of the ego." Under these circumstances it sometimes happens that the subject puts up a certain amount of resistance. The purely mechanical character of the executed movements then disappears: they take on the likeness of voluntary acts. It becomes possible to enter 'en rapport' with the subject. If an object is held up to the patient, the mere view of it will arouse in him a certain number of ideas which will be converted into movements. Nevertheless, the most efficient instrument remains suggestion by means of the word.[76]

Bernheim, for his part, contests the reproach that research in Nancy veered too rapidly to psychical phenomena instead of first mapping its somatic and physical characteristics. At the Salpêtrière one was of the opinion that Bernheim and his disciples interchanged the various hypnotic phases and that they failed to indicate in which phase the subject was. "I reply that if we have not taken the three phases of hysterical hypnotism, as Charcot describes them, for the starting-point of our researches, it is because we have not been able to confirm their existence by our observations. (...) I have never been able to induce in any of my cases, the three phases of the Salpêtrière school, and it is not for want of trial. I add, that even in three hospitals in Paris, I have seen subjects hypnotized in my presence and they acted as our patients do, and the doctors who were treating them fully confirmed our observations. (...) Once only did I see a subject who exhibited perfectly the three periods of lethargy, catalepsy and somnambulism. It was a young girl who had been at the Salpêtrière for three years, and why should I not state the impression which I retained of the case ? Subjected to a special training by manipulations, imitating the phenomena which she saw produced in other somnambulists of the same school, taught by imitation to exhibit reflex phenomena in a certain typical order, the case was no longer one of natural hypnotism, but a product of false training, a true *suggestive hypnotic neurosis*. Even if I am mistaken, and these phenomena are met with primarily, and without any suggestion, we must recognize that this "grand hypnotisme" is a rare condition. Binet and Frère say that only a dozen of these cases have occurred at the Salpêtrière in ten years. Should these cases, opposed to thousands of cases in which these phenomena are wanting, serve as the basis for the theoretical conception of hypnotism?"[77]

Freud's point of view

Freud understood perfectly what was at stake in this dispute. If Bernheim was right, very little of what was regarded as true in the Salpêtrière remained. And this was not only the case with respect to 'major hypnotism', but also with respect to the entire clinical tableau of hysteria: "If suggestion by the physician has falsified the phenomena of hysterical hypnosis, it is quite possible that it may also have interfered with the observation of the rest of hysterical symptomatology: it may have laid down laws governing hysterical attacks, paralyses, contractures, etc., which are only connected with neurosis through suggestion and which consequently lose their validity as soon as another physician in another place makes an examination of hysterical patients."[78]

However true these words will turn out to be, Freud still felt compelled to advocate Charcot's view. Bernheim's conception seemed to him to add grist to the mill of the German speaking community which persisted in discarding the laws governing hysterical phenomena. "Here we should have a splendid example of how neglect of the psychical factor of suggestion has misled a great observer [Charcot] into the artificial and false creation of a clinical type as a result of the capriciousness and easy malleability of a neurosis."[79]
In Freud's mind, the objectivity of the hysterical symptomatology can easily be proved. Bernheim's critique may well be pertinent as regards the work of some researchers, but Charcot was still the one who demonstrated the consistency of hysterical symptomatology through the centuries. By isolating objective physiological phenomena in hysteria, it is also possible to show that the phenomena of the 'great hypnotism' do not result from the suggestion of the researcher. "Thus it lies with the Salpêtrière school to prove that the three stages of hysterical hypnosis can be unmistakably demonstrated even upon a newly arrived experimental subject and even when the most scrupulous behaviour is maintained by the investigator."[80]

Freud thus subscribed to the postulate both of psychical as well as of physiological phenomena which could induce hypnosis. Yet he agreed with Bernheim that the partitioning of hypnotic phenomena leaves one with a most unsatisfied feeling. The necessity of a connecting link between the two classes of phenomena was urgently needed. In attempting to come up with such a link, Freud commented that the shifting and ambiguous use of the word 'suggestion' granted a misleading sharpness to this antithesis. What one calls suggestion implies some kind of psychical influence which distinguishes itself from other kinds of psychical influences (such as a command or giving a piece of information or instruction) by the fact that "in the case of a suggestion an idea is aroused in another person's brain which is not examined in regard to its origin but is accepted just as though it had arisen spontaneously in that brain."[81] The catalepsy of the arm aroused by direct suggestion is a classic example. One could still give other examples in which suggestion only plays a minor role. For instance, when one raises the arm of an hypnotised patient, he will maintain the posture. This is a case of spontaneous catalepsy of the arm which does not require the injunction "your arm is paralysed; you cannot move it". In Freud's opinion, the part played by the physiological condition of the subject is in this case evidently more substantial. The distinction between a directly psychical suggestion and an indirect physiological suggestion becomes even clearer when examining what Charcot called auto-suggestion. For instance, just by tapping the patient on the arm one can produce a physiological hypnotic effect: "[...] independently of any intervention on the part of the physician, paralysis has been suggested — if such an expression is still applicable here. In other words, it is a question in these cases not so much of suggestions as of *auto-suggestions*. And these, as anyone can see, contain an objective factor, independent of the physician's will, they reveal a connection between various conditions of innervation or excitation in the nervous system. It is auto-suggestions such as these that lead to the production of spontaneous hysterical paralyses and it is an inclination to such auto-suggestions, rather than suggestibility towards the physician, that characterises hysteria."[82]

According to Freud, these auto-suggestions can be regarded as psychical and physiological phenomena because "they are no longer exposed to the full light of consciousness which falls upon direct suggestion."[83] The antithesis between the two kinds of hypnotic phenomena is meaningful in so far as suggestion is understood as the direct psychical influence of the physician, but it vanishes as soon as one realises that the term also describes sets of manifestations based on the peculiarities of the hypnotised nervous system.[84]

It seems obvious that Freud's explanation was a desperate attempt to cling to the notion of the clinical entity of hysteria, which had been revised by the Nancy school. As we have seen, Bernheim paid no particular attention to neuroses or to their explanation. Following in Liébault's footsteps, the treatment was given the priority and hypnosis was massively and indistinctly applied to the most divergent diseases. Nonetheless, this attitude, i.e. the prescription of a psychical treatment in conjunction with the administration of classical medical care, comes across as being quite modern. What Freud esteems in Bernheim's book is its coverage of psychical treatment and the psychological explanation of its mode of operation.

Another reason why Freud embraced Charcot's view probably has to do with the fact that, at that stage, he had also acquired some experience in the field of hypnosis. Going beyond Bernheim's exposing of the clinical tableau of hysteria, Freud had reached the opinion that the symptomatology of hysteria was largely determined by the patient's life history and hence could not wholly be put down to the physician's direct suggestion.

Freud's advocacy of Charcot's view of hypnosis is not so much aimed at safeguarding the physiological explanation.[85] He too perceives that Bernheim's hypothesis is more likely to be true, as the operation of the mechanism of suggestion is much more transparent than the operation of the presupposed physiological processes. By attempting to 'safeguard' the entity of hysteria — because this is precisely what he was concerned with — Freud leaves the door open to a potential specific psychical mechanism: "The symptomatology of hysteria hints in many respects at a *psychical mechanism*, though that need not be the mechanism of suggestion."[86] Freud leaves us in the dark as to the nature of this mechanism, but the allusion to Charcot's auto-suggestion indicates that he had some hypotheses in mind.[87] When all is said and done, auto-suggestion still implies an idea, i.e. a psychical element, and for Freud it is very much a question of whether the qualification 'psychical' can be left to depend on whether the idea in question occurs in the patient's consciousness. "We possess no criterion which enables us to distinguish exactly between a psychical process and a physiological one, between an act occurring in the cerebral cortex and occurring in the subcortical substance; for 'consciousness', whatever that may be, is not attached to the very activity of the cerebral cortex, nor is it always attached in an equal degree to any particular one of its activities, it is not a thing which is bound up with any locality in the nervous system."[88]

Conclusion

Answering the question as to the influence of Bernheim's book on Freud brings to light two factors which will occupy an important role in his later work and which will develop into essential characteristics of his approach. Although the reference to hypnotic suggestion clearly transpires from the case study of Emmy von N., Freud nevertheless seems to adopt a fundamentally independent viewpoint in his psychical treatment. The nature of his therapy is particular, since his curiosity and attention are directed to the speech of his patient. The choice of this line of approach can be explained by the hypothesis that the hysterical symptom is determined by the 'forgetting' of ideas or recollections and by the observation that Emmy's speech is disrupted and falsely connected. The patient's speech accordingly not only paves the way for the talking cure but also reveals her symptoms. This conception, crystallised in Freud's annotations to Bernheim's book, implies a subversion of Bernheim's therapy of suggestion. While Freud abandons the 'rapport' or the influence of the physician's authority, he turns to eroticised 'transference' which materialises as both a condition for gaining knowledge of the psyche and as a phenomenon of resistance.

A first observation in this respect could be formulated as follows. Freud's object is not the patient, the symptom or the discovery of a cure. Instead he decides to turn his attention to the mechanisms operative in the psyche. Speech under transference — the analytical apparatus — represents in his opinion the instrument *par excellence* for the construction of his science on the psyche, or his psychology.

The second point ties in with the aforementioned and is at the same time connected with Freud's thirst for knowledge. It is undeniable that by translating Bernheim's book — as well as Charcot's — Freud intended to develop his private practice and to make a name for himself in Vienna. But, just as with the application of the techniques of treatment, Freud turns out to be a 'user' or 'borrower' of fragments of theory, formulated hypotheses and wielded concepts, rather than an adherent or a disciple. Freud is well able to make a distinction between the important and the subordinate. He transforms the allusion to the psyche (Charcot) and the postulate of a psychical mechanism (Bernheim) into a radical epistemological choice: the question about the psyche is a question about a psychical *mechanism.*[89] *This point of departure is by no means the result of a linear progression based on what he learned from Charcot and Bernheim. It signifies instead the subversion of the position which enabled both Masters to arouse these psychical phenomena in their respective institutes.*

CHAPTER 3

Studies on Hysteria

"Alas! I have explored
Philosophy, and Law, and Medicine;
And over deep Divinity have pored,
Studying with ardent and laborious zeal;
And here I am at last, a very fool,
With useless learning curst,
No wiser than at first!"

Goethe

3.1. Introduction

The *Studies on Hysteria* back up the thesis which holds that the *Project* can be interpreted as Freud's theoretical construction in response to the clinic of the excessively intense idea.[1] If one assumes that the *Project* can be read as a work on psychology and that it should not to be understood and discarded as Freud's ultimate attempt to provide a physiological explanation of psychopathology, this evidently raises the question as to the links between the *Studies* (clinic) and the *Project* (theory).

The chronology of both texts warrants a reading of this kind. In the period during which he sent the corrected draft for the *Studies* to his friend and colleague, Wilhelm Fließ, Freud regularly made mention of his laborious endeavour to write a "psychology for neurologists". Incidentally, it is possible to trace the genesis of both texts on the basis of Freud's correspondence with Fließ.

Amongst other things, my reading of the *Project* implies, that one cannot look upon this manuscript as being an isolated enterprise which only acquires significance within the frame of what is sometimes called the 'transference' between Freud and Fließ.[2] That this represents an inadequate approach, becomes apparent when considering the marginal glosses in a great number of Freud's later works directing the reader to this particular manuscript for a first formulation of some hypotheses. In these instances, this seminal text is implicitly ascribed the predicates 'psychological', 'metapsychological' and even 'psychoanalytical'. The same applies to the *Studies*: leaving aside the gap between the *Studies* and Freud's output, the *Studies* are constantly viewed as being the source of psychoanalysis.

The chronology and the qualifications of the *Studies* and the *Project* give grounds for setting both texts side by side; an exercise which up until now has not been endeavoured by many authors.[3]

However, a comparison between the two is not particularly straightforward. A closer examination reveals that the *Studies* contain *two* distinct theoretical assumptions. On the one hand, Breuer's theoretical chapter and on the other, Freud's theoretical conceptions in his chapter on psychotherapy. These two visions are so different and even contradictory at times, that one is forced to question the extent to which either can convey anything on the subject of the clinic of the excessively intense idea. It is primarily this blatant discrepancy that impels one to view the *Project* as also implying a critique of Breuer.[4]

Traditionally, two provisional reasons are invoked in connection with the theoretical divergence of opinion between Freud and Breuer. According to Freud, Breuer appointed too peripheral a role to the mechanism of defence and furthermore experienced difficulties in acknowledging the importance of sexuality as an etiological factor.[5] Is it then merely a question of the degree of importance they attributed to both factors, or is the difference between the two approaches due to a fundamental epistemological distinction?

Epistemological questions in Freud's early work are definitely not unequivocal. For instance, a presupposed continuity between Breuer's theoretical chapter and the *Project* leads all too easily to the idea that in 1895 Freud was as yet a purely materialistic-mechanistic thinker. An important argument in favour of this view is found in the frame of reference employed by Freud. How valid can this be said to be? In other words, does Freud employ a frame of reference to elucidate or represent clinical psychological insights, or does he employ this frame in order to infer psychological insights?

In the present chapter, I intend to do no more than to map the actual clinical and theoretical antecedents of the *Project*. My reading of the *Studies*, in addition, seeks to offer a contemporary answer to questions pertaining to the purpose of psychotherapy and to what can be expected or even demanded from a psychotherapist at present. These two subordinate questions seem to me to be legitimate, since the *Studies* are historically speaking one of the first texts dealing with psychotherapy. It would be a shame to ignore this line of approach, for what is the purpose of questioning older texts, if not to try to find answers to present day questions?

What is clear, is that the publication of the *Studies* was an arduous undertaking. Towards the end of June 1892, Freud informed Fließ that Breuer had agreed to a joint publication of their findings and hypotheses concerning hysteria.[6] A 'Preliminary Communication' which included their first attempt at explaining the aetiology of hysterical symptoms was already published in January 1893, but it was not until April 1895 that Freud sent the last drafts to Fließ.[7]

Yet the genesis of the *Studies* is somewhat more intricate than this would suggest. The *Studies* are clearly *not* the product of the combined efforts of two researchers sharing a passion for one and the same object of study, i.e. the psyche. This joint publication symbolises, to a certain extent, the inevitable and definitive estrangement between Freud and Breuer.

Breuer, who finally complied with Freud's insistent request to collaborate, had cast psychotherapy aside a long time ago. So his first task was to retrieve the peculiar history of Anna O.'s treatment. This in itself was no *tour de force*, as he could make use of the detailed notes he took during the progression of the treatment.[8] These notes cover the period running from November 1880 to June 1882. What is more, Breuer had already informed his 14 years younger colleague in November 1882 of his activities.[9] A second element is however new to his approach, namely the writing of a *theory* explaining hysteria and the mode of operation of the psycho-cathartic method. And even though Breuer did make a serious attempt to regain command of what had happened a decade ago and to follow Freud who had unleashed new views, his theoretical chapter can still be regarded as a sample of his moral resistance against what surfaces from Freud's case studies.

Freud's situation was totally different. On returning from Paris and through his reading of Bernheim, he found (or at least so he thinks) in Breuer a third individual of excellent reputation who, just like himself, deemed it possible — if not essential — to approach neuroses from a psychological vantage point, i.e. from the psyche and its mechanisms. In spite of Freud's further dedication to other issues, one can make out an undeniable continuity in his progression. The notion of the psyche gradually started to occupy a more prominent place in both the articulation of his theoretical viewpoint as well as in the mounting influence of the "Seelenbehandlung" (psychical treatment) in his praxis. It is not clear from either the *Studies* or from his correspondence with Fließ whether, between May 1886 and June 1892, Freud undertook the treatment of other patients besides Emmy von N. and Căcilie M. using the cathartic method. One reason for the delayed publication of the book could lie in the fact that both authors thought that they did not have enough clinical material at their disposal.[10] Whatever the case may be, when considering the different chapters of the *Studies* written by Freud, i.e. the four case studies and the chapter on psychotherapy, one's attention is caught by the progression which they display. Once again, this progression exhibits a characteristic trait, namely the dialectic between the empirical and the theoretical.

Therein lies the most important difference with Breuer's attitude. For him what represents an end — "never again"[11] — which Breuer could only reconsider from a strictly medical-ethical line of approach, is to Freud a point of departure. In Emmy's case the psycho-cathartic method was turned into a research instrument. And in the case of Căcilie, the findings of this method provided a direct impetus for his writing of the 'Preliminary Communication'. I will now take a closer look at both authors' conceptions. As far as Freud's progression is concerned, I will start with a fairly unknown publication from 1890.

3.2. "Seelenbehandlung"

In 1890, Freud published an inspired article on psychical treatment in the popular household medical book, *Die Gesundheit*.[12] At first sight, this text seems devoid of any scientific pretensions. Yet this article, written in the smooth, elegant and clear German which is characteristic of Freud, betokens a revelation, a declaration of principles, even a plea. Behind it, lay concealed a truly revolutionary epistemological viewpoint for that time.

What does this text reveal? It deals with the way in which *speech* is employed in a systematic manner as a therapeutical instrument and opens with the following excellent paragraph: "'Psyche' is a Greek word which may be translated '*mind*'. Thus 'psychical treatment' means 'mental treatment'. The term might accordingly be supposed to signify 'treatment of the pathological phenomena of mental life.' This, however, is not its meaning. 'Psychical treatment' denotes, rather, treatment starting in the mind, treatment (whether of mental or physical disorders) by measures which operate in the first instance and immediately upon the human mind. Foremost among such measures is the use of words; and words are the essential tool of mental treatment."[13]

This implies that, irrespective of what the psyche may be and of how Freud's later theory of it was to look, his object of study, the psyche, is something which one can only gain access to via *speech*. Psychical treatment or psychotherapy is not directed at the physical symptom or at behaviour, but essentially indicates the notion of influencing by means of the *word*.

From the outset, this speech is attributed a dual status. On the one hand, words themselves are the *instrument* par excellence for *treatment*. On the other, this basic assumption raises questions concerning the psyche as such: how is one to interpret the psyche and what should a *clinical psychology* look like if it is to account for the effects of speech? All this suggests that to Freud speech acquired the status of a *research instrument* from the very start.

This psychological approach is legitimised by the manifestly inadequate explanatory potential of medicine whose focus on the body was too exclusive. Freud speaks about a "reciprocal relation between body and mind" and argues that the physicians' fear of attributing a certain degree of independence to psychical life is no longer founded. For, indeed, has the practice of medicine itself not shown that numerous diseases do not have any tangible, i.e. organic, explanations?[14] "This condition has been described as 'nervousness' (neurasthenia or hysteria) and has been characterised as a merely 'functional' disorder of the nervous system."[15] Gradually one came to the understanding that the cause of obsessional and delusional ideas, as well as of delusional insanity in patients had to be looked for in "their minds".[16] What this means is that Freud postulated the existence of a domain where something can be observed and treated, a domain which lies beyond any 'functional disorder', i.e. beyond a presupposed physiological anomaly of the nervous system, namely the *psyche*.[17]

But what precisely does the psychical refer to? The epistemological view adopted by Freud doubtless implies that a particularly arduous task lay ahead of him. If we leave aside the weak hypotheses which we encountered in Charcot and Bernheim's works, amongst others, we realise that no elaborate clinical psychology was available in 1890. Such a psychological theory, based on the praxis of psychotherapy was yet to be constructed. In this respect it is, to say the least, surprising to find, in as early as 1890, a formulation of some understandings and concepts (such as those of the *affective idea, transference* and *resistance*) which are of essential importance to the psychoanalysis Freud later developed, and which are the direct result of his very first experience with the talking cure.

The first aspect to which Freud tags the appellation 'psychical' is the *affect.* He departs from the observation that the scientific examination of psychical suffering sheds a new light on normal mental life. The influence of the psychical on the physical has long been recognised; we need only think of what one understands by "the expression of the emotions". Almost all psychical states manifest themselves in changes in physical parameters. These concurrent physical changes are mostly ineffectual in the sense that they often thwart the intention of the person in question, which is to *conceal* his mental processes from other people. For other people the physical changes function as indications which allow one to infer these processes and which are often more reliable than the words which are expressed simultaneously.
The influence of psychical states (affects) on the body is even more striking. In the case of anxiety, anger, mental pain and grief, the physical changes are so drastic that numerous researchers thought that the essence of the affects lay in these phenomena. Freud, for his part, stressed that strictly speaking all psychical states, "including those that we usually regard as 'processes of thought', are to some degree 'affective' (...) Even when a person is engaged in quietly thinking in a string of 'ideas', there are constant series of excitations, corresponding to the content of these ideas, which are discharged into the smooth or striated muscles."[18]
Without resorting to any sort of physiological speculation, Freud defines the realm of the psychical as being that of the *affective idea.* To him, coupling the affect to the idea represents the first step towards a logos for the psyche. This fundamental hypothesis makes it possible to explain a series of peculiar phenomena. Freud alludes to the so-called "Gedankenerraten" (thought-reading) which, departing from the notion that the thought or idea is manifested by means of small, involuntary muscular movements, ought to be considered as a "Gedanken*ver*raten" (thought-betraying). But the influence of psychical processes such as those of *volition* and *attention,* also argue in favour of Freud's conception. It is also a well-known fact that just by directing one's

attention to a particular place on one's body, one can produce sensations or pains. Conversely, diverting one's attention from these mitigates their effect.[19]

However, the psyche is not simply an explanatory factor for peripheral medical phenomena. The psychical state of "faithful expectancy" which is in operation in the phenomenon of the miraculous cures, is also an essential component in the relationship of the patient to the physician. "The results of every procedure laid down by the physician and of every treatment that he undertakes are probably composed of two portions. And one of these, which is sometimes greater and sometimes less, but can never be completely disregarded, is determined by the patient's mental attitude. The faith with which he meets the immediate effect of a medical procedure depends on the one hand on the amount of his desire to be cured, and on the other hand on his confidence that he has taken the right steps in that direction — on his general respect, that is, for medical skill — and, further, on the power which he attributes to his doctor's personality, and even on the purely human liking aroused in him by the doctor."[20]

Freud observes that if we understand "mental treatment" as entailing the generation of mental states propitious for the patient's recovery, then we are bound to recognise that psychotherapy is the oldest form of treatment. In the past, i.e. before the advent of modern medicine, the physician had very little else at his disposal other than his personality which he would use in the same way. Modern "mental treatment" differs from its older form in that it "deliberately imposes a propitious state of mind by suitable methods". Freely choosing one's physician evidently plays an important part and is a precondition for the psychical influence, since the objective is to arouse the human liking and confidence of the patient.[21] At first sight, the means at the physician's disposal for systematic psychical influencing seem very limited. The physician has to renounce one of the most instrumental of all these means, namely the affects. For he cannot possibly compete with the vicissitudes of life which often manage to cure illnesses by satisfying needs and fulfilling wishes, which in these instances have positive consequences in daily life. Trying to act on the patient by using fear or fright does not seem to be appropriate either. The physician must also exclude any relations with a patient which are permeated with feelings of affection.[22]

What remains is the physician's focus on the *psychical functions* of the patient. And the scope of this is anything but restricted. Freud confines his analysis in the rest of this article to the technique of the hypnotic suggestion and thence follows in the footsteps of Bernheim, whom Freud believed to be one of the pioneers who put the use of the word on a par with any other medical intervention for the first time in the history of medicine. This means that hypnotic suggestion lies at the origin of every psychical treatment.

Hypnosis is primarily directed at the psychical function of *attention*. This is already apparent in the various ways in which hypnosis can be induced in patients. One can either hypnotise someone by holding up a bright object in front of his/her eyes or by talking the patient into hypnosis ("Einreden"). All these means have a fixing of the attention in common. The hypnotic state is also to be conceived of in this way. The most important characteristic that Freud perceived lay in the attitude of the hypnotised patient to the hypnotist. The patient behaves towards the outside world as if he were asleep, with one notable difference, namely that he remains awake for the person who brought on the hypnotic state. The patient hears and sees nobody else but the hypnotist; he understands him and replies to his questions. "This phenomenon, which is described as rapport in the case of hypnosis, finds a parallel in the way in which some people sleep — for instance, a mother who is nursing her baby. It is so striking that it may well lead us to an understanding of the relation between the hypnotic subject and the hypnotist."[23] Not only is the attention of the hypnotised subject exclusively directed at the hypnotist, but in addition, s/he subjects her/himself totally to the hypnotist and exhibits an unrestrained "obedience and credulity" which is characteristic of the 'rapport'. This, as a matter of fact, reveals the extraordinarily heightened influence of the psychical on the physical: words uttered by the hypnotist, such as "you can't move your arm" invariably and promptly lead the patient to assume the corresponding posture. The same also holds for sensory perception. The subject's 'credulity' reaches such high proportions that when the physician says that there is a snake, the patient effectively sees a snake.The conviction of seeing a snake has such a powerful effect on the patient's body that he sees or hallucinates the snake. Freud adds: "It may be remarked, by the way, that, outside hypnosis and in real life, credulity such as the subject has in relation to his hypnotist is shown only by a child towards his beloved parents, and that an attitude of similar subjection on the part of one person towards another has only one parallel, though a complete one — namely in certain love-relationships where there is extreme devotion. A combination of exclusive attachment and credulous obedience is in general among the characteristics of love."[24]

Freud puts forth a criticism of these characteristics. The credulous obedience can, within the frame of the therapy, lead the patient to be dependent on the physician, which surely is not the aim of therapy. A second limitation of hypnotic therapy lies in the physician's incapability of overcoming the "interfering autocratic element" which Freud was later to call 'resistance'. This element is preserved throughout the hypnosis and reveals itself already in the resistance that is put up against the attempt to hypnotise. For even under hypnosis, one remains conscious of oneself. "If we put a healthy person into deep hypnosis and then tell him to take a bite out of a potato under the impression that it is a pear, or if he is meeting one of his acquaintances and must greet him as such, he is to prove completely tractable, because the hypnotised subject has no serious reason for resisting the suggestion. But in the case of other instructions — if, for instance, we ask a naturally modest girl to uncover herself or if we ask an honest man to steal some valuable object — we may already find the subject putting up a resistance, which may even go to the length of his refusing to obey the suggestion. This teaches us that even in the best hypnosis suggestion does not exercise unlimited power but only power of a definite strength. The hypnotic subject will make small sacrifices, but, just as though he were awake, he hesitates before making great ones. If, then, we are dealing with a patient, and urge him by suggestion to give up his illness, we perceive that this means a great sacrifice to him and not a small one. Here the power of suggestion is contending against the force which created the symptoms and maintains them, and experience shows that that force is of quite a different order of strength from hypnotic influence."[25]

Like Bernheim, Freud observed that *neurotics* are difficult to hypnotise. The contention between the hypnotic influence and the strong forces which root the illness in the patient's mental life is often very unbalanced. Severe disturbances necessitate repeated hypnosis and even then it is very possible that the symptom will only disappear for a short period of time. In such cases, there exists a danger of abetting the aforementioned dependence on the physician as well as a kind of "addiction to hypnosis". In any case, hypnotic treatment remains as laborious and time-consuming as any other method. At the end of this article, Freud insinuates that hypnosis only marks a first step, albeit a fundamental one. He himself had no doubts that in the future other and better forms of psychical treatment will come into existence.

The declaration of principles is apparent in this article: psychotherapy implies the reinstatement of the use of *words* based on a *scientific medicine*. Freud notes that medicine had only managed to emancipate itself from natural philosophy during the past half-century due to the positive influence of the natural sciences. This could explain the reticence of medicine towards mental or psychical treatment.

There is no doubt that words are invested with 'magical powers' and that they can produce effects in a therapeutic setting. Nineteenth century scientists, for instance, refer indiscriminately to medieval and primitive 'healers'. These scientists were however faced with the problem of explaining how the healing process actually operates. Freud's attitude towards this question is ambivalent from the start. He pleas for words to be reinvested with 'magical powers', but this time from a scientific point of view. If the psychical treatment effects a change in reality, then it must also be governed by certain *rules*. It is then only a matter of disclosing these rules and of assigning to them a place within a theoretical framework.
This may sound fairly simple and obvious, yet as we have seen earlier on, the direction in which Freud conducted his research pointed towards the elaboration of a *clinical psychology*. In other words, this means that, for Freud, the first and the principal reference for this elaboration is contained in an *empirical* approach to psychotherapy. The notions I have just mentioned in connection with his article on the mental treatment (affective ideas, the relation between the patient and the physician, resistance, and the function of attention) are indeed not of a fictional nature, and they henceforth reappear systematically in Freud's work. Therefore, the emphasis on the scientific character of his approach need not be interpreted as an endorsement of the physicalistic manifesto of du Bois-Raymond and Brücke. The physical and physiological models present in Freud's work can be seen from a different angle, i.e. as useful frames of reference *orienting* the psychical rules he discovered in the clinic.

Bernheim already described the physician's suggestion as the "introduction of an idea into the brain of the patient". Obviously Freud, just like us today, was not satisfied with a metaphor of this kind. For instance, a tumour can be removed from the brain or a pacemaker can be inserted into the heart, but what we do not know is what the "introduction of an idea into the brain" means. Nevertheless, this metaphor imposed itself from the observation of traumatic neuroses. At the Salpêtrière, for instance, it was noted that the hysterical symptom seemed ultimately determined or maintained by an *idea* connected to a trauma and that such a symptom could be induced when the patient was in a state of hypnosis. Charcot spoke of the "powerful idea", or of "auto-suggestions", and reasonably concluded that what could be brought about by suggestion could be obliterated in the same way. The principle of the systematic psychical influence was thus created, and in Nancy Charcot's conclusions were consistently applied for the first time.

However, this first avatar of psychical treatment was not granted a long life. Before long, the hypnotic technique lapsed into the old "traitement moral" of the philanthropist Pinel, which consisted in creating a favourable environment for the patient and subjecting him to restful and benevolent impressions.[26] I have already indicated the principal reasons for this lapse: Bernheim's failure to recognise the climate of suggestibility in the institute, his boasting of authority which he ultimately derived from the group element and his lack of interest in the ideational life of his patients. In addition to this, Bernheim, unlike Freud, denied himself any possibility of simultaneously using this mode of treatment as an instrument to probe into the psyche. The creation of psychotherapy and the concomitant clinical psychology was to take place elsewhere.

3.3. From Anna O. to the 'Preliminary Communication'

As it was for Charcot and Bernheim, the 'intense idea' constitutes Freud's starting point, for his 'treatment' as well as for an embryonic theorisation. This is also an aspect which Freud encounters in Breuer's report on the treatment of Anna O.. The two most important observations in this report relate to the notion that each of the numerous symptoms are associatively linked up with an idea or memory, and consecutively that putting memories into words causes symptoms to vanish.

A second important notion that can be found in both Charcot and Bernheim's work as well as in Breuer's report, is of a 'topographical' nature. At the Salpêtrière and Nancy, the explanation of hypnotic experiments — after which the patient seemed to be ignorant of what had occurred — compelled one to postulate an 'elsewhere'. That is to say a topos or a place in the psyche

where an intense idea or auto-suggestion could exert its influence — a place not directly accessible to consciousness. Charcot speaks of the "dissolution du moi" and Bernheim perpetually refers to the various "states of consciousness" which, in his mind, do not vary greatly from each other, but whose contents or ideas still exert their influence next to each other or simultaneously. For instance, take the description of the unconscious "alarm" that goes off in order to explain post-hypnotic suggestion.[27]
This operative 'elsewhere' — impressively illustrated at the Salpêtrière by the hysterical attacks functioning as repetitions of the original trauma, and at Nancy by the scenes played out by the subjects of Bernheim's experiments — is also located by Freud in Breuer's hypothesis on the "hypnoid state" or in the idea of the "splitting" of consciousness. This concept imposed itself from the phenomenology of Breuer's case description.

In December 1880, when Breuer undertook the care of Anna O. and began the actual treatment, he encountered her in a severely disturbed psychical state.[28] Apart from several successive physical symptoms — such as headache, convergent squint, disturbances of vision, paresis of the muscles of the front of the neck, contracture and anaesthesia of the right lower arm — the relation of this intelligent girl to the outside world was at times thoroughly disturbed. She alternated between a state of anxiety and melancholy, which could still be considered as relatively normal, and a state of hallucination in which she was abusive and aggressive towards the people around her. Moreover, she would lapse into absence: her conscious perception of what occurred around her was incomplete. This 'absence' was, amongst other things, reflected in her speech. When telling somebody something she would stop abruptly in the middle of a sentence and could only go on talking after a short pause. These alternating states of consciousness gradually came into prominence in the syndrome during the course of the treatment. In the afternoons she would fall into a somnolent state which in the evenings gave way to a form of autohypnosis. Such 'absences' were accompanied by the emergence of frightening hallucinations and an increased excitement. She was, according to Breuer, completely unsuggestible and defended herself tenaciously against any intervention on his part. There was consequently no other alternative for Breuer than to listen to her description of the spectres roaming in her mind. A first observation is that Anna O. would regain her normal state after having

spoken about these spectres, which allowed her, at least for a short period, to write or draw.
This spontaneously occurring sequence gradually developed into a 'mould' for Breuer's method of treatment. When he visited her in the evenings, he encouraged her to give verbal expression to all the hallucinations and fantasies that had plagued her since his last visit. When this "chimney sweeping" succeeded, she would lose all her "energy" and her mood improved greatly. Breuer used this blueprint in a subsequent phase of the treatment to systematically remove her symptoms. He asked her to concentrate her thoughts on a symptom and to tell him all the occasions on which it had ever appeared. For instance, her 'absence' was characterised by her not hearing what was said to her. Under hypnosis she had to tell about all the previous occasions on which this phenomenon supervened, including the very first instance of it prior to the advent of her hysterical condition when she used to nurse her father.
The outcome of such a "talking cure" was promising. Her symptoms vanished one by one after a temporary increase of intensity during the "Absprechen". This does not mean that the psychocathartic method — which Breuer accredited to Anna O.[29] — was a simple undertaking. The treatment resembles a war of attrition. The successful outcome depends on the exhaustive character of the recollection and on an 'energetic' speech.
I should like to draw your attention to one particular point. In comparison to the remaining case histories published in the *Studies* — all of them written by Freud — that of Anna O. strikes one as being particularly streamlined. Although Breuer claims that he got to know Anna O. to an extent to which one person's life is rarely known to another, and although he draws attention to the close relationship his patient had with her father whom she deified, the fact remains that Breuer failed to go deeper into Anna O.'s personal tragedy and essentially paid attention to the formal characteristics of the cure and to the rich palette of symptoms.[30]

In Breuer's mind, this case was not an unusual instance of hysterical disease, but was especially interesting on account of the transparency of the aetiology. He mentions two factors explaining Anna O.'s hysteria. Firstly, the monotonous family life which offered this gifted patient no intellectual outlet for her "psychical energy" surplus, which was accordingly released through fantasy. Secondly, her systematic indulging in day dreams formed the basis for her "dissociation of personality", once the day dreaming gave way to the hallucinatory absence which was a first manifestation of the developing disease. The transitory dreams gradually organised themselves into a "double conscience" (dual consciousness), which formed the condition for the emergence of the various symptoms. Breuer thence agrees with Charcot's explanation of traumatic hysteria. The affect of fright cannot be 'abreacted' in an adequate manner if the trauma took place when the patient was in a hypnotic state.

The history of Anna O. is put forward in the 'Preliminary Communication'[31] as being paradigmatic for the psychotherapy of hysteria. In order to treat the hysterical symptoms, one course of action imposes itself, namely the systematic investigation of the patient's *life history* and more particularly the discovery of the first occurrence of the symptom so as to implement the 'abreaction'. The moment in question is often far removed in time and shedding light on it is seldom an easy job. The patient sometimes dislikes discussing the complex of recollections associated with the symptom, he may be unable to recollect it or may not immediately see the causal connection between the memories that surface and the symptom. The use of hypnosis is then necessary in order to arouse his memories.

It is argued that the moment of the accident is the determinant for the pathology of hysteria. This *causal connection* is evident in the case of traumatic hysteria.[32] The trauma brings about the hysterical syndrome, and in the case of a hysterical attack the traumatic event is hallucinated. This causal connection is, however, not always very obtrusive. It often consists in what might be called a symbolic relation between the precipitating cause and the pathological phenomenon. For example, a neuralgia may result from a mental pain or vomiting may result from a feeling of moral disgust.

Freud and Breuer discovered that the spontaneous and, at first sight, idiopathic[33] phenomena of hysteria were wholly the product of a trauma, just like traumatic hysteria. Furthermore, they pointed to the disproportion between the single occurrence of the trauma — frequently some event in *childhood* — and the perdurability of the symptom.

Both Breuer and Freud consequently found the extension of the Charcotian notion of traumatic hysteria to be legitimate. In traumatic neuroses the operative cause of the illness is not the mere physical injury, but is to be looked for in the *affect of fright* or the *psychical trauma*. If the life history of the patient is analyzed meticulously enough, it then becomes possible to trace back the

precipitating cause (which can often only be described as a psychical trauma) of every symptom. Any event which calls up affects such as those of fright, anxiety, shame, or mental pain may operate as a trauma of this kind.
The causal relation between the psychical trauma and the hysterical symptom is, however, not of a such a nature that it would imply that the trauma can merely be regarded as an "agent provocateur" in releasing the symptom, which afterwards leads an independent existence. The psychical trauma, or a recollection of the trauma, can be conceived of as a "Fremdkörper" (a foreign body) — just like a splinter — which long after its penetration into the organism continues to be regarded as an operative agent. The proof in support of this hypothesis was that each individual hysterical symptom immediately and irreversibly disappeared when "we had succeeded in bringing clearly to light the memory of the event by which it was provoked and in arousing its accompanying affect, and when the patient had described the event in the greatest possible detail and had put the affect into words".[34]

For the therapy to be effective two factors are of importance: *recollection* and the *putting into words of the affect*. But Breuer and Freud stress that "recollection without affect almost invariably produces no result" and the original psychical process must be repeated as vividly as possible, it must be brought back to its *statu nascendi* and be expressed in speech. They found support for this psychical treatment or psychotherapy of hysteria and the concurring theoretical conceptions in the works of Delboeuf, Binet and Janet, to name but a few.[35] The effects of these cannot be attributed to a random suggestion or to the expectation of being cured. Both authors of the 'Preliminary Communication' allude to the report of the treatment of Anna O. which stems from the "pre-suggestion period" and which was only made possible by the spontaneous autohypnosis on the part of the patient. This came as a great surprise to Breuer.
They both agree that "hysterics suffer mainly from reminiscences", a purely *empirical* fact which calls for elucidation. How does it come about that some memories do not fade and continue to be affective? And how can memories lose their affect? Breuer and Freud resort to the *reflexive model*. Whether a memory fades or loses its affect depends on whether there has been an "energetic" reaction to the event calling an affect forth.
A first instance of a reaction of this kind is found in the *reflex* which "releases" or abreacts the energy or affect. If someone bursts into tears as a

reaction of fright to an event, then this reflex causes the affect of fright to disappear. If this does not happen, the affect remains linked to the memory and, in the instance of an offence suffered in silence, develops into a "Kränkung". A second instance is an *act* — such as the act of revenge — which functions as an "adequate reaction". Hence, the insult that was avenged is recalled in a different way from the one that had to be endured. Finally, *speech* functions as a third instance. It serves as a substitute for action and with its help an affect can be most effectively abreacted.

'Abreaction', however, is not the only answer at the disposal of the 'psychism' of people experiencing a psychical trauma. The memory of a trauma can be inserted into the entire complex of associations and be placed alongside all other memories. An insult or an injury can, in such a way, be corrected by the presence of ideas 'contradicting' the psychical trauma. Breuer and Freud speak of the associative "Verarbeitung" of traumatic ideas.
Experience with hysterical patients suggests that the memories underlying the symptoms remain vivid or that they have not lost their affect. Yet — and this is a great mystery — these memories are not accessible to the patient. Only by means of hypnosis can the desired "extension of memory" be achieved, causing the recollections to surface in the patient's consciousness. What then thwarts the abreaction or the 'associative processing' of the trauma? Breuer and Freud put forward two different kinds of factors:
1. Firstly, there are the traumas precluding an adequate reaction, as in the case of the loss of a loved one or when social circumstances make such a reaction impossible. Also included in this first category, are the cases in which the subject *wishes to forget* and intentionally represses, inhibits or suppresses the traumas from his conscious thoughts. It is precisely distressing occurrences of this nature that come to light under hypnosis as being the basis of hysterical phenomena. In all these cases the content of the memory determines what causes the failure to react adequately.
2. Alternatively, it is the psychical state of the subject at the time of the trauma that makes the adequate reaction impossible. Ideas, which are not significant in themselves, can indeed determine hysterical symptoms. For even though the ideas are insignificant, their pathogenic effect results from the fact that the trauma originated during an affect of fright or during a semi-hypnotic twilight state of day-dreaming. In other words, these ideas were 'acquired'

during a modified state of consciousness and from then onwards led an existence independent of other ideas.

Thus two elements are adduced to explain the aetiology of hysterical symptoms: *psychical mechanisms* (resistance or the repression of ideas) and *psychical states* or innate disposition (the so-called hypnoid states). Thence both authors speak respectively of a psychically acquired hysteria in which the trauma engenders a psychical dissociation, and of hysteria that is a matter of innate disposition, in which case the dissociation precedes the trauma (cf. the case of Anna O.). The proposed psychotherapy "brings to an end the operative force of the idea which was not abreacted in the first instance, by allowing its strangulated affect to find a way out through speech; and it subjects it to associative correction by introducing it into the normal consciousness (under light hypnosis) or by removing it through the physician's suggestion."[36]

Let us now move away from the theory as expounded in the 'Preliminary Communication' to compare it to Freud's eponymous lecture delivered on 11 January 1893.[37] In this lecture, the *psychical mechanism* of *repression* seems to be the only new element in the explanation of the impossibility to abreact — at least when compared to that postulated by Charcot.[38] Charcot experimentally showed that the genesis of the symptoms of traumatic neurosis is analogous to that of the symptoms brought on in hypnotised patients by means of suggestion. Let us recall the patient whose arm was paralysed after having received a light blow to it.[39] The notion of the hypnoid state as a disposition prior to the trauma can thus not exclusively be attributed to Breuer. Charcot's "dissociation du moi" and his "condition seconde" and Bernheim's "different states of consciousness" are similar to what is described as "hypnoid states". For these three authors, it refers to an empirical postulation of something recalling a 'second memory' or an 'elsewhere' which assigns a place to the pathogenic and inaccessible idea in the psyche.

In an allusion to the case of Anna O. in his 'Lecture', Freud emphasises that the entire life history of the subject can be equated with the single trauma. This equation is by no means an exaggeration, since it has been shown that in the case of major traumas, it is not the *mechanical factor* (the physical injury), but rather the affect of fright or the psychical trauma that brings the effect about. In this respect Charcot's blueprint remains valid, for it refers to the operation, in this instance by summation, of the psychical traumata.

However, Breuer's method which integrates the subject's life history offers two new understandings.

Firstly, the attempt at discovering the determining cause of a symptom is at the same time a *therapeutic manoeuvre*. For when the physician establishes the first occurrence of the symptom and when a complete and vivid memory of it can be remembered or elicited, the symptom vanishes. Alternatively, one could argue that psychotherapy reveals itself as being a real *research instrument* probing the psyche.

Secondly, the empirical observation which propounds that giving verbal expression to ideas that form the basis of hysterical conversion symptoms makes them disappear, leads to the notion that "speech affords a bridge" between mental states and their expression, between the psyche and the somatic.[40]

The clinic to which both the 'Preliminary Communication' and Freud's lecture point, is not merely to be interpreted as that of *the idea*, for *the affect* also occupies an equally central position. For patients do not present themselves to the physician with only conversion symptoms, but also with their anxieties, guilt and ill-humour. Speech also has a cathartic influence on the mood of patients. A simple recollection is not enough. The pathogenic ideas need to be energetically "Abgesprochen" or abreacted. Content and force, idea and affect: these are the two aspects of speech that exert a therapeutic effect.

3.4. From the 'Preliminary Communication' to Breuer's 'Theoretical'

What is there to say on Breuer's theoretical chapter? A first reading leaves one with an uncomfortable feeling. This chapter follows immediately after Freud's clinical observations on Emmy von N., Lucy R., Katharina and Elisabeth von R. One is first struck by the gulf between Freud's empiricism and Breuer's theory. Yet the introduction of the chapter sounds promising: "In what follows little mention will be made of the brain and none whatever of molecules. Psychical processes will be dealt with in the language of psychology; and, indeed, it cannot possibly be otherwise. If instead of 'idea' we chose to speak of 'excitation of the cortex', the latter term would only have any meaning for us in so far as we recognised an old friend under that cloak and tacitly reinstated the 'idea'. For while ideas are constant objects of our experience and are familiar to us in all their shades of meaning, 'cortical excitations' are on the contrary rather in the nature of a postulate, objects which we hope to be able to identify in the future. The substitution of one term for another would seem to be no more than a pointless disguise. Accordingly, I may perhaps be forgiven if I make almost exclusive use of psychological terms".[41]

But in the subsequent 50 pages there is precious little of this psychological language. Breuer does not manage to emancipate himself from the viewpoint of the physiologist. Rather, one has the impression of witnessing a kind of Echternach procession in which every step forward is followed by two steps back. Breuer proceeds backwards and in his theory he also recoils from the notion of the psyche and from that of psychology.

3.4.1. Hysteria determined by the abnormal excitation of the nervous system

In effect, Breuer's theory of hysteria entails a 'regression' with respect to the 'Preliminary Communication'. For in the latter, the *psychical mechanism* of resistance was propounded for the first time as an explanation of the aetiology of hysterical phenomena. Besides this mechanism, the hypothesis of the hypnoid state was also alluded to. In Breuer's theoretical chapter, this second notion takes precedence and is described in physiological terms: a precondition to any form of hysteria is the hypnoid state which results from the intracerebral tonic excitation of the nervous system and which partakes of hysterical disposition. In fact, in Breuer's model, the psychical mechanism of defence features only as a potentiality.

Breuer's starting point is entirely Charcotian. Hysteria is discovered empirically, just like tubercular pulmonary phthisis, that is to say, it is a *syndrome* which originates from clinical observation. The syndrome is gradually made deeper and clearer by the progressing knowledge, but ought not be disrupted by it. Were it to turn out that hysteria was determined by various causes, as is the case for tubercular pulmonary phthisis, then the clinical unity of hysteria must be preserved at all costs.[42]

Breuer reacts against the illegitimate generalisation that all hysterical symptoms are *ideogenic*, i.e. determined by an idea. This view, which is advocated by the neurologist P.J. Möbius, threatens to do away with the clinical unity of hysteria. Breuer is firmly convinced that there also exists hysterical phenomena which are not determined by psychical mechanisms.

It is of course tempting to show some understanding for Breuer's criticism of Möbius's generalisation: "since ideas are very frequently the cause of hysterical phenomena, I believe that they always are". Firstly, I would like to say that, even when one is dealing with one single hysterical subject, it is not very easy to draw a link between hysterical symptoms and the corresponding ideas. Determining the paralysis of the arm by pointing to the idea entrenched in the psyche, only offers a *blueprint* for the possibility of determining the somatic by the psychical. In both the 'Preliminary Communication' and in Freud's lecture, it is stressed that the ways in which this psychical determining takes place can be particularly complicated. This also surfaces from the cases covered in the *Studies*. As far as psychotherapy is concerned, it is not so much a question of isolating the precipitating idea, as of getting the patient to process *complexes of ideas* and to put these into words.

Further, there is the great difficulty of assigning a place to the *affect*. As I emphasised previously, the clinic of hysteria is not confined to the notion of the idea or the recollection. In other words, it does not simply consider the purely psychical element and the symptoms caused by it. Anxiety and melancholy — the 'affective states' — belong just as much to the syndrome of hysteria, but they seem to call more for a physiological explanation than for a psychological one.[43]

It is then quite understandable that such an eminent physiologist as Breuer would veer towards physiology in his attempt to provide a theory of hysteria.[44] Yet again, he displays similarities to Charcot: physiology also reveals itself as the discipline enabling one to establish the clinical unity of hysteria more solidly.

This teaches us at least one thing about Breuer's epistemological viewpoint on hysteria. Another motive lies concealed behind the desire to safeguard the clinical unity of hysteria, namely, that of safeguarding the unity of the *knowledge* from which hysteria is to be approached. This means safeguarding medicine, in which physiology fulfils the role of an auxiliary discipline supporting it. It also implies that Breuer's theorisation of hysteria runs counter to Freud's progression towards a psychology. The argument Breuer evokes against Möbius's 'generalisation' is a case in point: "Let us consider an everyday instance. A woman may, whenever an affect arises, produce on her neck, breast and face an erythema appearing first in blotches and then becoming confluent. This is determined by ideas and therefore according to Möbius is a hysterical phenomenon. But this same erythema appears, though over a less extensive area, when the skin is irritated or touched, etc. This would *not* be hysterical."[45] What Breuer fails to see, is that the irritation or touching of the skin by the physician cannot be considered as an innocent, objective physical arousal of vasomotor reaction. And what Breuer calls an illegitimate 'generalisation', does not, in my opinion, imply that Möbius denies the existence of physiological processes and reactions. Rather it suggests the adoption of a psychological viewpoint in order to explain and to shed light on a well-defined phenomenon.[46]

Breuer is willing to acknowledge that a great number of hysterical phenomena are ideogenic. But the fundamental pathological change which is present in each individual case and which enables ideas as well as non-psychological stimuli to produce pathological effects lies *in the abnormal excitability of the nervous system*.[47]

3.4.2. The notion of 'psychical energy'

Breuer highlights a second hypothesis from the 'Preliminary Communication'. This is the concept of "Erregung", i.e. the excitations which "flow away or have to be abreacted". In 1893, Freud and Breuer had both been encouraged by their clinic to introduce this notion, for they were frequently confronted with the "Aufregung" (excitement, agitation), and their patients' affects, as well as with the favourable influence of abreacting the excitation by means of speech. Taking into account this *quantitative* process did not merely impose itself empirically, as the then-prevalent description of neuro-physiological processes was also invoked to support and legitimise the hypothesis of the psychical energy.

Taking the example of the two extreme conditions of the nervous system, i.e. dreamless sleep and the clear waking state, Breuer endeavoured to argue in favour of the concept of energy. There is not much to say about the first of these two states as the subject is totally unconscious, thus precluding any sort of inner observation or experience. The resulting analysis passes over to the condition of sleep accompanied by dreams[48] in which the psychical activity is apparently *less intense* than in waking life: sensory stimuli (from the outside world) may well be perceived, but they are not *apperceived*.[49] The ideas that emerge in dreams, unlike those emerging in waking life, do not activate all the ideas which are connected with them and which are present in potential consciousness. Incompatible ideas can be present alongside each other without mutually inhibiting each other. Breuer thence surmises that in the deepest sleep this severance of connection between the psychical elements is carried even further. During waking life, however, the brain operates as a unit with complete internal connections. "We shall perhaps only be describing these facts in other words if we say that in sleep the paths of connection and conduction in the brain are not traversable by excitations of the psychical elements (cortical cells ?), whereas in waking life they are completely so traversable. The existence of these two different conditions of the paths of conduction can, it seems, only be made intelligible if we suppose that in waking life those paths are in a state of tonic excitation (what Exner calls 'intercellular tetanus'), that this intracerebral excitation is what determines their conductive capability, and that the diminution and disappearance of that excitation is what sets up the state of sleep."[50]

Breuer thinks of the cerebral paths of conduction as resembling an electric network through which there is a constant flow of galvanic current: "Let us imagine a widely ramified electrical system for lighting and the transmission of motor power; what is expected of this system is that simple establishment of a contact shall be able to set any lamp or machine in operation. To make this possible, so that everything shall be ready to work, there must be a certain amount of excitation present throughout the entire network of lines of conduction, and the dynamo engine must expend a given quantity of energy for this purpose. In just the same way there is a certain amount of excitation present in the conductive paths of the brain when it is at rest but awake and prepared to work."[51]

The question as to the *origin* or the source of the psychical energy is, needless to say, essential. When one wakes up a person, one causes the extension of the local state of excitation by the intervention of a sensory stimulus. This state of excitation, in turn, brings about a higher facilitation in all the paths of conduction. Waking can also supervene spontaneously. This goes to show that the development of energy can be presupposed to exist in the *life processes* itself. The discharge of the stimulus is continuous and increases the tension in the 'network' provoking *unpleasure*.

As an illustration, Breuer takes the example of boredom ("Langeweile") brought about by a prolonged mental quiescence, i.e. a lack of perception, ideas or associations. An excitation ("Aufregung" — in this instance a feeling of unpleasure) of this kind always coincides with a certain "Bedürfnis" (need) from the part of the organism which does not find satisfaction and finds expression in a feeling of unpleasure. "Since these feelings disappear when the surplus quantity of energy which has been liberated is employed functionally, we may conclude that the removal of such surplus excitation is a need of the organism. And here for the first time we meet the fact that there exists in the organism a 'tendency to keep intracerebral excitation constant' (Freud)."[52] Hence, each surplus of excitation drives the organism to expend it. There are various outlets available; it can be eliminated through direct motor action or alternatively, it can be processed via ideational activity.

To which organic need does the *principle of constancy* respond? Breuer assumes that there is an optimum degree of intracerebral excitation. This optimum degree is determined by the working of the brain and corresponds, for instance, to the nervous system's accessibility to all external stimuli, to the optimal facilitation of reflexes, and to memory's optimal accessibility to arouse ideas and to bring them in joined association.

Each heightening of intracerebral excitation is accordingly brought to bear on the functions of the brain, for example, an alteration causing a hypersensitivity towards sensory stimuli or an inappropriate increase in the reflex excitability. An increase of this kind is not always useful and it can even damage the organism if it appears for no real purpose, as is the case when one is 'nervous'. By analogy with a number of other regulations in the human organism, e.g. the constancy of the water content in the blood this hypothesis concerning the constancy principle could be defined as the tendency in the organism to maintain the optimum of excitation or to return to it after it has been exceeded.[53] Breuer also finds a confirmation of this in everyday language: "Our speech, the outcome of the experience of many generations, distinguishes with admirable delicacy between those forms and degrees of heightening of excitation which are still useful for mental activity (i.e. in spite of rising above the optimum) because they raise the free energy of all cerebral functions uniformly, and those forms and degrees which restrict that activity because they partly increase and partly inhibit these psychical functions in a manner that is not uniform. The first are given the name of 'incitement', and the second 'excitement'. An interesting conversation, or a cup of tea or coffee has an inciting (stimulating) effect; a dispute or a considerable dose of alcohol has an 'exciting' one. While incitement only arouses the urge to employ the increased excitation functionally, excitement seeks to discharge itself in more or less violent ways which are almost or even actually pathological. Excitement constitutes the psycho-physical basis of the effects, and these will be discussed below."[54] Let me just point out that in this passage Breuer is referring to *exogenous* sources of excitation, i.e. located in the outside world. But there also exist *endogenous* sources, i.e. located within the organism.

What are these endogenous causes that provoke the increase in excitation? There are of course the major needs of the organism, the need for oxygen, hunger and thirst all of which function as a model. The transition between these endogenous increases of excitation and *psychical affects* in the narrower sense is effectuated by sexual excitation and sexual *affect*: "Sexuality at puberty appears in the first of these forms, as a vague, indeterminate, purposeless heightening of excitation. As development proceeds, this endogenous heightening of excitation, becomes firmly linked (in the normal course of things) with the perception or idea of the other sex — and, indeed, with the idea of a particular individual, where the remarkable phenomenon of falling in love occurs. This idea takes over the whole quantity of excitation liberated by the sexual instinct. It becomes an 'affective idea'; that is to say, when it is actively present in consciousness it sets going the increase of excitation which in point of fact originated from another source, namely the sex-glands."[55]

In Breuer's opinion the sexual instinct is to be regarded as the most powerful source of continuing increases of excitation and thus of neuroses. This increase is most irregularly distributed over the nervous system. It also influences the psyche directly in the sense that when it (the increase) reaches a high intensity, the chain of ideas or the associative activity is disrupted. And in an extreme form such as the orgasm, "thought is almost completely extinguished".[56]

Let us bear in mind that Breuer looks at the relation between the psyche and the soma from the vantage point of the influence that the physical-physiological exerts on the psychical. Sexuality — seen as a physiological process occurring only during puberty — is then looked upon as the great disrupter of psychical processes. Breuer does not go into any detail about its mode of operation. He hastens to say that he has no intention to formulate either a psychology or a physiology of affects.[57] He does, however, intend to provide a *physiological foundation* for hysteria and for the therapeutic phenomenon of *catharsis*. The abnormal excitation of the nervous system (a precondition for hysteria) and the increase of excitation (particularly through the agency of the sex-glands) are respectively described as being the first cause and the plane where a therapeutic intervention is possible. The negative increase in excitation can indeed be eliminated by abreacting it, either by means of words or through actions. This levelling then reinstates the psychical balance that was temporarily lost. If the abreaction or discharge is thwarted, it leads to a pathology, that is to say, one enters the field of the "abnormal expression of the emotions".[58] The result is then the same as with fright or anxiety: the intracerebral excitation is powerfully increased, but is used neither in associative nor in motor activity.

3.4.3. Hysterical conversion

One of the most important objectives Breuer sets himself in his theoretical chapter, is to explain hysterical physical symptoms. Although the nervous system is indeed an interconnected unit, the excitation present in it cannot simply cross over from, say, the field of ideas to that of the autonomous functions of the organism. This can, however, happen when the natural resistance which somehow keeps the nervous system's various functions separate is overcome. This leads to "an abnormal expression of the emotions", which can supervene when the intracerebral excitation increases substantially. The natural resistance is then overcome and something like a 'short circuit' ensues. As a result, the appropriate levelling down by motor discharge or by associative activity (ideational activity) fails to occur. A second cause can be an abnormal weakness of the resistance in particular paths of conduction, which, for Breuer, amounts to the notion of the innate hysterical disposition.[59] Breuer touches upon two kinds of abnormal expression of emotions which he observed in his clinic: the symptom of hysterical conversion and the hysterical attack. The hysterical attack can be interpreted as a motor reaction or a discharge. If an attack follows a strong and discernible affect having an objective basis we are not dealing with hysteria, for a hysterical attack appears with apparent spontaneity, just like the manifestation of an illness. However, a closer analysis shows that this apparent spontaneity is actually based on recollections which reactivate the original affect. Or, to put it in Breuer's words, an affect which would "*revive it if these reactions (the attacks) did not, in fact, occur instead*".[60] The abnormal expression of emotions thus surfaces as a sort of "Ersatz" for previous feelings like shame or anxiety.

The other outcome was also to be observed in the clinic. This can occur when the original idea, which was charged with an affect, reappears in consciousness, thus *renewing* the strong affect. The idea coloured with affect therefore re-emerges vividly in consciousness.

In order for hysterical conversion to occur, the affect has to be reiterated. This repetition, e.g. may be the result of the patient ending up in several situations arousing an affect of fright, but a mere renewal of the affect in the patient's memory is enough. Breuer directs us once again to Charcot's work. "During the days following the railway accident, for instance, the subject will live through his frightful experiences again both in sleeping and in waking, and always with the renewed affect of fright, till at the last, after this period of 'sychical working-out' (Charcot) or of *incubation*, conversion into a somatic phenomenon takes place."[61]

The strength of the affect created in this way depends on its 'wearing away' ("usurierenden") and on the extent to which the original affect was abreacted. For instance, the strength of an affect of anger which is conjured up by a recollection, depends on the way in which it was originally dealt with: was the action taken, was the anger vented or repressed? In the event of a 'psychical reflex' that was fully achieved (for instance, revenge in the case of an insult), the recollection of it releases a minimal quota of affect. However, if the original affect was released in an 'abnormal reflex', then the affect is also released or renewed by recollection, and the excitation arising from the affective idea is converted into a physical phenomenon. If this reflex is frequently repeated, it leads to a complete 'facilitation' accompanied by total conversion. This implies that the psychical process withdraws entirely from consciousness. The idea on which it was based is 'forgotten', and even the affect fails to be perceived. This explains why a hysterical symptom of this kind appears at first sight to be purely organic: conversion depletes the precipitating idea of its affect in the shortest possible time.

When discussing the possible vicissitudes of an affect, Breuer brings up the notion of 'discharge'. What determines how an affect is to be discharged? What determines whether the discharge of the affect is to take place via a normal or an abnormal reflex? Breuer posits that the discharge follows the path of 'the least resistance'; put differently, it opts for the best facilitated path. A pre-existing heart disease, for instance, facilitates the conversion of affects which are generated into heart pains. A similar mechanism determined Anna O.'s paralysis of the right arm by the sight of snake-like objects, as at the time of the original affect of fright, her arm had gone to sleep. Breuer speaks of association due to simultaneity, i.e. the facilitation of abnormal reflexes according to the general laws of association.

Alternatively, symbolism may determine which reflex is selected. Sequences of associated ideas link the affect and the concurring reflex. "What unites the affect and its reflex is often some ridiculous play upon words or associations by sounds, but this only happens in dream-like states when the critical powers are low."[62] This explains why in a great number of cases the determination remains unintelligible, because one has only a dim knowledge of the ideas on which it is based.

Breuer describes the events which release the original affect as psychical traumas, and the pathologic manifestations arising in this manner as hysterical symptoms of traumatic origin, hence differentiating them from traumatic hysteria which is caused by a physical lesion.[63]

The hysterical conversion of a psychical excitation which does not originate from external stimuli or from the inhibition of normal psychical reflexes, but from the inhibition of the course of association, takes place in an analogous manner. As an example of an inhibition of this kind, Breuer takes the case where one forgets a proper name or a word. Normally when someone reminds us of the word that had momentarily escaped us, the excitation vanishes because the chain of association is brought to an end.

It also happens that the course of association is inhibited on account of the *irreconcilability* of two groups of ideas. Religious torments can, for instance, bring about a heightening of excitation or a psychical pain and a feeling of unpleasure which supervenes when one's conscience struggles with moral ideas and the recollection of one's action. "It is a matter of everyday experience that a conflict like this between irreconcilable ideas has a pathogenic effect. What are mostly in question are ideas and processes connected with sexual life: masturbation in adolescents with moral sensibilities; or, in a strictly conscientious married woman, becoming aware of an attraction to an man who is not her husband. Indeed, the first emergence of sexual feelings and ideas is very often in itself enough to bring about an intense state of excitation, owing to its conflicting with a deeply-rooted idea of moral purity."[64] A conflict of this kind is usually the cause of pathological depression and states of anxiety, or of somatic phenomena.

What is the 'adequate reaction' or the 'normal reflex'? In the 'Preliminary Communication' we saw that the process of association ensures the 'wearing away' of an affect. This implies that the affectively coloured idea is gradually stripped of its affect through the intervention of the thought process and the rectification of other ideas. But when an affective idea is withdrawn from the "course of association" it retains its affective value and, as a result it also keeps its pathogenic influence.

Here, one can observe that the clinician is confronted with two similar forms of exclusion of the 'affective ideas' from the process of association — precisely as was the case two years earlier.

The first case of exclusion is the *defence* or the deliberate suppression of distressing ideas. "In his (first) paper on 'The Neuro-Psychoses of Defence' and in his case histories in the present volume, Freud has discussed this process, which undoubtedly possesses very high pathological significance."[65] Breuer adds to this that although it is not entirely clear how an idea of this kind can be repressed from consciousness, we are familiar with the corresponding positive process, namely that of concentrating one's attention on an idea. We do not know all the complexities of this matter either, but the fact remains that an idea from which consciousness is diverted is not subjected to the "wearing away process" and thence retains its quota of affect.

In the second case, the ideas are kept out of association "not because one does not *want* to remember the idea, but because one *cannot* remember it: because it originally emerged and was endowed with affect in states in respect of which there is amnesia in waking consciousness — that is, in hypnosis or in states similar to it. The latter seem to be of the highest importance for the theory of hysteria, and accordingly deserve a somewhat fuller examination."[66]

The aforementioned quotation is important for any reading of the *Studies* and for the interpretation I wish to advocate on the difference of opinion between Breuer and Freud. For Breuer, the hypothesis of the hypnoid state leaves the door open to a conception of psychopathology, and more particularly, of hysteria for which any responsibility or any subjective implication can either be rejected or at least circumvented. Breuer therefore remains limited to a strictly medical conception of hysteria which originates outside the subject: "There's nothing I *can* do about it, I *can't* remember it, I *can't* help it, I just happen to have weak and thus very excitable nerves." This indeed seems to be the viewpoint Breuer adopts for his treatment of Anna O.. Firstly, Breuer utterly misunderstood his patients' and his own desires, in spite of the fact that these desires were used as a principle of organisation for the therapy. Secondly, in his theoretical chapter, the initial juxtaposition of defence and the hypnoid state — which are both a cause of hysteria — merely appears as cosmetic.

3.4.4. Hypnoid state

For his proposition concerning hysteria, Breuer draws on Möbius's almost identical viewpoint, i.e. that hypnoid states form the basis of hysteria. As early as 1890, Möbius wrote that, "(...) the necessary condition for the (pathogenic) operation of ideas is, on the one hand, an innate — that is, hysterical — disposition and, on the other, a special frame of mind. We can only form an imprecise idea of this frame of mind. It must resemble a state of hypnosis; it must correspond to some kind of vacancy of consciousness in which an emerging idea meets with no resistance from any other — in which, so to speak, the field is clear for the first comer. We know that a state of this kind can be brought about not only by hypnotism but by emotional shock (fright, anger, etc.) and by exhausting factors (sleeplessness, hunger, and so on)."[67] To Breuer the importance of hypnoid states lies principally in the amnesia and in the "Spaltung" (the splitting of the mind) which they occasion and which play such an essential part in 'Major hysteria'. Yet Breuer somewhat qualifies the generalising claim of his proposition: "Conversion — the ideogenic production of somatic phenomena — can also come about apart from hypnoid states. Freud has found in the deliberate amnesia of defence a second source, independent of hypnoid states, for the construction of ideational complexes which are excluded from associative contact."[68] Deliberate amnesia is connected to *defence* or *repression*, two notions Breuer can only place reluctantly and with great difficulty. He remains of the opinion that hypnoid states are the cause of and precondition for most cases of major hysteria as well as for the most complex cases of hysteria. However, in the *Studies*, this view is manifestly at variance with the case histories of Emmy von N., Elisabeth von R. and Cäcilie M., who can scarcely be described as suffering from 'simple' hysteria.

Compared with the 'Preliminary Communication', one can thus detect a departure from any notion of equivalence between the two etiological hypotheses. Furthermore, Breuer's theoretical chapter only puts a series of physiological arguments to the fore, thereby underpinning not only the clinical unity of hysteria, but also the concept of the hypnoid state.

Hysterical conversion takes place far more easily in a hypnoid state than in the waking state or the normal state of consciousness, even though the mechanism itself is essentially the same. The reason for this is fairly obvious, a normal abreaction by means of speech is precluded.

However, the question as to whether these hypnoid states come into existence *before* the actual pathology is a crucial one. Since Breuer can only draw on his experience with Anna O., he cannot give a decisive answer to the subject. In the case of Anna O. there was indeed the question of daydreams, or her 'private theatre' as "Normalvorbild" of the hypnoid state. Nevertheless, Breuer, who was usually dismissive of generalisations, wrote: "It seems not improbable that this process holds good fairly generally."[69]

How do hypnoid states of this kind come into existence? Generally speaking, there are various situations which can induce an 'absence of mind' towards sensations and perceptions from the exterior. This is true for someone who studies, writes or engages in scientific research. In such instances, an energetic mental work is performed, and the excitation of the nervous system thus liberated is consumed in this activity. This, however, is not the case in a state of absent-mindedness where the intracerebral excitation sinks below its clear waking level. "If during such a state of absorption, and while the flow of ideas is inhibited, a group of affectively-coloured ideas is active, it creates a high level of intracerebral excitation which is not used up by mental work and is at the disposal of abnormal functioning, such as conversion."[70]

If the mechanism described above occurs once, the hypnoid state comes into being and if the affect is repeated, the hypnoid state will reoccur.

3.4.5. The 'splitting' of the mind

The existence of ideas which are operative at a given moment, yet which remain 'unconscious' or 'subconscious', is to Breuer a common fact of everyday life. He cites as an example the occasion when he forgot to make one of his medical visits. Until he remembered the appointment, he was plagued by a feeling of unrest. This continuous unrest can only be explained by the fact that the idea went on being operative outside consciousness. Breuer, unlike Freud at a later stage, does not touch on the actual cause of a forgetfulness of this kind which occurs by means of unconscious ideas, but stresses its influence on the 'mood' of an individual. "A great deal of what we describe as 'mood' comes from sources of this kind, from ideas that exist and are operative beneath the threshold of consciousness. Indeed, the whole conduct of our life is constantly influenced by subconscious ideas. We can see every day how, where there is mental degeneration, as for instance in the initial stages of general paralysis, the inhibitions which normally restrain certain actions become weaker and disappear. But the patient who now makes indecent jokes in the presence of women was not, in his healthy days, prevented from doing so by conscious memories and reflections; he avoided it 'instinctively' and 'automatically' — that is to say, he was restrained by ideas which were called up by the impulse to behave in this way, but which remained beneath the threshold of consciousness, though they nevertheless inhibited the impulse."[71]

Whether an idea does or does not penetrate into consciousness depends first and foremost on its intensity. But how is one to explain the fact that an idea which is intense enough to produce a lively motor action, is not intense enough to become conscious? The conversion mechanism can offer an explanation. The clarity of an idea — thus its capacity to be observed by our self-consciousness — is also determined by its *quota of affect*, i.e. the feeling of pleasure or unpleasure which it arouses. In the event of a feeling of unpleasure, the conversion into a somatic symptom ensues as a kind of 'short circuit'. Put differently, in cases of conversion, ideas are stripped of their affect. However, this elementary explanation accounts only for a small part of the phenomenology of the clinic of hysteria.[72] Patients do not simply present themselves with well-delineated conversion symptoms, but also with their mood swings, sorrows and anxiety. This means that the affect aroused by unconscious ideas is not immediately converted integrally into somatic symptoms, but that it also manifests itself as a patient's affective state. In this instance, the ideas remain just as unconscious. "In patients like these we found that it was the rule for the emotional disturbance — apprehensiveness, angry irritability, grief — to precede the appearance of the somatic symptom or to follow it immediately, and to increase, either until it was cleared up by being given utterance in words or until the affect and the somatic phenomenon gradually disappeared again."[73] When the patient manages to put the ideas determining the affect into words, then not only does the affect disappear, but the patient also acquires an understanding of its excessiveness. Breuer emphasises that hypnosis or the physician's intervention is required to bring intense ideas of this kind into consciousness. He revealingly describes unconscious ideas which nonetheless display a great degree of liveliness, as ideas that are *inadmissible to consciousness*. The existence of ideas of this kind then is pathological.

What Breuer observed in his clinic and what he describes here, is related to the *splitting of the mind*. What this implies is that, in the event of a pathology, the ideational psychical activity does not coincide with potential consciousness. The psychical activity consists of a conscious and an unconscious part, and the ideas are divided into those which are 'admissible' and 'inadmissible' to consciousness. Breuer therefore speaks of a splitting of the mind into two relatively independent parts.

Of course, the question that remains unanswered is, what causes a splitting of this kind to be occasioned? Nonetheless the hypothesis allows one to explain certain aspects of the clinic, and not just the occurrence of isolated hysterical phenomena like conversion symptoms. "I do not assert that everything that we call hysterical has a splitting of this kind as its basis and necessary condition; but I *do* assert that the splitting of psychical activity which is so striking in the well-known cases in the form of "double conscience" is present to a rudimentary degree in every major hysteria, and that the liability and tendency to such a dissociation is the basic phenomenon of this neurosis."[74] Somatic phenomena which last continuously for years, also seem to be explicable in terms of the operation of unconscious ideas. The portion of the mind that contains these ideas is so sealed off, that Breuer also concludes that they are of a permanent nature. Take, for instance, a subject suffering from melancholia who is immersed for a long time in the same distressing idea.

Like Binet and Janet, Breuer places a portion of psychical activity at the centre of hysteria. What is the explanation for this? "It is only too easy to fall into a habit of thought which assumes that every substantive has a substance behind it — which gradually comes to regard 'consciousness' as standing for some actual thing; and when we have become accustomed to make use metaphorically of spatial relations, as in the term 'sub-consciousness', we find as time goes on that we have actually formed an idea which has lost its metaphorical nature and which we can manipulate easily as though it was real. Our mythology is then complete."[75]

Inevitably, the question as to the localisation of psychical functions arises.[76] Breuer is in favour of using spatial metaphors, so long as one refrains from allocating a specific place in the brain to consciousness and unconsciousness. If this principle is respected, then the use of spatial metaphors enables one to articulate what is observed in cases of hysteria. One must accept as a fact that part of hysterical patients' psychical activity remains inaccessible to perception and to their own self-consciousness. This leads us to the conclusion that the hysterical attack is caused by a splitting of the mind. Consider, for instance, patients who seem to 'observe' and reproach themselves when they have hysterical attacks: "They need not have behaved like that". Breuer finds these reproaches illegitimate since the patients cannot prevent them. Their ego, i.e. the conscious rectifying thought, is in no position to influence either the attack or the psychical activity. "Here we have a situation in which the thought and ideation of the conscious waking ego stands alongside of the ideas which normally reside in the darkness of the unconscious but which have now gained control over the muscular apparatus and over speech, and indeed even over a large part of ideational activity itself: the splitting of the mind is manifest."[77] The concept of the splitting of the mind is accordingly indispensable for Breuer's theory; there seems to be no other possible way to account for the clinical picture of hysteria.

To Janet the 'splitting of personality' rests on an innate mental weakness or an "insufficance psychologique". Whereas normal mental activity shows a possibility for 'synthesis', i.e. the ability to unite various ideas into a complex, this function appears to be severely disrupted in the case of hysteria. Janet describes this as the 'restriction of the field of consciousness'. In the present instance, this function is connected to sense-impressions (sensory perception) that make up a "Gestalt". For consciousness does not only presuppose perception, but also apperception. If the latter is lacking, the separate perceptions either disappear and produce no further consequence, or they aggregate and form subconscious ideational complexes which, when considered in their entirety, make up the subconscious. Hysteria is thus a "maladie de faiblesse". This is why it is more likely to develop in an innately weak mind when it is being subjected to influences that weaken it even further. Normality or pathology are both related to the strength of the psyche. Hence the notion of a hysterical disposition. Janet therefore considers that hysteria is a particular form of congenital mental weakness.

Breuer does not agree with Janet on this point. To Breuer, the splitting of the consciousness does not come about as a consequence of the patient's innately weak mind. Patients only appear to be weak-minded because their mental activity is divided, and only a portion of the psychical functions is at the disposal of their conscious thought. Breuer puts Janet's view down to the fact that he based his observations on patients found in hospitals or institutions,

i.e. on patients who were unable to cope with life on account of their mental weakness. However, the case descriptions in the *Studies* go to show that hysteria need not necessarily coalesce with weak-mindedness. Breuer and Freud regularly found amongst their patients "the clearest intellect, strongest will, greatest character and highest critical power".[78] It is after all no mere coincidence that St Theresa is the patron saint of hysteria.[79]
Breuer eventually formulates an answer to the question about the origin of the splitting of the mind. He alludes once more to Anna O.'s day-dreaming as a paradigm for the 'other psyche'. He considers day-dreaming, which also occurs in normal individuals and whose content is often of a sexual nature, as the "Normalvorbild" of the hypnoid state, because it implies a similar splitting of the mind. "In complete opposition to Janet's views, I believe that in a great many cases what underlies dissociation is an excess of efficiency, the habitual co-existence of two heterogeneous trains of ideas."[80] Such a duplication of the psychical activity can be observed in people, or else it can be triggered off by strong emotional conditions.[81] It is essentially this duplication that predisposes one to developing a "splitting of the mind". One passes over from one state to the other when the content of the two co-existing clusters of ideas is no longer of the same kind or when one of them encapsulates ideas which cannot enter consciousness. In other words, it has to do with ideas which have been *fended off* or which have *arisen* from a *hypnoid state*. Only then can a permanent split occur, that is to say, the ideational complexes from each half of the mind cannot link up.

I would like to make two observations on this matter. Firstly, there is a certain *circularity* in Breuer's reasoning, as the 'splitting of the mind' can be brought back to an innate split. Secondly, the mechanism of resistance comes across as only being a *secondary* etiological factor in the duplication of the psyche, although Breuer does seem to admit that this is not always the case. "Freud's observations and analyses show that the splitting of the mind can also be caused by 'defence', by the deliberate deflection of consciousness from distressing ideas: only, however, in some people, to whom we must therefore ascribe a mental idiosyncrasy. In normal people, such ideas are either successfully suppressed, in which case they vanish completely, or they are not, in which case they keep on emerging in consciousness. I cannot tell what the nature of this idiosyncrasy is. I only venture to suggest that the assistance of the hypnoid state is necessary if defence is to result not merely in single converted ideas being made into unconscious ones, but in a genuine splitting of the mind. Auto-hypnosis has, so to speak, created the space or region of unconscious psychical activity into which the ideas which are fended off are driven."[82] Therefore a splitting of the mind logically occurs *prior* to resistance or repression.

3.4.6. Innate disposition and development of hysteria

Breuer admits that most of the hysterical phenomena which he dealt with in his theoretical chapter can partially be based on an *innate idiosyncrasy*. Yet the actual capacity to acquire hysteria undoubtedly also depends on an individual's idiosyncrasy ("Eigenart"), which Breuer attempts to describe more accurately.

Earlier on, Breuer criticised Janet's view that a predisposition to hysteria stems from an innate psychical *weakness*. Any family doctor knows from experience that a disposition of this kind lies in an 'excess' rather than in a 'deficiency' — it is an incapacity to bear monotony and boredom for a prolonged period. Hysterical subjects are people whose nervous system liberates a surplus of excitation which needs to be used up. At puberty "this original excess is supplemented by the powerful increase in excitation which arises from the awakening of sexuality" and is made available for pathogenic phenomena.[83] Whether or not these phenomena take the shape of hysterical phenomena, depends on the idiosyncrasy of the individual. Once again Breuer aims at the *abnormal excitation of the nervous system*.

In fact, he goes even further. He argues, falling back on the notion of physiological disposition, that in such people "the excitation of the central organ can flow into the sensory nervous apparatuses which are normally accessible only to peripheral stimuli, as well as into the nervous apparatuses of the vegetative organs which are isolated from the central nervous system by powerful resistances".[84]

A series of pathological phenomena are thence explicated, such as the mechanism that brings the neurosis of the organ into existence. When one's attention is sufficiently concentrated on some part of the body, then the "attentionelle Bahnung" exceeds the normal amount. This means that attention facilitated a passage for the excess of excitation. The abnormal excitation also explains the exaggeration of the normal organic link between cause and effect. Breuer takes the example of excessive vomiting during pregnancy when a minimal stimulus of the uterus occurs. In this sense, he does not do away entirely with the old 'reflex theory'.

Breuer refrains from making generalisations about his newly acquired understanding, yet for him the idiosyncrasy of the nervous system and the mind seem to explain numerous familiar properties of patients suffering from hysteria. The surplus of energy not only determines the patient's inability to lead a monotonous life, but also their craving for sensations in order to break the monotony of their lives and the 'need for being ill', or their inclination to display other symptoms. To Breuer, this is a long way from the simulation that hysterical patients were previously accused of. If it is a question of actual simulation "that is based, not on the hysterical disposition but, as Möbius has so aptly said, on its being complicated by other forms of degeneracy — by innate, moral inferiority".[85]

The surplus of excitation also brings about numerous pathological phenomena in the motor sphere, such as the very early development of nervous tics in children. Breuer does not discard the possibility that motor phenomena of this kind can also come about without any ideational intervention. For instance, a convulsive attack can only be caused by the summation of an amount of excitation.

Puberty is an extremely precarious condition as regards the excitation of the nervous system. Indeed, one could even suggest that puberty in effect creates the aforementioned disposition, since one can observe that some people remain healthy until the onset of puberty when they become ill. "We must ask ourselves whether that process may not create the disposition to hysteria where it was not present innately. And in any case we must attribute more to it than a simple raising of the quantity of excitation. Sexual maturation impinges on the whole nervous system, increasing excitability and reducing resistances everywhere. We are taught this from the observation of adolescents who are not hysterical and we are thus justified in believing that sexual maturation also establishes the hysterical disposition in so far as it consists precisely in this characteristic of the nervous system."[86] Breuer recognises once more the importance of sexuality as one of the major components contributing to hysteria.

To Breuer, hysteria is to be thought of as a building several storeys high, the foundation of which is the idiosyncrasy ("Eigenart") of the nervous system. Ideogenic as well as non-ideogenic phenomena are then constructed on this foundation. He therefore opposes the view that allots a central place to psychi-

cal factors in the aetiology of hysteria, clinging to a purely physiological conception of hysterical stigmata, like various pains, vasomotor phenomena and purely motor convulsive attacks. He does, however, leave room for ideational phenomena and the prevalence of sexuality in these. When an idea is fended off or repressed, it is often of a sexual nature. A resistance of this kind underlies a great deal of hysteria at puberty. The attitude of young girls towards sexual ideas and feelings often varies greatly. Some girls ignore them, while other girls tend to be very receptive, like boys "(...) and lastly there are natures of a refined organisation who, though their sexual excitability is great, have an equally great moral purity and who feel that anything sexual is something incompatible with their ethical standards, something dirtying and smirching. They repress sexuality from their consciousness, and the affective ideas with a content of this kind which have caused the somatic phenomena are fended off and thus become unconscious."[87] Thus hysterical phenomena in young women can often be traced back to traumas during their honeymoon, or an insufficiently satisfactory sexuality may result in a conversion of sexual excitation into hysterical symptoms.[88] Although non-sexual affects can be equally hysterogenic, it is clear to Breuer that the sexual factor is by far the most important and that it is the most productive for the pathology.
As well as the abnormal excitation of the nervous system, Breuer names the hypnoid state as the third constituent of the hysterical disposition. This state, which largely favours the conversion of symptoms, can also yield auto-hypnosis which eventually completes the 'splitting of the mind'. According to Breuer, it is in this split that one has to look for the demon that springs from a former idea of the 'possessed' hysterical patient.

3.5. Freud's clinic of the excessively intense idea

3.5.1. Introduction

A reading of Freud's chapter on the 'Psychotherapy of Hysteria' should enable one to formulate an answer to three different questions.
Firstly, that of the discrepancy between the theoretical material developed by Breuer and the clinic of the "Seelenbehandlung" which Freud took upon himself. As far as Freud's view on psychotherapy is concerned, one can draw substantially on the subject matter of the case histories of Emmy von N.,

Lucy R., Katharina and Elisabeth von R, as well as on the chapter on psychotherapy.[89] The feeling of uneasiness that the 'Freudian' reader experiences when approaching Breuer's theoretical chapter is counterbalanced by a sense of wonderment on reading the theory developed by Freud in this chapter. This sense of wonderment springs from the originality and the linearity of the text, as well as from the topicality of the issues raised in it. A juxtaposition of both chapters reveals that Breuer's was not developed from the notion of the 'excessively intense idea'.

This leads to a second question. Freud's chapter on psychotherapy has a particular historical relevance, as it is the first text which paid attention to speech within the frame of a therapeutic environment for neurotics. It therefore merits a second reading in order to find an answer to the following questions: "What is psychotherapy?", or even, "What must psychotherapy be?" These questions are especially relevant today. I should like to draw the reader's attention to the draft that the *Association for Psychoanalysis and Psychotherapy* sends to its members. In this text the view that psychotherapy is too important to be left to non-analysts is put to the fore. "The place of psychotherapy in relation to other adjoining fields is contingent; even though it occupies a prominent place with respect to these fields. Psychoanalysis and psychotherapy can by no means be equated, but to deny that there are and must be links — albeit only because a psychotherapy that does not owe a debt to psychoanalysis in one way or another is inconceivable — would represent the negation of an important cultural phenomenon. Psychotherapy in the literal sense of the word, i.e. the potential completion of a cure, and not in the societal-economic meaning, is a theoretically based point of departure whose slogan-like formulation does not exempt analysts from dutifully outlining the relation between both. If analysts were to neglect their duty, they would notice much to their surprise that society compels them to fill this blank by using the ruthless language of adaptation and efficiency in order to erase this untimely theory formation."[90] This quotation is directed at analysts in particular and urges them not to pass over the field of psychotherapy flippantly because of the manifest differences between psychotherapy and the actual psychoanalytical 'cure'.[91]

I will demonstrate that, within the frame of this discussion, it is pertinent to refer to the *Studies* and more particularly to Freud's chapter on psychotherapy. Even if one goes beyond the differences between psychoanalysis and psychotherapy, the fact remains that the psychoanalytical apparatus grew from one of the first attempts (if not from the very first one) to act systematically on the psyche by means of the 'word', namely Freud's "Seelenbehandlung". Not only psychoanalysis, but any contemporary conception of psychotherapy would do well to question their assumptions on the basis of this text, unless of course they opt to renounce their origins so as not to see the gap between their own praxis and the question of the psyche as it presents itself today (or 100 years ago for that matter) by means of speech. I thus advocate the idea that a contemporary clinical psychology, in so far as it wishes to be recognised as such, should answer the same questions raised by the clinic of the 'excessively intense idea'.

The third question is contiguous to the two previous ones and relates to Freud's progression. In my approach to Freud's work, I favoured the notion of the *epistemological breach* or *choice*. This does not mean that no continuity can be descried in the evolution of Freud's thinking on the psyche from the moment that the question of the psyche emerged. What it does mean is that this continuity pertains to the gradual development of a psychology, and has no connection whatever with the alleged continuity between, for instance, physiological or neurological disciplines and his psychology. Psychology, as it was conceptualised by Freud, is instead determined by the epistemological choice which is already apparent in his early work where it was predictably always linked with his *clinic*. To Freud it had already been plain from his stay at the Salpêtrière and from his reading of Bernheim's book, that the question of the psyche could only be answered by constructing a completely new psychology. His 'declaration of principle' can be traced back to his 1890 article on the "Seelenbehandlung", even though the article in question was discretely published in a popular book about medicine. Freud's chapter on psychotherapy (1895) unambiguously announces that the 'talking cure' logically entails a *new clinical psychology*, a new science, one far removed from the physiological foundation of a syndrome as propounded by Breuer. The need for a psychology of this kind becomes apparent in this chapter and serves as my starting point for a reading of the *Project* as an expression of a similar attempt to provide a clinical psychology.

3.5.2. Freud versus Breuer

Freud posed several questions concerning the therapeutic method which yielded the aetiology of hysterical symptoms and which had already been described in the 'Preliminary Communication': what is the scope of this method? How can it be said to differ from other methods? What is the technique employed? What difficulties does it come up against? His answers to these questions display three essential points which are at variance with Breuer's conception.

On the subject of the *scope* or application of the method, the gap between what is described in the 'Preliminary Communication' and Breuer's chapter, is apparent from the start. For, the declared intention of this joint publication dating from 1893 focussed on the "psychical mechanism of hysterical *phenomena*".[92] In Breuer's chapter, the psychical mechanism of defence or repression is allotted a place in function of the physiological concept of the *clinical unity* of hysteria. Freud's application of the technique in conjunction with the difficulties he experienced with it, impelled him to adopt an original viewpoint.
What exactly were these difficulties? Freud touches upon two of them, one of which was of a practical nature and the other of an epistemological nature. Firstly, he found that not all patients who exhibit hysterical symptoms can be hypnotised. This means that an almost immediate change to the hypno-cathartic method imposed itself. Let me remind you that this method corresponds to Breuer's notion of the hypnoid state. The hysterical symptom is determined by a trauma that occurred during an altered state of this kind, which results in the withdrawal from consciousness of ideas appertaining to this trauma. The hypno-cathartic method attempts to create an access to this 'other psyche' by putting the patient in a comparable state by means of hypnosis. The same reasoning could be found in Charcot, who showed that what could be brought about by means of hypnosis could also be undone using the same method. With the exception of Breuer's treatment of Anna O. (who, as we have seen, spontaneously fell into autohypnosis, an ideal state of consciousness for the therapy), Freud's own experience corroborates Bernheim's view: hysterical patients are often unsuggestible, especially when the suggestion — and thus hypnosis — is used with a therapeutic aim in mind.[93]

These practical difficulties raise questions about the essential characteristics of hysteria. As we have seen, Breuer's answer to this lies in physiology, i.e. in the abnormal excitation of the nervous system, in the increase of excitation caused by the sex-glands, as well as in the hypnoid state, which is part and parcel of the innate hysterical disposition. Freud, however, does not find evidence of the third characteristic in his actual practice.[94] Instead, all the cases he comes across seem to point in favour of the postulate of the mechanism of repression.

How suitable can Breuer's method be if the hypnoid state does not corroborate clinical findings? Freud rightly points out that it is impossible to make a precise diagnosis of actual neuroses *before* one has acquired a thorough understanding of the particular case, that is to say, before one has submitted the case to a "thorough analysis — an analysis which can, in fact, only be brought about by the use of Breuer's method".[95] Yet the decision on the diagnosis and the sort of therapy to be adopted has to be made before such an in-depth knowledge of the case has been acquired. In other words, Freud highlights the problem of the decision to be made relating to the treatment once faced with an actual patient. Should one opt for "Seelenbehandlung" or for a classical medical treatment?

Freud goes as far as disconnecting the new method of treatment from the diagnosis of 'hysteria'. He thence moves away from the idea that each particular disorder deserves a specific therapy to the idea of a choice of principle for *one* therapeutic treatment for all cases of neuroses. This choice is no longer determined by the patient's symptomatology and it is here that his epistemological shift becomes apparent.[96]

As an argument Freud uses the progression he himself had made since he had undertaken the study of neuroses. He observed that the cathartic method he initially employed for patients who exhibited one or more characteristic symptoms of hysteria often failed to produce any results. "On other occasions again, I tried applying Breuer's method of treatment to neuroses which no one could have mistaken for hysteria, and I found that in that manner they could be influenced and indeed cleared up. I had this experience, for instance, with obsessional ideas, genuine obsessional ideas of the Westphal type, in cases without a single trait which recalled hysteria. Consequently, the psychical mechanism revealed by the 'Preliminary Communication' could not be pathognomonic for hysteria."[97]

To Freud, the generalised application of psychotherapy also implies a displacement of the status of the treatment that goes from being pure therapy to becoming a sort of research tool for the psyche. He soon came to the idea of looking for the aetiology and the specific psychical mechanism of all forms of neurosis in this way. The first findings of this research assigned a central place to sexual factors. He made a distinction between neuroses which could only be explained in terms of these factors (the "Aktualneurosen", such as neurasthenia and anxiety neurosis) and neuroses in which a psychological mechanism, comparable to the one which operates in hysteria, could be traced (obsessional neuroses).[98]

Having introduced a distinction between the 'simple' clinical picture of neurasthenia, anxiety neuroses and obsessional neuroses, he went on observing other neuroses commonly included under the heading of hysteria. He remarked that there was a profusion of diseases listed under this heading, which he opined was used too often. It is not because a few hysterical symptoms are apparent — e.g. anaesthesia or a hysterical attack — that one can rightly define the disease as being a form of hysteria. The conception holding that neuroses are mostly mixed is closer to reality. Neurasthenia and anxiety neuroses, however, are found in more or less pure forms in young people. Hysteria, however, is more problematic, as one is usually confronted with a *combination* of two etiological factors: the sexual factor and the psychical mechanism of repression. "As regards hysteria, however, it follows that this disorder can scarcely be segregated from the nexus of the sexual neuroses for the purposes of study, that as a rule it represents only a single side, only one aspect, of a complicated case of neurosis, and that it is only in marginal cases that it can be found and treated in isolation."[99] In other words, Freud replaces the physiological foundation that safeguarded the clinical unity of hysteria with a question concerning the psychical mechanism characteristic of every neurosis. A more explicit refutation of Breuer's theory is unthinkable.

This leads me to the second important difference with Breuer's view, namely the *status of Eros*. Freud decided to submit the case studies collected in the *Studies* to his newly acquired viewpoint, i.e., to submit them to the incidence of sexuality which emerged from the examination of the "Aktualneurosen". This point of view seems indeed to be new, for he writes that the case histories date from a period during which he did not focus on the tangles of sexuality, at least, not in the field of hysteria. "And if, instead of these four,

I did not report twelve cases whose analysis provides a confirmation of the psychical mechanism of hysterical phenomena put forward by us, this reticence was necessitated by the very circumstance that the analysis revealed these cases as being simultaneously sexual neuroses, although certainly no diagnostician would have refused them the name of hysteria. But an elucidation of these sexual neuroses would overstep the bounds of the present joint publication."[100] Yet on a second reading, it seems easy to uncover the cases belonging to the realm of mixed neuroses.

The generalisation that all neuroses result from a sexual factor, which Breuer disapproved of, involves much more than a simple transposition from another field of research. The underlying signification will become clearer later in this chapter. When Freud argues that a psychoanalysis of every case of neurosis reveals the part played by Eros, it is certain that he is not merely referring to the sex-glands of the patient, but that he is also alluding to the phenomenon of *transference*.

Freud still does give Breuer some credence as regards the treatment of Anna O., although the case does seem to contradict the hypothesis of the mixed neurosis. What Freud deplores is the fact that Breuer did not examine his patient from the angle of the "Seksualneurose" (sexual neurosis).[101] The expectation of a sexual neurosis was as yet also fairly remote during the treatment of Emmy von N. "I had come fresh from the school of Charcot, and I regarded the linking of hysteria with the topic of sexuality as a sort of insult —just as the women patients themselves do."[102] But when Freud goes through his notes, it seems plain to him that sexual abstinence fulfils an important role in the development of hysteria. In the case of Lucy R., the sexual aetiology is obvious, as it also was for Katharina who suffered from hysteria accompanied by 'virginal anxiety'. Freud leaves it up to the reader to interpret the case of Elisabeth von R., but again the sexual foundation of this case was never investigated at the time.

A first observation concerning Freud's retrospective 'evaluation' relates to his examination of the sexual factor. Is the sexual factor something that can be recorded in the same way as a doctor takes his patient's body temperature in order to diagnose a sore throat? Or is the dimension of Eros inextricably intertwined with psychotherapy?

Freud indirectly proposes an answer when he expounds upon the difficulties he encountered in the clinic. "The procedure is laborious and time-consuming for the physician. It presupposes great interest in psychological happenings, but *personal concern* for the patients as well. I cannot imagine bringing myself to delve into the psychical mechanism of a hysteria in anyone who struck me as low-minded and repellent, and who, on closer acquaintance, would not be capable of arousing human sympathy; whereas I can keep the treatment of a tabetic or rheumatic patient apart from personal approval of this kind."[103] The treatment also makes demands on the patient, aside from a certain level of intelligence "(...) the complete consent and complete attention of the patients are needed, but above all their confidence".[104] This is because psychoanalysis regularly veers towards the most intimate and secret psychical processes. It is therefore not suitable for all patients. Some withdraw from the treatment as soon as they realise in which direction the research is going. "For patients such as these the doctor has remained a stranger. With others, who have decided to put themselves in his hands and place their confidence in him — a step which in other such situations is only taken voluntarily and never at the doctor's request — with these other patients, I say, it is almost inevitable that their personal relation to him will force itself, for a time at least, unduly into the foreground. It seems, indeed, as though an influence of this kind on the part of the doctor is a sine qua non to a solution of the problem. I do not think any essential difference is made in this respect whether hypnosis can be used or whether it has to be by-passed and replaced by something else. But reason demands that we should emphasise the fact that these drawbacks, though they are inseparable from our procedure, cannot be laid at its door. On the contrary, it is quite clear that they are based on the predetermining conditions of the neuroses that are to be cured and that they must attach to any medical activity which involves intense preoccupation with the patient and leads to a psychical change in him."[105]

On the one hand, Freud unambiguously indicates that transference is unavoidable within the frame of psychotherapy. Any intensive research into the life history or relationships of the patient leads to an improper relation of this kind. "Just like a new love rekindles old memories, the in-depth exploration of the memory cause previous stirrings of the mind."[106] On the other hand, Freud draws a connection between the appearance of transference and the factors contributing to neuroses. In other words, something that makes up the transference phenomenon is simultaneously a constituent of the neurosis. Before long, Freud was to point to this constituent by using the famous reference to Oedipus, though there is no explicit allusion to it in the *Studies*.[107]

The fact that the notion of transference was recognised in 1895 is significant. It proves — at the very least — that one cannot reduce Freud's conception about sexuality to Breuer's speculations.

A third difference is related to the psychical mechanisms of *defence* or *repression*. In the *Studies*, one can trace how Freud actually discovered that this mechanism is not an abstract postulate, as it falls in line with the empirical approach of the talking cure. From the start, the clinic of the excessively intense idea exposed itself as one of repression and of an unwillingness to know. Interestingly, it was a technical difficulty that gave Freud the idea of assigning a central position to repression in his conception of the aetiology of neuroses.

Earlier on, we saw that Freud extended the *scope of application* of psychotherapy to all neuroses — unlike Breuer whose main concern was to maintain the clinical unity of hysteria. The reason for Freud's move lies in his detection of the mechanism of defence in patients who could not be suspected of suffering from hysteria. A second modification concerned the therapeutic *technique*. Freud observed that a lot of hysterical patients were difficult to hypnotise, although hypnosis was essential for the application of Breuer's technique. To him, hypnosis was vital to attain the required 'extension of memory' which had not been abreacted.

The case of Lucy R. offers a good illustration of this difficulty and of the solution provided by Freud. Amongst other things, this patient was plagued by continually recurring "subjective olfactory sensations". Every state of excitation led to her smelling "burnt pudding". Naturally, Freud assumed that this excessively intense idea was associatively linked to the recollection of an original trauma. He thus tried to use hypnosis to probe into her mind so as to isolate the first apparition of the hysterical symptom. However, it was impossible to bring Lucy R. into a state of somnambulism. Freud was then faced with the choice of either abandoning the treatment or of looking at other ways to conjure up the memories. "I therefore did without somnambulism and conducted her whole analysis while she was in a state which may in fact have differed very little from a normal one."[108] Freud found himself comforted in his choice by his Nancy experience and by his reading of Breuer. For, hadn't he heard Liébault, the *doyen* of hypnosis, sigh: "If only we had the means of putting every patient into a state of somnambulism, hypnotic therapy would be the most powerful of all."[109] And hadn't Bernheim said that he could only achieve the desired results within the walls of his institute? Freud also recalled one of Bernheim's experiments in which hypnosis was not required to bring events that took place during hypnosis back to consciousness. Keeping this at the back of his mind, Freud assumed that his patients themselves actually knew everything that could possibly harbour a pathogenic significance. Hence the technical modifications he implemented were purely devices aimed at producing a state of attention which allowed the patients to look within in order to describe the images that were going through their minds.

Let me point out that this approach does not essentially differ from what is understood today by 'free association'. For ultimately, the ritual pressure of the hand, which Freud used at the beginning, merely gives more weight to the question "what occurred to you?" Why this deceptively open question? The cases listed in the *Studies* lead me to put forward two reasons.

Firstly, Freud noticed that every time he asked a patient when the symptom occurred for the first time, he received an answer along the lines of "I really don't know". This is where free association comes in; it plays the part of a technical device which, via an associative by-pass, allows one to bring the desired memory into consciousness. A case in point is the therapy followed by Lucy R. One witnesses that by using the free associative process in a relatively fluid way Freud was led to the memory and could therefore eradicate the symptom. When Lucy R.'s olfactory hallucinations disappeared, the treatment was brought to an end. However, the reader remains with an unanswered question: to what extent was the patient liberated from the morbid vow she took at her aunt's deathbed?[110]

A second reason stems from the fact that the effect of psychotherapy is not determined by simply turning memories into words. If this were the case, psychotherapy would simply be a mechanistic affair. What is far more important is the articulation of what has been left unsaid — a procedure in which memories only serve as an impetus.[111]

The difficulties Freud experienced when applying hypnosis revealed a crucial aspect of both the psychopathology of neuroses and psychotherapy. For Freud perceived that in a large number of cases, the cause of his failure to hypnotise his patients went back as far as their refusal of the attempt to hypnotise. "The idea occurred to me one day that the two cases might be identical and that both might signify an *unwillingness*; that people who were not hypnotisable were people who had a psychical objection to hypnosis, whether their objection was expressed as unwillingness or not."[112] When Freud asked when the symptom had occurred for the first time, some patients replied that they couldn't remember, while others had some vague recollections, onto which they couldn't graft anything. By-passing the technique of hypnosis by resorting to the rule of free association was certainly no mean feat. It required a high degree of involvement on Freud's part to obtain the attention and concentration of his patients. "And since this insistence involved effort on my part and so suggested the idea that I had to overcome a resistance, the situation led me at once to the theory that *by means of my psychical work I had to overcome a psychical force in the patients which was opposed to the pathogenic ideas becoming conscious (being remembered)*. A new understanding seemed to open before my eyes when it occurred to me that this must no doubt be the same psychical force that had played a part in the generating of the hysterical symptom and had at that time prevented the pathogenic idea from becoming conscious."[113]

Psychotherapy or the clinic of the excessively intense idea therefore presents itself as a clinic of repression and resistance. In other words, the apparent 'not-knowing' of the neurotic patient ultimately turned out to be an 'unwillingness to know'. For weren't the ideas in question likely to arouse affects of shame, reproach and mental pain? Hence, neurotic patients seem to prefer to accept more suffering and 'mock fighting' rather than confronting the actual ideas.[114]

Freud emphasises that it would however be erroneous to believe that the device of free association enables one to master all the psychical obstacles in the path of a cathartic treatment. "But to believe this would be to make a serious mistake. Gains of this kind, so far as I can see, are not to be looked for in treatment. Here, as elsewhere, a large change requires a large amount of work. The procedure by pressure is no more than a trick for temporarily taking unawares an ego which is eager for defence. In all fairly serious cases the ego recalls its aims once more and proceeds with its resistance."[115]

Resistance can occur under a variety of forms, ranging from "the patient putting himself on his guard" to "completely forgetting their undertaking, though they had agreed to it beforehand. They promised to say whatever occurred to them under the pressure of my hand, irrespectively of whether it seemed to them relevant or not, and of whether it was agreeable to them to say it or not — to say it, that is, without selecting and without being influenced by criticism or affect."[116] However, Freud's patients rarely keep this promise. The work keeps on being interrupted and they keep on insisting that nothing has come to their mind. Freud argues that the psychotherapist ought not to believe them; one must always assume that the patients have kept something back because they thought it trivial or found it distressing. When they do come out with it, they often add: "I *couldn't* believe it could be that. It was only when it came back every time that I made up my mind to say it."[117]

Furthermore, excuses of all sorts, such as the ticking of the clock and lack of concentration are invoked to put an end to the associations. The most important elements are often announced as being insignificant, just like in an opera where the prince appears in the guise of a beggar. "Something has occurred to me now, but it has *nothing* to do with the subject. I'm only saying it because you want to know everything."[118] Freud alludes to other typical reactions of the unwillingness to know or "Verneinung". For instance, there are cases in which the patient deems the ideas unreal and the responsibility for the recurrence of the ideas is disowned. "Something has occurred to me now, but you obviously put it into my head". Or, "I know what you expect me to answer. Of course you believe I've thought this or that". Or even, "Something has occurred to me now, it's true, but it seems to me as if I'd put it in deliberately. It doesn't seem to be a reproduced thought at all."

Freud opposes to such a "Verneinung" or an 'unwillingness to know' the idea of the unconscious knowledge of the patient. Every technical modification he implements is prompted by the will and the necessity to bring this knowledge to light. Hence this attitude towards the patients differs fundamentally from Breuer's. As we have seen, Breuer's "hypnoid state" and the subsequent splitting of the mind imply a *not being able to know* rather than an *unwillingness to know.*[119]

What is more, hypnosis — the method Breuer puts forward to bring the patient back to a state akin to the one in which hysteria originated — seems to have no influence at all on the defence or resistance Freud experienced. On this subject the example of Emmy von N. is telling. Although Freud could make use of hypnosis, he observed that she would bristle up every time a mention of eroticism was made. "But it is also true that I learnt from that lady nothing whose telling might have called for any special overcoming of objections, nothing that she could not have told me even in a waking state, supposing we had been acquainted for some time and she had thought fairly highly of me. I never reached the true causes of her illness, which were no doubt identical with the causes of her relapse after my treatment (for this was my first attempt with this method); and the only occasion on which I happened to ask her for a reminiscence which involved an erotic element I found her just as reluctant and untrustworthy in what she told me as I did later with any of my non-somnambulistic patients."[120]

Let me go back to the findings Bernheim derived from his experiments with hysterical patients. Some of them appeared to be extremely prone to be hypnotised or extremely suggestible, but only so long as the suggestion did not bear on their symptoms. In other words, even under a "general climate of suggestibility", hypnosis seemed anything but an appropriate instrument for the treatment of hysteria.[121]

Freud's experience with neurotics paved the way for his conception of repression mechanisms. In the case of 'conversion hysteria' the defence is directed at distressing ideas, which afterwards persist as a weak trace of memory. The affect that was stripped, is 'discharged' through a somatic innervation. Hence, in such cases Freud would speak of *defence hysteria*. He also stressed that all the cases of hysteria he had treated so far belonged to this category.

A different category encompasses hypnoid hysteria, even though Freud is only familiar with one such case. "I could not, indeed, find a better example of it than Breuer's first case, which stands at the head of our case histories. Breuer has put forward for such cases of hypnoid hysteria a psychical mechanism which is substantially different from that of defence by conversion. In his view what happens in hypnoid hysteria is that an idea becomes pathogenic because it has been received during a special psychical state and has from the first remained outside the ego. No psychical force has therefore been required in order to keep it apart from the ego and no resistance need be aroused if we introduce it into the ego with the help of mental activity during somnambulism. And Anna O.'s case history in fact shows no sign of any such resistance."[122] Freud does add that his own clinic systematically meets with this resistance and thence concludes: "In short, I am unable to suppress a suspicion that somewhere or other the roots of hypnoid and defence hysteria come together, and that there the primary factor is defence."[123] I thus hope to have demonstrated the essential difference between Freud's conception and that of Breuer.

3.6. Conclusion: what is psychotherapy?[124]

Is it legitimate to look upon the *Studies* as a text on psychotherapy? Although neither author mentions psychoanalysis, they do both speak about "psychotherapy", and at times about "psychological analysis" or "psychological treatment". In addition, this 1895 publication is unmistakably one of the earliest writings on the subject of psychotherapy in the modern sense of the word, and as such one cannot let it go unnoticed in a historical approach to psychotherapy. An important question that therefore arises is that of the requirements the authors set themselves as psychotherapists, and more particularly, about what really animated them for becoming involved with psychotherapy. What desire can be detected on the part of psychotherapists? Are they driven by a desire to cure or by a desire to know?

The point of departure of the entire work is centred on a simple chance observation. In some cases it appeared that therapy — which favoured a recovery or the disappearance of symptoms — was determined by the patient's speech. Anna spoke... and, to the bewilderment of Breuer, she recovered from her hysterical symptoms.

That psychotherapy is principally determined by speech is today commonly recognised — or at least so would one like to assume. However, this was not the case a hundred years ago. At that time, one could only make use of several primitive instruments such as the rest-cure, electrodes and hydrotherapy to treat hysteria. The prevailing belief was that even if these methods did not cure, they would certainly do no harm. On the basis of this observation and of some reading on hypnosis, the possibility of creating a new instrument arose, namely that of the *talking cure*. And indeed, why not if the rest did not work anyway?

What sort of speech did these pioneers of psychotherapy have in mind? From the *Studies*, it would appear that one is dealing with a specific sort of speech, namely the "Aussprechen" or *speaking out* of the recollections linked to the first occurrence of a particular symptom. If a patient can achieve this, then the hysterical phenomenon disappears.

This explanatory blueprint propounded by Breuer and Freud is as elementary as the empirical observations themselves: at a particular moment, something happened to the patient which left a residual idea charged with affect. And as the affect was never sufficiently abreacted it remained operative. The quota

of affect may then be turned into a physical symptom. *Psychotherapy*, accordingly, consists in *turning the patient's attention* to this symptom in the hope that the ideas and affects intertwined in it can find expression in speech.
The blueprint which marshalled Breuer and Freud's progression logically led them to focus on the patient's *life history* and initially on the first occurrence of the symptom.
Let us however not be misled by the simplicity of the blueprint they departed from. Neither author leaves any doubt at all as to the *laborious and time-consuming nature* of such a mode of operation. In most cases the "(...) question is often some experience which the patient dislikes discussing; but principally because he is genuinely unable to recollect it and often has no suspicion of the causal connection between the precipitating event and the pathological phenomenon."[125] The major problem these budding psychotherapists encountered was precisely the laborious process entailed in the patient's speech and recollections. This process needs to be explained, and we may deem ourselves lucky as two explanations for it are proposed in this book.
On the basis of his treatment of Anna O., Breuer assumes that hysterical patients *cannot* remember the psychical material which provoked their symptoms. This, for the very simple reason that they acquired that material, i.e. ideas and their concurrent affect, and accumulated it in the psyche during a hypnoid state. In short, from the start, their consciousness exhibits an unbridgeable 'split' which explains why the pathogenic material that ends up there at a given moment cannot be abreacted. This splitting of the mind belongs to what he terms the hysterical disposition which is the ultimate cause of all the misery.
The remedy Breuer proposes to palliate this *not being able to remember* or *not being able to abreact* by means of speech, consists in artificially bringing on the hypnoid state of the mind. The technique of hypnosis is employed in order to achieve this.
Freud's conception is diametrically opposed to this. While he initially heeded Breuer's advice in attempting to gain access to this other state of consciousness or pool of pathogenic ideas by means of hypnosis, he was forced to recognise that he was not very successful. Nevertheless, he did not seem to have too much trouble admitting that he was by no means a good hypnotiser. The two subsequent observations he made are interesting in this respect.
Firstly, he found that he was not entirely to blame — indeed in my opinion, not at all. And what is more, he also held his patients accountable to an equal

degree, for they simply did not want to be hypnotised. "I noticed, however, that in some patients the obstacle lay still further back: they refused even any attempt at hypnosis. The idea then occurred to me one day that the two cases might be identical and that both might signify an *unwillingness*; that people who were not hypnotisable were people who had a psychical objection to hypnosis, whether their objection was expressed as unwillingness or not."[126] Secondly, hypnosis is by no means the only technique which can be used to gain access to pathogenic memories. These memories also surfaced when Freud asked his patients to direct their attention to or to concentrate on the symptom, thereby causing the memories to become conscious. The split postulated by Breuer, which is proper to the hysterical psyche and ultimately takes root in an inherited or acquired deviating disposition of the nervous system, is not as absolute as it seemed.

However, this understanding did not mean that the question of *unwillingness* was solved. It only elicited the fact that the notion of the hypnoid state was a superfluous one, both from a theoretical and a practical therapeutic angle. But it is principally the *status* of Freud's alternative explanation that makes it radically distinct from Breuer's. The patient's unabated resistance against speech and the emergence of the recollection, forces Freud to conjecture that a *psychical* mechanism was operative, one that bore no resemblance to an organically or physiologically determined state of consciousness. In the *Studies*, Freud uses a range of terms to describe this. He speaks of the *defence* issuing forth from the ego and of the *repression* from consciousness of unpleasant or unbearable reminiscences. For Freud spared no effort in attempting to get his patients to speak. It was the necessity of this application that led him to the notion that a resistance was operating in the psyche, which needs to be pushed aside in the course of the psychotherapy. 'Something' is resistant to ideas becoming conscious.

The difference between both conceptions is undeniably of an epistemological nature. When Feud asks questions about the *psyche* with an eye to disclosing *psychical mechanisms*, he is bound to arrive at a *psychology* of speech and of the *unwillingness to know*, in short, a psychology of recollecting and repressing.

Breuer, for his part, was content to push ideogenically determined hysterical symptoms aside, employing the psycho-cathartic method he had at his disposal. It is however true that in his theoretical chapter, he paid *lipservice* to the idea of the psychical mechanism of defence. He was willing to recognise that in some cases, a mechanism of this kind could be invoked as an explanation. Yet he laid the emphasis on the dispositional nature of both the hypnoid state and hysteria. To Breuer, driven by a desire peculiar to physicians, the *Studies* only deal with a new *therapeutic technique* for hysteria.

Freud was much more ambitious. Encouraged by the effects which he could empirically observe (beyond any resistance), and driven by his *desire to know* the psyche, he gradually started to map the psyche and its mechanisms. The means par excellence to constitute this new psychology, this new science was to be found in psychotherapy itself. In other words, in answer to his patients' *unwillingness to know* Freud responded by the converse: he *wanted to know.* The postulate of a disposition linked to some sort of clinical picture never impinged on his endeavour. On the contrary. From a therapeutic point of view, he underlined the triviality of diagnosing hysteria on the basis of one or more hysterical symptoms.

A first conclusion I gleaned from my reading of the *Studies* can be phrased as follows: *one witnesses a displacement from a minimalist option in the field of praxis to an epistemological choice on a scientific plane.* This choice, which bears on the constitution of a new science, entails everything but minimalist consequences at the level of the clinic. At the same time, Freud extends the field of application of psychotherapy to the domain of neuroses as a whole. In his eyes, the title of the book, *Studies on Hysteria,* only refers to the point of departure of his intellectual journey.

Let me come back to the initial question: what can we expect from a psychotherapist, even today? A desire to cure or a desire to know? The least one can expect of a therapist who essentially works with the word, with speech, is that he knows that the speech of neurotics — just like their symptoms — is determined by *memory* and by an *unwillingness to know.* One can furthermore expect him to know that his psychotherapy, regardless of the one chosen, ought to be pursued in accordance with this understanding and with its concomitant theory.

A second conclusion drawn from my reading of the *Studies* relates to the ultimate aim of psychotherapy. What is the objective of psychotherapy or the talking cure? Is it recollection or judgement?

On the basis of elementary observations from which the talking cure emerges, I arrived at the understanding that therapy is *determined by recollections*. This condition, although necessary, is in itself insufficient. Upon a reading of the case of Anna O., one is fleetingly tempted to accept that psychotherapy is, in point of fact, as simple as this outline suggests. However, Freud continually warns one not to labour under any delusions on the time-consuming and laborious nature of psychotherapy.

It is true that in the initial phase, the devices such as hypnosis, the focusing of attention and concentration which are employed to deal with the unwillingness to know, suffice to arouse a mass of psychical material to have "the camel" appear "through the eye of the needle".[127] This procedure in itself requires laborious effort and courage on the part of the patient, as well as patience on the part of the psychotherapist. Nonetheless, psychotherapy, as it was empirically outlined by Freud, encompasses much more than just listening to the memory of patients.

What else is indispensable aside from recollection? Or put differently, how is one actually to interpret the recollection and the psyche from which all these reminiscences stem? Is it not enough to look upon the psychism as being a deep pool, which doubtless is difficult to gain access to, but which, after all, is no more than this?

Freud cannot imagine the psyche as being anything other than *stratified* and therefore avails himself of a spatial metaphor. Furthermore, it seems that to him one sort of recollection cannot not simply be equated with another. "Things that belong to the external strata are *recognised* without difficulty; they had, indeed, always remained in the ego's possession, and the only novelty to the ego is their connection with the deeper strata of the pathological material. Things that are brought to light from these deeper strata are also recognised and acknowledged, but often only after considerable hesitations and doubts. Visual memory-images are of course more difficult to disavow than the memory-traces of mere trains of thought. Not at all infrequently the patient begins by saying: 'It's possible that I thought this, but I can't remember having done so.' And it is not until he has been familiar with the hypothesis for some time that he comes to *recognise* it as well; he remembers — and confirms the fact, too, by subsidiary links — that he really did once have the thought."[128] Freud adds to this that he pays no attention to the patient's judgement during the psychoanalysis. That is to say, that when the patient expresses doubts about the authenticity or the accuracy of a certain memory, he reserves his own judgement until the treatment has progressed further.[129]

Freud proceeds by writing that "The ideas which are derived from the greatest depth and which form the nucleus of the pathogenic organisation are also those which are acknowledged as memories by the patient with greatest difficulty. Even when everything is finished and the patients have been overborne by the force of logic and have been convinced by the therapeutic effect accompanying the emergence of precisely these ideas — when, I say, the patients themselves accept the fact that they thought this or that, they often add: 'But I can't *remember* having thought it.' It is easy to come to terms with them by telling them that the thoughts were *unconscious*. But how is this state of affairs to be fitted in our own psychological views? Are we to disregard this withholding of recognition on the part of the patients, when, now that the work is finished, there is no longer any motive for their doing so? *Or are we to suppose that we are really dealing with thoughts which never came about, which merely had a possibility of existing, so that the treatment would lie in the accomplishment of a psychical act which did not take place at the time?*"[130]

The preceding passage shows that the status of speech in psychotherapy stretches far beyond recollection and reproduction. In what Freud terms the psychical "Verarbeitung" (processing) and "Durcharbeitung" (working through), which refer to a repeated processing of the life history and to a working through of all the associative connections present in the life history, as well as in what he says about the patient's "Anerkennung" (judgement), one finds that the status of speech coalesces exactly with that of the *judgement*. Psychotherapy, as Freud sees it here, leads at a never previously articulated judgement, at an enunciation of the nature of "this I have been" or "this I will have been".[131]

A further requirement of the psychotherapist is thus that he is able to assist someone else in arriving at a judgement of this sort.

Here, there is little one can add on the subject of speech, except perhaps one last observation which Freud briefly mentions as being a significant aid in this process: "In the next place, we may reckon on the intellectual interest which the patient begins to feel after working for a short time. By explaining things to him, by giving him information about the marvellous world of psychical processes into which we ourselves only gained insight by such analyses, we make him himself into a collaborator, induce him to regard himself with the objective interest of an investigator, and thus push back his resistance, resting as it does on an effective basis. But lastly — and this remains the strongest lever — we must endeavour, after we have discovered the motives for his defence, to deprive them of their value or even to replace them by more powerful ones."[132] As this passage makes clear, we can expect the psychotherapist's desire to know to be 'contagious'.

My third conclusion brings me around to the question of whether psychotherapy ought to be approached with or without taking Eros into account. The *Studies* provide one with an even more explicit answer, if that is at all possible. For there is no psychotherapy possible without Eros. With such a conception, Freud follows in the footsteps of Apuleius, who expressed an eternal truth in his fairly tale about *Amor and Psyché*. In his mind, the only way to gain access to the psyche is via love[133] — a view which, as is commonly known, Breuer found difficult to accept. Within the framework of the *Studies*, the scope of Eros is contained in two different understandings.

Firstly, there is the understanding that the sexual factor plays a crucial role in the aetiology of every neurosis. Pure hysteria and the purely "Sexualneurose" are merely abstractions and are therefore not found in the clinic. One is always confronted with "gemischte" or mixed neuroses whose pathogenic nucleus (the aetiology) is to be located in childhood and which is connected to sexuality. When sexuality *could not* adequately be understood in childhood, psychotherapy offers the opportunity to repeat the psychical processing ("psychische Verarbeitung") and to lead it to a recognition in the form of a judgement ("Anerkennung").

As Freud admitted, it took him quite some time to reach this understanding. Only later was he in a position to point to the hiatus present in a number of case studies collected in the *Studies*, while at the actual time of the treatment he left them untouched.

The second understanding implied in Eros relates to the notion of *transference*. What astonishes me is not so much the presence of this theme in the *Studies,* as the caution — or should I say the typically British sense of understatement — with which it is mentioned in Strachey's editorial in the English translation. One reads that Freud "(...) had already had a *glimpse* of its formidable nature and had even, *perhaps* already *begun* to recognize that it was to prove not only an obstacle but also another major instrument of psychoanalytic technique".[134]

The origins of the 'perhaps' are not quite clear to me when I read, for instance, that psychotherapy "(...) is laborious and time-consuming for the physician. It presupposes great interest in psychological happenings, but *personal concern* for the patients as well. I cannot imagine bringing myself to delve into the psychical mechanism of a hysteria in anyone who struck me as low-minded and repellent, and who, on closer acquaintance, would not be capable of arousing human sympathy; whereas I can keep the treatment of a tabetic or rheumatic patient apart from personal approval of this kind."[135]

The total consent ("Einwilligung") and undivided attention is further required from the patient. By this I mean not only a readiness from the patient to look within, thus casting aside any form of *unwillingness to know*, but also the courage to put whatever surfaces into words. But Freud principally stresses that the trust ("Zutrauen") in the therapist is indispensable since the analysis regularly leads one to the most intimate and secret psychical processes.

Even today this strikes one as being obvious. As the talking cure is concerned with 'warding off' the unwillingness to know, it needs the intervention of another passion, namely that of the Eros in order for this to take place. "In not a few cases, especially with women and where it is a question of elucidating erotic trains of thought, the patient's co-operation becomes a personal sacrifice, which must be compensated by some substitute for love."[136]

While transference represents a necessary condition for psychotherapy, it can also function as an obstacle to the advancement of the therapy, as is reported in the *Studies*, when a patient recoils from transferring the distressing ideas that emerge in the course of the analysis to the physician. Freud puts the following typical example forward. In one of his patients, the origin of a hysterical symptom lay in a wish that had arisen many years earlier, but which the patient had at once relegated to the realm of her unconscious. This wish was that the man with whom she was talking at the time would make a passionate move and kiss her. At the end of a session, a similar wish manifested itself in her, but this time in relation to Freud. However, he forewarns that it is not appropriate for the therapist to take everything upon himself, and he further urges physicians to take a note of when "the third person coincided with the physician".[137] Yet if this transference is not given verbal expression, it blocks the therapy.

What is the moral of the story? One is compelled to declare Apuleius to be right, for there is no *Psyché* without *Amor*, i.e. no psychotherapy without a theory on psychosexuality and transference.

To conclude, if I were to sum up the partial answers I derived from the *Studies* and to reiterate the questions about what one is to expect from psychotherapists — regardless of the problems they have to deal with and irrespective of the institute where they work — the answer would be relatively simple. One can expect them to have an understanding of their own psyche and of the mechanisms operative in it. Even Freud did not escape from this. In the summer following the joint publication of the *Studies*, Freud started his analysis.

The discrepancy between Breuer and Freud can be summed up as follows. While Breuer's theory remains essentially physiological, Freud adopts a clinical-psychological position. By putting the psychical mechanism of defence in a central position Freud presupposes the patient's speech as a point of departure. This speech seems to be characterised by two fundamental passions: Eros and the unwillingness to know. This dual observation logically calls for a *psychological theory* which assigns a central place to speech and which can explain both characteristics.
A *clinical psychology*, i.e. *a psychology stemming from the praxis of the talking cure*[138], can never be a question of taste or preference. Rather, it needs to result from a meticulous scientific approach to its object, i.e. the psyche and the rules governing it as they transpire through the subject's speech. When Freud realised that hysteria did not correspond to the laws of neuroanatomy and neurophysiology, he was still thoroughly convinced that there existed only one neuroanatomy and one neurophysiology. As a result, he lucidly opted for the construction of a psychology in which he made use of the talking cure as a therapeutic instrument to probe into the human psyche. When — prompted by the first information on the psyche brought to light by a setting of this kind — one brings up questions such as "what should one expect from a psychotherapist?" and "what should one demand from clinical psychology?", one ought not to lose sight of the fact that these are borne from the conviction that there is only one psyche whose laws can essentially be discovered. This seems to me to be the only appropriate scientific approach.

CHAPTER 4

On Aphasia

> "But for us, workers, scholars, doctors, technicians, what direction does this return to the truth of Freud indicate ? It is the direction of a positive study whose methods and forms are given to us in this sphere of the so-called human sciences, which concerns the order of language, linguistics. Psychoanalysis should be the science of language inhabitated by the subject. From the Freudian point of view man is the subject captured and tortured by language."
>
> *Jacques Lacan*[1]

4.1. Introduction

As Freud was later to comment, the theoretical understanding implied in the *Studies on Hysteria*, accurately conveys what is empirically observable in the talking cure. This, however, does not alter the fact that the major axes of Freud's late theory are already discernible in the *Studies*. By 1895, Freud had already progressed a long way from the Charcotian notion of the clinical unity of hysteria. To Freud, the *Studies* is not so much a book about the so-called syndrome of hysteria, as a first elaborate exploration of the way in which *hysterical speech* materialises in a therapeutic setting. While Breuer, still thinking in terms of categories proper to medicine, made an effort to prescribe the psycho-cathartic method as a means of treating hysteria, Freud, guided by his first clinical experience, made a choice of principle in taking hysterical speech as a point of departure for his yet to be constructed clinical psychology. The second axis of his developing theory formation consists in that which is aroused by and intertwined with this hysterical speech, namely the *affect*.

For the therapeutic clinic presents itself as being one of the *excessively intense idea.*

The speech of the hysterical patient, however, is not merely charged with affect, it is also *falsely connected.* Freud makes a distinction between two aspects.

First, the speech of his patients always confronts him with a rational-cognitive problem, that of understanding. There exists a wide gap between the premises and the conclusions and it is in this gap that the 'elsewhere', the driving force behind speech, is located. The hypothesis of an operative *unconscious* seems thus logically and inseparably linked with a clinic rooted in speech. On a theoretical plane, the topographical idea of the psychical apparatus will have to account for the *repression* or for the passion of the *unwillingness to know.*

Second, the speech of any hysterical patient appears to be *addressed* to someone. That is to say that the therapeutic speech which produces effects can only be grasped when the function of the addressee, of the other, is recognised. The initial impetus for such a conception is found in Freud's description of the phenomenon of transference, which has only one possible mode, that of the false connection.[2]

I have just summed up Freud's first clinical insights and the theoretical hypotheses which arose from them. It is apparent from these, that speech occupies a central position. Hence, one ought not to be surprised to observe that, alongside his very first therapeutic experiences, Freud displayed a profound interest in various anomalies of human speech. His voluminous monograph on aphasia bears witness to this.[3]

When the first edition of his *Gesammelte Werke* was in preparation, Freud looked upon this monograph as being part of his 'pre-analytical' period and thence preferred not to have it appear alongside *The Interpretation of Dreams* and *The Psychopathology of Everyday Life.*[4] Several arguments can be invoked for this. The book, unlike his psychoanalytical writings, was not written by using clinical material which he collected himself during the course of the 'talking cure'. Instead, it sets the then-prevailing neuroanatomical model of explanation side by side with the descriptions of cases of organic aphasia found in scientific literature. His repudiation of the model of explanation follows from a strictly neurological criticism and not from a purely psychological perspective. However, Freud does not confine himself to a critical questioning of this deductive theoretical model; he also proposes an alternative system of classifying the various forms of aphasia, based on psychological criteria. Today, his model is still regarded as provocative and well thought out from a neuropathological perspective, and it is still a source of inspiration for many a neurologist.[5] In any case, it offered Freud the advantage of finding an explanation for both organic and hysterical aphasia within one and the same "psychological schema of the word presentation". This observation leads me to regard his monograph as being conditioned by his quest for the psyche. An argument in support of this view lies in the fact that Freud's interest in aphasia, the *not being able to speak*, coincides with the emergence of this very subject in his own intellectual progression.

4.2. Aphasia at the Salpêtrière

In 1885 at the Salpêtrière, Freud was confronted with a particular form of aphasia for the first time when Charcot dedicated a number of lectures to the phenomenon of hysterical mutism. The letter to Charcot in which he proposed his services to translate his *Clinical Lectures*, implicitly alludes to these particular lectures. In this letter, Freud assures Charcot that, as far as his knowledge of French is concerned, he only suffers from the motor variant of the disease.[6] So Charcot may rest assured, his book will be properly translated into German. The difference between organic and hysterical (or functional) diseases of the nervous system postulated by Charcot, is furthermore conveyed in Freud's monograph as a critique of a purely localisationist conception of psychopathology.
In this respect, it is informative to take a closer look at Charcot's lectures on hysterical mutism. Is it not symptomatic of hysteria that it defies the anatomy of the nervous system? This, at any rate, is perfectly illustrated when hysterical patients reveal themselves as champions of the fantasy which localises various psychical functions in the cerebral cortex. Freud will ascribe the status of 'false connection' to this theory.

The last lecture of the *Clinical Lectures on the Diseases of the Nervous System* contains Charcot's clinical presentation of a case of male hysterical mutism. In the appendix there is also a paper written by M. Cartaz on this disease. It gives an account of the lectures given by Charcot in December 1885 and includes various observations recorded in the literature on this subject.[7] It is also interesting to realise that Freud attended several of these lectures during his short stay in Paris. As we read this article, let us accompany Freud to Charcot's clinical demonstrations.

"Gentlemen, — It is in order to compare one with the other that I present to you two patients whose diseases imply a prognosis so essentially opposed. In the first, the recovery will be complete, that is absolutely certain, and I may add that in all probability it will happen quite suddenly in a few days, perhaps tomorrow.[8] In the second, on the other hand, the verdict is *prognosis pessima, exitus lethalis*, and I might also add *properatus*."[9]

Charcot justifies his claim by diagnosing an incurable and progressively deteriorating organic bulbar lesion in the second patient. According to Charcot, the lesion in the first patient probably originates from the cortex and, in any case, is of a purely dynamic and essentially transitory nature.

"However, gentlemen, the affections from which they are suffering present certain traits in common, and on certain points they have such marked resemblance that even an experienced physician may be excused for confounding them. It is precisely for this reason that I have brought them before you at the same time on the present occasion."[10]

Both patients experience difficulty in producing sounds in general and in expressing themselves in articulate speech in particular. Hence we are faced with two cases of mutism. However, on closer inspection, the differences become apparent. In the case of the first patient, mutism and aphonia are *absolute*. He is unable to emit either words or sounds. His even more unfortunate colleague, however, is capable of producing some grunting sounds after considerable effort.

"The first patient is the principal object of our lecture today; the second only having been placed beside him by way of comparison. Gentlemen, I may at the onset state that in my opinion this man, thirty-three years old, a gas-fitter by occupation, is a very good example of what is generally termed hysterical mutism. (...) Hysterical mutism is not an extremely rare affection; it has often been described, and you will find it mentioned in all writings devoted to hysteria. However, I think that the characteristics of the disease were not sufficiently isolated until the delivery of the lectures to which I have just made allusion. And the details into which we shall now enter may possibly present to some of you the appearance of novelty."[11]

In the vast majority of cases hysterical mutism sets in abruptly, often as the result of an affect of fright or a violent emotion of some sort. The syndrome can also follow a hysterical attack or may supervene in the course of an ordinary laryngitis. The duration of the disease is extremely variable; it can last for several hours, days, months or even years, and the recovery is almost as sudden as the appearance of the mutism. The most noteworthy characteristic, Charcot stresses, is that hysterical patients, even though integrally preserving the possibility of moving the tongue and mouth muscles, are not capable of emitting any sound at all. In other terms, they are even more mute than the deaf-mute who still manages to produce wild inarticulate yells. What is more, these patients are not even able to whisper. This, then, is the peculiar nature of hysterical mutism.

"Whispering is nothing else than spoken and articulate language. The phenomenon is, note it well, absolutely independent of the laryngeal voice. The truth of this fact was demonstrated experimentally in the laboratory of M. Marey, in 1876, and again in 1879 by M. Boudet, of Paris. These authors have clearly shown by means of the graphic method that the larynx takes no part in whispering; the vocal cords do not vibrate, the air traverses the larynx as it traverses the trachea, it passes along a motionless tube, nothing more."[12]

Charcot furnishes the following explanation for the hysterical patients' incapacity to whisper: they are deprived of the *motor representations* necessary to put articulate speech into action. However, a similar hypothesis was put forward for organic motor aphasia, after Broca's discovery of the phenomenon in 1861. But the cause of this form of aphasia is an *injury* of a certain part of the cerebral cortex which is responsible for the loss of motor word-presentations. Furthermore, in the case of hysterical mutism, the observed motor aphasia is *absolute* and *pure*, which it never is in its organic counterpart, for, in this case, speech is maintained at a constant level, albeit to a very limited extent. In most severe forms of organic mutism patients can still emit cries and utter clear and distinct syllables or even words. This is absolutely not the case with hysterical patients. Their lips have been completely sealed. Yet, in hysteria, the faculty of the intellect and the remaining speech functions (signs, etc.) have been preserved, which again is not the case in organic diseases. Charcot notes that other speech disorders can occur in concurrence with aphasia and with a general lowering of intelligence.

"The hysterical mute has not only preserved all the faculties of his intellect, not only does he readily comprehend all that is communicated to him by means of his ear or his eye, but he is perfectly able, as I said at the commencement of this lecture, to make himself understood by pantomimic signs, and of communicating his thoughts by writing."[13]

In the case of an organic lesion, the subject is unable to read or can only do so with the greatest difficulty. Furthermore, he does not understand or only partially understands what is said to him in his ear. One also observes in patients of this kind a loss of the faculty of making themselves understood by gesture. Writing, if indeed these patients are still able to write, is also a slow and laborious process. The difference between these two forms of aphasia is, according to Charcot, so distinct that the physician should have no problem making a diagnosis. Observing the loss of voice and articulate speech, in conjunction with strikingly graphic and vivid facial movements, is enough to recognise hysterical mutism.

"Founded on the preceding considerations, and on all that I have since learned of this subject in an experience by no means short, I think that I am justified in affirming that the condition, hysterical mutism, is sufficiently well characterised, sufficiently original, to be recognised by itself, even in the absence of all information furnished by concomitant symptoms. And you also, gentlemen, when you have become thoroughly acquainted with the characteristics, you in your turn will achieve diagnoses of such rapidity as to be considered by the uninitiated as a sort of magic."[14]

The "concomitant symptoms" he mentions refer to the known hysterical stigmata. In cases of hysterical mutism, symptoms such as the retraction of the visual field, and single or double hemianaesthesia are regularly observed in conjunction with the classical hysterical attacks. The presence of these can only confirm the diagnosis of hysteria. Hence hysteria is, in a great majority of cases, "polymorphous". This however does not preclude that hysterical mutism can occur as the only symptom of the illness. What is more, the physician who has acquired a solid knowledge of the syndrome of hysterical mutism ought not to fear being deceived by a possible simulation.

"Generally speaking the malingerer may be considered to be a fantastic person. He gives the reins to his imagination, and he adds all sorts of embellishments. Recall to your minds the conversation between Sganarelle and Lucinde, who may perhaps be considered as a perfect simulator.

Sganarelle. — 'What is the matter? What pain is it that you feel?'
Lucinde (replying by signs, carrying her hand to her mouth, to her head, and to her chin). — 'Han, hi, hon, han.'
Sganarelle. — 'Eh! what do you say?'
Lucinde (continuing the same gesture). — 'Han, hi, hon, han, han, hi, hon.'
Sganarelle. — 'What?'
Lucinde. — 'Han, hi, hon.'

Well, gentlemen, these han, hi, hon, han, are evidently superfluous, and reveal simulation. The legitimate mute remains silent, as I have told you, and if he carries his hand often towards his throat, it is to show you where in his idea the obstacle is; he would not point to his head and to his mouth. This is the way, as it seems to me, by considerations of this sort, that simulation often unmasks itself."[15]

Alternatively, in some situations when simulation seems to be the most obvious explanation, a closer inspection rules it out. The patient named Hélène G. is a case in point.

"Hélène G., a young prisoner of about twenty-four years of age, had directed to a priest, who she believed had wronged her, the dead body of a newly born child well wrapped up and placed in a basket. The parcel, labelled cheese, arrived by post just at the moment when the priest was receiving friends. Enclosed with the body was a small note, thus worded: — "*Pray for what you have lost.*" Was not that the act of an hysterical lunatic? Arrested soon afterwards, Hélène G. suddenly lost her speech after the very first interrogation. This time you will say the mutism was evidently simulated. Well no, gentlemen, it was not so in my opinion. (...). Hélène G. was mute and aphonic; she did not emit the least sound even when startled or excited to laughter by surprise. Not the least sound, no hin, hi, hon, han; not the least unnecessary gesture. The onset was quite sudden. The hysterical stigmata were, moreover, very pronounced, and of such a nature as did not admit of simulation; complete general anaesthesia; anaesthesia of the pharynx; retraction of the visual field, etc. And lastly, there was a feature that is absolutely peremptory; as in the case of other hysterical mutes. The patient wrote fluently and correctly, and it was in this way that she was able to communicate with the magistrate, and, at least in great part, confess her crime. A malingerer, without any doubt, would have pushed matters to the bitter end, she would have ceased to be able to write."[16]

Charcot eventually concludes his lecture with an experimental demonstration in which he artificially induces hysterical mutism by means of hypnotism. The technique itself is very simple. One starts by having a friendly chat with the hypnotised patient. Then one gradually approaches closer to the patient, pretending neither to hear nor to understand him/her. The patient will invariably attempt to raise his/her voice. If one continues pretending not to hear or understand him/her, the patient's voice will become progressively lower, which will ultimately lead to complete aphonia and an impossibility to articulate. Mutism thus obtained persists after awaking from hypnosis.

"Gentlemen, the possibility of giving rise to the syndrome of hysterical mutism artificially by means of suggestion, appears to us to indicate sufficiently clearly the point of departure of all the phenomena; and one is thus able to suppose the mechanism of its development. *It is in the grey cortex of the cerebral hemispheres that we must seek for the dynamic lesion whence emanate the symptoms in question*; and the mechanism that is to be invoked in such conditions is none other than that which acts in the production of psychical, or, if you like it better, mental paralysis. This theory, which is now founded on a considerable number of facts and on experience, is applicable, as you know, to a large number of hysterical affections, particularly those which arise under the influence of an occasional cause, such as a violent emotion, a traumatism, etc."[17]

Charcot reacts against the view holding that the syndrome is determined by the hysterical paralysis of the muscles of the speech apparatus, by explaining hysterical mutism in terms of a dynamic lesion of the cerebral cortex. A paralysis of this kind can, in this instance, account for a certain degree of aphonia, but cannot explain the incapacity to whisper. Consequently, hysterical mutism forces one to locate the dynamic lesion in the cerebral cortex.

Charcot proposes two possible conceptions of a lesion of this kind. Firstly, there is the point of view inspired by the traditional explanation of organic aphasia, which conjectures a *loss* of memories or *ideas*, as hysterical patients seem to have 'forgotten' how to speak. This forgetting is transitory and can therefore not be explained by the *destruction* of the nerve cells in which the ideas in question are said to be stored. Secondly, the symptomatology of hysterical mutism seems to be entirely determined by the impression the patients have of *what it is to have lost one's voice*. The well-delineated symptomatology *can only be made explicit* by a *subjective judgement* or a statement such as 'I have no voice' or 'I can no longer speak'. Charcot's conception of the dynamic lesion clearly appears to be located on the border between a neurophysiological and a psychological explanation of psychopathology.

I pointed out earlier that Charcot's notion of 'auto-suggestion' (amongst other things) veered towards a psychological approach to hysteria. Auto-suggestions of this sort allude to the ideational life of patients, which in turn functions as a point of departure for and an explanation of their symptoms. Charcot usually looks for this ideational life in the immediate antecedent of the hysterical disease, i.e. in the preceding trauma or in a scene in which a strong emotion or affect gripped the patient in question. In this respect, Charcot could be said to have paved the way for Freud's quest for the psyche, even though he never dealt with ideational life in a proper and systematic manner. The vast majority of the case descriptions collected in his *Clinical Lectures* are only weakly backed up from a psychological perspective. In other words, the notion of 'auto-suggestion' had not yet expanded so as to incorporate the *life history* of the patient. This expansion would later come about as the direct result of the praxis of the "Seelenbehandlung". However, there was precious little psychotherapy at the Salpêtrière.

On the basis of a case of hysterical mutism which Charcot revealed to his audience in December 1885 and which is included in the appendix, I will now illustrate how an actual clinical psychological perspective was still there for the taking when the patient's life history was taken into consideration.

The case Ch.

Ch., 37 years old, was admitted in November 1885 to Charcot's ward, where his family background was recorded.[18]

Family history. — Paternal grandfather died of an affection of the oesophagus. The brothers and sisters of the grandfather enjoyed good health; one of them died at seventy-eight. One of his nephews was bad-tempered, somewhat hypochondriac, and finally committed suicide. The paternal grandmother was very nervous, died at seventy-two of a catarrh. In her family there was a lunatic who died in an asylum. The maternal grandmother had an inebriate son who was not considered responsible. The father of the patient had epileptic fits and died of laryngeal tuberculosis at the age of fifty-seven. The patient's mother, who was very passionate, died of phthisis. She had eight children of whom Ch. was the eldest. Of his seven brothers and sisters, one brother died of croup at three years of age; two sisters died of phthisis at twenty-four and twenty-six years. One of them was subject to nervous attacks, and attacks of cataleptic sleep; "on waking she was aphonic; she articulated quite clearly, but very low, so low that it required extreme attention to understand her." Four sisters are living; two are delicate but without any definite complaint. One of the latter has a rachitic and choreic son.

Ch. was always ailing in childhood. When twelve he was confined to bed for five or six months with weakness. The doctor treated him for anaemia. "The least sound", he says, "caused me to faint; they were *unable to converse* beside my bed." On two occasions when he was at school he had haemoptysis. He was nicknamed the philosopher on account of his *taciturn character*. On leaving school he went to a college as assistant tutor; and subsequently went for some time into a large private horticultural establishment. After some family disagreements and disappointments in love, he quitted Switzerland, his native country, and joined the Foreign Army Corps. During his sojourn in Algeria he drank absinthe to excess, and contracted intermittent fever. When the war of 1870 broke out his regiment came to France. At Vierzon he remained eight days in a delirious condition, caused, so he says, by an attack of fever. He rejoined his regiment and in the Eastern Campaign he received a bullet-wound in the left elbow (January 17th, 1871) for which his arm was amputated by Dr. Mollière, of Lyons. He then returned to Switzerland and was appointed manager of a post-office. It was at this time (end of 1871) that the first important nervous manifestation made its appearance. While at supper with some friends he was seized, towards the end of the repast, with invincible sleep, and slept with his elbow on the table. His comrades were quite unable to awaken him. Towards the morning a nervous attack came on attended with terrible delirium. The doctor suspected an acute meningitis; and Dr. Mayor, called into consultation, confirmed this diagnosis. The second day afterwards, the patient recovered, but relapsed a few days later. Leeches were applied, but a nervous attack, still more terrible than the first, came on. However, the fever and the delirium disappeared at the end of two days.

Up to the year 1875 nothing abnormal occurred in Ch.'s condition. In this year he departed for Algeria, where he had obtained a post of clerk in the Prefecture of Oran. Shortly before his departure he experienced for the first time sudden and violent attacks of palpitation which would sometimes oblige him to sit down.

Then strange symptoms occurred. "I was unable for whole days to bear any clothes on my body. My skin seemed on fire and I had contractions of all my limbs. When I attempted to put on my clothes it seemed as though I had millions of pins pricking me." During his journey to Lyons on his way to Algeria he was seized with feelings of suffocation, and on going into a chemist's shop he was taken with a nervous fit similar to the preceding, but which only lasted about two hours. In December, 1877, he had a slight attack of smallpox.

In the spring of 1878, while on circuit with my chief, I was found one morning senseless in my bed. Bleeding and doses of calomel restored me, but my larynx was almost completely paralysed. I continued for seventy-two days *to articulate my words with difficulty*, though I could make myself understood." The patient allowed himself to indulge in both venereal and alcoholic excesses. To escape the frequent attacks of ague he went to the province of Algiers, and after staying there three years he returned to Geneva.

In 1880 he traversed Europe on foot, staying for some time with his brother-in-law in Prussia. There he was taken a second time with cataleptic sleep, which disappeared under the influence of bleeding. On waking he had paralysis (with insensibility) of the left leg and he had also *complete mutism*. Not a single word could he speak. "But my intelligence was unaffected, my memory, alone, was a little at fault, for recent events." After this he left Prussia and returned to Geneva.

We take the details of his story in Geneva from the case as published by Dr. Revilliod. On admission into the hospital, February 11th, 1881, the only pathological phenomena he presented were absolute mutism and slight numbness of the left side.

On laryngoscopic examination, which was rendered very easy by reason of the anaesthesia of the pharynx, the following condition was made out (Dr. Wyss). Abduction and adduction of the vocal cords are normally performed when the patient pronounces *e*, *i*. The only act which is faulty is the tension of the cords.[19] Although they approach, they remain festooned and slack, flapping more or less according to the force of the inspiratory or expiratory current of air. If under these conditions the patient is requested to increase the effort necessary to produce a sound, the vocal cords, instead of becoming stretched as they approach, close suddenly, as though by a spring, and then stick together as it were all along, so that not only is no sound produced but the impeded respiration requires a great inspiratory effort, like the sigh, to restore matters to their former condition.

The patient passes his days reading, and in writing veritable memoirs describing his different impressions. On February 15th, he wrote that he had pronounced the words "No, do you want any..." and then that he was unable to continue, the throat being contracted, and as though it were obstructed by an obstacle. His respiration was also more impeded than before.

After several applications of faradism of the crico-thyroid muscles and along the course of the superior laryngeal nerve, he was able to emit a few sounds, then some vowels, though without

precision, and intonation only occurred at the end of expiration. The same thing happened when he was made to bend his head forcibly, or when the inferior border of the cricoid was raised. But these exercises fatigued him very much, although he performed them willingly enough, being convinced that they promoted his cure.
On March 30th he pronounced the vowels easily enough, consonants with more difficulty. (...) On June 18th, 1881, Ch. quitted the hospital, speaking spontaneously and fluently without difficulty. He only experienced dryness of the throat after a long conversation. (...) On September 11th, 1882, he was found unconscious in his bed. (...).
He entered the Salpêtrière on November 8th, 1885. (...) He had nightmares, and hallucinations during his delirious attacks, sometimes terrible sometimes agreeable, and the latter were accompanied by involuntary emissions. Charcot thoroughly examined the patient and eventually came to the conclusion that he was confronted with a case of hysterical mutism. After some time the patient was released without having recovered his speech capacity. Several days later he regained his speech faculty and a few days later he was found dead in his bed.

The syndrome of hysterical mutism is, according to Charcot, one of the numerous diseases that come under the heading of hysteria. All that this meant at the time, was that one presumed the cause to be a dynamic or functional lesion. Yet one may observe a double displacement with respect to the problem of hysterical paralyses, which Charcot had previously focused on. Charcot localised the dynamic lesion in the *cerebral cortex* and invoked two arguments in support of this hypothesis. The then-prevailing neuropathology had already shown that the so-called higher psychical functions could be linked to this structure. Clinical observations had also demonstrated that the symptomatology of hysterical mutism could not be explained at the level of the larynx. Let me point out in passing that Charcot does not specify the localisation of the lesion and that the postulate of distinct speech centres, later criticised by Freud, is already present in the *Clinical Lectures*. Charcot was further unable to provide any additional details on the dynamic lesion as a neurological process. He merely mentioned the loss of ideas and of speech movements. The dynamic lesion can therefore be considered as a last 'trump' for a neurophysiological approach to hysteria and as a substitute for something resembling the *idea* or the *psychological*.
Yet, the syndrome of hysterical mutism does open up the way to a conception which looks upon hysteria as being an anomaly of *speech*. One is clearly not dealing with a conversion symptom, for here hysteria manifests itself only at the level of speech. And it is only at this level that the rules governing hysteria, and *ipso facto* those governing the psyche, can be disclosed.

That 'not being able to speak' is a *telling* fact in itself, appears from Charcot's case description of Ch.. One notices, for instance, that the symptom of hysterical mutism is over-determined in his life history. His suffering is, as it were, already encoded in the cause of death of his father and brother, in the symptomatology of his nervous sister and in his 'taciturn character'.

A similar case is that of a 20 year old sculptor of Polish extraction who was struck with aphasia on reading a letter in which his father reproached him for his conduct and refused to continue to send him money.[20] On his arrival at the clinic, the usual tests were carried out and note was taken of the fact that he could write perfectly in both French and Polish. When, after a certain time, his speech gradually came back, the word Warsaw was written for him in both languages ("Varsovie" and "Varchava") in order to get him to pronounce them. He failed to do this and instead said "Vavie" and "Vava", despite the fact that he understood and was able to write both words perfectly. For Charcot, this was definitive evidence of hysterical mutism. Should we interpret this as "Vava ne veut plus sauver ma vie!" ("Father no longer wants to save my life!")? Of course we have no substantial grounds for such a reading. However 'dense' a case description is, in the absence of a psychology, of attention to the patient's speech, or of a theory connected to speech and to the symbolical in which every tragicomedy or every human life is anchored, one is still a long way from an actual 'psychical treatment'. In Charcot, there is precious little evidence of a clinic of the excessively intense idea. Accordingly, there is very little attention devoted to the content of delusions or dreams in the various case descriptions. Only in exceptional cases does one have the words or comments of the patient at one's disposal. No room was made for the psyche at the Salpêtrière.

Freud, who was one of Charcot's attentive listeners, left Paris with the well-defined assignment — and the ambition — of finding an explanation for the distinction between hysterical and organic paralyses. However, the paper dealing with the result of his research was not published until 1893. Two striking points emerge from the reading of the paper in question.[21] The first one is Freud's *interpretation* of Charcot's functional lesion as a *psychical mechanism* which dissociates ideas from the associative activity. In actual fact, this dissociation bridges the gap between the neurophysiological and psychopathological approach. The second point to be made is that the arguments developed in this paper issue forth entirely from his monograph on aphasia. Freud had apparently grasped the message, i.e. in order to penetrate into the psyche and especially to understand hysteria, one needs to turn one's attention to *speech*.

I will come back to this paper later and for the time being I will focus on Freud's monograph. If we are to take Freud's progression into consideration, we cannot regard this work as being disconnected from his ambitions in the fields of the psyche and of psychotherapy. On the contrary, the fact that he displayed such an interest in the subject of the incapacity to speak seems to me to be congruent with his clinic of the excessively intense idea.

4.3. Freud's *On Aphasia*

Before formulating his conception on the various forms of aphasia, Freud painstakingly researched the subject. However, his monograph goes far beyond a mere formulation. Indeed, it is still regarded as an excellent overview of the literature published on this subject in 1891. The most reputed neurologists from Germany and elsewhere (Wernicke, Kussmaul, Lichtheim and Grashey, Hughlings Jackson, Bastian and Ross, Charcot and others) had already written extensively on the topic and Freud consulted all of these works.

The study of aphasia was very popular at the end of the 19th century. In 1861, Broca presented his findings before the 'Paris Société Anatomique', where he argued that a lesion in the third left frontal cerebral convolution caused a loss or a severe reduction of articulate speech.[22] Thirteen years later, Wernicke published *Der aphasische Symptomencomplex* in which he described another speech disorder. Patients affected by this particular speech disorder lost the faculty to understand, but retained the capacity to use articulate speech.[23] The 'sensory aphasia' described here, functions in a way as the logical counterpart of Broca's 'motor aphasia'. Wernicke explained the observed loss of function in an analogous manner, by pointing to a lesion in the first left temporal cerebral convolution. Both discoveries simply betokened the triumph of the localisationist approach within psychiatry. It seemed legitimate to nurse the hope of one day tracing all the clinically perceived speech disorders to precisely localised injuries. In accordance with this view, the psyche was split up into its elementary functions and classified into as many delineated centres in the cerebral cortex.

In this context, Freud's monograph levels the first thorough criticism at the localisation theory in the German speaking world.[24] Freud distanced himself from his Master's viewpoint, i.e. Meynert's, by following a strictly scientific line of approach: his monograph reflects an exhaustive study of the scientific literature on the subject and a systematic testing and refutation of the prevailing theoretical models on the basis of clinical case descriptions.[25]

According to Freud, the majority of theories on aphasia entail two hypotheses which were in urgent need of revision and which could just as well have been replaced by others. The first is the traditional distinction in the literature between centre aphasia and conduction aphasia. The former was thought to be caused by the destruction of certain cerebral centres while the latter was thought to result from the destruction of paths of conduction between cerebral centres. The second hypothesis, which derives from Wernicke, evaluates the topographical relation between various speech centres.
As we shall see, both hypotheses are connected. Localising different speech functions in clearly demarcated centres in the cerebral cortex, implies for Freud a certain view on the mode of operation of what he terms the "Sprachapparat", i.e. a conception of the *speech apparatus*. Freud's alternative model focuses principally on this very point, as his monograph looks at speech that may or may not be disrupted by an affect. The refutation of the first hypothesis, which is clearly the easiest part, draws on clinical observations derived from the literature on this topic.

4.3.1. Wernicke's theory as 'false connection'

Wernicke's schema postulates a distinction between centre aphasia and conduction aphasia. *Centre aphasia* can be explained by a lesion in a speech centre. This injury implies the loss of recollections or ideas which are stored in the centre in question. Conversely, *conduction aphasia* denotes the destruction of pathways of association conducting to a speech centre or between speech centres. A lesion of this kind, consequently disrupts an 'association', e.g. the association between the acoustic image (stored in the sensory speech centre) and the image of the speech movements (stored in the motor speech centre).
In departing from this distinction — which is in effect an extrapolation on the approach adopted by the localisation theory — Wernicke attempts to account

for the different forms of speech disorders. He conjectures that every speech disorder springs from a specifically determined lesion of one of the various speech centres or of a path of conduction between, to or from these centres. Wernicke designed his schema — as Broca had done before him in 1861 — when he thought he had established a connection between a speech disorder and an injury in the cerebral cortex. Wernicke discovered a cortical lesion of the first left frontal cerebral convolution in a patient who had lost the faculty to understand, but who was still able to use articulate speech — albeit with confusion of words or sounds.[26] It seemed normal then to interpret this lesion as a direct cause of the elimination of one of the speech functions. To Wernicke, 'cortical sensory aphasia' indicated the existence of a sensory speech centre — which could furthermore easily be placed in a schema alongside the so-called motor speech centre. For Broca had demonstrated that in the event of a lesion in the third frontal cerebral convolution, the function of articulate speech was seriously, if not entirely impaired.

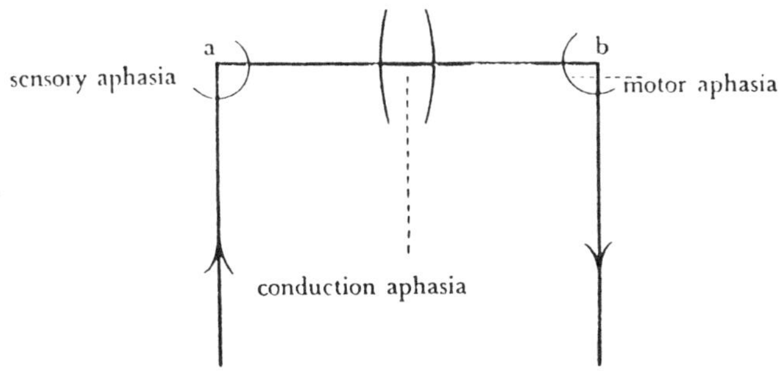

Fig. 1[27]

Wernicke's schema is in fact a hypothetical representation of the speech pathway and is based on a theoretical conception of language acquisition. Linguistic sounds find their way to the sensory speech centre (*a*) via the auditory nerve (nervus acusticus). The stimulus is then transferred via the paths of conduction to the motor speech centre (*b*) which then sends the impulse of articulate speech to the periphery of the body. It is in this way that Wernicke attempts to understand the physiological process of repeating words, in conjunction with what he deemed legitimate to presuppose from pathology.

Wernicke also entertains a very definite idea on the way in which sounds are stored in the sensory speech centre. To Freud, Wernicke's view holds far-reaching implications for the whole localisation theory. The sensory stimuli which reach the cerebral cortex, leave lasting impressions which are all stored in separate cells. Drawing on Meynert's analysis, Wernicke states that the cerebral cortex consists of approximately 600 million cells, and that it is therefore a satisfactory storage place for external perceptions. The cerebral cortex is accordingly conceived of as being filled with the residues of past stimuli, or memory images. Wernicke consequently distinguishes between the memories of speech sounds, located in the sensory centre, and the memories of movements performed during speech, located in the motor centre.

The two speech disorders mentioned above surface as a sort of disruption of memory provoked by the lesion of one of the speech centres concerned. A disruption of the sensory speech centre eventuates in the loss of acoustic images — which explains the impossibility of understanding speech (i.e. word deafness). A disruption of the motor centre brings about a loss of the images of the speech movements, which is conveyed by the loss of articulate speech.

Freud distinguishes two main areas of criticism of this explanation of speech disorders.

On the first level, Freud refutes Wernicke's distinction between centre and conduction aphasia by setting the findings derived from the schema against those brought to light by clinical observations.

The weakness of this simple, yet coherent schema, lies in Wernicke's postulating of a third form of aphasia, i.e. conduction aphasia, which is brought on by an interruption of the path of association *a-b*. According to Wernicke, this injury finds expression in the so-called 'paraphasia', that is, the substitution of words and the uncertainty concerning their use. Despite this, a patient affected by paraphasia still maintains the faculty of understanding and articulating words. This speech disorder, however, cannot be derived from the schema. Freud writes that when "(...) we ask what ought to be the result of this interruption the answer would have to be as follows: via the tract *a-b* the ability of reproducing perceived word sounds has been learned; its function is that of repetition of words heard; its interruption ought to result in a loss of that ability while spontaneous speech and understanding ought to remain intact. Yet everybody will admit that such a dissociation of speech functions has never been observed nor is it very likely to be observed. The faculty of repeating is never lost as long as speaking and understanding are intact."[28]

It is for the very same reason that Freud criticises and repudiates Lichtheim's schema. For Freud, this schema is in effect a refinement of Wernicke's, complemented with five different conduction aphasias.[29]

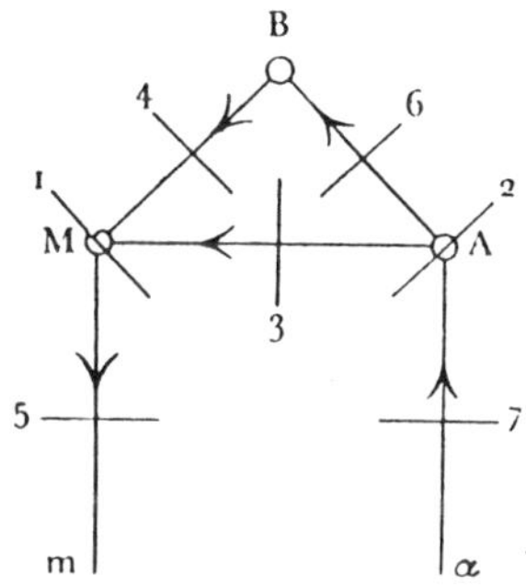

Fig. 2[30]

Freud raises the following objections to Lichtheim's schema: firstly, it was arrived at by means of deductive reasoning, in the sense that it postulated paths of conduction which were yet to be discovered. Secondly, a number of known speech disorders do not fit, or barely fit into the schema. The clinic shows, for instance, that distinct speech functions can be disrupted to very different degrees and that some speech disorders can be put down to combined injuries. Thirdly, the schema claims to be exhaustive and thus ought to be able to account for every kind of speech disorder, which is clearly not the case.[31]

Freud introduces another neuroanatomical argument into his critique. Wernicke drew on Meynert's conception of neuroanatomy and neuropathology — more precisely on the notion of the 'point-by-point projection' of the periphery of the body in the cerebral cortex — in order to posit the existence of distinctive and localisable speech centres. In contrast to this idea, Freud records a diminution of the masses of fibres at the level of the grey matter of the spinal cord, which signifies that not every point of the periphery of the body (not every perception) corresponds to a point in the

cortex.[32] The relation between the periphery of the body and the cerebral cortex is thus more complex than Meynert had imagined.
A second argument against Meynert's view relates to the cortical paths of conduction. Departing from the notion of a point-by-point projection, Meynert conjectures that the 'identity' of every nerve fibre or pathway, remains equal over its entire length, irrespective of, for instance, its passage through the cerebral nuclei. Against this, Freud argues that the nerve fibres "contain the body periphery in the same way as — to borrow an example from the subject with which we are concerned here — a poem contains the alphabet, i.e., in a completely different arrangement serving other purposes, in manifold associations of the individual elements, whereby some may be represented several times, others not at all."[33]
By repudiating Meynert's conception, Freud does away with one of the essential arguments in favour of the postulate holding that speech centres are separated from each other by functionless areas in the cerebral cortex.

On the second level, Freud's critique is directed at the *epistemological foundation* of such a schema. If one takes a closer look at Freud's reasoning, one can see that his rejection of Wernicke's distinction between centre aphasia and conduction aphasia amounts to a rejection of the speech centres as such. For what is a speech centre? According to Wernicke, a follower of theoreticians like Meynert, a speech centre can be defined as a well-demarcated field in the cerebral cortex, where some nerve fibres of the speech pathway terminate. Stimuli occurring along the speech pathway bring on an alteration in that field which turns previously 'untouched' brain cells into a storing place for a memory or an idea. For instance, hearing "no" would propagate acoustic vibrations via the auditory nerves to the centre end point of this afferent nerve path, to the so-called sensory speech centre where the acoustic image is stored as a memory. A schema constructed in a similar fashion might seem acceptable if one is only preoccupied with finding an explanation for the interaction between a biological organism and the physical stimuli coming from the outside world. Freud, however, aims his critique at the amplification of this idea so as to include *linguistic psychical processes*. It then ought to come as no surprise to see that Freud deems this explanatory model as insufficient or even totally irrelevant when applied to speech, i.e. the psychical function par excellence.

Yet Wernicke had offered an answer along the same lines concerning the possibility of localising psychical functions of this kind. He admitted that the schema was only acceptable for the most elementary functions such as visual or auditory perceptions. "Everything beyond this, such as the association of various ideas to a concept, was a function of the association systems connecting different parts of the cortex; they could no longer be localised in one particular area."[34] This pronouncement is, however, not to be reconciled with the implications of Wernicke's theory on aphasia which instead reflects the far reaching claims of the localisation theory.

Freud notes that, under Meynert's influence, the speech apparatus was seen as consisting of a number of distinct and mutually interconnected cortical centres containing ideas. However, he harbours serious doubts about the legitimacy of the hypothesis which locates ideas in the brain cells. "Considering the tendency of earlier medical periods to localise whole mental faculties, such as are defined in psychological terminology, in certain areas of the brain, it was bound to appear as a great advance when Wernicke declared that only the simplest psychical elements, i.e., the various sensory perceptions, could be localised in the cortex, the areas concerned being those of the central terminations of the sensory nerves. But does one not in principle make the same mistake, irrespective of whether one tries to localise a complicated concept, a whole mental faculty or a psychical element? Is it justified to immerse a nerve fibre, which over the whole length of its course has been only a physiological structure subject to physiological modifications, with its end in the psyche and to furnish this end with an idea or a memory? Now that "will" and "intelligence", etc., have been recognized as psychological technical terms referring to very complicated physiological states, can one be quite sure that the "simple sensory impression" be anything else but another such technical term?

The relationship between the chain of physiological events in the nervous system and the mental processes is probably not one of cause and effect. The former do not cease when the latter set in; they tend to continue, but, from a certain moment, a mental phenomenon corresponds to each part of the chain, or to several parts. The psychical is, therefore, a process parallel to the physiological, "a dependent concomitant".

I am well aware that the writers whose views I am opposing here cannot have been guilty of thoughtless mistakes in their scientific approach. They obviously mean only that the physiological modification of the nerve fibre through sensory stimuli produces another modification in the central nerve cells which then becomes the physiological correlate of the "concept" or "idea". As they know a lot more about ideas than of the physiological modifications, which are still undefined and unknown, they use the elliptic phrase: an idea is localised in the nerve cell. Yet this substitution at once leads to a confusion of the two processes which need have nothing in common with each other. In psychology the simple idea is to us something elementary which we can clearly differentiate from its connection with other ideas. This is why we are tempted to assume that its physiological correlate, i.e., the modification of the nerve cells which originates from the excitation of the nerve fibres, be also something simple and localisable. Such an inference is, of course, entirely unwarranted; the qualities of this modification have to be established for themselves and independently of their psychological concomitants."[35]

These memorable paragraphs clearly reflect the epistemological concern which shed a new light on the serviceability of the localisation theory, and what is more, which focused on the boundary between neurology and psychology. The alternative model proposed by Freud, as a response to the existing theories of the localisation theory, has implications for both a neurological and a psychological approach to speech disorders.

4.3.2. Freud's alternative

Freud identifies the speech area as a well-demarcated and interconnected region of the cerebral cortex located in the left hemisphere. The so-called speech centres are found in the outer part of this speech area. An injury in this region causes speech disorders. A lesion affecting the demarcation lines of this area provokes an even more profound effect — a more serious speech disorder — than a lesion occurring at the centre of the field. This is simply because the links with the cortical fields of the optic, auditory and motor cranial nerves are situated along those demarcation lines. It is this stronger effect which seems to suggest the existence of separate and well delineated speech centres. Freud therefore emphasises that the particular signification of the centres is relevant only for the pathology, but not for the physiology of the speech apparatus.[36]

This alternative view ensues from Freud's refusal to separate the ideational process from the associative process or, put differently, from the refusal to locate both processes in different places.

An approach of this kind also seems to be better able to account for the large variety of clinically observed speech disorders. On the one hand, it explains the more 'spectacular' speech disorders, such as sensory and motor aphasia which cause the loss of specific speech functions. This loss, however, is not seen as a consequence of the obliteration of a function-specific 'speech centre', but rather as the result of the interruption of an important field of association. On the other hand, Freud's approach provides an explanation for the numerous and often milder intermediate forms, which do not eventuate in the loss of the capacity to function, but rather in an impairment of them.[37] In other words, apart from a topical element, Freud invokes a *functional* element. The entire problem rests on the relation between an organic lesion and a functional disruption, since the organic lesion can only manifest itself via a functional disruption. It then leads to a weakening of the function, and only very rarely does it provoke the actual elimination of a specific function. It thence never comes to pass that a minor lesion in the 'motor centre' results in, say, the disappearance of a hundred words. A partial lesion of this kind always expresses itself through a generalised weakening of the function of the 'centre' in question.

Freud proceeds by writing that "In assessing the functions of the speech apparatus under pathological conditions we are adopting as a guiding principle Hughlings Jackson's doctrine that all these modes of reaction represent instances of *functional retrogression* (dis-involution) of a highly organized apparatus, and therefore correspond to earlier states of its functional development. This means that under all circumstances an arrangement of associations which, having been acquired later, belongs to a higher level of functioning, will be lost, while an earlier and simpler one will be preserved."[38]

The advantage of Freud's explanatory model consists in looking upon *paraphasia* as a purely functional symptom. As we have seen previously, Wernicke added to the two forms of centre aphasia he proposed (motor and sensory aphasia) a third form, the so-called conduction aphasia, which occurs when the paths of association between both speech centres are interrupted. According to Wernicke, this third form could explain paraphasia. However, it was this very speech disorder which impelled Freud to discard Wernicke and Lichtheim's schemata as being unsuitable and as having, at the very most, only a didactic interest. Not only does paraphasia not correspond to the symptoms suggested in the schema, but what is more, Freud remarks that one also comes across cases of paraphasia where no organic lesion is involved. "We propose to postpone discussion of the symptom of paraphasia (mistaken use of words), and also of the reasons which caused Wernicke to regard it as characteristic of an interruption between *a* and *b*. At this stage we only want to mention that the paraphasia observed in aphasic patients does not differ from the incorrect use and the distortion of words which the healthy person can observe in himself in states of fatigue or divided attention or under the influence of disturbing affects, the kind of thing that frequently happens to our lecturers and causes the listener painful embarrassment. It is tempting to regard paraphasia in the widest sense as a purely functional symptom, a sign of reduced efficiency of the apparatus of speech associations. This does not exclude that they may occur in most typical form as organic focal symptoms."[39]

One commonly attributes the cause of *lapsus linguae*, a *slip of the pen* and other formations of the unconscious to fatigue, a state of diffused attention or the influence of disruptive affects. Freud's monograph is still a long way from an effective endeavour to penetrate the actual sense of 'everyday' paraphasia.[40] Yet what Freud puts forward for this speech disorder functions as a signpost for his further progression towards an alternative model of the speech apparatus. The operation of the speech apparatus can be disrupted in two fundamentally different ways: either by an organic lesion or by a general and dynamic lesion which amounts to an alteration in the capacity to function. Here, another question emerges, i.e. can Freud's 'functional conception' be considered as an attempt to account for hysterical aphasia?

It is not because one tends to classify Freud's monograph under the heading 'pre-analytical', when reviewing the entire body of his work, that the poles of interest which emerge from it cannot encompass the psyche.[41] Some authors do indeed adulterate the issues at hand. Buelens, for instance, argues that Freud's interest in aphasia derives purely from the attention this subject commanded at the turn of the last century. The main reason for this popularity was that the field of aphasia seemed to corroborate the far reaching claims of the localisation theory. The very fact that in his monograph Freud cuts the localisation theory down to size, therefore appears as quite a paradox.[42]

Freud's study acquires a totally different meaning when seen in the light of a number of other facts. Earlier on, I pointed out that Freud's alternative model provided an explanation for aphasia which could not be assigned to an organic lesion. At this juncture, the concept of the functional 'Rückbildung' offers additional merit to Freud's schema. This theoretical framework provides an explanation for a number of linguistic phenomena of the psychopathology of everyday life as well as of speech disorders (such as hysterical aphasia) which have a purely psychical aetiology.

The previously mentioned article, 'Some Points for a Comparative Study of Organic and Hysterical Motor Paralysis' in which Freud, upon Charcot's request, eventually carried out the task of explaining the difference between organic and hysterical paralysis, demonstrates that this was the intention of his study on aphasia. I mentioned earlier on that Charcot used the notion of the dynamic or functional lesion as a sort of temporary expedient. He conjectured the existence of a dynamic lesion which could still be interpreted in physiological terms in cases of hysterical diseases which did not display any organic lesion. In the above mentioned paper, Freud does not simply recuperate this notion, but proceeds to *interpret* it on the basis of his study on aphasia.

Freud departs from the notion that two sorts of organic motor paralyses can be distinguished: periphero-spinal paralysis and cerebral paralysis. This distinction is in perfect agreement with the anatomy of the nervous system which shows that the motor conductive fibres consist of two parts. The first part runs from the peripheral nerves to the spinal cord, while the second part goes from the spinal cord to the cerebral cortex. Freud argues that the anatomical differences between both parts of the 'route' explain very clearly the various symptomatologies emerging from a lesion of each part. An injury at the level of the first part results in a paralysis responding to the point-by-point projection. An injury in the cerebral cortex, however, causes a more generalised paralysis. Referring to his own study, Freud proposed a different appellation for the two injuries mentioned above: projection paralysis and representation paralysis.[43]

Hysterical paralysis always involves a 'simulation' of the more global representation paralysis, and never that of projection paralysis. In other terms, hysteria always 'simulates' cerebral, and especially cortical paralyses.[44] Yet hysterical paralysis differs from its organic counterpart, for instance by the fact that it does not follow the rule according to which the distal segment is always more affected than the proximal one. Hysterical patients also have no problem in artificially producing an isolated paralysis. In this respect, hysterical paralysis can be said to be intermediate between projection paralysis and representation paralysis; the symptoms of cortical paralyses are, as it were, fragmented in hysteria. As an argument for this Freud alludes to hysterical aphasia — where the speech disorder is limited to articulate speech ('motor aphasia') — something inconceivable in organic aphasia. He also mentions cases in which both motor and sensory aphasia exist for one particular language only. He further indicates that the symptoms of hysterical paralysis exhibit an intensity unknown in the organic disease. Finally, Freud takes the example of hysterical patients who are unable to produce a single word, whereas the organic aphasiac still manages to utter "yes" or "no" or even a swear-word. To sum up, *hysterical paralysis and hysterical aphasia are characterised by a precise delimitation and excessive intensity.*

This raises the pressing question of how hysterical paralyses, which perfectly mimic cortical paralyses, still differ very clearly from them. And what is the general nature of the particular representation with which they are connected? Freud writes that "Since there can only be a single cerebral anatomy that is true, and since it finds expression in the clinical characteristics of the cerebral paralyses, it is clearly impossible for that anatomy to be the explanation of the distinctive features of hysterical paralyses. For that reason we must not draw conclusions on the subject of cerebral anatomy that are based on the symptomatology of those paralyses."[45] According to Freud, the answer to the problem lies in the nature of the lesion causing hysterical paralysis.

In Charcot's view this lesion is a purely dynamic or functional cortical one. This still leaves the question of how one ought to interpret the nature of this lesion. The notion is defined negatively, since Charcot argues that there are never any tissue changes found in the post-mortem. He advocates the idea of a lesion which leaves no trace in the autopsy, such as is the case, for instance, with an oedema or an anaemia. The notion 'dynamic lesion' thus conceals the idea of a transitory organic disorder.

To this Freud remarks that "(...) the lesion in hysterical paralyses must be completely independent of the anatomy of the nervous system, since *in its paralyses and other manifestations hysteria behaves as though anatomy did not exist or as though it had no knowledge of it.*"[46] Hysteria is ignorant of the distribution of the conductive fibres and it is precisely for this reason that it simulates projection paralysis. "It takes the organs in the ordinary, popular sense of the names they bear: the leg is the leg as far up as its insertion into the hip, the arm is the upper limb as it is visible under the clothing. There is no reason for adding paralysis of the face to paralysis of the arm. A hysteric who cannot talk has no motive for forgetting his understanding of speech, since motor aphasia and word deafness are unrelated to each other in the popular mind, and so on."[47]

Freud accordingly proposes to interpret the phrase 'functional or dynamic lesion' in its proper sense, i.e. as an 'alteration in function or dynamics', as an alteration of a functional property. An alteration of this kind could refer to a diminution in excitability or in physiological quality which normally remains constant or else fluctuates within fixed limits. It should, however, still be an organic or physical alteration governed by known laws of nature. Freud therefore felt compelled to cross over to a *psychological interpretation.* "I will try to show that there can be a functional alteration without a concomitant organic lesion — or at least without one that is grossly palpable even by the most delicate analysis. In other terms, I will give a suitable example of an alteration of a primitive function; and for that purpose *I only ask permission to move on to psychological ground — which can scarcely be avoided in dealing with hysteria.*"[48]

In hysterical diseases one is always confronted with the banal or popular conception of the body and its organs, which is not founded on a solid knowledge of the anatomy of the nervous system, but rather on tactile and visual perceptions. "The lesion in hysterical paralysis will therefore be an alteration of the conception, the idea, of the arm, for instance. But what kind of alteration must this be in order to produce paralysis? Considered psychologically, the paralysis of the arm consists in the fact that the conception of the arm cannot enter into association with the other ideas constituting the ego of which the subject's body forms an important part. The lesion would therefore be the *abolition of the associative accessibility of the conception of the arm.* The arm behaves as though it did not exist for the play of associations. There is no doubt that if the material conditions corresponding to the conception of the arm are profoundly altered, the conception will also be lost. But I have to show that it can be inaccessible without being destroyed and without its material substratum (the nervous tissue of the corresponding region of the cortex) being damaged."[49]

The psychological explanation propounded by Freud postulates at least two places in the psyche.
On the one hand, there is the locus of the normal associative activity, from which certain conditions, or ideas can sometimes be excluded. This exclusion, however, is not comparable to an obliteration of the idea. Instead, the idea is transferred to another place, or better, it is included into a second chain of associations. This is the way in which Freud introduces the dimension of *subjective meaning* into his explanation of hysterical symptomatology. For the hysterical patient is at heart not so different from the loyal servant who did not want to wash his hand after the king had touched it. "The relation of this hand to the idea of the king seemed so important to the man's psychical life that he refused to let the hand enter into any other relation. We are obeying the same impulse when we break the glass in which we have drunk to the health of a young married couple. Savage tribes in antiquity, who burnt their dead chief's horse, his weapons and even his wives along with his dead body, were obeying this idea that no one should ever touch them after him. The force of all these actions is clear. The quota of affect which we attribute to the first association of an object has a repugnance to letting it enter into a new association with another object and consequently makes the idea of the (first) object inaccessible to association."[50] It is just the same in Herbartian psychology. For instance, when the arm is integrated in an unconscious association with a large quota of affect (for instance the recollection of a trauma), it will remain inaccessible to the conscious associative activity.
The crucial point of this reasoning lies in Freud's answer to the initial question about the particular representation operative in hysterical paralyses. The hysterical symptomatology gives expression to the fact that the body is, psychologically speaking, represented in an idea, i.e. it is represented *linguistically*. For the subject can only relate to the body via speech. Furthermore, in Freud's interpretation of the functional lesion as a psychical process which excludes an idea from association, one can recognise the precursor to the *psychical mechanism* of *defence* or *repression*. I will now return to Freud's monograph on aphasia for a more accurate formulation of his *linguistic theory*.

Freud's repudiation of the difference that Wernicke postulated between centre aphasia and conduction aphasia, as well as his endorsement of the hypothesis of the functional "Rückbildung" do not amount to a rejection of all classifications in the field of aphasia. Starting with his representation of the speech apparatus which he coupled with a philosophical-psychological analysis of the relationship of the word-presentation to the object-presentation, Freud arrived at a tripartite classification of aphasia.

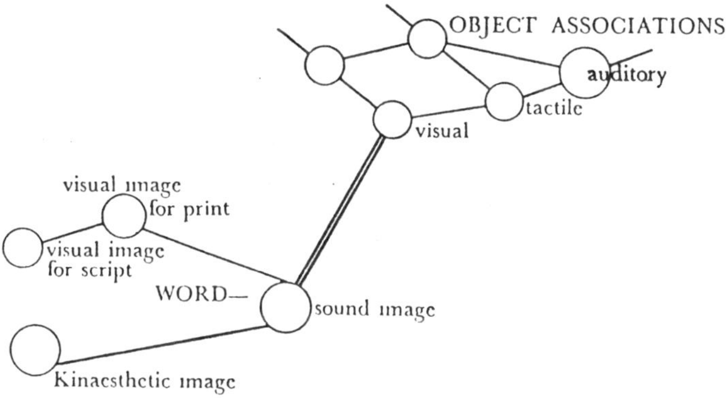

Fig. 3[51]

A word acquires meaning by being linked to what he calls the object-presentation: "The idea, or concept, of the object is itself another complex of associations composed of the most varied visual, auditory, tactile, kinaesthetic and other impressions. According to philosophical teaching, the idea of the object contains nothing else; the appearance of a "thing", the "properties" of which are conveyed to us by our senses, originates only from the fact that in enumerating the sensory impressions perceived from an object, we allow for the possibility of a large series of new impressions being added to the chain of associations (J.S. Mill). This is why the idea of the object does not appear to us as closed, and indeed hardly as closable, while the word concept appears to us as something that is closed though capable of extension. In the light of observations in speech disorders we have formed the view that the word concept (the idea of the word) is linked with its sensory part, in particular through its sound impressions, to the object concept."[52]

On the basis of this Freud distinguishes between two classes of speech disorders: 1. aphasia of the first order, or verbal aphasia, entailing a disruption of the association between the separate elements of the word-presentation; 2.

aphasia of the second order, or asymbolic aphasia, i.e. the disruption between the word-presentation and the object-presentation. Freud also refers to a third form of aphasia which he terms 'agnostic aphasia'. This form is characterised by a disruption of the association between the object and the object-presentation. A patient suffering from this form of aphasia can only recognise objects with great difficulty. These disruptions need however to occur in conjunction with speech disorders.

Stephan indicates that Freud was certainly not the only one to adhere to this conception.[53] As well as John Stuart Mill, Stricker also advocated this approach to semantics. A word is also invested with meaning because the ideas of a given object in reality were associatively linked with the appropriate word-presentation.

As I pointed out above, Freud takes the 'psychological schema of the word-presentation' as a point of departure for the classification of the aphasias he proposed in his monograph. This text accounts, amongst other things, for the cases of aphasia in which the effect of a lesion can be obliterated in an *indirect* way, that is, via other associative paths. For instance, if in the word-presentation, the associative path was interrupted between the sound image and the motor image, then one can still call upon the associative paths of the writing image or of the reading image in order to preserve the motor image which is required for articulate speech. However, Freud does describe cases of patients who are entirely incapable of finding the word they wish to utter at a particular moment — not even when drawing on alternative associative paths. In such cases of amnesia, the patients make use of a *circumscription* of the expression they cannot find. Freud will later explicitly use this theory of semantics in order to explain the aetiology of hysterical symptoms and of dream formation. The case study of Dora is a case in point. "The symptom cannot occur more than once and the capacity for repeating itself is one of the characteristics of a hysterical symptom unless it has a psychical significance, a meaning. The hysterical symptom does not carry this meaning with it, but the meaning is lent to it, soldered to it, as it were; and in every instance the meaning can be a different one, according to the nature of the suppressed thoughts which are struggling for expression."[54] A thought process — which would have led to a verbal expression of thoughts and ideas if the course of association had been left unhindered — always precedes the manifest hysterical symptom. Due to a psychical conflict, the associative path is

blocked and the corresponding idea is thence repressed. As with aphasias, the associative process must thenceforth follow a course that differs from the usual one. Instead of stimulating the speech centre it generates object-presentations (in the case of dreams) or it changes course to the associated motor ideas (in the case of hysteria).
The meaning of a symptom includes the associative intertwinement of complexes of ideas with the concurrent somatic reaction (motor ideas) resulting from a trauma. According to Freud's semantics, the somatic processes display the same content as the one that the word-presentations associated with these would have shown, had they not been repressed.[55]

The linguistic theory or semantics wielded by Freud belongs to the field of analytical philosophy. It is a well known fact that Freud was familiar with Mill's semantics, for, on the advice of Franz Brentano — his philosophy teacher when he was a student of medicine — Freud had translated the twelfth volume of Mill's complete works.[56] Nevertheless, it must be said that this volume does not include an exposition of his semantics, but Freud's bibliographical references in *On Aphasia* leave one with no doubt as to his familiarity with the subject. However, another champion of this science was spatially and temporally closer to Freud: the Viennese experimental pathologist, Salomon Stricker.[57]
Freud's conception that a word is invested with meaning by means of associative intertwinement with the appropriate object-presentation, corresponds entirely with Mill's definition of the function of proper names "which is to arouse in the mind the ideas with which they are associated."[58] Freud shares Stricker's conception of the word as being a word-presentation and furthermore only attributes meaning to a word on the basis of its associative interconnection with other ideas.

What then is the scope of the theory of semantics which Freud introduced into the field of the pathology of the speech function, and eventually also into the field of psychopathology? Taking stock of the above mentioned way in which Freud provided an explanation for the organisation of hysterical symptoms — an explanation that indicated their treatment — one could argue that this semantics, this linguistic theory also accounts for the *subjective* element. Freud's 1891 study reflects his long-standing fascination for clinical-psychological questions. As one can see, the subjective implication, the subject and his life story, surfaces from this piece of writing, differentiating it from the anatomical-materialistic conceptions of scholars like Meynert or Wernicke.

Gottlob Frege's philosophical criticism levelled at Mill and Stricker emphasises the subjective aspect of their approach and by extension it also qualifies Freudian semantics as subjective.

"His critique was directed at the influence of psychological thought in mathematics and logic; yet its intent was not to discard the results of psychological research as being totally irrelevant. Rather, it was aimed at the exaggerated claims that psychological research could tackle and solve the fundamental problems of arithmetic and logic."[59]

That Frege recognised the subjective idea becomes apparent in his fundamental text 'On Sense and Reference': "The reference and sense of a sign are to be distinguished from the associated idea. If the reference of a sign is an object perceivable by the senses, my idea of it is an internal image, arising from memories of sense impressions which I have had and acts, both internal and external, which I have performed. Such an idea is often saturated with feeling; the clarity of its separate parts varies and oscillates. The same sense is not always connected, even in the same man, with the same idea."[60]

4.4. Conclusion

Ludwig Binswanger once wrote that Freud's monograph on aphasia is indispensable for whomever wants to grasp the subsequent theoretical development of psychoanalysis.[61] This is certainly true. The psychological schema of the word-presentation offers a theory of semantics which Freud himself was later to use, without however explicitly referring to it.[62] Freud was himself quite satisfied with his book and described it as "a really good thing". Even though its reception was not overwhelming, this evaluation was eventually to be corroborated by the scientific forum.[63]

The most substantial gain lays perhaps in another domain, namely that of the epistemology of psychoanalysis and its transference through education. For it is a known fact that it is not a simple task to transpose knowledge about the unconscious, be it only because both teacher and student are themselves saddled with it. If one persists in wielding the so-called distinction between pre-psychoanalytical texts and the actual psychoanalytical writings, one ultimately does no justice to the teachings mentioned. If, for instance, one takes *The Interpretation of Dreams* (regarded as a fall out of Freud's "Aha-experience" in 1897 and which belongs to his own Oedipus, i.e. the product of his self-analysis) as the starting point of psychoanalysis, then one grants it a particular status that is all too easily predicated with "you either believe in it or you don't".

Let us rather opt for Freud's so-called scientism and let us assume that — as there is only one anatomy of the nervous system — there is only one psyche whose laws can be discovered. However problematic it may be, the psyche, as an object of study, has nothing mystical or supernatural about it. Still, one cannot dispose of it by describing its logos as the study of behaviour.

The monograph on aphasia teaches us something new about Freud's scientism. I have demonstrated how this work — rather than just reflecting the fact that in 1891 he was still divided over and preoccupied with his transition from neurology to psychology — pursues his quest for the psyche. The "Seelenbehandlung", or the psychotherapy reveals speech itself as the instrument for the therapy and as an 'access door' to the psyche as an object of study. There is thence nothing surprising in the fact that Freud almost immediately went in search of usable frames of reference for a clinical psychology which attributes a central part to speech. In this context he scrutinises the neuroanatomy and the neuropathology of the 'incapacity to speak' from the point of view of their serviceability for his psychology of the 'not wanting to speak'. Better than any other work, Freud's monograph shows how he *translates* and *twists* physiological concepts into psychological concepts in function of, and in a dialectical process with his object of study. This is at any rate the significance he himself attributes to his monograph, when looking back at it in 1893 and when interpreting Charcot's 'functional lesion' as defence or repression.

PART II

FREUD'S

PROJECT FOR A SCIENTIFIC PSYCHOLOGY

INTRODUCTION

> "Freud's intellect is soaring at its highest. I gaze after him as a hen at a hawk."
>
> *Josef Breuer*[1]

The least one can say about the opening paragraph of the *Project* is that it catches one's attention:
"The intention is to furnish a psychology that shall be a natural science: that is, to represent psychical processes as quantitatively determinate states of specifiable material particles, thus making those processes perspicuous and free from contradiction. Two principal ideas are involved: (1) What distinguishes activity from rest is to be regarded as Q, subject to the general laws of motion. (2) The neurones are to be taken as the material particles. N and $Q\acute{\eta}$ — Similar experiments are now frequent."[2]

How is this disconcerting introduction to be interpreted? In the itinerary I have followed so far, which has covered the works of Charcot (*Clinical Lectures*), Bernheim (*Suggestive Therapeutics*), Breuer and Freud's joint publication of the *Studies* and Freud's monograph *On Aphasia*, I have attempted to demonstrate that Freud was driven and possessed by his quest for the psyche. And suddenly in 1895, he started to discourse upon quantities subjected to the laws of motion and neurones as material particles encompassing psychical processes. Is there an alternative or, is one to read this manuscript in accordance with its opening sentence, i.e. as an endeavour to revamp psychology by rooting it in neurophysiology? Or are we to interpret this as just a provisional regression to a reductive view of the human psyche?

Another possibility does exist. The following discussion is divided into two parts, each of which is articulated around one of the two basic hypotheses put forward by Freud in the aforementioned paragraph.

In the first part, I will take a closer look at the concept of *quantity*, or the hypothesis *Q*, and I will attempt to explain the status this concept occupies in Freud's text. I will draw links between the clinic of the excessively intense idea, as described in the *Studies*, and his view on the sexual aetiology of the "Aktualneurosen". Freud's correspondence with Fließ will serve as my main guide-line for this task. Before dealing with these topics, I will dwell on various conceptions of the concept of energy. I will base this discussion on the fourth chapter of *Zeven avonden met Jacques Lacan* (*Seven Evenings with Jacques Lacan*), as it sheds light on the general discontent with respect to the concept of energy, which was seen as a repudiation of the affect and, *ipso facto* of the talking cure.[3]

In secondary literature, a plethora of influences on Freud are readily enumerated, and the most diverse and respected sources are invoked to show that the genius of the father of psychoanalysis lay in his fantastic and seemingly mounting powers of *synthesis*. Yet, for instance, a direct comparison of the *Project* with Exner's book, which after all is temporally and geographically the closest to Freud, is lacking, while the influence of Darwin, Herbart, Helmholtz, Fechner, Griesinger, Brücke and du Bois-Reymond, to name but a few, is confidently held out. In addition, an attitude of this kind departs from the assumption that the reader is capable of recreating Freud's alleged construction.[4]

From the line of approach I have adopted, the result of an endeavour of this kind is negligible, for the significance of Freud's work and the question of the psyche become lost. The numerous interpretations and comments on the *Project* would lead one to suppose that "something is rotten in the state of Denmark!" This allusion to the approaching confrontation with the father — for is there not a bit of Hamlet in all of us?[5] — is probably not unfounded if one considers that the interpretation of this particular text often debouches on evaluations with respect to Freud and his creation, psychoanalysis. Accordingly, the *Project* is certainly interesting and even provocative, but ultimately it reveals Freud as being "midway between neurology and psychology"[6], and as a "crypto biologist"[7], a "materialistic-mechanistic thinker"[8] who had succumbed to a peculiar "regression to neurophysiology"[9],...

However well sustained, such interpretations raise serious questions. For instance, every single one of these readings implicitly departs from the notion that the status of the *Project* can be determined on the basis of the *conceptual frame of reference* employed.[10] The occurrence in the text of concepts such as quantity, stimulation and the principle of constancy function as a decisive argument for inscribing Freud's project alongside those of the *Berliner Fysikalische Gesellschaft* of Bois-Reymond, Helmholtz and Brücke. By the same token, Freud's *Project* is turned into a biological *tractatus* in which he draws on Darwinian evolutionary principles for his outline of the differentiation of the nervous system. The concepts of the neurones and of the contact barriers undeniably encourage one to look upon this work as belonging to the fields of neurology and neurophysiology.

I however take a different approach, I argue that the epistemological status of the text is determined by the *question* it manifests, that is to say it is determined by the field of tension between the frame of reference used and the text's object of study, and not exclusively by the conceptual frame of reference it makes use of.

I will employ the same line of reasoning in the second part of my analysis. In this second part I will start off from Freud's hypothesis of the neurone *N*, and read the *Project* as a clinical-psychological text, i.e. as a text that seeks to provide an explanation for the effects of speech.

CHAPTER 1

The concept of quantity

> "The way you present sexual etiology, you are attributing to the audience a knowledge which it, after all, possesses only in latent form. It knows, and yet behaves as though it knew nothing."
>
> *Sigmund Freud*[1]

1.1. Discontent with the concept of energy

When considering the epistemological roots of Freud's theory, one invariably notices a certain discontent that can often be pinned down to the conceptual frame of reference he employed. The concept of energy is obligingly welcomed as the quarry. The scandal is consensual, for surely one cannot conceive of the human soul as a machine, and of humans as a pleasure apparatus that recharges itself in the sexual glands and that is in perpetual search of discharge. Such expressions of unease can be found in works dealing with the Freudian epistemology solely on the basis of the conceptual frame of reference.[2]

Freud's correspondence with Fließ, as well as the *Project*, make up an outstanding material for responding to the two criticisms levelled at psychoanalysis. Here, Freud does indeed mention "Nervenkraft", the "Seksualaffekt" and "endogene Erregungen". For the first group of critics this represents an argument — whose degree of subtlety varies across the spectrum — to serenely rid themselves of any materialistic conception of the essence of human beings. For the second group, it offers a good reason for disregarding Lacan's teachings. Despite this, at the same time, they pass over the fact that Lacan gave a seminar for a year on the affect of anxiety.[3]

Quackelbeen, on the other hand, argues that the *Project* needs to be read from the understanding of the necessities which presented themselves to Freud and hence opposes this convenient solution whose restriction is clearly reflected in the results it produced, i.e. the rejection of analytical discourse.[4] What this means is that one ought not to be fixated on Freud's use of the concepts of energy and quantity and their occurrence in other disciplines, but rather that one should pose the question as to what the use of the concept of energy produced for the elaboration of a psychology derived from the clinic of the talking cure.

Jan Buelens's book, *Freud, kind van zijn tijd* (*Freud, Child of his Time*), is pertinent to the present discussion.[5] It is relevant because it shows how little one obtains when opting for an adulterated form of Freud's epistemology. The author's view on psychoanalytical theory is encapsulated in the title of his publication. He opposes those who wish to accredit psychoanalytical theory to Freud's personality and genius. Instead he advocates the idea of his capacity for synthesis. Freud's genius then lies in his ability to *synthesise* a great number of currents of thought that prevailed in the late nineteenth century. In other words, Freud's psycho*analysis* blends in a unique way the sciences of physiology, neurology, biology, psychology and psychiatry, but also (!) the liberal economic trend of that age. Buelens backs up his claim by setting works of various authors from these disciplines side by side with Freud's early writings and by pointing to the correspondences and, according to circumstances, the differences between both.

Generally speaking, one could argue that this modus operandi does produce some results. For it is indeed true that in the *Project* Freud applied a pre-existing conceptual frame of reference which he borrowed from neurology and physiology. It is thence certainly enlightening to learn something about the theories from which these concepts originate. The reader could turn to Buelens's book for a succinct discussion or an introduction to the conceptions of Griesinger, Fechner, Herbart, Meynert, etc. However, it is an entirely different matter whether one can draw conclusions about Freud's epistemology on the basis of these references.

Buelens' method suggests that the conceptual frame of reference is the only criterion to assess Freud's theory. He thus looses sight of an essential reference, namely that of the clinic. Let me qualify this statement by referring to some aspects dealt with by Buelens.

First and foremost there is the *psycho-physical parallelism*. In his study on aphasia, Freud leaves no doubt about his conviction that psychical processes run parallel to physiological ones. However, Buelens indicates that two different understandings of this parallelism have to be distinguished. Spinoza and Leibniz, for example, held the view that for every physical phenomenon there existed a psychical counterpart, and vice versa. A second conception puts the view forward that for every psychical phenomenon there is only one nervous process, in the sense that for each psychical condition there exists a nervous equivalent. In this instance, reciprocity is not applicable, for nervous activities and *a fortiori* physical-chemical actions can exist without corresponding psychical actions. In Buelens's opinion, Freud adheres to the second conception, be it only "that he is fairly inconsistent in his use of the term and that he sometimes veers to interactionism". He further stresses the historical importance of Freud's viewpoint. This marks a rupture with Meynert, who claimed that the realm of the psychical starts where that of the physical stops: "Freud's novel conception is much broader in scope, because the psychical is seen to encompass a field that coalesces with the physiological, at least in the central nervous system. This view is better able to pave the way for the transition to a conception of the unconscious as appertaining to the province of the psychical."[6]

This is a fairly surprising reasoning in the light of my own reading of Freud. Yet it is true that in his book on aphasia Freud refers to Jackson's psycho-physical parallelism, and it is entirely to Buelens's credit to have unearthed the expression "dependent concomitant" in Spencer's work.[7] However, he fails to see that the study on aphasia, even though it contains a psychological questioning, is related to an entirely different clinic from that of neuroses. For once, it would consequently be wise to take a totally divergent conception of the psycho-physical parallelism into account when evaluating Freud's later work. For is it not so that every psychologist is at the same time a psycho-physical parallelist, to the extent that he is aware that no psychical processes are possible without the brain? However, as regards the talking cure, one can expand this parallelism, since beyond any form of interaction between the physiological and psychical level, there is a need for a psychology which is understood purely on the basis of speech and its effects. Freud's scepticism of what physiology could offer to psychotherapy and its concomitant psychology has already been reported in my discussion of his article on the 'Psychical Treatment', which was published one year before his study on aphasia. Strangely enough, Buelens does not mention this particular article while, in keeping with the intention of his book, he takes into account just about all the writings published before 1900.

Buelens is apparently attached to the idea of describing Freud's early writings as being physiological. This is somewhat paradoxical because, for an approach guided by the notions of 'evolution', 'continuity' and 'synthesis', Freud's itinerary then inevitably seems to follow a winding path. As a result, upon analyzing Freud's first publications on hysteria Buelens comments that the allusions to physiology are rather *vague*.[8] Seen from a different angle, the explanation for this is obvious: hysteria does not respond to the rules governing anatomy, but to the idiosyncratic ideational life. Why then should it correspond to physiological rules? But Buelens goes on to write: "This renunciation of the neurophysiological point of departure is explained when Freud argues that hysteria manifests itself through its symptoms as though it were ignorant of the structure and operation of the nervous system: hysteria is a psychical disorder. This point is again of historical interest as it bears witness to Freud's first doubts concerning the relevance of a neurological approach to neuroses. In spite of the fact that shortly after he had written these words down he was engaged in an ultimate attempt (in the *Project*) to find a neurological explanation for psychopathological phenomena, he gradually moved on from a neurological approach to a purely psychological one."[9] This paragraph foreshadows the chapter that he dedicates, "with a certain degree of apprehension", to the *Project*. Since he interprets Freud's *Project* as his ultimate attempt at constructing a physiological psychology, Buelens is bound to attribute the theoretical chapter in the *Studies* to both Breuer and Freud in order to hold on to the viewpoint according to which "(...) one is confronted with a work which is, in spite of the separate signatures, the product of a long and intense collaboration and which should accordingly be considered as a joint publication. It will be possible to make out what Freud retained and shed from the later evolution of his conceptions."[10] In this statement, he utterly overlooks the discrepancy between the case histories and Breuer's theoretical chapter, which is indeed predominantly physiological.[11]

Buelens alludes once again to the applied conceptual frames of reference to support his interpretation of the *Studies*, according to which the book only reflects an energetic and physiological conception of hysteria. Concepts such as energy, tension, conduction, charge and discharge unequivocally hint at the influence of technical progress in the fields of electricity, telegraphy and telephony.[12] There is also the influence of German psychology in the figure of J.F. Herbart, who regards psychology as the science of ideas which also displays similarities with physiology: "Just as physiology constructs the body from fibres, psychology constructs the mind from series of ideas. Just as the stimulation of fibres is a major issue in physiology, so too is the stimulation of the series of ideas precisely the element on which all knowledge of the mental activity depends."[13] However, Buelens seems totally unaffected by the enduring role played in psychoanalytical theory by the Herbartian concepts of energy, defence, resistance and repression.

Buelens also refers to G.T. Fechner, who elaborated on Herbart's views in his *Psychophysik*, while departing at the same time from the latter's theory by resorting to physiology and experiments. What is of interest to Buelens, is that Fechner departed from the notion of a psycho-physical parallelism in the sense that physiology constituted the basis of psychology. The notion of the displacement of energy and the principle of constancy are also symptomatic of Fechner.

Finally, we can turn to Griesinger's work to illustrate the influence of German psychiatry. For instance, the reflex model that Breuer and Freud made use of can be traced back to Griesinger's writings. He merged Herbartian psychology and English association psychology: "(...) the intensity of ideas determines the strength of volition and hence of actions. Fortunately, not every idea is strong enough to incite us to act. This (action) results from associations between ideas which lead to a heightening or a weakening of the idea in question. In the event of conflicting ideas, the ego appears as a sort of referee. The ego consists of a permanent nucleus and ultimately determines human actions in conjunction with the association of ideas."[14] Griesinger was also the first author to use the concept of psychical tonus which, according to Buelens, greatly influenced Breuer and Freud's notion of the intracerebral tonus and the conception of psychical energy which it implied.

Not only do inconsistencies emerge in the interpretation of Freud's work when Buelens attempts to explain the development of Freud's theory on the basis of other theories and in terms of his potential to synthesise these, but the reader is also left with a fragmented image of psychoanalysis, which is seen as the sum of various epistemologies. Yet, surely the best way to define the epistemological foundation of a theory is to base it on the most adequate relation it holds with the object of study on which the constructed theory wishes to shed light: is this adequacy not more important and does it not precede the language in which it was couched? It seems as though Buelens wishes to deny the impossibility Freud had to face, i.e. that of progressing from the level of physiology to the level of psychology. This becomes apparent in his systematic postponement of the inescapable epistemological choice facing anyone dealing with the question of the psyche. Ever since his return from Paris, Freud was preoccupied by this question and by the epistemological choice, even though he continued to make use of conceptual frames of reference familiar to him in order to develop a theory on what the talking cure revealed about the psyche.

For his reading of Freud, Buelens resorts perforce to the postulate of intermediary stages and transition periods, yet he also suggests that psychoanalysis exhibits the lasting legacy of neurophysiological terminology, "(...) which constitutes for some authors a serious obstacle in the way of the development of psychoanalytical theory formation".[15] A theory which is an obstacle to itself strikes one as being rather peculiar. This would only be possible if one was to neglect the very object of one's theory. By contrast, my reading of Freud's early writings reveals an author who was always willing to adapt his theory to his object of study, that is to say the clinic. I will now illustrate this in respect to the *Project*.

1.2. The *Project* as an experiment of thought

Freud's *Project* can only be appreciated if it is read as an experiment of thought through which he hoped to grasp on both pathological and normal psychical processes.[16] This experiment consists in verifying the degree to which these psychical processes can be understood and explained when conceptualised "as quantitatively determinate states of specifiable material particles".[17] Already when writing to Fließ on 25 May 1895, Freud had explicitly set himself the task "(...) of examining what shape the theory of mental functioning takes if one introduces quantitative considerations, a sort of economics of nerve forces; and, second, to peel off from psychopathology a gain for normal psychology".[18]

This basic assumption was not only elementary, it imposed itself from his "psychical treatment": the quantitative conception "derived directly from pathological clinical observation especially where excessively intense ideas were concerned — in hysteria and obsessions, in which, as we shall see, the quantitative characteristic emerges more plainly than in the normal. Processes such as stimulus, substitution, conversion and discharge, which had to be described there [in connection with those disorders], directly suggested the conception of neuronal excitation as quantity in a state of flow."[19] This reference to the clinic is by no means an exaggeration. By 1895, ten years practice of "psychical treatment" had brought Freud closer to an answer to the question that had preoccupied him ever since adolescence, i.e. the question relative to the essence of Man.

His clinic taught him first and foremost that man is "over-cathected". However, this bears no resemblance with what is at present understood by the term "stress", for which family and work environment is traditionally held responsible and in which case a rest or a "break from the suffocating environment" would offer a solution. According to Freud, human beings are indeed poorly adapted to their environment, milieu or outside world, lest this outside world is interpreted in a particular way, an interpretation which, at face value, even seems contradictory.

One can indeed gather from the *Studies on Hysteria* that in the talking cure patients convey their physical afflictions by means of complaints about both their professional and emotional lives. But it is precisely in the gulf between the physical afflictions (the excessively intense organ or the conversion symptom) and the complaint (the excessively intense idea) that the quantitative features described by Freud materialise. This is what characterises human beings as agitated or affected, swamped by an *affect* of fright or literally crushed by an unexplainable feeling of melancholy, inhibited by irrational anxieties or marked by elusive physical symptoms. In other words, to Freud the most important cause of the evil is located *within* the organism proper, i.e. in the endogenous stimulation or, more accurately, in the psyche of the neurotic person who is unable psychically to process reality in an adequate way.

In the *Project*, Freud carries this analysis even further by reinterpreting the notion of endogenous excitation or, quantity $Q\eta$. The affect human beings have to deal with is the sexual affect ("Sexualaffekt"). In clinical terms, this means that both the physical ailments and complaints of his patients ultimately serve as an inadequate processing of or, as a means to convey the way in which their *sexuality* was psychically represented.

This point of view is the first key for my reading of the *Project*. Freud himself offers this key in his letters to Fließ anterior to the text and relative to the problem of the "Aktualneurosen". One could argue that in the *Project*

Freud blends the notion of repression present in the *Studies on Hysteria* and the hypothesis on the sexual aetiology of the "Aktualneurosen". This fusion is a crucial point in Freud's theoretical development. It coincides with the creation of the concept of the *drive* which lies halfway between the somatic and the psychical. This in itself suffices to look upon the *Project* as being a metapsychological text.

1.2.1. The sexual affect of hysteria and obsessional neurosis

All of this leads me once again to explore the problem of *sexuality*. I already touched upon this subject when dealing with Freud's conception of psychotherapy and the accompanying clinical psychology. A psychology of this kind is bound to leave room for Eros, as the talking cure invariably discloses the import of sexuality in the ideational life and psychical processes of human beings. It also demonstrates the necessity of exploiting eroticised transference as a therapeutic instrument. This clinical viewpoint is still prevalent in contemporary psychoanalytical practice: the repression of the sexual idea and the repetition of it in the process of transference are by no means hypotheses, but clinical-empirical *facts*.[20]
It took Freud ten years to recognise the dual importance of Eros. However, the *explanation* for the two ways in which human sexuality manifests itself is an entirely different matter. In this respect, the *Studies on Hysteria* fall short of our expectations. From a purely clinical perspective, this book is still modern and nobody would deny it its place in the corpus of psychoanalytical literature. Yet the need for a more coherent and more abstract theory is blatant.[21] In my opinion, the essence of psychoanalytic praxis reached its final form in 1895, and as an instrument of research it had already shed light on a substantial number of elements. What was missing then was the most complex facet of psychoanalysis: a theory.
The *Project* contains the first attempt at constructing a comprehensive and explanatory theory of psychoanalysis. However, I should like to enter a caveat: this manuscript which is the product of an advanced and extensive experiment of thought can certainly not account for everything. That being said, the text contains no less than the creation of the concepts of the *drive* and of the *unconscious* which, along with those of *transference* and *repetition* constitute the four essential concepts of psychoanalysis.[22]

On the eve of the last century a plethora of physicians maintained that hysteria was in some way connected to sexuality. Young unmarried girls appeared particularly prone to contract this disease and the hysterical attacks they suffered from often displayed overtly sexual traits. The oversensitiveness of the genitals and the occurrence of other genital symptoms legitimised the making a link between hysteria and organic abnormalities and/or certain features of sexual behaviour, such as abstinence. The reinterpretation of hysteria as a functional disorder of the nervous system need not contradict this emphasis on the genitals. A functional disorder of this kind may just as well supervene as secondary to a non-neural disease: the affected organ can bring about physiological changes in the neural canals which innervate the organ concerned. In other terms, hysteria acquires the status of a reflex-neurosis. This view was also propounded by the Viennese neurologist and contemporary of Freud, Moritz Benedikt.

There is barely any trace of this conception in Freud's book, even though in his letters he sometimes praised Fließ for his concept of the nasal reflex neurosis.[23] One does find the notion of the somatic compensation in the aetiology of some hysterical symptoms, but the genital disorder itself plays no part at all in his theory on hysteria. This can not be said of the role played by sexual behaviour, which over a hundred years ago was generally recognised as an important etiological factor for neuroses. In Freud's writing, this subject receives the full attention it deserves, though initially not within the frame of his examination of hysteria but within that of the "Aktualneurosen".

As for hysteria, Freud initially shared the viewpoint of Charcot who had disconnected this disease from the uterus, thence paving the way for a more psychological approach to this affliction. But in 1888, Freud still stressed the importance of the hereditary factor: "The aetiology of the *status hystericus* is to be looked for entirely in heredity. Hysterics are always hereditarily disposed to disturbances of nervous activity, and epileptics, psychical patients, tabetics, etc., are found amongst their relatives. Direct hereditary transmission of hysteria, too, is observed, and is the basis, for instance, of the appearance of hysteria in boys (from their mother). Compared with the factor of heredity all other factors take a second place and play the part of incidental causes, the importance of which is as a rule overrated in practice. The accidental causes of hysteria are, however, to this extent important in that they release the onset of hysterical outbreaks, of acute hysteria. As factors calculated to encourage the development of a hysterical disposition may be mentioned: a mollycoddling upbringing (hysteria only in children), premature awakening of mental activity in children, frequent and violent excitements. (...). As regards what is often asserted to be the preponderant influence of abnormalities in the sexual sphere upon the development of hysteria, it must be said that its importance is as a rule over-estimated."[24]

However, before long, Freud abandoned the Charcotian emphasis on heredity, on the "famille névropathique", and the attribution to all other factors of the status of "agent provocateur".[25] In his 1894 theory on the neuro-psychoses of defence, Freud ascribed a central position to the sexual nature of the ideas that were repressed. In this essay, he wrote that for female patients the distressing ideas usually originated in the realm of sexuality and sensation. Hence Freud's female patients had very clear recollections of their attempts at defence, and their explicit intention to push the content of these ideas away ("fortzuschieben") and forget them. Freud illustrates this with two examples from his clinic, but stresses that he could easily have alluded to a score of similar cases.[26] One patient, Elisabeth von R., reproached herself because while nursing her sick father she had thoughts about a young man who had made an erotic impression on her. Lucy R., another patient, attempted to dispel the thoughts she had for her employer with whom she had fallen in love.

The attempt at defence or 'forgetting' of distressing ideas is in any case doomed to fail and it leads indirectly to the constitution of symptoms. Both the memory-trace and the affect that was coupled to the distressing idea continue to exist. The ego's attempt at defence only succeeds in weakening the distressing idea by withdrawing its sum of excitation ("Erregungssumme"). The weak idea will then have virtually no part to play in the work of association. In other terms, it will have been excluded from conscious psychical processes. The affect detached from the idea inexorably chooses another 'discharge route'. I should like to observe that up to this point the mechanisms of conversion hysteria, phobias and obsessions have run parallel, but henceforth their path will diverge.[27]

In the case of conversion hysteria the distressing idea is made innocuous by having the sum of excitation 'converted' into the physical. This course is called the "psycho-physical process" of hysteria.[28] However, in other cases the affect stripped from the idea that was fended off lives on in the "psychical sphere" and attaches itself to other ideas, which in themselves are not distressing but which "thanks to this false connection" are "turned into obsessional ideas".[29] A similar psychical mechanism operates for phobias. This mechanism contains two empirical elements. First, there is the observation that, just as in hysteria, the source of the phobia lies in the subject's sexual life: "Theoretically, it is not impossible that this *affect* should sometimes arise in other fields; I can only report that so far I have not come across any other origin. Moreover, it is easy to see that it is precisely sexual life which brings with it the most copious occasions for the emergence of incompatible ideas."[30] Second, the "effort of will", or the attempt at fending off clearly transpires from the patient's speech. In certain cases they report that the obsession or phobia appeared for the first time after a seemingly successful effort of will: "Something very disagreeable happened to me once and I tried very hard to put it away from me and not to think about it any more. I succeeded at last; but then I got this other thing, which I have not been able to get rid of since."[31] However, the origin of obsession is not as clear as this to every patient. Usually the response one meets when drawing the patient's attention to the original idea of a sexual nature is sometimes like: "It *can't* come from that. *I didn't* think at all much about that. For a moment I was frightened, but I turned my mind away from it and I haven't been troubled by it since."[32] In Freud's eyes the patients' own judgement furnishes evidence of the surrogate nature of obsessions which substitute for the distressing sexual ideas.

However, his theory is not entirely the product of his clinical observation. "Between the patient's effort of will, which succeeds in repressing the unacceptable sexual idea, and the emergence of the obsessional idea, which, though having little intensity in itself, is now supplied with an incomprehensibly strong affect, yawns the gap which the theory here developed seeks to fill. The separation of the sexual idea from its affect and the attachment of the latter to another, suitable but not incompatible idea — these are processes which occur without consciousness. Their existence can only be presumed, but cannot be proved by any clinical-psychological analysis. Perhaps it would be more correct to say that these processes are not of a psychical nature at all, that they are physical processes whose psychical consequences present themselves as if what is expressed by the terms 'separation of the idea from its affect' and 'false connection' of the latter had really taken place."[33]

Freud reveals himself as anything but a naive thinker. He accurately distinguishes between that which is empirically or clinically observable and that which needs to be presupposed theoretically in order to explicate the observed information. Freud elaborates on the precise status of his construction in the conclusion to this article. "I should like, finally, to dwell for a moment on the *working hypothesis* which I have made use of in this exposition of the neuroses of defence. I refer to the concept that in mental functions something is to be distinguished — a quota of affect or sum of excitation — which possesses all the characteristics of a quantity (though we have no means of measuring it), which is capable of increase, diminution, displacement and discharge, and which is spread over the memory-traces of ideas somewhat as an electric charge is spread over the surface of a body. This hypothesis, which, incidentally already underlies our theory of 'abreaction' in our 'Preliminary Communication', can be applied in the same sense as physicists apply the hypothesis of a flow of electric fluid. It is provisionally justified by its utility in co-ordinating and explaining a great variety of psychical states."[34]

1.2.2. "Aktualneurosen" and sexual excitation

Freud's recognition of the dual import of Eros in both hysteria and obsessional neuroses, prompted him to approach sexuality from a different angle. In the first letter that Freud sent to Fließ in November 1887, there are already references to the field of the "Aktualneurosen".[35] In early Freudian nosology this appellation designates the clinical pictures of neurasthenia and anxiety neurosis. At the end of the past century, neurasthenia in particular drew a lot of attention in neurological literature where it was often mentioned in the same breath as hysteria. In addition, Freud often received patients whose symptoms could be said to originate in what he called their sexual *behaviour*. Practices such as abstinence, frequent masturbation and coitus interruptus seem to be anything but conducive to the psychical well being of Man who as a result falls prey to attacks of anxiety, mood swings and physical ailments of all kinds. This phenomenon had already been acknowledged and described in the medical literature, but one can surmise from Freud's correspondence with Fließ that both its explanation as well as its delineation with respect to other diseases left a lot to be desired. He therefore set up a sort of experimental project with Fließ in order to clarify this subject. On February 8, 1893, Freud entrusted Draft B to Fließ advising him to conceal the 'story' in question from his young wife. As is characteristic of

Freud he goes straight to the point and audaciously asserts that *every* neurasthenia is a sexual neurasthenia. In his etiological outline Freud draws a distinction between the preconditions in the absence of which the disease cannot come into existence and the precipitating factors. For neurasthenia this means that the sexual "Abnützung" (exhaustion) is either sufficient in itself to bring on the disease, or that it predisposes the *nervous system* so that physical illness, a depressive affect or overwork can directly conduce to neurasthenia. However, without the role played by sexual exhaustion, these factors can in no way be conducive.[36]

In males neurasthenia is acquired[37] at puberty, and takes effect in the twenties. Its origin is masturbation, the frequency of which runs in complete parallel with that of neurasthenia. Besides, "(...) one can observe in the circle of one's acquaintances that (at least in urban populations) those individuals who have been seduced by women at an early age have escaped neurasthenia".[38] Freud emphasises that the most important generative factor is onanismus conjugalis, i.e. incomplete intercourse in order to prevent pregnancy.

However, neurasthenia in women usually derives from or concurs with that of the male partner whose potency is impaired by his sexual neurasthenia. Female neurasthenia is thus always mixed with hysteria, "the traditional mixed neuroses of women". An admixture of this kind issues directly forth from "the holding back of the excitation of the act". Therefore, the weaker the male's potency, the greater the incidence of hysteria.

A second thesis in this draft deals with the difference between neurasthenia and anxiety neurosis. For instance, anxiety which finds expression in "(...) a certain lowering of self-assurance, by pessimistic expectation and an inclination to distressing antithetical ideas (...)", also definitely occurs in neurasthenia. However, Freud wonders whether the occurrence of anxiety with no other symptoms cannot be sufficient argument for the separation of anxiety neurosis from neurasthenia.[39] Freud does not provide any conclusive answer as to the hereditary factor here either. The fact remains that in both male and female anxiety, neurosis often has its roots in the marital bed and coitus interruptus can offer once again an explanation.

Freud is totally pessimistic about the therapy. As in cases of neurasthenia and anxiety neurosis the physician's intervention relies entirely on prophylaxis. "The first part of this task, prevention of the sexual noxa of the first period, coincides with prophylaxis against syphilis and gonorrhoea, since they are the noxae that threaten anyone who gives up masturbation. The only alternative would be free sexual intercourse between young men and unattached young women, but this could only be adopted if there were innocuous methods of preventing conception. Otherwise, the alternatives are masturbation, neurasthenia in the male, hysteroneurasthenia in the female, or syphilis in the male, syphilis in the next generation, gonorrhoea in the male, gonorrhoea and sterility in the female. The same task — an innocuous means of controlling conception — is set by the sexual trauma of the second period; since the condom provides neither a safe solution nor one acceptable to someone who is already neurasthenic."[40]

In order to test his hypothesis and determine the weight of the hereditary factor, Freud was even willing to turn to experiments. He thus set out to record one hundred cases of anxiety neuroses and just as many cases of male and female neurasthenia. One hundred non-neurotics were to serve as a control group.[41]

In his letters and drafts during the years to follow, Freud repeatedly endeavoured to decipher and circumscribe the aetiology of neurasthenia and anxiety neurosis.[42] Let me point out that from the start Freud's approach of these "Aktualneurosen" was quite different from the one he had adopted when dealing with hysteria. In the latter Freud, unlike numerous other authors, only gradually came to a recognition of the importance of the sexual factor.

The major distinction between both categories is the *status* Freud ascribed to sexuality. In the case of hysteria and anxiety neuroses it is the *content* of the ideas which have been fended off which is sexual. This suggests that the problem is located at a *psychical* level and that it should be interpreted as the failure to acknowledge a sexual desire. This desire is at most *denied* or repudiated.[43] In neurasthenia and anxiety neurosis on the other hand, one is dealing with a "purely affective aetiology". His patients do not come to him to deny something but rather, or so it seems, to confirm that they have sexual problems. The sexual problems mentioned concretely refer to the actual intercourse. Freud's attention to the "sexual history" even seemed to attract customers. Rather relieved and surprised, his patients told him about their unhappy marriage, remarking that "(...) no one had ever asked [them] about that before."[44]

Strangely enough, the key to a more plausible explanation of the "Aktualneurosen" is given to Freud by a particular category of patients whose symptoms do *not* originate in their sexual behaviour. The patients in question are "young persons who must be presumed to be virgins and who have not been subjected to abuse".[45] I will not expound on what Freud means by the expression "subjected to abuse", but it may refer to either masturbation or seduction by a third party. However, what Freud adds in this letter about two analyses he had recently undertaken, is significant: "(...) it was a *presentient dread* of sexuality, and behind it things they had seen or heard and half-understood — thus, the aetiology is purely emotional but nevertheless of a sexual nature."[46] In other words, for the paradigm of the "Aktualneurosen" Freud avails of material which strictly speaking lies outside this category, for here we are dealing with a fear *of* sexuality, rather than a fear *caused* directly by sexuality.

Katharina

One of the case histories in the *Studies on Hysteria* is particularly relevant to this subject. It is the case of Katharina, the young daughter of the landlady of the inn where Freud spent his holidays in August of 1893.[47]

One day during one of his excursions Freud was consulted by a girl of about eighteen. She said that she suffered from her nerves and was plagued by a difficulty in breathing, for which she had received a prescription from a doctor, which was of no avail. "So there I was with the neuroses once again — for nothing else could very well be the matter with this strong well-built girl with her unhappy look. I was interested to find that neuroses could flourish in this at a height of over 6,000 feet; I questioned her further therefore."[48] Freud inferred from Katharina's description of her ailment that what she regarded as shortness of breath was in fact an anxiety attack. Out of all the complex of sensations of such an attack she had only stressed her difficulty in breathing. Freud diagnosed this shortness of breath as being hysterical attacks characterised by anxiety, and speculated as to whether these attacks were not connected with another content.

If one takes into account the schemata outlined in Freud's correspondence with Fließ, then it seems at the very least premature to diagnose hysteria at this stage. Only later in her narration does the diagnosis become legitimate. One is apparently dealing with a case of mixed neurosis in which the 'pure affect' was liberated by and coupled to a sexual idea at a given moment. This most engaging excerpt (which is the fall out of one single conversation) is not only of significance for Freud's theoretical development in connection with the "Aktualneurosen" and the hypothesis *Q*. It also reveals Freud as a particularly subtle clinician. One surmises from his interventions that he is quick to 'see through' the reason Katharina gives for her affliction. These interventions give evidence of the 'knowledge' he had acquired through experience: they are decisive and they encourage Katharina to develop her narrative further. At the same time he leaves a certain leeway to his patient in the sense that any progression in the conversation results from a judgement or statement from her part, with the exception of one intervention which can only be described as a genuine construction, as defined by Freud in 1937![49] This case description thus considered illustrates how one single conversation is patterned in the same way as an entire treatment. It accordingly implies a stance on the finality of the cure which is then described as *guiding towards a judgement*.[50] The passage I quote extensively shows that the affect can only be conveyed by means of a subjective judgement, i.e. an enunciation that incorporates the subject. Put differently, it demonstrates how that which was never before put into words can only take on the form of a judgement.[51]

— 'When you have an attack do you think of something? and always the same thing? or do you see something in front of you?'
— '*Yes. I always see*[52] *an awful face that looks at me in a dreadful way, so that I'm frightened.*'
— 'Do you recognise the face? I mean, is it a face that you've really seen sometime?'
— 'No.'
— 'Do you know what your attacks come from?'
— 'No.'
— 'When did you first have them?'
— 'Two years ago, while I was still living on the other mountain with my aunt. (She used to run a refuge hut there, and we moved here eighteen months ago.) But they keep on happening.'

Up to this point the conversation with Katharina brought very little to light. Freud therefore resorted to an intervention relying on the memory of his treatment of another young lady. The young patient in question persistently denied that her affliction had anything to do with her married life. She defended herself by retorting that she already suffered from these attacks as a girl. After a certain lapse of time she suddenly conceded that the origin of these attacks was connected with sexuality. As a child she used to sleep in a room contiguous to her parents' and on numerous occasions she had caught a glimpse of her father getting into bed next to her mother and then overheard something which aroused her. Soon after that the attacks of anxiety started. For Freud other cases too pointed to a similar causal link, which he summed up by arguing that anxiety in young girls often results from the horror that strikes their virginal minds when they are confronted with the world of sexuality. Freud, weighing his words, thus guessed:

— 'If you don't know, I tell you how I think you got your attacks. At that time, two years ago, you must have seen or heard something that very much embarrassed you, and that you'd much rather not have seen.'
— '*Heavens, yes!*' she replied, '*that was when I caught my uncle with the girl, with Franziska, my cousin.*'
— 'What's this story about a girl? Won't you tell me all about it?'
— 'You can say anything to a doctor, I suppose. Well, at that time, you know, my uncle — the husband of the aunt you've seen here — kept an inn on the --kogel. Now they are divorced, and it is my fault they were divorced, because it was through me that it came out that he was carrying on with Franziska.'
— 'And how did you discover it?'
— 'This way. One day two years ago some gentlemen had climbed the mountain and asked for something to eat. My aunt wasn't at home, and Franziska, who always did the cooking was nowhere to be found. And my uncle was not to be found either. We looked everywhere and at last Alois, the little boy, my cousin, said: "why, Franziska must be in Father's room!" *And we both laughed; but we weren't thinking anything bad.* Then we went to my uncle's room but found it locked. That seemed strange to me. Then Alois said: "There is a window in the passage where you can look into the room." We went into the passage; but Alois wouldn't go to the window and said he was afraid. So I said: "You silly boy!" I'll go. *I'm not a bit afraid." And I had nothing bad in my mind.* I looked in. The room was rather dark, but I saw my uncle and Franziska; he was lying on her.'
— 'Well?'
— 'I came away from the window at once, and lent up against the wall and couldn't get my breath — just what happens to me since. Everything went blank, my eyelids were forced together and there was a hammering and buzzing in my head.'
— 'Did you tell your aunt that very same day?'
— 'Oh no, I said nothing.'
— 'Then why were you so frightened when you found them together? Did you understand it? Did you know what was going on?'
— '*Oh no. I didn't understand anything at that time. I was only sixteen. I don't know what I was frightened about.*'
— 'Fraülein Katharina, if you could remember now what was happening in you at that time, when you had your first attack, what you thought about it — it would help you.'
— 'Yes, if I could. But I was so frightened that I've forgotten everything.'
— 'Tell me, Fraülein. Can it be that the head that you always see when you lose your breath is Franziska's head, as you saw it then?'

— '*Oh no, she didn't look so awful. Besides, it's a man's head.*'
— 'Or perhaps your uncle's?'
— 'I didn't see his face as clearly as that. It was too dark in the room. And why should he have been making such a dreadful face just then?'
— 'You're quite right.'
— 'And what happened then?'
— 'Well, those two must have heard a noise, because they came out soon afterwards. I felt very bad the whole time. I always kept thinking about it. Then two days later it was a Sunday and there was a great deal to do and I worked all day long. And on the Monday morning I felt giddy again and was sick, and I stopped in bed and was sick without stopping for three days.'
— 'If you were sick three days later, I believe that means that when you looked into the room you felt disgusted.'
— 'Yes, I'm sure I felt disgusted,' she said reflectively, 'but disgusted at what?'
— 'Perhaps you saw something naked? What sort of state were they in?'
— 'It was too dark to see anything; besides both of them had their clothes on. Oh, if only I knew what it was I felt disgusted at!'

Freud was also unable to provide an answer. The only option open to him was to encourage her to go on with her narration and to tell him whatever occurred to her. He carried the firm conviction that whatever came to her mind would prove instrumental in shedding light on her case. Katharina went on to tell him about how her aunt managed to find out her secret, the ensuing dispute between her aunt and her uncle, and the eventual divorce.
However, then she interrupted the thread of her story and picked up two sets of older stories which took place two or three years before she had looked in through the window. The first series dealt with memories of how her uncle had approached her when she was only fourteen. On that occasion she was sharing a room with him in a valley inn and he tried to get into bed next to her. Suddenly awoken by his body, she sprang up and reproached him for not letting her sleep.

— 'Go on, you silly girl, keep still. You don't know how nice it is.'
— '*I don't like your "nice" things; you don't even let one sleep in peace.*'

The nature of her defence seems to indicate that she failed to recognise the sexual aspect of the offence. Upon Freud's question as to whether she was aware then of what his intentions were, Katharina answered that she was not. It did not dawn on her till much later. She had only confronted him then because she did not like her sleep to be disturbed and because "it wasn't nice". She also recalled a second similar incident in which she had to repel

him and confirmed that in both instances she felt a pressure on the eyes and chest, although not as intense as in the scene of discovery.
The second set of stories is relative to her realisation that there was something going on between her uncle and Franziska.
After having reached the end of both sets of stories she paused. It was as if she had undergone a metamorphosis. Her sulky, suffering face came alive and her eyes were bright and exalted again. In the meantime, Freud realised that what Katharina told him seemingly spontaneously explained her behaviour at the scene of the discovery. At that time she was impregnated with two sets of experience which she remembered but did not understand and from which she thus could not draw any conclusions. When she caught a glimpse of the couple having sex, she made a link between both sets of recollections. She began to understand them and at the same time to repress them. Thereupon followed a short period of incubation which gave way to symptoms of conversion. Vomiting functioned as a substitute for her moral and physical disgust. Freud had solved the riddle. She did not feel disgust at the sight of the couple, but at the memory that it stirred in her. This surely could only be the memory of the nocturnal incident when she felt her uncle's body. Freud tentatively put the following construction forward in which he articulates the judgement which was left unsaid by Katherina:

— 'I know now what it was you thought when you looked into the room. You thought: "*Now he's doing with her what he wanted to do with me that night and those other times.*" That was what you were disgusted at, because you remembered the feeling when you woke up in the night and felt his body.'[53]
— 'It may well be,' she replied, 'that that was what I was disgusted at and that that was what I thought.'
— 'Tell me just one thing more. Your a grown-up girl now and know all sorts of things...'
— 'Yes I am.'
— 'Tell me just one thing. What part of his body was it that you felt that night?'

Katharina did not give any clear answer to this and just smiled in an embarrassed manner, like someone who is convinced, or who is forced to admit that the heart of the matter has been reached and that there is not much more to say. Freud writes that he "(...) could imagine what the tactile sensation was which she had later learned to interpret. Her facial expression seemed to me to be saying that she supposed that I was right in my conjecture. But I could not penetrate further, and in any case I owed her a debt of gratitude for having made it so much easier for me to talk to her than to the prudish ladies of my city practice, who regard whatever is *natural* as *shameful*."

The case thus seemed to be solved. Yet there remained one question: to whom did the face that haunted her in her hallucination belong? Freud put the question again to Katharina and, it seemed as though she had expanded her own understanding through the conversation, for she promptly replied:

— 'Yes, I know now. The head is my uncle's head — I recognise it now — but not from that time. Later, when all the disputes had broken out, my uncle gave way to a senseless rage against me. He kept saying that it was all my fault: if I hadn't chattered, it would never have come to a divorce. He kept threatening he would do something to me; and if he caught sight of me at a distance his face would get distorted with rage and he would make for me with his hand raised. I always ran away from him, and always felt terrified that he would catch me some time unawares. *The face I always see now is his face when he was in a rage.*'

Freud perceptively adds that it is quite understandable that the mnemic symbol originated from the period during which her aunt's interest was absorbed by entirely different matters (the court, the divorce). Her aunt was not in a position to listen to her and there was nobody else to help her in her "Verarbeitung", that is until now when she happened to meet an unknown doctor. By means of conclusion Freud writes: "I hope this girl, whose sexual sensibility had been injured at such an early age, derived some benefit from our conversation ("Aussprache"). I have not seen her since."

In his discussion of the case, Freud emphasised that the solution was not so much the result of his *analysis* than of *guesswork*. He referred to the fact that Katharina merely confirmed his inquiries (what I called construction), but that she was unable to recognise these as something she actually had experienced, or, if I may add, thought. Hypnosis would have been required for this. Or indeed perhaps not. Maybe another conversation, or a series of conversations based on a similar pattern, would have been sufficient, not so much to conjure up *memories*, but to allow Katharina herself to pass the suspended judgements.

Whatever the case may be, in Freud's eyes this was a instance of acquired hysteria. The two series of traumatic experiences she remembered made up the traumatic factor which left behind the content of consciousness, which in turn was excluded from the normal thought process of the ego. Here the cause is not the 'will', but rather the 'ignorance' on the part of the ego. In this respect, Freud qualifies the case of Katharina as being typical: in the case of every analysis of hysteria caused by sexual traumas one finds that the impressions form the pre-sexual period which produced no effect then, do exert an effect when the girl or married woman has acquired an understanding of sexual life. Consequently, the "splitting off of psychological groups" is to be regarded as a normal process in the development of the adolescent, and it is understandable that their later reception in the ego can engender psychical disturbances. Freud entertains doubts as to whether the mechanism of the "splitting of consciousness" due to ignorance on the part of the ego differs essentially from either the will of the ego or defence. Who knows whether adolescents do not know more about sexuality than others, or even they themselves, suspect.

Freud does not provide any explanation for the fact that suspicions and premonitions about sexuality can arouse affects of fright in virgins. It was not until the *Project* that Freud was to venture to formulate such an explanation on the basis of the case of Emma.

1.2.3. Anxiety neurosis

> "There are still a hundred gaps, large and small, in the matter of neuroses; but I am getting closer to an outline and some general perspectives."
>
> *Sigmund Freud*[54]

Let us resume our quest for the status of the concept of quantity. From a case such as Katharina's it appears that Freud ascribes a *psychical causality* to the sudden emergence of the affect. It is the confrontation with sexuality — which consists in the association of two groups of ideas — which conjures up a feeling of anxiety which is subsequently grafted or coupled to particular ideas, such as the hallucination of the awful face in Katharina's case. This suggests that the quantitative factor should essentially be interpreted as the anxiety or the pure affect and that its cause is psychical.

Freud came up with a new hypothesis in November 1893: "I have hit upon the idea to tie anxiety not to a psychic but rather to a *physical consequence* of sexual abuse. I was led to this by a wonderfully pure case of anxiety neurosis following coitus interruptus in a totally placid and totally frigid woman."[55] Freud thence rejected the hypothesis according to which every anxiety must be a recollected or hysterical anxiety, since the anxiety that emerged after the "sexual abuse" cannot be traced back to an anxiety experience during the coitus.[56] This is the first allusion to what Freud was to call his toxicological theory on anxiety to which he was not to give a clearer interpretation until May 1894. By that time, he was deeply engrossed in his ambition to construct a general theory of neuroses which would accommodate every clinical entity.[57] The cornerstone of this new theory was affect combined with the various mechanisms holding sway over this affect. Freud initially distinguished three mechanisms: 1. that of affect transformation ("Verwandlung") for conversion hysteria; 2. that of affect displacement ("Verschiebung") for obsessional ideas; and 3. that of exchange of affect ("Vertauschung") for anxiety neurosis and melancholia. However, "(...) *in every case* it should be *sexual excitation* that undergoes these transpositions, but the impetus to them is not in every case something sexual."[58] In other terms, the basic affect is considered as on a par with sexual stimulation: "Sexual affect is of course taken in its broadest sense, as an excitation having a definite quantity."[59]

Freud goes into great detail about the question of the genesis of the affect of anxiety. To that effect, in draft E, he drew up a sort of classification of all the clinically distinct groups of cases involving anxiety which seemed to be connected to sexuality in some form or other.[60] All these groups have one thing in common, namely the accumulation of physical sexual tension which is caused by an obstructed discharge. Consequently, anxiety neurosis, like hysteria, should be considered as a form of *damming up neurosis*, in which the accumulation of sexual tension is converted into anxiety.[61]

But why does the transformation have to debouch on anxiety? To answer this, Freud introduces a passage that is adumbrative of his experiment of thought in the *Project*, namely the distinction between endogenous and exogenous excitation. In what he terms a normal mechanism, the excitation emanates from the outside world and is conducive to an accretion of excitation in the psyche. This accretion is discharged by any reaction as long as it reduces the inner psychic excitation by the same quantum. Endogenous excitation follows a different course. Its source is located in the body (hunger, thirst, sexual drive) and in this case *specific reactions* suffice. These prevent the further occurrence of the excitation in the end organs in question: "Here we may picture the endogenous tension as growing either continuously or discontinuously, but in any case as only being noticed when it has reached a certain *threshold*. It is only above this threshold that it is deployed *psychically*, that it enters into relation with certain groups of ideas, which then set about producing the specific remedies."[62] In other words, the essential precondition for the specific reaction to the sexual tension is present in a psychical group of ideas. It is fairly obvious to gather what sort of specific reaction Freud had in mind. The discharge of the sexual tension can only take place during intercourse for which the psyche needs to have an adequate idea in order to put the sexual object in a favourable position.[63]

But we have not quite reached that point. Yet again the clinic puts spokes in the wheel of an overly mechanistic reasoning and impels Freud to further qualify his conceptual apparatus. Freud's patients invariably react with indignation with regard to this coherent outline, retorting that they have no sexual desire whatsoever. How then can there be obstructed discharge of accumulated sexual tension? Freud, who at the time was not entirely convinced that indignation is an avatar of the lie, resolved this problem by arguing that physical sexual tension is aroused by a value of "psychical libido" which then leads to coitus. If this specific reaction fails to occur, the physico-psychic tension (the sexual affect) increases and becomes disruptive. The physical and the psychical can therefore influence each other up to a certain threshold. However, in the case of anxiety neuroses one is confronted with a derailment ("Entgleisung"): "The physical tension increases, reaches the threshold value at which it can arouse psychic affect; but for several reasons the psychic linkage offered to it remains insufficient; a sexual affect cannot be formed, because there is something lacking in the *psychic determinants*."[64] The physical tension that is not psychically bound is accordingly transformed into anxiety. *Anxiety neurosis is thus characterised by a deficit of "sexual affect" or psychical libido.*

Freud subsequently checks whether the proposed mechanisms fit the different groups involving associations between sexuality and anxiety. To his great satisfaction, he realised that his reasoning was accurate: where the physical "sexual tension" is richly developed, but cannot be turned into affect by psychical processing — because of an underdeveloped psychical sexuality, or because of an attempt to repress it (i.e. defence), or even because of a reduction of it or an ordinary alienation of physical or psychical sexuality — the sexual tension is transformed in anxiety.[65]

We may ask ourselves once again why is it that this transformation debouches in anxiety? "Anxiety is the sensation of the accumulation of another endogenous stimulus, the stimulus to breathing, a stimulus incapable of being worked over psychically apart from this; anxiety might therefore be employed for accumulated physical tension in general. Furthermore, if the symptoms of anxiety neurosis are examined more closely, one finds in the neurosis disjointed pieces of a major anxiety attack: namely, mere dyspnoea, mere palpitations, mere feeling of anxiety, and a combination of these. Looked at more precisely, these are the paths of innervation that the physical sexual tension ordinarily traverses even when it is about to be worked over psychically. The dyspnea and palpitations belong to coitus; and while ordinarily they are employed only as subsidiary paths of discharge, here they serve, so to speak, as the only outlets for the excitation."[66]

In the case of anxiety neurosis, as in hysteria, a kind of conversion takes place. But whereas hysteria is characterised by a conversion of psychical excitation into the somatic, anxiety neurosis is a physical tension which cannot be processed psychically and hence must remain in the register of the physical.

Interpretation

So much for Freud's first attempt at explaining anxiety neurosis. He is aware that it is not entirely satisfactory, but for the time being he effects no major changes to his explanation.[67] Indeed, he saw no reason why he should. When he initially tested the construction of his diagram of sexuality to see whether it fitted cases of anxiety neurosis and neurasthenia, he obtained positive results.[68] Whether his approach is mechanistic or not, no clinician — even a contemporary one — can deny that psychopathology in general, but particularly the form which supervenes during the honeymoon, initially manifests itself in the marital bed. As a result, in his later nosography Freud never abandoned the category of the "Aktualneurosen".

In the subsequent period, i.e. from June 1894 to May 1895, one observes a major shift in Freud's poles of interest, which was most reflected in the way he defined the problem. The diagram of sexuality suggested in Draft E contains two problems which Freud left unanswered. Firstly, there is the question as to *how* the conversion mechanism of *physical sexual tension* into *physical anxiety* operates. Strictly speaking, only a physiological explanation could offer a solution, as one could incidentally conjecture for the conversion mechanism accounting for hysterical symptoms. Secondly, there is the problem of the *psychical processing* of the physical sexual tension.

I will be brief with regard to the first question, since Freud never once attempted to solve this problem, even though he sometimes hoped and wished that a physiological explanation of this kind would be undertaken which would account for this *excess of physical sexual tension.*

At this point, I should like to remind the reader of my previous discussion on Breuer's physiological explanation of hysteria. According to Breuer, hysteria results from an *excessive excitation.* Freud's diagram of sexuality, by contrast, contains the seed of his later approach to psychopathology, i.e. from the clinic of the "psychical treatment". This necessity is apparent in the schema, even if in some cases — such as in those of the "Aktualneurosen" and conversion hysteria — the physical or somatic register is explicitly displayed. The embryonic form of his approach is also visible in the fact that anxiety neurosis can just as well be observed from a psychological vantage point, that is to say from the *deficiency at the psychical level.*[69]

This brings the analysis around to the second problem which deals with the transition from the physical to the psychical. Unlike what a perfunctory reading of his "diagram of sexuality" would suggest, Freud's notion of the *deficiency* or the *insufficiency* of the psychical questions the unequivocal explanation which postulates a causal connection between both levels, as if to say that the psychical were determined by the physical. Or put differently, whereas the "psycho-physical parallelism" conveniently seeks to cloak the problem, Freud's schema opens an avenue for a resolutely psychological approach to it. Again, the first point of reference is the clinic. For, even though the quantitative factor unmistakably transpires from their speech and symptomatology, Freud's patients do not complain about an excess of excitation or sexual tension. On the contrary, they lack any sort of drive or sexual desire. What is more, the lack of "rapport sexuel" can only be treated on a psychical plane. Hysterical or actual neurosis, obsessional or phobic, melancholic or paranoid: the "Seelenarzt" can only access the sexual knot by means of psychical processing ("Verarbeitung").

Melancholia versus paranoia

It is therefore not surprising that Freud's theoretical considerations emphasise the various modes of psychical processing. This is already disclosed in Draft H with respect to paranoia. However, for the sake of completeness, I will start by discussing the draft on melancholia which Freud based on the diagram of sexuality initially drawn up for anxiety neurosis.

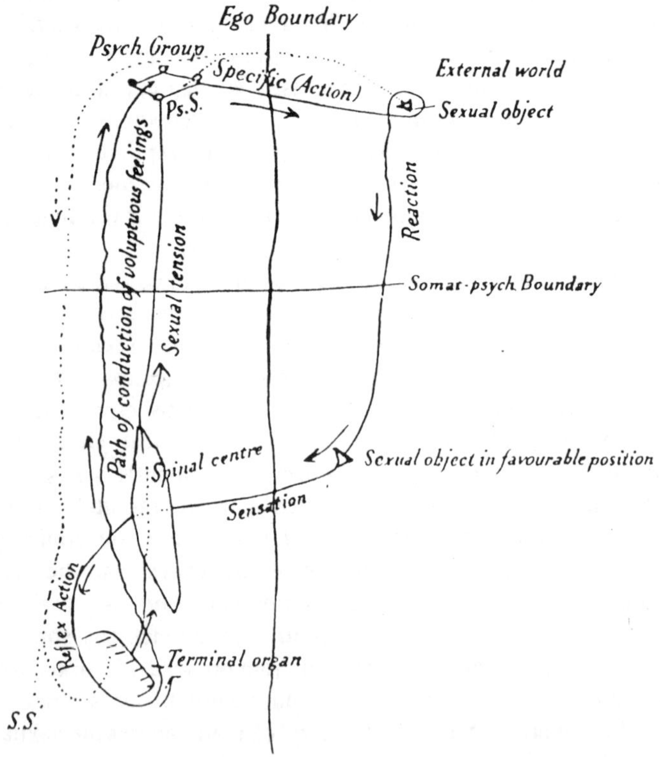

Fig. 1: Schematic diagram of sexuality[70]

The outline of melancholia focuses mainly on mapping out a reflexive interaction between the psyche and the soma, along the lines of that of the anxiety neurosis.[71] The affect that corresponds with melancholia is that of mourning, i.e. a longing for something lost: "*Thus in melancholia it must be a question of a loss — that is, a loss in instinctual life.*"[72] Freud further invokes the clinically observed frequent concurrence of melancholia and anaesthesia to formulate the following point: "(...) melancholia consists in mourning over the loss of libido."[73] Or put differently, the psychical "sexual group" does not receive any excitation from the somatic. This occurs when: 1. the production of somatic excitation sinks or ceases; 2. the sexual tension emanating from the somatic is derived from the psychical sexual groups, as is the case with masturbation; 3. the somatic excitation is put to some other use, for example when it is transformed into anxiety. The anaesthesia that often accompanies melancholia stems from the fact that the feeling of lust is suspended as a normal consequence of the discharge of the sexual tension from the end organs in the psychical "sexual group".

Despite the fact that Freud did retain some elements from his original draft, for his later description of melancholia, the emphasis lay primarily on the somatic and the reflexive.[74] By means of illustration I refer to his schematic diagram of sexuality, which served as guide line in mapping anxiety neurosis, neurasthenia and melancholia.

The driving force behind the entire process is the end organ functioning as the source of the somatic sexual tension which needs to be discharged in the appropriate way, i.e. via coitus.

Freud's next draft on paranoia is of an entirely different nature. He introduces his explanation by drawing a parallel between the delusional and the obsessional idea, both of which are traditionally interpreted as a disruption of the intellect. "If once obsessions have been traced back to an affective disturbance and it has been proved that they owe their strength to a conflict, then the same view must apply to delusions and they too must be the outcome of affective disturbances and must owe their strength to a psychological process."[75]

Chronic paranoia is a "(...) *pathological mode of defence*, like hysteria, obsessional neurosis, and hallucinatory confusion. People become paranoid over things they cannot put up with, provided they possess the peculiar psychic disposition for it."[76] Freud illustrates the nature of this disposition by referring to the following case, which he diagnosed as a case of paranoia.[77]

"An ageing spinster (about thirty) shared a home with her brother and (elder) sister. She belonged to the upper working class; her brother was working his way up to becoming a small manufacturer. Meanwhile they rented a room to a fellow worker, a much-travelled, rather enigmatic man, very skilful and intelligent, who lived with them for a year and was on the most companionable and sociable terms with them. Then the man went away, only to return after six months. This time he stayed for only a comparatively short time and then disappeared for good. The sisters often lamented his absence and could speak nothing but good of him. Nevertheless, the younger sister told the elder one of an occasion when he made an attempt at getting her into trouble. She had been tidying up the rooms while he was still in bed. He called her to his side, and when she unsuspectingly went, put his penis in her hand. There was no sequel to the scene; soon afterward the stranger left.

In the course of the next few years the sister who had this experience fell ill, began to complain, and eventually developed unmistakable delusions of observation and persecution with the following content. The women neighbours were pitying her for having been jilted and for still waiting for this man to come back; they were always making hints of that kind to her, kept saying all kinds of things to her about the man, and so on. All this, she said, was of course untrue. Since then the patient has only fallen into this state for a few weeks at a time; from time to time she becomes rational, explaining that it is all the result of the excitement; though even in the intervals she suffers from a neurosis which can without difficulty be interpreted as a sexual one. And soon she succumbs to a fresh thrust of paranoia.

The elder sister was astonished to notice that as soon as the conversation turned to the scene of the temptation, the patient denied it. Breuer heard of the case, the patient was sent to me, and I endeavoured to cure her tendency to paranoia by trying to reinstate the memory of that scene in its legitimate place. I failed in this. I talked to her twice; in concentration hypnosis got her to tell me everything to do with the lodger; in reply to my pressing inquiries about whether something "embarrassing" had happened, I received the most decided negation as an answer; and — saw her no more. She sent me a message to say that it upset her too much. Defence! That was obvious. She *wanted* not to be reminded of it and consequently intentionally repressed it.

There could be no doubt whatever about the defense; but she could just as well have acquired a hysterical symptom or an obsessional idea. What was the peculiarity of paranoid defense?

She was sparing herself something; something was repressed. We can guess what it was. Probably she had been really excited by what she saw and its memory. So what she was sparing herself was the reproach of being a "bad woman." That same reproach she then came to hear from outside. Thus *the factual content remained undisturbed*; what was altered, however, was something in the *placing* of the whole thing. Earlier it had been an internal self-reproach, now it was an imputation coming from outside. The judgement[78] about her had been transposed outward: people were saying what otherwise she would have said to herself. Something was gained by this. She would have had to accept the judgement pronounced from inside; she could reject the one arriving from outside. *In that way the judgement, the reproach, was kept away from her ego.*

The purpose of paranoia is thus to ward off an idea that is incompatible with the ego, by projecting its substance into the external world."

According to Freud paranoia involves the misuse of a commonly employed psychical mechanism, that of transposition ("Verlegung"), or projection. This mechanism offers an explanation for neurotic or normal delusions. "Whenever an internal change occurs, we have the choice of assuming either an internal or an external cause. If something deters us from the internal derivation, we naturally seize upon the external one. Second we are accustomed to our internal states being betrayed (by an expression of emotion) to other people."[79] In Freud's view, pathology can only occur when one is no longer conscious of these inner changes. When these elude one, one is left with a syllogism, i.e. the false connection as it is suggested in the projection mechanism.[80] "If we forget it and we are left with only the leg of the syllogism that leads outward, then we have paranoia, with its overvaluation of what people know about us and of what people have done to us. What do people know about us that we know nothing about, that we cannot admit? It is therefore an *abuse of the mechanism of projection for purposes of defence*."[81]
Unlike his theoretical approach to neurasthenia, anxiety neurosis and melancholia, Freud's draft on paranoia places his investigation at the very heart of the clinic of the excessively intense idea.[82]

1.2.4. The *Project* and the hypothesis *Q*

> "We can only say: 'We must call the Witch to our help after all.' — The Witch Metapsychology. Without metapsychological speculation and theorising — I had almost said 'fantasising' — we shall not get another step forward."
>
> *Sigmund Freud*[83]

Freud clings to his initial project to construct a comprehensive theory for all neuroses, even though the final outcome marks a substantial shift from it. As we can see from Draft D, this project dates from May 1894. Freud started by outlining the "Seksualschema" which seemed to provide a satisfactory explanation for the "Aktualneurosen". In this instance, the aetiology appeared to be almost wholly connected to the sex-glands and the vicissitude of the sexual excitation the glands produced. This immediately granted a certain status to the quantitative factor. However, an entirely different explanation needs to be provided for what surfaces in Freud's so-called clinic of the excessively intense idea.

Let us bear in mind the chronology of the development of Freud's line of reasoning. In early 1895, he discontinued his research on the diagram of sexuality as well as on neurasthenia, anxiety neurosis and melancholia, the explanation of which he had grafted onto this very diagram. As I argued earlier, Draft H on paranoia can be placed under the heading of the clinic of the excessively intense idea. During the first half of 1895, Freud understandably directed his attention to this field, as the imminent publication of the *Studies on Hysteria* suggests. The case descriptions collected in this work in progress had already been written at the time. The only missing part was Freud's own chapter on psychotherapy, which I have already examined extensively in this book. Freud wrote this particular chapter in March 1895.[84] This chapter reflects the shift in Freud's line of reasoning which was ultimately to lead to his writing of the *Project*. By writing down his conception of what psychical treatment can and should be, he paved the way for the construction of a psychological theory. The combination of some hypotheses he employed in his "Seksualschema" for the "Aktualneurosen", and what he learned from the clinic of the excessively intense idea plays an essential role in his undertaking. This shift is also apparent in the tone adopted by Freud in his letters to Fließ from April 1895 onwards. Here we learn that he no longer wished to develop a comprehensive theory of the major neuroses, i.e. a theory which focuses on the different vicissitudes of the actual sexual excitation. Instead he wished to develop a clinical psychology, that is to say, a psychology based on the clinic of the excessively intense idea. The letters written to Fließ from April to October 1895, i.e. the time during which he was working on the *Project*, indicate that this period was one of truly intense creativity. The psychology "torments" and "consumes [him] totally". At times he is "really exhausted" and "overworked". At end of April 1895 Freud writes: "Scientifically, I am in a bad way; namely, caught up in "The Psychology for Neurologists," which regularly consumes me totally until, actually overworked, I must break off. I have never before experienced such a high degree of preoccupation. And will anything come of it? I hope so, but it is difficult and slow going."[85] And a month later: "The main reason, however, was this: a man like me cannot live without a hobbyhorse, without a consuming passion, without — in Schiller's words — a tyrant. (...) It is psychology, which has always been my distant, beckoning goal, and which now, since I have come upon the problem of neuroses, has drawn so much nearer.[86]

His activity was indeed intense. For the difficulty facing him, i.e. that of explaining the talking cure, was overwhelming. The clinic required a theory to account for repression and its annihilation in speech, a theory which could explain the unmistakable determination of speech disrupted by the affect, a theory which could provide an explanation for the passion of the 'not-knowing' and of the 'unwillingness to know'. Finally, this theory was also to explain the purpose of the psychical treatment. What was required was a clinical psychology constituting the basis for a general psychology, since the demarcation line between pathological and normal psychical processes was ultimately quite arbitrary: "I am tormented by two aims: to examine what shape the theory of mental functioning takes if one introduces quantitative considerations, a sort of economics of nerve forces; and, second, to peel off from psychopathology a gain for normal psychology. Actually, a satisfactory general conception of neuropsychotic disturbances is impossible if one cannot link it with clear assumptions about normal mental processes. During the past weeks I have devoted every free minute to such work; I have spent the hours of the night from eleven to two with such fantasising, interpreting, and guessing, and invariably stopped only when somewhere I came up against an absurdity or when I actually and seriously overworked, so that I had no interest left in my daily medical activities. It will still be a long time before you can ask me about results."[87]

Freud takes the excessively intense idea as a point of reference for his scientific psychology.

An important question to ask is — just what is this clinic? "I start off from things which occur in hysteria without necessarily being peculiar to it. — Every observer of hysteria is struck in the first place by the fact that hysterical patients are subjected to a *compulsion* which is exercised by *excessively intense ideas*. An idea will, for instance, emerge in consciousness with particular frequency without the passage [of events] justifying it; or the arousing of this idea will be accompanied by psychical consequences that are unintelligible. The emergence of the excessively intense idea brings with it consequences which, one the one hand, cannot be suppressed and, on the other hand, cannot be understood — release of affect, motor innervations, impediments. The subject is by no means unaware of the striking character of the situation."[88]

With the reading of the *Studies on Hysteria* at back of one's mind, one can relatively easily form an idea of what Freud meant by excessively intense ideas. For example, let us recall the case of Lucy R. whose affliction can be seen as a prototype: although there was no pudding in sight, olfactory sensations of burnt pudding kept imposing themselves upon her mind. In other words, the *idea* of burnt pudding was so *intense* that it took on the form of an olfactory hallucination.

Nevertheless, in the *Studies* the expression "clinic of excessively intense ideas" is invested with a broader meaning. In a very general sense, this expression refers to psychotherapy or the psychical treatment based on the excessively intense speech which operates as the means par excellence to influence the psyche. In this respect, as Freud reports in the *Project*, the clinic of the excessively intense idea goes beyond that of hysteria, and includes that of obsessional neurosis, phobias and even that of paranoia.[89]

Apart from the quantitative factor, speech as it manifests itself in psychotherapy exhibits a second prominent characteristic: "Hysterical *excessively intense ideas* strike us, on the contrary by their oddity; they are *ideas* which in other people have no consequences and of whose importance we can make nothing. They appear to us as intruders and usurpers, and accordingly as ridiculous. Thus, *hysterical compulsion* is "(...) (1) *unintelligible*, (2) *incapable of being resolved by the activity of thought*, (3) *incongruous* in its structure".[90] The three aspects enumerated by Freud can essentially be boiled down to one characteristic. I will again draw on the case of Lucy R. to illustrate this. Firstly, in the initial stage of treatment her symptom was *unintelligible* to both herself and Freud, i.e. there was no rational explanation for her incidental olfactory perception of burnt pudding. Secondly, the symptom appears to be *incongruent*, in the sense that its connection to the general affect of mourning was grossly exaggerated: the loss of the pudding — or the mnemic idea of this loss by no means legitimises Lucy R.'s melancholia. Thirdly, her symptom cannot be resolved by the *activity of thought*, i.e. the symptom did not vanish until after the analysis when it had been "*explained* (made intelligible)".[91]

Broadly speaking, the statement 'after the analysis' denotes at least two things. On the one hand, it implies that she remembered the scene during which the olfactory hallucination originated and on the other, that she articulated the judgement or enunciation of the erotically coloured desires which she had repressed. For as we have seen, recollection on its own was not enough to cause her symptomatology and general state of mourning to disappear. For this to occur, she had to come to terms with her desire in the judgement. In other words, the three implications for the judgement are: the 'dissolution' or disappearance of the symptom, an understanding of it and an insight into its legitimacy.

In the *Project* Freud reconstructs this process as follows: "Before the analysis, *A* is an excessively intense idea, which forces its way into consciousness too often and each time gives rise to weeping. The subject does not know why he weeps at *A*; he regards it as absurd but cannot prevent it. After the analysis, it has been discovered that there is an idea *B*, which justifiably gives rise to weeping and which justifiably recurs frequently so long as a certain complicated psychic action[92] has not been performed against it by the subject. The effect of *B* is not absurd; it is intelligible to the subject and can even be combated by him.[93] *B* stands in a particular relation to *A*. For there has been an occurrence which consisted of *B+A*. *A* was an incidental circumstance; *B* was appropriate for producing the lasting effect. The reproduction of this effect in memory has now taken a form of such a kind that it is as though *A* had stepped into *B*'s place. *A* has become a substitute, a *symbol* for *B*. Hence the incongruity: *A* is accompanied by consequences which it does not seem worthy of, which do not fit in with it. (...) The *hysteric*, who weeps at *A*, is quite unaware that he is doing so on account of the association *A-B*, and *B* itself plays no part at all in his psychical life. The symbol has in this case taken the place of the *thing* entirely. "[94]

This reference to the clinic of the excessively intense idea makes substantial demands on clinical psychology, as a psychology of this kind needs perforce to provide an explanation for the *mechanism of repression*, the operation of repressed memories and the degree of efficiency of speech. For, "(...) analysis has led to the surprising conclusion: that for every *compulsion* there is a corresponding *repression*, that for every excessive intrusion into consciousness there is a corresponding amnesia."[95]

In other terms, pathological psychical processes exhibit an empirically observed pattern, and in Freud's mind, it is incumbent on psychology to conceptualise this pattern as it finds expression through speech. A point of departure for such an explanation is the unmistakably quantitative aspect of psychical processes: "The term 'excessively intense' points to quantitative characteristics. It is plausible to suppose that repression has the quantitative meaning of being denuded of *Q* and that the sum of the two [of the compulsion and the repression] is equal to the normal. If so, only the distribution has changed. Something has been added to *A* which has been subtracted from *B*. The pathological process is one of *displacement*, such as we have come to know in dreams — a primary process therefore."[96]

An important question to pose is what is the *motive* behind repression or the passion of the unwillingness to know, which seems to prevail in the talking cure. Put differently, what is the *regulating principle* of repression? Again, Freud finds an answer to this question in the clinic, more precisely in the characteristics of the repressed ideas. Firstly, after the analysis and the concurrent 'dissolution' of the ideogenically determined symptoms, one always seems to discover that "repression is invariably brought to bear on ideas which evoke a distressing affect (unpleasure) in the *ego*".[97] This means that the pathological process — repression — can only be explained if one accepts the *pleasure principle* as a regulating mechanism.[98]

Let me add at once that in Freud's view this is a quite common principle: "It is quite generally the case that we avoid thinking of what arouses only unpleasure, and we do this by directing our thoughts to something else. If, however, we accordingly manage to bring it about that the incompatible [idea] *B* seldom emerges in our consciousness, because we have so far as possible kept it isolated, yet we never succeed in forgetting *B* in such a way that we could not be reminded of it by fresh perception. Now an arousal of this kind cannot be precluded in hysteria either; the difference consists only in the fact that then, instead of *B*, *A* always becomes conscious — that is, cathected. Thus it is *symbol-formation* of this stable kind which is the function that goes beyond normal defence."[99] In other terms, the pleasure principle implies that defence is the general regulating mechanism of psychical processes.

The distinctive nature of pathological defence or hysterical repression must therefore be linked to a second characteristic of the repressed ideas, for as Freud's psychological analyses indicate, "sexual ideas are alone subjected to repression".[100] Freud refutes the most obvious explanation for the difference between normal defence and hysterical repression, namely that the difference would be of a quantitative nature. "It is quite impossible to suppose that distressing sexual affects so greatly exceed all other unpleasurable affects in intensity. It must be another characteristic of sexual ideas that can explain how it is that sexual ideas are alone subjected to repression."[101]

Emma

Freud refers to the analysis of Emma in order to disclose this distinctive "characteristic of sexual ideas". This case could be described as one of hysterical anxiety in virgins.[102] Emma came to Freud because she suffered from phobia. She was not able to go into shops *alone*. The reason she invoked for this was the memory of an incident that occurred to her when she was twelve years old, i.e. shortly after puberty.

"She went into a shop to buy something, saw the two shop-assistants (one of whom she can remember) laughing together, and ran away in some kind of *affect of fright*. In connection with this, she was led to recall that the two of them were laughing at her clothes and that one of them had pleased her sexually."

Freud could make nothing out of this:

"If she felt unpleasure at her clothes being laughed at, that must have been corrected long ago, ever since she has been dressing as a [grown-up] lady. Moreover, it makes no difference to her clothes whether she goes into a shop alone or in company. That she is not simply in need of protection is shown by the fact that, as happens with agoraphobia, even the company of a small child is enough to make her feel safe. And there is the quite incongruous fact that one of them pleased her; it would make no difference to this either, if she were accompanied."

Further investigation brought a second memory to light, once again a scene in a shop:

"On two occasions when she was a child of eight she had gone into a small shop to buy some sweets, and the shopkeeper had grabbed at her genitals through her clothes. In spite of the first experience she had gone there a second time; after the second time she stopped away. *She now reproached herself for having gone there the second time, as though she had wanted in that way to provoke the assault.*[103] In fact a state of 'oppressive bad conscience' is to be traced back to this experience. We now understand Scene I (shop-assistants) if we take Scene II (shopkeeper) along with it. We only need an associative link between the two. She herself pointed out that it was provided by the *laughing*; the laughing of the shop-assistants had reminded her of the grin with which the shopkeeper had accompanied his assault. The course of event can now be reconstructed as follows. In the shop the two assistants were *laughing*; this laughing aroused (unconsciously) the memory of the shopkeeper. Indeed, the situation had yet another similarity [to the earlier one] she was once again in a shop alone. Together with the shopkeeper she remembered his grabbing through her clothes; but since then she had reached puberty. The memory aroused what it was certainly not able to at the time, a *sexual release*, which was transformed into anxiety. With this anxiety, she was afraid that the shop-assistants might repeat the assaults, and she ran away."[104]

Emma's symptom is thus determined, like all hysterical symptoms, by the syllogism of the 'proton pseudos', located in both false connections, namely that "she was being laughed at on account of her clothes and that one of the shop-assistants had excited sexual pleasure in her".[105] Freud proceeds with his explanation:

"It might be said that it is quite usual, as happens here, for an association to pass through unconscious intermediate links until it comes to a conscious one. In that case, the element which enters consciousness is probably the one that arises special interest. In our example, however, it is noticeable precisely that the element which enters consciousness is not the one that arouses interest (assault) but another one, as a symbol (clothes). If we ask ourselves what may be the cause of this interpolated pathological process, only one presents itself — the *sexual release*, of which there is also evidence in consciousness. This is linked to the memory of the assault; but it is highly noteworthy that it [the sexual release] was not linked to the assault when this was experienced. Here we have the case of a memory arousing an affect which it did not arouse as an experience, because in the mean time the change [brought about] in puberty had made possible a different understanding of what was remembered. Now this case is typical of repression in hysteria. We invariably find that a memory is repressed which has only become a trauma by *deferred action*. The cause of this state of things is the retardation of puberty as compared with the rest of the individual's development."

Interpretation

The excerpt from Emma's case study serves as a prototype for what is invariably the substance of the psychical treatment as conceived of by Freud in 1895. There is a symptom, a complaint or problem for which the patient seeks his advice and which, so much is clear, needs to be promptly resolved. The cure, or to use Freud's words, the "dissolution" of the symptom is effectuated by *speech.*

This raises a first question as to the status of this speech. From both the *Project* and the *Studies*, it appears that in psychotherapy its status does not differ from that of the symptom: it is hysterical or falsely connected speech.[106] This speech is not only "falsely connected", in the sense that it is said to be "unintelligible, incapable of being resolved by the activity of thought and incongruous". To Freud, this predicate alludes to two other characteristics of speech, namely the falsely assessed or repressed erotic desires comprised in it, and the fact that it is determined by an equally falsely connected transference onto the physician.[107] These two characteristics are in essence two sides of the same coin: it is by recognising that the process of transference involves a false connection that one can come to the understanding that *speech is determined* by an unconscious erotic desire. This and no other is the lesson to be learned from the reading of the *Studies*.

Clinical psychology thence needs to offer first and foremost an explanation for the *determinant influence of the unconscious*. I should like to argue that Freud undertook the first systematic attempt at formulating such an explanation in the *Project*.

The sense or direction of this explanation is already discernable in the excerpt of Emma's case description, as well as in that of Katharina, which I discussed earlier on. What is the crucial element in these cases? In both cases, the symptomatology is determined by the repression of a sexual desire. However, this repression is doomed to fail, in the sense that the sexual desire finds expression in the symptomatology as determined by a *past* period, by memories or ideas as reminiscences to the desire, not of oneself, but of someone else.[108] This is the only meaning one can ascribe to the discrepancy between the periods preceding and following puberty. Puberty does indeed impose an 'altered understanding' of the sexual desire. In this connection, two essentially different possibilities are offered: the repudiation or repression of a sexual desire which leaves one at the mercy of the desire of another, or the assumption in the judgement of one's own sexual desire. Logically, in psychotherapy Freud is confronted with the first solution: it is a common fact of experience that coming to terms with a sexual desire is not an easy matter. No clinician will contradict the fact that often the onset of neuroses occurs during or shortly after puberty.

The problems he then had to face has three facets. Firstly, there was the need for a theory which could account for the law or determinants of the symptomatology which emerges in the absence of individual desire. Secondly, he faced the practical difficulty involved in accompanying neurotics whilst they assume their own desire. One can observe on reading the *Studies* that Freud was fairly competent as far as this field of psychotherapy was concerned. A third and entirely different possibility was the theoretical explanation of the operation of speech. It is obvious that the two theoretical nodal points are closely interconnected: for the first problem has to do with repression which only manifests itself in what one can interpret as the sudden recurrence of the repressed idea, whereas the second problem is concerned with the obliteration of this repression by speech.

Freud's φ-ψ-ω model of the psyche

In so far as one acknowledges that the aforementioned questions tie in with the issues proper to the "psychical treatment" or psychotherapy, one can then venture to verify the extent to which they are explained by Freud's theoretical construction as outlined in the first part of the *Project*, i.e. in the *General scheme*.

The actual object of this elaborate experiment of thought is to describe the modus operandi of psychical processes in general. This suggests that Freud does not confine his analysis to the pathological psychical processes but that, in keeping with his long cherished ambition, his outline is also conducive to an understanding of normal psychical processes.[109]

Contrary to what an initial, naive reading of the *Project* might suggest, it is not difficult to trace back to the clinic the materials Freud used for the construction of his system.

In the previous paragraphs, I have brought up enough arguments in connection with the quantitative factor, i.e. the hypothesis *Q*. There is undeniably a quantitative aspect to be distinguished in psychical processes. Hence the allusion to the clinic of the excessively intense idea does not seem to be a hyperbole. Freud, however, does leave aside the connotation he attached elsewhere (in his correspondence with Fließ for example) to this quantitative factor. The factor *Q* is tersely introduced as "what distinguishes activity from rest", "subjected to the general laws of motion".[110]

The second basic hypothesis, that of neurones *N* which are defined as the "determinate states of specifiable material particles", deceptively suggests that Freud was concerned with the elaboration of a strictly neurological theory.[111] This could have been the case were it not for the fact that a neurone cathected with a quantity *Q* is at one stage interpreted as an excessively intense idea. However, one ought *not* to evaluate this as an attempt by Freud to provide the material substratum of psychical processes. Rather, as his scepticism about a materialistic approach of this kind would suggest[112], he was intent on

constructing a model within which he could ascribe a *place* to the dynamic of the psychical processes he had observed.
This excessively intense idea needs to be allocated a place in the psychical apparatus. To this end Freud turned to neuroanatomy and neurophysiology, two fields he was familiar with and which, it seemed, could be put to use to achieve his end. Yet it soon becomes apparent that this text cannot simply be regarded as a neurological tractatus. Using these two frames of reference with admirable consistency and parsimony, Freud constructs the text from a psychological questioning. This transpires right from the beginning of the text where he gradually outlines his psychical apparatus with an eye to allocating a place to the *psychical* functions of *memory* and *consciousness*. But it becomes even more relevant halfway through the first part of the manuscript when he puts the apparatus in operation in his discussion of *the experience of satisfaction*. One is thenceforth face to face with what Freud was later to call "the witch of Metapsychology", or the theory of the psyche which is as essential as the brew of the witch whom Faust encountered when (still in the company of Mephistopheles) he was in his search for the truth.

In my view, the ratio between psychology and neurology in the *Project* can be formulated in the following way: the dynamic of the psychical processes as observed by Freud in the clinic of psychical treatment are, at first sight, governed by a number of factors and operational principles that belong to the field of neuroanatomy and physiology. One could thence argue that Freud's experiment of thought was prompted by his expectation that an orientation of his psychical apparatus to known neurological data could yield results for psychology. This conviction is echoed by what Freud contends at the beginning of the text: "Processes such as stimulus, substitution, conversion and discharge, which had to be described there [in connection with those disorders], directly suggested the conception of neuronal excitation as quantity of flow. It seemed legitimate to attempt to generalise what was recognised there."[113] It is certainly not the actual view held by Freud that was original, for this was a widespread idea in neurological circles at the end of the last century. However, what was original, was the use of neurology for a psychological questioning. I should like to direct your attention to the beginning of the second part of the book which deals with psychotherapy, where Freud writes: "The first part of this project contained what could be deduced from the basic hypotheses, more or less a priori, moulded and corrected in accordance with various factual experiences. This second part seeks to infer from the analysis of pathological processes some further determinants of the system founded on the basic hypotheses; a third part will hope to construct from the two preceding ones the characteristics of the normal passage of psychical events."[114]

An epistemological contrivance of this kind is not new in Freud's work. Earlier on, I pointed out how he managed to grasp the difference between organic and hysterical paralyses by redefining the concept of the "functional or dynamic lesion" in psychological terms. As with the *Project*, Freud reflected carefully upon the idea and only theorised the above distinction after having carried out a thorough scrutiny of the literature on neurology and more precisely on aphasia. Freud's advanced knowledge of neurology not only provided him with the indispensable auxiliary hypothesis, but it also made him aware of the limits of the explanatory potential of neurology.

Freud defines his object of study, the human psyche, as being in essence an organism exposed to influences from the outside world. In terms of the two auxiliary hypotheses *Q* and *N*, this implies that the nervous system of human beings is subjected to quantity *Q*, meaning that the organism absorbs the quantity *Q* to which it is exposed. This produces the image of a nervous system charged or cathected with quantity. The primary operational principle of this system is indicated by that of neuronal inertia: "(...) the principle of inertia explains the structural dichotomy [of neurones] into motor and sensory as a contrivance for neutralising the reception of $Q\dot{\eta}$ by giving it off."[115] In other words, the absorbed quantity is disposed of as quickly as possible. The argument and inspiration for this basic hypothesis comes from the clinical observation of the vicissitudes of the quantitative factor.[116]

However, the complexity of the human organism puts a limitation on the hypothesis of the principle of inertia. For the nervous system also receives endogenous stimuli which "have their origin in the cells of the body". These are responsible for the exigencies of life such as hunger, respiration and sexuality.[117] In order to eliminate needs of this kind the organism has to use a certain amount of quantity $Q\dot{\eta}$ which eventuates in alleviation, albeit a temporary one, of these exigencies. In the event of hunger, for instance, an amount of work needs to be carried out to absorb food.[118] As a result of this,

"(...) the nervous system is obliged to abandon its original trend to inertia (that is, to bringing the level [of *Qή*] to zero). It must put up with [maintaining] a store of *Qή* sufficient to meet the demand for a specific action. Nevertheless, the manner in which it does this, shows that the same trend persists, modified into an endeavour at least to keep the *Qή* as low as possible and to guard against any increase of it — that is, to keep it constant."[119]

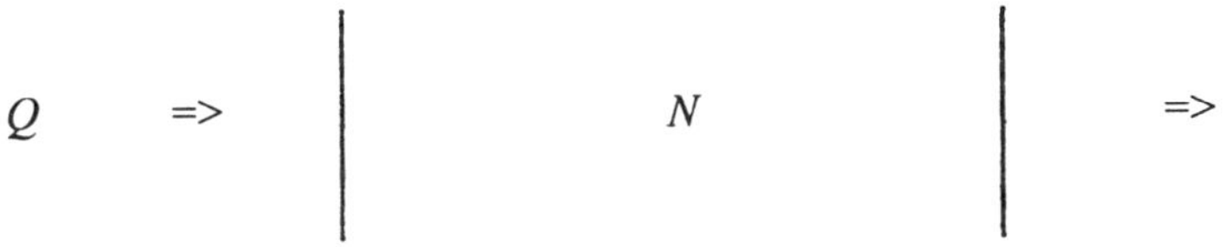

Fig. 2: The single neurone

Freud departs from the idea that the entire nervous system is comparable to a neurone, both in its structure and in its operation. In order to accommodate the psychical functions of respectively memory and consciousness, Freud is forced to extend this schematic representation of the nervous system to include the ϕ-ψ-ω model.[120] He constructs this model in stages and, in the course of his development, attributes the various parts to just as many neuro-anatomical entities. The representation of the dynamics of the apparatus thence refers to the way in which this complex deals with quantity *Q* which still affects it.

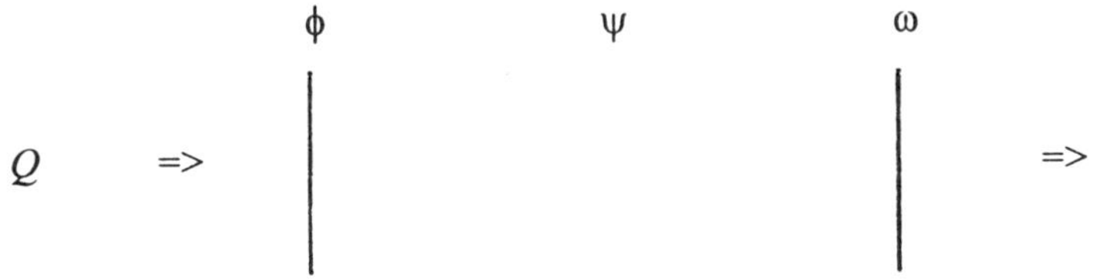

Fig. 3: The ϕ-ψ-ω model

The system ϕ is used to refer to the sensory neurones, i.e. the neurones which are in contact with the exterior world. They are the first to be exposed to physical quantities affecting the organism. However, the structure of the

human organism is such that it only absorbs a small fraction of the exterior physical vibrations. First, a selection is made: only certain periods from the existing continuum of physical vibrations can be absorbed and sent to ψ from which they proceed to ω where the sensation of quality is generated. Indeed, we only have a limited number of senses, each one of which functions as a sort of receptor for vibrations located within a well-defined period.
Secondly, the human organism functions as a sort of transformer, in this sense that quantities absorbed in the sensory nervous system are reduced to lower levels. The large quantities Q reaching one from the physical external world are converted in smaller psychical quantities $Q\eta$. Freud does not have the slightest idea about the absolute magnitude of these quantities, but he postulates the existence of a reduction formula for this conversion.[121] The system ϕ is accordingly the part of the neuronal apparatus that is the least able to lay claim to the appellation 'psychical'. It refers to the neuro-anatomical part of the nervous system which connects the organism to the external world. Its function is confined to the efficient conduction of the stimuli it receives.

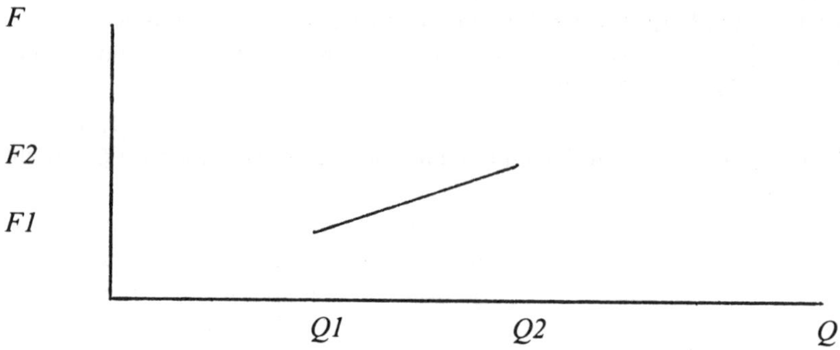

Fig. 4: The physical vibrations of the exterior world[122]

However removed from psychology it may be, a reasoning of this kind compels one to make some philosophical observations. The relation of human beings to reality seems extremely complex, even purely in terms of physical quantities. One has a very partial and distorted perception of physical reality. Indeed, by far the largest part of the vibrations which constantly affect human beings are not perceived at all.

However, the term 'perception' implies a part of the system where this perception is generated. For Freud argues that an actual psychology ought to account for what one calls in general perception or 'consciousness'.[123] This function impels Freud to postulate a second neuronal system located in the higher regions of the nervous system, which functions as the neuro-anatomical seat of consciousness. System ω or that of conscious perception, which is in direct connection with system ϕ, takes over the quality of the vibrations it receives, i.e. the frequency of the vibrations. For instance, the specific frequency of vibrations of a beam of light conjures up the quality 'green' in consciousness.[124]

This relatively simple and coherent system offers as yet no explanation for any psychical phenomenon whatsoever. The definition of consciousness as a place or structure where quality is absorbed and at the same time generated, leaves one none the wiser about consciousness as a psychical function. This reasoning is, so to speak, only relevant to the consciousness of a totally autistic organism, which admittedly absorbs quality, but which will never utter the word 'green'. For the time being, one also has to deny system ω the appellation 'psychical'.

The third system is introduced when Freud attempts to account for the second major psychical function, namely that of memory. For, "(...) a psychological theory deserving any consideration must furnish an explanation of 'memory'. Now any such explanation comes up against the difficulty that it must assume on the one hand that neurones are permanently different after an excitation from what they were before, while nevertheless it cannot be disputed that, in general, fresh excitations meet with the same conditions of reception as did the earlier ones. It would seem, therefore, that neurones must be both influenced and also unaltered, unprejudiced. We cannot off-hand imagine an apparatus capable of such complicated functioning; the situation accordingly saved by attributing the characteristic of being permanently influenced by excitation to one class of neurones, and, on the other hand, the unalterability — the characteristic of being fresh for new excitations — to another class."[125]

This lasting change consists in facilitating the association between various neurones through which quantity passes as it travels from ϕ to the motor innervation. Since the organism always needs to be restored to its former state for the quantity that continues to affect it, it is necessary to supply memory with a separate system, i.e. system ψ. This means that the neurones from the various systems must be ascribed different characteristics. The neurones from system ϕ are entirely permeable — i.e. the quantity meets no resistance at all — whereas those of system ψ are impermeable and accordingly in a position to accommodate memory or recollections. More particularly, "(...) memory is represented by the facilitations existing between the ψ neurones", or more accurately by "the *differences* in the facilitations between the ψ neurones".[126]

Metapsychology

The theoretical construction described above offers Freud a strictly neurological-mechanistic explanation for memory and consciousness. Both the neurology and the mechanics he draws upon are now considered as quite rudimentary. The contents of a book on natural sciences and an undergraduate course on neurology are sufficient to show that the ideas borrowed from these fields are not a figment of Freud's imagination.[127] Having said this, I should like to add that the neurological concepts employed were not especially elementary for that time. The notion of the contact barriers, essential to his explanation of memory, preceded the discovery of the synapse by years.[128] Even more striking is that this explanation of memory and consciousness has not as yet been refuted. Today it is still deemed acceptable to give a neurological explanation for memory in terms of attrition and to explain consciousness in terms of conversion of quantity in quality.[129]

Seen within the framework of the entire text, one could argue that Freud simply delineates and signposts the field within which the dynamic of psychical processes was to unfold. He would thenceforth no longer take biology, neurology and mechanics as a point of reference for the construction of his theory, but would lean towards what had to be explained clinically. To say the very least, the task he was faced with carrying out was daunting, as it was concerned with explaining the *fundamental determinant* of psychical processes.

The clinic sheds light on two aspects of the *nature* of this determinant. It is invariably of a *sexual* and *temporal* nature: it is sexual in the sense that every psychological analysis points at an essential junction, i.e. the relation of the subject to sexuality. And it is temporal in the sense that every neurotic problem seems to be determined by the *past*. A clinical psychology worthy of any attention must therefore offer an explanation for the determinant of psychical processes by combining these two, i.e. the '*sexual past*'.

I therefore wish to advocate the following thesis: *Freud equipped himself with a topos to represent this sexual past in his φ-ψ-ω model. The system ψ yields a place impervious to consciousness where sexuality as a mainspring can only appear when represented and hence determined by mnemic images or memory-traces. In other words, sexuality acquires the status of an unconscious drive, which is halfway between the physical and the psychical.*

Let me clarify this statement. After having constructed the φ-ψ-ω model Freud was mainly intent on putting it into operation. The first step he took in this direction was to redefine the fundamental principle of neuronal activity in connection with quantity *Q*. "Since we have certain knowledge of a trend in psychical life towards *avoiding unpleasure*, we are tempted to identify that trend with the primary trend towards inertia. In that case *unpleasure* would have to be regarded as coinciding with a raising of the level of *Qή* an increasing quantitative pressure: it would be the ω sensation when there is an increase of *Qή* in ψ."[130] Freud thence locates the essence of psychical processes in system ψ, the nexus of which "(...) is connected with the paths by which endogenous quantities of excitation ascend. Without excluding the possibility of these paths being connected with φ, we must nevertheless hold to our original assumption that a direct pathway leads from the interior of the body to ψ neurones. If this is so, however, ψ is exposed to Qs on this side without protection and in this fact lies the *mainspring* of the psychical mechanism."[131] And later on he writes: "ψ is at the mercy of *Q*, and it is thus that in the interior of the system there arises the impulsion which sustains all psychical activity. We know this power as the *will* — the derivative of the *instincts*."[132]

The status Freud ascribes to consciousness also shows that the system ψ contains the nucleus and source of psychical processes: "A word on the relation of this theory of consciousness to others. According to an advanced mechanistic theory, consciousness is a mere appendage to physiologico-psychical processes and its omission would make no alteration in the psychical passage [of events]. According to another theory, consciousness is the subjective side of all psychical events and is thus inseparable from the physiological mental process. The theory developed here lies between these two. Here consciousness is the subjective side of one part of the psychical processes in the nervous system, namely of the ω processes; and the omission of consciousness does not leave psychical events unaltered but involves the omission of the contribution from ω."[133] The "advanced mechanistic theory" is, for example, found in Meynert, who equated the psyche with consciousness and thus believed that consciousness was entirely determined by the physical — the psychical being only an epiphenomenon. In the *Project*, Freud counters this with the notion of consciousness as the epiphenomenon of unconscious ψ processes.

However, the notion of the endogenous quantity *Qή* conceived of as a driving force only highlights one aspect of the unconscious determinants Freud wanted to explain. In order to determine the course of these psychical processes more accurately, Freud turned to an indication from the clinic at his disposal according to which the drive, i.e. the affect, only occurs when linked or coupled to ideas.[134] The system ψ offered the possibility of ascribing a place to what one could call the representation of the drive. By postulating the connection between the system ψ and the source of the quantity *Qή* within the organism one ipso facto determines psychical processes in terms of memory. By doing this, Freud attributed a place to what I referred to as the 'sexual past'.

Freud carried this analysis even further by querying the origin of the very first barrier the endogenous quantity *Qή* inexorably had to cross. He pertinently located the origin or the very first 'facilitation' in the dialectic between the mother and the child, more precisely in what he called the first experience of satisfaction which dictates the course followed by all the subsequent psychical processes.[135]

One can thus see that at this point Freud unmistakably and definitively veers toward psychology. He no longer speaks about an abstract ϕ-ψ-ω model, but about a new born child exposed to quantity on both sides (i.e. exogenous and endogenous quantities).

On the one hand, there are the large quantities emanating from the external world which affect the child. For instance, the fatherly slap given by the physician to the child's buttocks, or the sudden change of pressure which it experiences when it leaves the amniotic fluid for the outside air.[136] The new-born child's reaction occurs by means of reflex contrivances and it is a natural reaction in its attempt to rid himself of the quantity *Q* via motor innervation: this is of course the first cry.

However, the child's organism is very complex. Quantities *Qή* are also released from within the body. These endogenous *Qή* are very small and released constantly. For instance, such quantities $Q\eta$ are operational when the child is hungry or thirsty; in other words when its life is in danger. It also wishes to discharge these quantities $Q\eta$, but it is clear that for this endogenous source of excitation to cease to exist, a specific action needs to be performed in the external world. The child, who is premature by definition, is incapable of doing this. It is unable to employ the constant accumulation of endogenous quantities in an efficient manner. It must thence rely on the kindness of what Freud calls the "Nebenmensch", i.e. the fellow human being.[137]

The sequence of events occurs as follows. The accumulated quantities are first discharged via motor innervation, i.e. when the child cries. The mother, as a fellow human being 'interprets' these cries as 'hunger' or 'thirst' and breast-feeds it, which brings about a temporary alleviation of the excitation. "In this way this path of discharge acquires a secondary function of the highest importance, that of *communication* ["Verständigung"], and the initial helplessness of human beings is the primal source of all *moral motives*."[138]

This event constitutes the child's first 'mythical' experience of satisfaction, and has a lasting influence on system ψ. Initially, the discharge of quantity $Q\eta$ occurs with as a result the disappearance of unpleasure. In addition, the two pallium neurones are cathected with quantity. These two neurones correspond to the perception of the object of satisfaction (the breast) and the perception of the reflexive movement (sucking) respectively. Here, Freud invokes the law of association by simultaneity. In the event of simultaneous cathexis, quantity $Q\eta$ passes over from neurone α to β. In other words, a facilitation or association is established between α and β.[139]

At a second stage, the primary state of urgency or longing reappears and the cathexis is transferred to the two mnemic images. This state produces a result that is identical to the initial perception, but in this instance it is to be described as a hallucination. The difference lies in the failure to discharge quantity $Q\eta$. The urgency therefore persists and unpleasure is produced.

This suggests that the course in ψ is informed by an original experience of satisfaction and consequently that all subsequent passages of quantity are determined by the primary dialectic between the child and its fellow human being. Every increase of quantity $Q\eta$ in the nucleus of ψ cathects the associated neurones, which results in a primary attraction to the object of desire or, more accurately, to the mnemic image of it.[140]

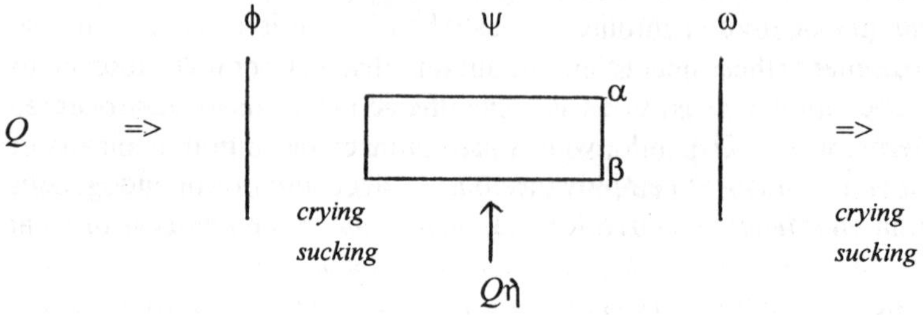

Fig. 5: The experience of satisfaction

The second prototype Freud alludes to in order to illustrate the effect of quantity on the new-born child is the experience of pain. With pain large quantities *Q* break through φ and pass over to ψ, again leaving a lasting influence.

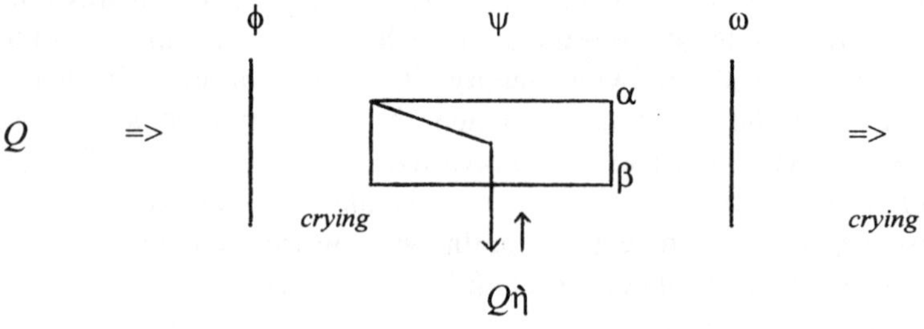

Fig. 6: The "Verpönung" or punishment

In the initial stage the large rise in the level of *Qή* in ψ is perceived as unpleasure in ω, which is conducive to the inclination to discharge in a certain direction, and initiates a facilitation between the latter — the direction of the discharge — and a mnemic image. In order to explain how unpleasure is nevertheless experienced in the absence of such a large rise in quantity *Qή*, Freud postulates the existence of secretory neurones located in the nucleus of ψ. These secretory neurones are only excited when a certain level is reached — as in the case of pain — and they release additional quantity *Qή* into the body. This produces a fourth effect in ψ, i.e. the facilitation between mnemic images and the secretory neurone.

At this juncture Freud makes an important observation with respect to sexuality. The sexual quantity *Qή* is also released via secretory neurones. In other words, when a sufficient rise of quantity takes place in the nucleus of ψ. *This means that for Freud it is possible to trace the origin of sexuality back to the first mythical primeval age when the primary experience of satisfaction or pain took place. This accordingly implies that he defines sexuality as an affect, i.e. something which is suddenly released as the consequence of an association with experiences of this kind.*[141]

Alongside the primary experiences of satisfaction and pain, Freud introduces the notion of the ego.[142] The ego is defined as the sum of the ψ cathexes at a given time, i.e. a group of associated or well cathected neurones. The ego is the organisation that orientates, directs or interferes with the passage of quantity, depending on the course followed by the primary experience. The primary function of the ego is thus to divert the passage of quantity. This can occur in two ways depending upon whether the primary experience was one of satisfaction or pain. For the primary experience is then repeated: "Both states are of the greatest importance for the passage [of quantity] in ψ, for they leave behind them motives for it which are of a compulsive kind. The wishful state results in a positive *attraction* towards the object wished-for, or, more precisely, towards its mnemic image; the experience of pain leads to a repulsion, a disinclination to keeping the hostile mnemic image cathected. Here we have primary *wishful attraction* and primary *defence* [fending off]."[143]

In the first case the initial mnemic image procuring satisfaction is recathected. This process has two possible outcomes: in the presence of the object the experience of satisfaction follows, whereas in the absence of the object unpleasure sets in in the long run.[144] In the second case, the mechanism of attention indicates to the ego that the mnemic image of the hostile object is going to be cathected. Again, this has two potential outcomes.[145] If the hostile object is effectively present, then the child starts to cry. Alternatively, the mnemic image is discharged as quickly as possible. Freud terms this mechanism as that of the primary defence, which is only made possible by the intervention of the ego which enables a side-cathexis to occur.

One can thence argue that the prototypical experience of satisfaction or pain is conducive to the constitution of the ego which in turn dictates the course of all the subsequent psychical processes by means of the mechanisms of wishful attraction and defence. This suggests that all psychical processes can be conceived of as either a repetition of the primary experience of satisfaction or as an attempt to obviate the primary experience of pain.[146]

Every psychical process is determined by the possibilities the ego has at its disposal to rid itself of quantity. If this organisation cannot rely on side-cathexis, or if the function of judgement fails, hallucinatory satisfaction or a feeling of unpleasure devoid of external reality materialises. Both states result strictly from the ego's incompetence to master the endogenously released quantities.

1.3. Conclusion

The theoretical model of the psyche propounded by Freud is certainly audacious and speculative, but decidedly not naive.

An important achievement of his attempt at providing an explanation for defence or repression lies in the *notion of the drive as being halfway between the somatic and the psychical.* In this respect, the *Project* can be interpreted as a combination of what Freud could observe in the clinic of the excessively intense idea and the schematic diagram of sexuality drawn up for the alleged clinical entity of the "Aktualneurosen". The clinician can only gain access to this drive, which is essentially directed at the original object of satisfaction that was lost, by means of its representations, i.e. the recollections retained in system ψ as a fall-out of the initial experience of satisfaction and as the direction of the passage or the motive.

Secondly, Freud's use of the primary experiences of satisfaction or pain locates the pleasure principle — a concept he claimed to have borrowed from Fechner — in the *early stage of the life history* of the subject.[147] Without doing away with the clinical view of the importance of puberty in the aetiology of neuroses, Freud paves the way for a theory on *infantile sexuality* and even on *the Oedipus complex* which betokens the ultimate motive of repression. For it is impossible to allocate another signification to the impact of the attribution of meaning by the fellow human being — who is "simultaneously the first satisfying object and further his first hostile object" whose desire is signified to the neonatus.[148]

CHAPTER 2

The hypothesis of the neurone N

"A man like me cannot live without a hobbyhorse, without a consuming passion, without — in Schiller's words — a tyrant. (...). It is psychology which has always been my distant, beckoning goal, and which now, since I have come upon the problem of neuroses, has drawn so much nearer."

Sigmund Freud[1]

2.1. Introduction

I will now introduce the second pillar of my discussion of the *Project*, namely the concept of neurone *N*. Just what is the status of this concept within Freud's experiment of thought? What does it yield for the "psychology for neurologists"?[2] Which of the questions brought up by his clinic of the excessively intense idea find an answer thanks to this concept, and which of those do not?
The reader may observe that these questions are analogous to those formulated with respect to the concept of quantity. Whether these questions are formulated in an adequate way, is another matter which, I hope, will become more tangible by the end of my discussion. From all that has gone before, one can surmise that it is not necessary to turn to neurology for the question about the meaning of the neurone as it poses itself within the *Project* considered as a clinical psychological text. I therefore maintain the reference to Freud's clinic.
The construction of the *Project* offers a clue to the questions posed above. This text departs from the clinical observation of the excessively intense idea which can be conceived of as a "*cathected* neurone filled with a certain $Q\eta$, while at other times it may be empty".[3] Having constructed a model for the

psyche on the basis of his fundamental hypothesis, in the second part of his study Freud returns to "the analysis of pathological processes" in order to "infer further determinants of the system".[4] Here the status of the neurone *N* as an aid or an instrument of thought finally becomes clear, as the description of the psyche as consisting of various systems of neurones enables one to attribute a *place* or *topos* to repressed ideas within the psyche.[5] In this respect, Freud's psychology is not so much an economics of *neurones*, but rather an economics of *ideas*, an economics which is only accessible via speech as it materialises under transference, via hysterical speech or via falsely connected speech. In other words, by means of the metonymy "*idea — neurone — idea*", Freud attempted to insert a *linguistic* aspect into his theory.

However, this working hypothesis still leaves the question about the *sense* of attributing an idea to a neurone unanswered. In other terms, what does one achieve by directing one's attention to neurology for the problem of speech? Does Freud's 'epistemological operation' or experiment of thought entail more than just an orientation? At this point it would be wise to go back once more to some aspects of this speaking as it presents itself in Freud's clinic in order to highlight the relevance of the *Project*.

First of all, in psychotherapy one is dealing with a falsely connected *speech*, i.e. a form of speech that is anything but intelligible to the listener. This status is incontrovertibly disclosed when the hysterical patients' "belle indifférence" towards their own suffering disappears and their excessively intense symptoms seem to become invested with meaning, i.e. they henceforth appear as a "symbol formation" for the repressed memories or ideas.[6] However, this same explanation can also be found elsewhere in Freud's writings dating from about 1895, and it does not in itself necessitate the attribution of an idea to a neurone.[7] Indeed, Freud could have chosen to restrict himself to Herbartian psychology, and by so doing would perhaps have excluded neurology from his theory.

However, on a closer reading of the *Project* one discovers the distinct advantage of his neurologically inspired model, especially with respect to the efficiency of the rule of *free association*. Clinical psychology, defined as the psychology of speech, must after all provide an explanation for the *effect* of speech. In a general sense, this effect can be described as *the obliteration of repression* by means of speech which in turn constitutes the conditio sine qua non for *recollection*. Freud's analysis of the *mechanism of attention* will shed more light on this matter.

Two other features of the speech under transference present a more serious problem.

Firstly, there is the element of catharsis which remains an essential part of speech — in spite of the fact that in the *Studies* Freud had already distanced himself from the conception of the psychical treatment as involving a pure discharge of the contracted affect. The energetic "utterance" [absprechen] and "speaking out" [aussprechen] indicate that the effective verbal expression is affective and prompt Freud to describe the aim of the talking cure as the "Affekt Worte geben", i.e. *putting* the affect *into words*.

Secondly, therapeutic speech is typified by the structure or form of the *subjective judgement*, which can be described as a judgement or statement which incorporates the speaker, or even better, as *a judgement or statement relative to the subjective desire*. In his chapter on psychotherapy, Freud hints at this characteristic, arguing that "(...) the treatment would lie in the accomplishment of a psychical act which did not take place at the time".[8] This raises the question as to what this psychical act could be. If one looks for the answer to this in the case histories featured in the *Studies*, one is forced to see this psychical act as the *subjective judgement*.[9] A second argument in favour of this interpretation can be drawn from the fact that Freud stresses that the "Verneinung" or negation is an inescapable avatar of judgement which helps the subject come closer to his/her own truth. Indeed, Freud's concepts of defence and repression reflect the very processes he was confronted with in all of his "psychological analyses", i.e. the passion of the *unwillingness to know*. The field of the negation lies between two poles: that of the conversion symptoms which operate like an "Ersatz" or substitute for the idea and its concomitant affect, and that of a coming to terms with one's own desire in the judgement. "Something has occurred to me now, but it has *nothing* to do with the subject. I am only saying it because you want to know everything."[10] Negative judgements of this kind abound in psychotherapy, and to Freud they form a welcome indication that the truth is impending.

Therefore, one ought not to be surprised to see that the *Project*, as an answer to the clinic of the excessively intense idea, makes room for the psychical function of the act of judging. If one accepts that in the *Studies* Freud ascribed the status of judgement to the therapeutically effective speech and to the coming to terms with a subjective desire, as seems to be suggested in his case descriptions, then his metapsychology of the judgement, as described in the *Project*, satisfies an important requirement which clinical psychology needs to meet. A psychology of this kind has to account for the determining influence of the subjective life history on the desire. It is in this context that Freud masterfully makes use of the fundamental hypothesis of neurone *N*. The neurone *N* and the system of neurones, which he gradually developed in his experiment of thought, provide a 'substratum' in which the life history can be inscribed — the life history being the result of the primary dialectic between the subject and the fellow human being ("Nebenmensch"). This implies that Freud not only evaluated the effects of speech in the course of the psychical treatment, but that he also attempted to provide a metapsychology of *language acquisition.*

The three aspects of speech or judgement in psychotherapy are: remembering the affect, putting it into words and the assumption of a subjective desire in the judgement. The first two aspects can be explored on the basis of the *function of judgement* as described by Freud in the *Project*. However, it will prove much more difficult to account for the third aspect, whose theoretical degree of complexity is reflected in clinical practice.

2.2. Wilhelm Jerusalem's theory of judgement

> "All that thy fathers leave to thee,
> At once enjoy it — thus alone
> Can man make anything his own;
> A hindrance all that we employ not —
> A burden all that we enjoy not."
>
> *Goethe*

In his correspondence with Fließ, Freud reports that Wilhelm Jerusalem's book was the source of two crucial insights leading to his *psychology of judgement*. On 25 May 1895, he feverishly wrote to his friend: "A book by W. Jerusalem, *Die Urtheilsfunction* [*The Function of Judgement*], has greatly advanced me; in it I discovered two of my principal ideas: *that judging consists in a transference into motoric sphere, and that internal perception cannot claim to be 'evidence'*."[11] That Freud's enthusiasm was well-founded, and that in addition to the two ideas mentioned, more arguments in support of his theory were to be found in Jerusalem's work, will I hope emerge from my review. I will explore Jerusalem's theory of judgement fairly extensively, not only because I believe that it is a masterful piece of scholarly work, in both form and content, and because it possesses a limpid style of reasoning which makes the study of this book really enjoyable, but also to form an idea about the elements Freud borrowed from it for his metapsychology of speech and its concurrent effects.[12]

What is a judgement? — The statute of the theory

The observation that "all our understandings take on the form of a judgement" forms the point of departure of this book.[13] For instance when, on the basis of sensory perceptions, one says: "it's raining", "it's thundering", "the sea is stormy", and also when one sums up the product of a prolonged reflection in simple sentences such as, "Kant's *Critique of Pure Reason* represents a turning point in the history of philosophy", one is making a judgement or statement. In a general sense, a judgement can be defined as "(...) the form in which one shapes, formulates, expresses and makes accessible to others both the simplest as well as the most complicated thought-contents".[14]
To Jerusalem the question about the essence of judgement is first and foremost a *psychological* question. This means that when the components involved in the act of judging have been revealed through a psychological analysis and when the relations that exist between judgement and other psychical processes have come to light, then and only then does one have the necessary foothold for the research into the logical and epistemological meaning of these modes of thought.[15] The *psychology of judgement* thence constitutes the bedrock and condition for the entire field of theoretical philosophy. Kant's question — "what is our contribution to the coming into existence of experience?"— cannot be answered, devoid of any transcendental and a priori elements, before one has penetrated the problem of judgement.[16] Questions of logic and epistemology do not as such come under consideration in this book. Nevertheless Jerusalem expects his psychological research into the act of judging to yield something for these fields, "in any case, this must fall into our lap like a ripe fruit and it must by no means have a predetermined goal".[17]

Description of psychical processes

The necessary demarcation of *psychical* and *physical* phenomena represents the first step in the construction of his theory. Jerusalem criticises the widespread belief holding that "psychical processes are known to us via inner perception".[18] This explanation is not satisfactory since physical processes also take place in inner organisms. Where then does the distinction between the two lie? "I believed it could be found in consciousness. Physiological processes take place without consciousness whereas psychical ones acquire their existence ("Dasein") by becoming conscious. I explained this characteristic in my *Lehrbuch der Psychologie* and it also proved extremely useful for didactic purposes. However, the issue of unconscious psychical processes either remained wholly unsolved, or it had to be decided in the manner of the French School. Ribot, the main representative of this school, only considers the physiological process as that which actually occurs, while consciousness (i.e. the psychical) seems to him to be a quite secondary appendage (surajouté)."[19]

Nonetheless there must exist a distinct feature that differentiates the psychical from the physical. Both are *processes* and Heraclitus's *panta rei* is applicable in all instances: "Only when one subjects physical occurrences to judgement (...) does it appear that the physical is always bound to a substratum. Even the child who looks into the world sees all around him things which he cannot but interpret as bearers of qualities and states. (...) An occurrence devoid of substratum is completely incomprehensible in nature."[20]

However, when on the other hand one takes a closer look at mental life, one invariably observes that one is dealing with occurrences which are utterly devoid of substratum. Thus the 'soul' can, at the very most, be regarded as the logical subject. On a more meticulous analysis we see that "(...) putting the ego forward as the subject of our psychical predicates leads to the immediate evaporation of this ego, which then appears as a group of processes which isolate themselves from the rest of the content of our consciousness on account of their constant nature, and which thereby acquires a certain autonomy".[21]

This distinction between physical and psychical phenomena can ultimately stake no major claims. "Physical phenomena *cannot be thought* without a substratum and conversely, psychical phenomena cannot be thought with a substratum. At the end of my description, I will investigate to what extent one is allowed to eliminate the factor 'be thought' on either side of this inequality and also, whether one may conclude, on the basis of the diversity of the mental phenomena, that this diversity is mirrored in the actual processes. Here I will only deal with phenomena and it may be readily admitted that this distinction exists."[22] This is a truly subtle reasoning![23]

From a scientific point of view, one could argue that the brain does provide a substratum for psychical processes. Jerusalem however repudiates this argument by arguing that the brain can only be regarded as the substratum for physiological processes. Due to the singular character of psychical phenomena, one cannot regard a non-psychical substratum as being their bearer. "I therefore maintain that psychical occurrences are essentially devoid of substrata and are only revealed as being linked to a substratum when empirically observed in conjunction with a physical occurrence."[24]

If one bears this difference in mind, "(...) then the hypothesis of *unconscious psychical phenomena* no longer presents any noteworthy difficulty. The characteristic of the lack of substratum remains when the property of consciousness is omitted. Let us further remember that we know of no other processes devoid of substratum apart from psychical ones, which enables us to assert, free of any contradiction, that all processes devoid of substratum are psychical, but that they are not all conscious."[25] Everyday experience impelled Jerusalem to take into account the existence of unconscious psychical processes. For example, when older ideas suddenly re-emerge, one can assume that they existed as unconscious psychical phenomena in the meantime.

He quotes an excellent example of this phenomenon from the autobiography of Grillparzer. It describes how Grillparzer's work on his trilogy *Das goldene Vlies* was interrupted in 1819 by the death of his mother and a trip to Italy. On his return, the writer took a holiday in order to finish his work. However, the entire plan he had previously devised had sunk into oblivion. Only by chance, when playing some of Beethoven's symphonies with a lady friend, was his plan brought back to his mind. He then recalled having played the same symphonies on a number of occasions with his mother before his departure.

How can a 'forgetfulness' of this kind be explained? A physiological monist might contend that the music notes conjured up cerebral processes along with the concurring psychical phenomena. But where did these psychical phenomena reside in the meantime? A physiological monist, such as Ribot, could reply that there must have been a physiological disposition available which was actualised anew by the musical notes. Jerusalem does not share this view. Such a disposition could not account for the repetition of a psychical act or memory.

Jerusalem's stance is clearly that a specific explanation has to be found for each of the two series. The presupposed *Dph* cannot be proposed as an explanation for the two *Aps*. Conversely, he militates in favour of accepting a psychical disposition. In the example of Grillparzer, Jerusalem neither indicates what he believes the psychical disposition to be, nor does he explain forgetting. However, from a clinical view point, it is not difficult to interpret the association between the forgetting of the draft of his literary project and the death of his mother as the motive of his forgetfulness, while the presupposed physiological disposition still needs to be discovered. "Whether one calls these unconscious processes psychical dispositions or whether one wishes to describe them as residing below the threshold of consciousness, is only a question of terminology which in essence alters nothing to the heart of the matter. However, since the imagery created a certain degree of confusion in the field of psychology, I propose to use the term 'unconscious processes' or the 'unconscious' which is of course not remotely connected to any form of metaphysics along the lines of Hartmann's. As well as concision, the term offers the advantage of being easily subdividable into excited and non-excited unconscious, a distinction which Benno Erdmann wielded rather successfully."[26]

Aph Dph Aph
Aps Dps Aps

In which:

Aps = the occurrence of the idea
Aph = the corresponding physiological process
Dps = the psychical disposition
Dph = the physiological disposition

Jerusalem proceeds with the following passage which, to say the very least, would not clash with Freud's work: "The unconscious, whose existence cannot be ascertained by means of direct experience, is to me an instrument of thought, which I cannot do without for understanding mental life. An instrument of thought is expected to be freed of contradiction and serviceable. Since the essence of psychical processes is not revealed in consciousness, but in the absence of a substratum, we can construct the concept of unconscious psychical processes and implement it without any contradiction. I conceive of this unconscious as being also devoid of a substratum and as a constant occurrence permanently affecting mental life. Indeed, one is continually exposed to the effect of unconscious psychical processes, and precisely these processes constitute the main component of our mental personality. Verbal expression can show us at any time the operation of unconscious processes, and hypnotic phenomena[27] too point in the same direction. I cannot do without the unconscious, and I believe I have achieved the right to put this instrument of thought to use in my theory of judgement."[28]

These inspiring words testify to the fact that Jerusalem was on the same wavelength as Freud. However, the use Jerusalem was to make of this instrument of thought remained very restricted. This can be explained by the fact that his investigation did not depart from the "constant effect of unconscious psychical processes". The difference from Freud's project is best formulated as follows: while Jerusalem is driven by his attempt at understanding the *successful or adequate judgement,* which could help him draw conclusions about the Kantian question of the extent of Man's contribution to the coming into existence of experience, Freud essentially starts from the *judgement disrupted* by the affect or Eros, from the syllogism or the false connection. Freud substituted the psychological question of *denying* for the philosophical question of *knowing*. Jerusalem's great merit is his acknowledgement of the operative unconscious which lends his book an additional dimension. However, unlike Freud's work, it cannot be said to represent a demonic theory.

The genetic and the biological viewpoint

For Jerusalem the psychology of the act of judgement involves first and foremost its *analysis*. This presupposes that the act of judgement, as a composite process, lends itself to an analysis of this kind.[29] However, every psychological analysis not only reveals something about the components of the process, but also about its *genesis*. As a result, the analytical method leads to a *genetic conception.*[30] "If ideas, feelings and desires are the basic elements of mental life, then one is forced to ask one self: 'what comes about first?' With the help of inner perception, experiment and even more effectively, the observation of a child's mental life and that of primitive people, one must attempt to advance hypotheses about the origin of Man's conscious mental life.[31] If Horwicz turns out to be right in asserting that mental life is founded on "pleasure and unpleasure along with the immediate reaction they produce", and if one could make acceptable the view that it is only the differentiation of this process which in turn creates sensations, perceptions and ideas, then the more complex thought processes could probably be understood as links in this chain of development."[32]

In the *Project*, Freud shares Jerusalem's view on this point. As we have already seen, the pleasure principle makes up the bedrock of the operation of the ϕ-ψ-ω model. The development mentioned in Jerusalem's work is described in terms of the "differentiation of this original sense of life" for which "the reactions of our psycho-physical organism, the movements with which our organism responds to the effects of the external world, are normative".[33]

Even more pertinent for the first of the two crucial ideas that Freud gleaned from this book, i.e. that every judgement consists in a transference in the motoric sphere, is the acknowledgement that what Jerusalem terms here the "sense of life" (the pleasure principle) is a fundamental constituent of judgement: "The way in which we react to external impressions has, as it gradually appears to me with more clarity, an essential and normative influence on the way in which we conceive of these impressions. 'We conceive of the world as we shape it', said Lazarus, and one might perhaps argue in a more general and accurate sense: that we conceive of the world in function of how we react to it. In this way, it would appear that, psychologically speaking, our contribution to the coming into existence of experience is substantial and that this contribution is made up of appropriate reactions to external impressions. A particular case of this general law is perhaps that *language* — which originally is undoubtedly nothing but an expression of emotion, (...) — remained for a long time confined to the *expression of emotional judgements* which contributed substantially to the formation of a world view, i.e. the structuring of our ideational contents, by means of connection between these judgements and other available elements. The aim of my investigation is to demonstrate that such a connection of various reactional modes exists in the act of judgement and that the essence of the act of judgement can only be laid bare by establishing these elements."[34] Independently of the philosophical implications it carries for Kant's question, Freud found an argument in favour of the view holding that every linguistic expression — as an avatar of judgement[35] — is accompanied by movement, i.e. a discharge of quantity $Q\eta$. Or as he put it in a letter to Fließ, that "*judging consists in a transference into the motoric sphere.*"[36] This notion could easily be inserted into Freud's quantitative model: "The example of judgement gives us for the first time a hint of the difference in their quantitative characteristic which is to be discovered between *thought* and the primary process. It is justifiable to suppose that during *thought* a slight current of motor innervation passes from ψ — only, of course, if during the process a motor or key neurone has been innervated."[37] It is clear here that Freud gives shape to at least one aspect of the speech which produces therapeutic effects, i.e. speech accompanied by *catharsis*. Further on, Freud reports that "(...) nevertheless it would be wrong to take this discharge for the process of thought itself, of which it is only an unintended subsidiary effect".[38]

The idea of *development* brings Jerusalem around to a biological viewpoint: "If a consideration about the original, primitive state of consciousness would make it probable to locate the origin of mental life in the feeling of pleasure and unpleasure and the corresponding movements of aggression and defence, then a cursory look at the effect of these movements already makes it plausible to look upon them as being remarkably well adapted to protecting life. There is undeniably also a close connection between aggression and the feeling of pleasure on the one hand and unpleasure and defence on the other. These elementary and peremptory facts illustrate the biological character of psychical phenomena and thus oblige by so doing the researcher to account for the biological factor in complex phenomena."[39] I would like to make just one observation in this respect. In the *Project*, Freud also uses the "biological viewpoint" as an argument for differentiating ϕ and ψ, and as a motivation for using the "biological rules" of *primary defence* and *attention.*[40]

Logic and grammar

I will now dwell on Jerusalem's conception of meaning, despite the fact that Freud did not adopt any explicit stance on this problem. Jerusalem's view was by no means naive and some of its aspects recall Lacan's linguistic theory.[41]

Jerusalem noted that one ineluctably had to address the problems of logic and grammar when undertaking a psychological research into the act of judgement, even though the object of his research was essentially not concerned with these two disciplines. In this respect, what Jerusalem had to say about the famous autonomy of words is of interest: "I protest vehemently against the psychological autonomy one is wont to ascribe to the semantic field of words and which is even regarded as self-evident. A word only comes to life in sentences, i.e. in formations in which language first acquires a real and lively character. It is principally Lazarus and Steinthal who deserve credit for having pointed out that the first apparition of language is a reaction to the observation of an entire process, and that the roots of speech are not words but sentences. In language words only exist as elements of sentences and only the branch of grammar which deals with syntax is able to unveil the laws governing actual linguistic life."[42]

Jerusalem thus opposes the doctrine holding that words are invested with well-defined ideas. The second widespread conception he criticised is related to the link between speech and thought. It is traditionally believed that judgement finds verbal expression in sentences, whereas concepts find expression in words. As a rule, this is interpreted as being indicative of the fact that judgement and concepts exist independently of language as a psychical phenomenon, and that the linguistic expression is only used to communicate these phenomena to others. According to Jerusalem, this is completely inaccurate: "If one also takes into consideration the meaning of words, one realises that sentences are no longer the expression of judgement, but the judgement itself. Judgement cannot come into being without language, and only in and simultaneously with language does it live and exist. Whether the speech movements are reinforced by audible sounds or whether they are inhibited by other impulses is wholly immaterial."[43]

The relation of words to ideas is also far from equivocal. It is usually advanced as a matter-of-course that words correspond to ideas and vice versa.[44] Jerusalem stresses that this postulated link is neither of a general nor permanent nature "I have already observed that as far as sensory ideas are concerned, words are secondary and are often only loosely connected to the idea. It is decidedly not the case that every idea corresponds to a word, and the converse is even less applicable. What ideas are conjured up when the words 'and', 'but', 'with', 'from', 'until' etc. are pronounced? (...) However, words which are even more material and apparently denser in ideational value do not always arouse ideas and certainly not always the same ideas. What is the mental image one has in one's mind when words like 'to walk, to sit, to lie, to fight, to grow' are uttered? (...) These example illustrate how preposterous it is to say: 'in the judgement *the boy is growing*, the idea of *the boy* is linked to that of *growing*'. For the idea of *to grow* does not exist at all and hence cannot be linked to that of the boy. The examples I have given go to show that, as a rule, the function of these words is not to arouse ideas."[45] To Jerusalem words are components of the judgement and they only fulfil their role in context, i.e. in a sentence. The connection between words and ideas seems to be less problematic in the case of substantives, yet the mental image that is conjured up is more varied and divergent than it may seem at first sight. When one hears the word 'plate', then a certain type of plate with a certain colour may appear in our mind. The aroused idea may look different for each one of us. However, Jerusalem is not interested in this subjective factor and thus concludes: "In psychical terms, words do not correspond to ideas, but to a component of the judgement. The semantic field of words does not encompass that of the ideas it evokes but the judgements of which it is a component."[46]

Idea

A crucial element brought to light by the analysis of the act of judgement is that of the *idea*: "Every judgement presupposes and contains an ideational act."[47] By this, Jerusalem understands the image of an object that is revealed to consciousness, either by means of sensory impressions or recollection. Let us take an example to illustrate this view on the relation between the ideational act and judgement. "When perceiving a blossoming tree, I can record an image of it even though I am ignorant of its name and I have never passed a judgement on it. The idea of the blossoming tree reveals itself as an entity and the idea of the tree may call up the most varied associations, in accordance with the disposition of the person performing the ideational act. It can remind him of other trees which bear a similarity with the one perceived or it can bring to mind connected experiences."[48] The associations that were triggered by the idea only come to an end when the judgement 'the tree is in bloom' is expressed. This judgement differs essentially from the various processes of association, for "(...) in the judgement 'the tree is in bloom' no new ideational components accede to the idea of the blossoming tree. All that is represented in the judgement, was already represented and the essence of association consists precisely in arousing, by an idea, other previously unrepresented ideas."[49]

The idea undergoes a drastic *change* when a judgement is passed, i.e. "(...) the whole ideational complex or the unstructured process is formed and structured by the fact that the tree is represented as an individual being endowed with power, the actual expression of which is conveyed by the very process of blossoming".[50] Jerusalem describes the outcome of this 'processing' as *objectification.* In the judgement 'the tree is in bloom', the tree is perceived as an independent centre of power which we invest with the power to bring about the blossoming. In more general terms, one could argue that the contents represented in a judgement are subdivided into a subject (the centre of power) and a predicate (the activity)[51]. Let us compare this with Freud's description of judgements in the *Project*: "The perceptual complex, if it is compared with other perceptual complexes, can be dissected into a component portion, neurone *a*, which on the whole remains the same, and a second component portion, neurone *b*, which for the most part varies. Language will later apply the term *judgement* to this dissection and will discover the resemblance which in fact exists between the nucleus of the ego and the constant perceptual component [on the one hand] and between the changing cathexes in the pallium and the inconstant component [on the other]; it [language] will call neurone *a* the *thing* and neurone *b* its activity or attribute — in short, its *predicate.*"[52]

Pleasure and unpleasure

If the ideational act (the representation) is said to constitute the receptive or passive side of judgement, it is equally possible to distinguish an active side. For passing a judgement is an "action, an act of will".[53] However, every act of will or inner drive of this kind presupposes pleasure and unpleasure. We have seen that Jerusalem too regarded pleasure and unpleasure as a rationale. He interprets them in a fairly straightforward way: the satisfaction of a need produces pleasure, whereas its non-satisfaction produces unpleasure. The question that arises in this respect is, to which need does a judgement correspond? A judgement is accompanied by a feeling of pleasure, which actually motivates it. An idea gives rise to a judgement because this idea generates an interest, namely "the pleasure involved in judging".[54]

How is the need to judge satisfied? "Firstly, it finds satisfaction in the fact that [judgement] comprises an activity of its own, it activates inner forces, unlike the ideational activity which merely implies a being subjected to the affect; but principally in the fact that [the judgement] terminates the process which was stimulated by ideas and gives it shape in accordance with our consciousness and turns this content into our mental property. 'That is the roof', means in fact that the visual impression I have just experienced is the effect of the centre of force the 'roof', known from a previous experience. The need to activate our intellectual force operates as a motive for judgement. However, the interest or pleasure derived from the satisfaction of this need is an element of the act itself, which as a rule accompanies and permeates it [the act]. Every judgement is thence permeated with pleasure since it satisfies a need. However, the frequent use we make of this function of judgement causes the accompanying feeling of pleasure to become blunted rather rapidly. (....) When the child cries out with joy upon seeing his father returning, 'father is coming back!', then the purely formal pleasure produced by the judgement cannot find a conscious expression alongside the joy produced by the father's return and the expectations linked to it. Alternatively, when a sad experience is recorded by a judgement, such as 'father is dead', then the distressing emotions linked to this judgement far outweigh the feeling of pleasure involved in the act of judging. In addition, there is the fact that we, children of a millennial culture, receive the largest part of our ideational contents already in the form of judgements and hence rarely experience the joy of making even one judgement from raw material. This being said, the pleasure originally linked to judging continues to be an element of this function, which proves to be still operative today."[55]

I would like to make two observations with regard to this quote. As far as judgement is concerned, Jerusalem does not escape from a strictly teleological reasoning: we pass judgements because there is a need to judge. Freud evades this pitfall by advancing his quantitative conception of psychical processes, that is the concept of the drive. Adopting the line of reasoning in the *Project*, one could argue that one judges because it represents an *adequate reaction* for the discharge of quantity. Or to formulate this even more accurately, the conquest of the world around us by means of judgement is sexually motivated. This aspect only comes to light if one takes as a point of departure the formation of judgement as it manifests itself in the clinic ("the false connection" or syllogism and the accompanying feeling of unpleasure). Jerusalem, vaguely mentioning the "activation of inner forces", swiftly glosses over the demon of Eros, which, in clinical-psychological terms, is not possible. Having said this, what Jerusalem describes meets one of the criteria for the adequate reaction, namely the catharsis produced by speech.[56]

Will

Along with the idea and the feeling of pleasure or unpleasure, the *will* constitutes a third element of the act of judgement. As I have already argued, in the initially unstructured process the *thing* and the *predicate* are divided by judgement in such a way that the activity takes on the shape of an expression of force on the part of the thing. How does Man arrive at an act of judgement of this kind? At this juncture, Jerusalem is impelled to take a closer look at the development of the process of judgement. "However, this thing, the subject of the judgement, appears to the original consciousness of primitive men as it does today to a child, like a being endowed with life and will, whose activities are expressions of the will of this thing. For a primitive man, as for a child, the tree blossoms because the tree has willed it. When the sensory perceptions offer nothing, then fantasy conjures up a being endowed with will in order to conceive of processes as expressions of will. This very basic form of anthropomorphism is unanimously acknowledged by researchers and it is conceived of as a preliminary stage of knowledge to be quickly overcome. Efforts are made to show that in order to achieve exact results one must emancipate oneself form this anthropomorphism."[57] However, according to Jerusalem the understanding of the essence and origin of this "error" is more important than the fact that Man attempts to free himself from it in the course of his development, something which in his view can never really be achieved.

Where does the idea of attributing a will to everything come from? It undoubtedly results from personal experience which teaches one that movements always follows after inner impulses and that they frequently coalesce with these impulses. When a moving object is perceived in the external world, the movement appears to the observer as the end point of a series whose starting point (the "volitional impulse") is invariably looked for in the moving thing. "The movements of one's own body have, ever since early childhood, created the apperception-mass which had to interpret the movements of external objects. (...) By apperception I understand the perception of ideational mass excited by attention. Judgement is the most primitive and most frequent mode of apperception and the stimulated ideational masses are themselves the recollected volitional impulses. (...). This apperception has a biological rationale because it is propitious to the knowledge of the environment, the preservation of the individual and species. There is in addition another important circumstance: the vivid tendency to mimic, which impels one to perform the observed movements."[58]

If one brings these passages to bear on Freud's *Project*, one can trace what Jerusalem terms "apperception mass" back to the primitive ego as it is engendered as a result of the primary experience of satisfaction or pain.[59] More importantly, there is the fact that this 'pleasure ego' or primitive subject seems to be constituted in a *pre-linguistic* act of judgement. This viewpoint, which Freud recuperated in the *Project* and to which he added a further qualification by distinguishing between *primary* and *secondary* judgement, becomes even clearer when Jerusalem introduces the linguistic element in his analysis.

Language

"The expression of emotion occurring in the cry is above all else representative of the formation of language, whereas its development is more determined by the need to make oneself understood ("Verständigung"). (...) Hence, the formation of language could be thought of in the following way. In the case of people and animals, intense emotions are expressed by sounds. A dog barks, a lion roars, and a horse neighs when excited in one way or another. A frail child in its cot is already in a position to attract the attention of the people around him by crying. The sounds emitted by animals are acknowledged as expressions of needs and already at that stage there are differences between sounds which other animals recognise and interpret correctly. Similarly, a child's cry is not always the same and a caring mother is well able to determine the nature of the need expressed by the child from the tone of its cries."[60] Thence in Freud's discussion of the experience of satisfaction it is not surprising to encounter the function of the attribution of meaning by the fellow human being: "At first, the human organism is incapable of carrying out the specific action. It takes place by *extraneous help*, when the attention of an experienced person is drawn to the child's state by discharge along the path of internal change. In this way this path of discharge acquires a secondary function of the highest importance, that of *communication*, and the initial helplessness of the human being is the *primal source* of all *moral motives*."[61]

To Jerusalem it is also from such elementary phenomena that language develops, or rather that language acquisition takes place in the subject. For instance, in the cry of anxiety Jerusalem descries the association between an emotional element (anxiety, unpleasure) and an idea (that of the enemy). What other factor is required for language to exist? "In physiological terms, articulation and in psychological terms, the emancipation of the sound from its emotional value and from the fixed association with ideas."[62] The 'numbing' of emotion and the development of articulation go hand in hand. It is important to stress that Jerusalem is not just dealing with a theoretical construction. For instance, he alludes to what he observed in the language development of Laura Bridgman, a deaf-mute and blind person. Listening to her primary utterance of sounds which were charged with emotions, he could follow the process whereby she formed real 'names' to the people around her.[63]

If one withdraws the emotional value from the primary cry, there remains simple, usually monosyllabic, sound complexes. These "roots of language" serve as indicators of a whole process of experience and should by no means be interpreted as verbs or substantives, but rather as *sentences*. "The root indicates, just like the initial speech sounds uttered by a child, a whole process in which the separation between the activity and the thing has not yet become totally conscious. The emotion excited by the ideational content in question which is expressed in sounds which in turn become roots, has at this stage of language development not entirely disappeared; the root is still expressed very vividly and is thus readily repeated. The content is however not yet formed; this still has more to do with emotion than with judgement."[64]

A second phase in language development is the connection between a verbal and a pronominal root. "For instance, when a root sound reflects the impression an approaching wolf makes on a primitive man, then the addition of a pronominal root ("Pronominal- oder Deutewurzel"), undoubtedly accompanied by a movement, would produce something like: 'wolf come — there!' In psychological terms, adding the pronominal root simply signifies the objectification already implied in the observation. As such it represents an important component in the function of judgement. While the expression 'wolf come' still represents more of an expression of emotion than the actual process perceived by the speaker, the presence of 'there' indicates that the sensation of anxiety or joy has to be looked for in the direct environment: that which brought me around to produce the sounds "wolf come" is over there, in this very place."[65]

However, this process is not yet formed or structured. This will only happen when the root will no longer be sufficient for the speaker to be understood by the listener. As long as *one* root sound suffices, Man will have no reason to strive for more. In other words, this suggests that a judgement is formed when "a process is expressed by two root sounds [of which] one root is spontaneously invested with the activity (and becomes the thing), while the other signifies the activity of the thing. (...). As one can still observe in children today, the indication of one process by two sounds constitutes an important phase in the development of the human intellect. Personally, I still have vivid memories of the day when my eldest son used a full sentence for the first time. He was familiar with the words "daddy" and "eat" and he frequently used them to indicate a full process. One day, in March 1881, he saw me eating, and cried out loud "daddy eat!" and one could read on his face the joy the entire indication of the process procured him. The boy, born on 17 September 1879, was one and a half years old at the time and from that day on he almost always used complete sentences, when he could find the words. *By the occurrence of the second sound the act of judgement acquires, the isolation that is so symptomatic of it.* As long as only one sound is used, a play of association remains possible; however when a second sound is added, every possible association is cut off. The act then acquires an isolating character which calls a halt to all associations."[66]

Jerusalem's view of language development is a splendid rendition of how a human being is able to get some grip, through wording, on the world that surrounds him. To him the relationship of man to his outer world is fundamentally *mediated by language*.

2.3. Freud's use of the theory of judgement

The aim of my discussion of *Die Urtheilsfunction* was to show how this book must have stirred Freud's ambition to use some of the elements highlighted in it in his own clinical psychological project. Some aspects of Jerusalem's theory seem to provide the necessary building blocks for an explanatory model for what Freud had learnt from his empirical approach and the talking cure. So far I have merely touched upon a few features shared by Jerusalem's book and the *Project.* I will now move on to discuss the way in which Freud actually made use of Jerusalem's theory of judgement.

I will tackle this at two distinct levels: 1. on an essentially *epistemological* plane in the passing of a judgement relative to the psyche; 2. on a *clinical* plane in the explanation of the effect of speaking.

2.3.1. Epistemology: Freud's 'primary judgement' *N* and *Q*

The best way to form a good idea of Freud's epistemological innovation, is probably to focus on the marked *differences* between both authors. I have already underlined the fact that in the *Project* Freud seems completely to overlook an important viewpoint adopted by Jerusalem, namely that "psychical phenomena cannot be thought of with a substratum". This epistemological point of departure is, to say the least, at the antipodes of Freud's experiment of thought which sets out from the conception of psychical processes as "quantitatively determinate states of specifiable material particles". How should one interpret this manifest contradiction?

Firstly, I would like to stress the distinction that exists in both authors' approach to the question. In spite of the fact that Jerusalem was conversant with psychology and at least aware of the clinic of neuroses, he was primarily driven by philosophical-epistemological questions. Jerusalem *wants to know*, he wants to *construct a theory* which deals with the function of judgement as "the activity that is applied generally and that is the most important and by means of which we mentally conquer the physical world in order to subsequently shape it into a biologically serviceable form".[67] But, unlike Freud, his frame of reference is not the psychopathology of knowing, that is to say, *thought disrupted by the affect.* In so far as this can be evaluated, Jerusalem's psychological analysis of the *psychical formation* of judgement and of the *psychical function* of the act of judgement ultimately lead him to formulate a coherent answer to the Kantian question of our "contribution to the coming into existence of experience".

However, Freud — who was perhaps even more ambitious — focused on the *psyche* and the mechanisms active in it. The *Project* attempts to put forward a solution for the mechanism of *repression*, i.e. for the essential passion of the *unwillingness to know* as a disrupter of the thought process which finds expression in the *false connection* or the hysterical *proton pseudos*, itself an avatar of speech under transference. The *sexual affect* also constitutes a factor that is indispensable for the clinical psychology which Freud wanted to construct. As a matter of fact, the drive itself constitutes the most important characteristic of psychical processes (which are invariably "excessively intense"), as they manifest themselves in the clinic. What is more, Freud's psychological analyses allocate a central place, not only to speech, but also to the psychical functions of *memory* and *consciousness*, whereas these only played a peripheral role in Jerusalem's conception.

In other words, Freud's declared intention was to fully grasp his object of study, the psyche, on the basis of the way in which it presented itself to him in the clinic, that is to say on the basis of the psyche as a process or "Vorgang". Rather unexpectedly, and in spite of the aforementioned manifest contradiction, *Die Urtheilsfunction* provides a key to the epistemology of the *Project* which falls into our lap like a ripe fruit. For Freud reacts according to the purest 'Jerusalemian' tradition with respect to the psyche seen as a process: in order mentally to perceive something of the reality of his object, *he passes a judgement*, or makes a statement, thence subdividing the psyche so as to make it visible and usable. He subdivides the psyche into a *thing* and an *attribute*, neurone *N* and quantity *Q*.

In the course of this experiment of thought, neurone *N* undergoes a differentiation and becomes model ϕ-ψ-ω out of the necessity to accommodate the psychical functions of memory and consciousness. Freud accordingly manages to construct a psychical apparatus which enables him to account for the unconscious determination of psychical processes. Formulated in a more pertinent way: in his clinical psychological theory, Freud comes to terms with the *subjective erotic desire* by means of a judgement, i.e. by subdividing of the psyche into a neurone *N* and a quantity *Q*. In my view, this represents both the essence and the first germ of Freud's psychology of judgement.

In the *Project*, this signification diverges when the course of psychical processes — i.e. the thought process or the secondary and ultimately linguistic judgement — is conceived as being 'marked', 'signed' or 'facilitated' by the first dialectic with the object of satisfaction. This dialectic is "originally an associative process between cathexes coming from outside and arising from one's own body — an *identification of information or cathexes from ϕ and from within*".[68] The primary judgement, i.e. the logical moment during which the pleasure ego is constituted, serves as the 'mould' in which the fellow human being imparts a linguistic desire to the child.[69] When the subject as a speaking being is later confronted with the reality of sexuality (perhaps at puberty), he will only be able to master it and to come to terms with a sexual desire by resorting to a verbal expression or judgement, which must transit via the desire signified to him, through his own life history.

This brings my analysis around to the second level, i.e. that of the clinic where Freud offers an interpretation for the theory of judgement. The discussion of speech in psychotherapy is best introduced with what Freud termed the *mechanism of attention.*

2.3.2. Clinic: the effects of speech[70]

In the first part of the *Project*, the mechanism of attention is allocated a place within the very first formulation of what is known in Freud's later work as reality-testing. This consists in the activity of the ego — the reality ego — which makes comparisons between the inside and the outside, between a memory or idea and a perception.[71] In the *Project*, the mechanism of attention acquires the signification of a feedback-principle within Freud's theoretical representation of the coming into being or the extension and protection of the psyche, once the primary experiences of satisfaction and pain took place.[72]

In the second part, which deals with the psychopathology of hysteria, the mechanism of attention is put forward as being the best instrument which the ego possesses for preventing the development of affects. In this part on the basis of a clinical excerpt, Freud illustrates how this mechanism of attention was perforce put on the wrong track in hysteria, because in the transition from childhood to puberty memories which initially could not release any unpleasure suddenly do so.[73]

Finally, in the third part which deals with what Freud termed the normal psychical processes, the mechanism of attention, featured in the first part, is taken up again in a very particular way. In a real tour de force the mechanism of attention is split into: (1) the very principle by which the subject acquires an understanding of the surrounding world — by the *act of judging*; and (2) the very "raison d'être" of psychical treatment — i.e., the treatment of psychical and physical disorders by speech.[74]

In order to shed light on the relevance of the mechanism of attention and perhaps also on the necessity of theorising it, I should like to dwell on a number of phenomena which we are all undoubtedly familiar with, before going over to the examination of it in the *Project*. These phenomena, although we may not be aware of them, are very common and accordingly belong to the normal psychical processes. What is more, they have also acquired a special significance within psychotherapy.

Let us take an example from the psychopathology of everyday life: upon leaving the house, one cannot find one's key. A feeling of unpleasure and a feverish search for the precious object ensues.[75] From experience one could say that in a situation of this kind the search for the key follows a specific pattern. One asks oneself specific questions such as: "when did I come in?", "what did I do then?", "where did I go in the house?", "where did I sit?" ... Sometimes this exercise of attention is sufficient. However, one is often only able to find the keys if one puts the questions that arise into words, while directing one's attention to the various places. One notices that *by articulating* or putting these questions into words, it becomes possible to extend the field of association and to carry it a stage further, which is not possible if one remains silent.[76]

A second similar example comes from analytical experience. One arrives at a session charged with the dreams of the previous night, but then realises that one can only manage to remember one element from these dreams. In his *Interpretation of Dreams*, Freud reassuringly argues that, if need be, one element suffices to reconstruct the entire dream. The conditio sine qua non for this operation to succeed is to focus one's attention on the mnemic image and to name it.[77]

The elementary observation that for recollection attention and articulation are closely interconnected and that they represent as it were two sides of one coin, throws a different light on what one normally understands by the appellation suspended attention ("gleichschwebende Aufmerksamkeit"). What is this suspended attention like when a patient relates a dream? What can the analyst's attention focus on? In any case not on the meaning of the dream as this meaning is not known; it is only presupposed out of necessity and as such should not command the attention of the analyst. His attention can accordingly only be directed at the articulated speech, or on the signifiers, which emerge in the interpretation as the indispensable counterpart of suspended attention.[78] Thus in the eyes of the analyst too, the functions of attention and articulation are indissolubly linked. After all, psychical treatment acquires its status and efficiency in this dialectical process.

Freud's case studies, his shorter clinical excerpts, as well as *The Interpretation of Dreams*, *The Psychopathology of Everyday Life* and *Jokes and their Relation to the Unconscious*, all bear witness to this fundamental point of departure. One can also find this viewpoint in Freud's early writings, for instance in the clinical excerpt published in the second part of the *Project*, and even earlier in his 1890 paper on 'Psychical Treatment'. These two texts show that Freud had already substituted the question of the psyche with that of language and its mechanisms, with the question of the efficiency of speech. However, it was not enough for him to simply take note of this efficiency and the dialectic of the function of attention and articulation, and to employ this in his clinical work. He also engaged in a serious attempt to grasp these operations in a theoretical construct.

Freud introduces the psychical mechanism of attention in the following way. The ego is formed in ψ after the primary experiences of satisfaction and pain and is defined as "the totality of the ψ cathexes at a given time".[79] This group of well-facilitated neurones cathected with a certain quantity $Q\eta$ constitutes the residue of the primary experience and influences all the subsequent psychical processes.

What the ego guarantees above all is repetition. For, in accordance with the principle of facilitation, a second psychical process or a second cathexis of quantity $Q\eta$ leads to a renewed cathexis of the mnemic image of both the primary object of satisfaction and the primary hostile object. Freud stresses that a total and renewed cathexis of these mnemic images is highly ineffective and even detrimental to the psyche. Let us take as an example the renewed cathexis of the mnemic image of the object of satisfaction.

When the mnemic image of the object of satisfaction is freshly cathected via a particular path, with exogenous quantity Q in the case of a new perception or with endogenous quantity $Q\eta$ by summation, then it is important to know whether the object of satisfaction is actually present in the external world. In other terms, the ego needs a criterion or an indication to enable it to distinguish between a perception and an idea.

This criterion is what Freud terms the indication of reality. According to the principle that for every external perception quantity Q passes over from ϕ to ψ and to ω, "a qualitative excitation occurs in ω".[80] The excitation or cathexis of a neurone in ω results in a discharge of perception of which ψ is informed.

"The information of the discharge from ω is thus the indication of quality or of reality for ψ."[81]
It is important to emphasise how Freud conceived of this discharge. A discharge of quantity is always accompanied by motility or movement. Take for instance the new-born baby who clearly has no other means to rid himself of quantity than by crying or moving (which in point of fact are identical). This discharge of quantity *Qή* will also be implied in *judging* or *speech* later in life. A second important principle is that such an information of discharge never occurs when only one mnemic image is cathected with quantity *Qή* in ψ.[82]
The indication of reality or of quality transmitted by ω represents for the ego a sign that it must cathect perception with additional quantity *Qή*, so as to focus attention on the perception. Here, attention is portrayed as a pure feedback principle for the organisation of the pleasure ego, i.e. for the ego intent on restoring the original situation of satisfaction as quickly as possible. Two possibilities are open to this pleasure ego: either the perception and memory coalesce (in which case the cathexis of the perception in the ego immediately produces the known release of satisfaction), or they only correspond partially. In this case, perception in ψ is cathected with quantity from both sides, i.e. form the external world and from the ego. This results in what Freud calls the 'process of thought', which in fact amounts to installing the identity between perception and recollection, via the shortest possible route.

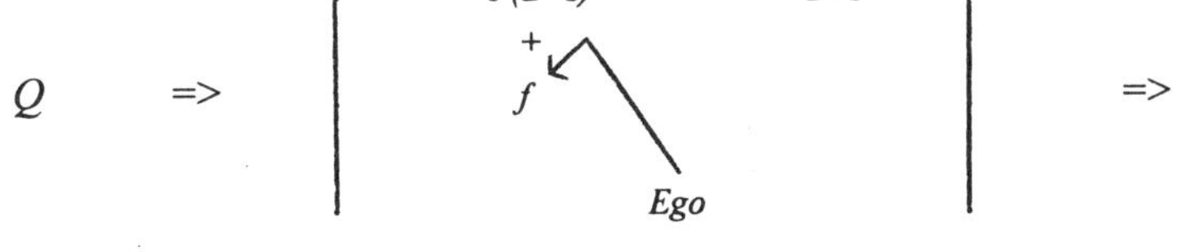

Fig. 1: The feedback mechanism

An example from the first part of the *Project* may be more enlightening. For the sake of clarity, let us assume that both perception and the mnemic image are made up of just two components.[83] Perception accordingly consists in a thing and an attribute: for example, a side view of the mother's breast (*B+s*).

The mnemic image is the front view of the same breast (*B+f*). Here, perception and memory only correspond partially. The perceptual complex *B+s* is cathected with additional quantity *Qή* because of the indication of reality originating from ω. This generates a passage of quantity which leads to an abundant cathexis of the complete mnemic image *B+f* along with a release of satisfaction.

However, a third possibility exists when perception does not correspond at all with the memory. The pleasure ego, whose aim is to ensure the repetition of the original satisfaction, is then confronted to an impossible task. Freud has to admit that even his mechanism of attention cannot deal with this. He is thus impelled to refine it and uses this opportunity to introduce the *language function.* This means that we are no longer dealing with the pleasure ego, but with the reality ego.

Freud assumes that it is in the interest of the reality ego (which permanently lost the object of satisfaction long ago, and for which the perception and memory of this object differ), to cathect the perception with quantity *Qή* from the ego. For one never knows, one might find the primary object of satisfaction again. This suggests that, even though the motive of the reality ego is still the same, the result of the mechanism differs greatly from the situation of satisfaction. Freud defines this result as an "Erkennen" — in the sense of knowing or recognising — of the external world. In this respect, one can consider Freud not only as a neurologist or analyst, but also as a refined cognitive psychologist; and what is more, one who uses a linguistic theory.

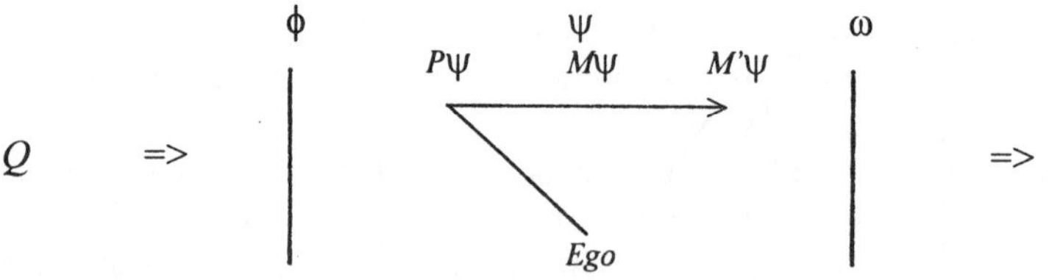

Fig. 2: The process of "Erkennen"

After the indication of reality occurred, the ego also cathects the perception (*P*) with additional quantity. Again, the result of this is the passage of quantity in the direction of the mnemic images (*M*): i.e., from *P*ψ to *M*ψ. If Freud discontinued the passage of quantity, this would result in an extremely unpleasurable situation for the reality ego. Why is this so? Because such a minimal passage of quantity would understandably result in a minimal discharge of quantity $Q\eta$. Freud therefore assumes that the passage of quantity continues. An indication is also required to redirect the attention cathexis of the ego to the mnemic image $M\psi$ for the passage of quantity to be able to pass through the mnemic image $M\psi$. This time, the indispensable indication can be neither an indication of quality nor of reality, because these can only supervene in the event of the discharge of a perception neurone in ω. A similar indication of discharge needs therefore to be provided in a different way.

How does Freud account for this indication of discharge or movement? He writes: "This purpose is fulfilled by *speech associations*. This consists in the linking of ψ neurones with neurones which serve sound-presentations and themselves have the closest association with motor speech-images."[84] Let me remind you that to Freud only an indication of motility or movement is capable of steering the attention cathexis of the ego.

Only at this stage does the meaning of the mechanism of attention become intelligible. Indeed, this second meaning is totally different from the first. The mere feedback mechanism determined by the reflexive discharge, has become the language function itself, seen as the conditio sine qua non for establishing a path of conduction along which the reality ego can guarantee a passage of quantity by putting the mnemic images into words.

This speech offers the reality ego an enormous advantage which can be described as follows: 1. it enables one to reach an "Erkennen" or understanding of the external world; 2. it simultaneously offers the possibility of escaping from the reflexive release while still providing the necessary but gradual discharge of quantity $Q\eta$.

The "Erkennen" of the external world becomes on a par with cognition, even though the cognition concerned must occur through the prism of language or mnemic images, in other words via a recognition. This accentuates the disjointed status of psychical reality and reality.

However, providing a passage of quantity that is distinct from reflexive discharge is not merely an explanation, but also the "raison d'être" of the rule of free association and its efficiency.

2.4. Conclusion

Having reached the end of this discussion, I must evaluate the scope of Freud's *Project* and the psychology of judgement it entails. My approach was motivated by the feeling of unease I experienced upon witnessing the contradiction which features prominently in the secondary works which interpret the epistemology of the *Project*. One has every reason to feel strongly about the implicit repudiation of this text which is regarded as the development of a materialistic-mechanistic theory, as a regression to a neurophysiological explanatory model, be it only because, by extension, it is also a repudiation of both psychoanalytical theory and praxis. However, the authors I object to are right on one point: the *Project* does attempt to throw light on the understanding of Freudian epistemology. Nonetheless, this epistemology is not the result of the conceptual frame of reference used by Freud, but can only be understood when his nascent theory formation is seen as emerging from the demonstrable dialectic with the clinic of psychotherapy. Only when departing from the 'primary judgement' which Freud passed on his object of study, can one explain why so many passages from his later work refer back to the *Project*.[85] This judgement, i.e. the subdivision of its object — i.e. the psyche — into a *thing* (neurone *N*) and a *predicate* (quantity *Q*), leads Freud to formulate the fundamental concepts of both the *unconscious* and the *drive*. A psychology based on the clinic of the talking cure is inconceivable without these concepts, at least if it wishes to account for what manifests itself in every psychotherapy, i.e. *repression* and *transference*. In the clinic "the question of psychology" is of necessity translated into "the question of the unconscious".[86]

Freud's metapsychology of judgement also offers an explanation for the empirical fact that every psychical treatment is inevitably structured by the recuperation and reformulation of the parental desires as they were signified to the child. Combining this with the fact that the concept of the drive enables one to situate the sexual desire in early childhood, allows one to regard the *Project* as a prelude to the theory of the Oedipus complex and infantile sexuality.[87]

CONCLUSION

"I love you,
But, because inexplicably
I love in you something
more than you
— the objet petit *a* —
I mutilate you."

Jacques Lacan[1]

Freud loved science. To him science was not just a fantasy. But greater than his love for science was his love for what had been the object of his desire ever since his youth, namely the human soul. His love of the human soul was scientific, that is to say, he assumed that the psyche and the rules governing it could be identified.

Freud loved medicine. But greater than his love for medicine was his love for psychical treatment, which formed the basis for his research into the psyche.

Freud loved the word. But greater than his love for the word was his love for putting into words that which had been left unsaid.

In Paris, at the Salpêtrière institute headed by Charcot, he realized for the first time that it was possible to *systematically influence* the psyche. The hypnotic technique operated mainly by means of articulated suggestions and highlighted the magical power of words. At the same time, Freud became convinced of the possibility of making the power of words cognisable.

Freud left Charcot with the well-defined assignment of elucidating the difference between hysterical and organic paralyses.

When he looked back on this period in 1893, he was grateful to the Master of hysteria for pointing him towards psychology. All of this surfaces from Charcot's *Clinical Lectures on the Diseases of the Nervous System* which was translated by Freud.

Back in Vienna, Freud focused on the therapeutic potential of the *talking cure*. This led him to the works of Hippolyte Bernheim and to a close collaboration with Breuer. However, unconvinced by Bernheim's book and aware of the impossibility of generating a "climate of suggestibility" akin to that prevailing in the Nancy institute within his own private praxis, he turned to Breuer for the support he needed to develop a new therapeutical device. However Freud soon substituted the psycho-cathartic method which Breuer had reserved for the treatment of hysterics, with a psychical treatment which was effective for all neurotics and which simultaneously functioned as the *research instrument par excellence* for the human psyche.

His patients' speech brought to light phenomena which hitherto had never been examined systematically.
His first empirical observation was *repression*. Strangely enough, the patients who consulted Freud for their psychical afflictions seemed to be driven by the passion of the unwillingness to know.
The second phenomenon inextricably linked to psychotherapy is Eros. Freud acknowledged two aspects that play an important part in Eros. Firstly, he emphasised *sexuality* as being a cause of the psychical suffering and secondly, he perceived the importance of *transference* and its dual status as both a means of defence and as an aid to the actual treatment.
Thirdly, there is the question of the *effects* produced by speech, which he identified in the *Studies on Hysteria* as involving the recollection and putting into words of the affect and the assumption of a subjective desire in the judgement.
Clinical psychology, defined as a psychology geared to the 'talking cure', consequently must provide an explanation for the passion of the unwillingness to know, Eros and the triple effect of speech under transference. I advocate the thesis that Freud already had this objective in mind when he wrote the *Project* in 1895.
A few years prior to this, in 1891, he published a study on organic aphasia which sanctioned his views on the limitations of the explanatory potential of neurology. I have shown that, in the course of this study, Freud made an essential step towards a psychological theory: his reinterpretation of the nebulous physiological notion of the functional or dynamic lesion led him to the *psychical mechanism* of defence.
In the *Project* Freud constantly refers to the scientific fields that were so familiar to him. The most telling passage in this connection is perhaps the opening paragraph of the text, where he conceives of psychical processes as "quantitatively determinate states of specifiable material particles". Yet one

cannot look upon this manuscript as an attempt at offering a materialistic-mechanistic theory of the psyche. Although he borrows concepts from other fields, Freud remains committed to the clinic. In other words, *Freud does not mutilate the object of his research. Instead he mutilates the existing sciences he knew so well in order to do justice to this object.*

I have shown that the quantity Q and the neurone N can be interpreted as *theoretical* concepts which enabled Freud to do justice to his object of study. The concept of the quantity Q accounts for the *affect*, whereas neurone N provides a *topos* or a locus from whence the psychical processes are determined.

The concept of the quantity Q, halfway between the physical and the psychical, proved instrumental in fusing the clinic of the excessively intense idea and that of the "Aktualneurosen". As such it was the forerunner of the concept of the *drive.*

The progressive differentiation of neurone N to the ϕ-ψ-ω model of the psychical apparatus implied the creation of the concept of the *unconscious.*

Finally, I interpreted Freud's epistemological tour de force, or the birth of metapsychology, as issuing forth from an *experiment of thought*, namely the act of passing a judgement which involved the division of his object of study, the psyche, into a thing (neurone N) and an attribute (quantity Q). The key to this insight was Wilhelm Jerusalem's *Die Urtheilsfunction*, which in my view is essential for a reading of the *Project.*

Only when the *Project* is seen as an experiment of thought, can one grasp why so many crucial passages from Freud's later work refer back to this manuscript.

In this metapsychology, Freud's 'primary judgement' is transformed into a theory on *language acquisition* which results from the primary dialectic between the mother and her child. This, in turn, paves the way for the determination of psychical processes by infantile sexuality and the Oedipus. These two discoveries cannot therefore be exclusively attributed to Freud's so-called self analysis.

In addition, I have demonstrated that the dual sense of Freud's theory of judgement is coherently connected with a view on the purpose of the talking cure which, on the basis of the *case studies*, could be described as the guiding of the subject towards a judgement. A judgement of this kind can take on the form of "this I have been", indicating a distancing from one's past, or "this I will have been", as the assumption of a desire.

The fact that this conception was present in Freud's early works, repudiates the widespread view holding that 'psychoanalysis' was not developed until much later. I have shown that by 1895 two aspects of his psychical treatment had reached a final form: psychical treatment as a therapeutical instrument and as a research instrument. In the *Project*, Freud puts this conception into theory.

My examination aspires to more than a mere historical rectification. I believe that it also urges one to raise questions on the status of psychotherapy in general. Irrespective of the category of patients s/he deals with or of the institute where s/he works, a psychotherapist is expected to have a theory on the psyche and the mechanisms operative in it. This implies that s/he has at her/his disposal a theory which accounts for what her/his praxis (the talking cure) can bring to light. Furthermore, one can expect her/him to guide some else towards a judgement. In other terms, the psychotherapist is expected to have an insight into his/her own psyche.

NOTES

PREFACE

1. J. Lacan, *The Seminar, Book VII, The Ethics of Psychoanalysis, (1959-1960)*, Edited by J.-A. Miller, Translated with notes by Dennis Porter, London, Routledge, 1992, 342 pp.
2. S. Freud, Ontwerp van een natuurwetenschappelijke psychologie, (1950*c*), (Translated into Dutch by G. Van de Vijver and F. Geerardyn), Ghent, Idesça, Pegasosreeks nr. 8, 1992, xxx + 81 pp. "The cartel is the basic working unit on which Lacan based his school of psychoanalysis, the *Ecole Freudienne de Psychanalyse* (EFP), and most Lacanian associations continue to organise work in cartels today." Cf. D. Evans, *An Introductory Dictionary of Lacanian Psychoanalysis*, London, Routledge, 1996, p. 20.
3. G. Van de Vijver, Terugblik op een interview, *Psychoanalytische Perspektieven*, 1987, no. 11, pp. 267-270; Tussen een fenomenaal en een noumenaal onbewuste — vragen naar de constitutie van het object van de psychoanalyse. Een interview met Jean Petitot, *Psychoanalytische Perspektieven*, 1988, no. 12, pp. 143-156; De receptie van wetenschappelijk-epistemologische werken in de psychoanalyse. Naar aanleiding van 'ntre le temps et l'Eternité', *Rondzendbrief uit het Freudiaanse Veld*, 1989, nr. 38, pp. 33-37.
4. J. Quackelbeen, *Zeven avonden met Jacques Lacan, Psychoanalytische commentaren bij 'Télévision'*, 2nd. edition, Ghent, Academia Press, 1993, p. 105.

PART I

THE CLINIC OF THE EXCESSIVELY INTENSE IDEA

INTRODUCTION

1. S. Freud, Project for a Scientific Psychology, (1950*c* [1895]), *S.E.*, vol. 1, p. 295.
2. See the letter to Fließ dated 27 April 1895, in which he describes the *Project* as a psychology for neurologists in S. Freud, *The Complete Letters of Sigmund Freud to Wilhelm Fließ 1887-1904*, (1985*c* [1887-1904]), (English translation by J.M. Masson), Cambridge, The Belknap Press, 1985, pp. 127-128.
3. S. Freud, Project for a Scientific Psychology, *o.c.*, pp. 347-359.
4. *Ibid.*, p. 347. This particular aspect is dealt with in the third part of his manuscript. *Ibid.*, pp. 360-387.

5. As far as this aspect is concerned, I will examine what can be interpreted as a mechanistic explanation in the *Project* and, in the light of this, the significance of his use of concepts derived from scientific frames of reference such as physics, physiology, biology and neuroanatomy. This epistemological interrogation permeates my entire investigation, even though I will only formulate an answer to it in the second part of this book.
6. To be more precise, Freud actually stayed in Paris from 13 October 1885 to 28 February 1886. Cf. E. Jones, *Sigmund Freud, Life and Work*, (1953), London, The Hogarth Press, vol. I, 1972, p. 227.
7. J. Breuer and S. Freud, *Studies on Hysteria*, (1895*d*), *S.E.*, vol. 2.
8. O. Mannoni, L'analyse originelle, *Clefs pour l'imaginaire*, Paris, du Seuil, 1969, p. 115.

CHAPTER 1

Clinical Lectures on the Diseases of the Nervous System

1. Letter to Minna Bernays dated 3 December 1885. Cf. S. Freud, *Letters of Sigmund Freud 1873-1939*, (1960*a*), English translation by T. and J. Stern, London, The Hogarth Press, 1961, p. 191.
2. J.-M. Charcot, *Clinical Lectures on the Diseases of the Nervous System*, (1887), (English translation by T. Savill), (ed. Ruth Harris), London & New York, Tavistock/Routledge, 1991, p. 1.
3. Because of the type of education he enjoyed in Vienna, Freud had originally planned to carry out laboratory research. But due to the lack of space and research facilities, he was forced to abandon this idea. For instance, his first project, namely the examination of secondary atrophies and degenerations resulting from affections of the brain in children, soon fell through. On the third of December 1885, Freud wrote to Martha that he was going to abandon his research, letting her know that one cannot only give up neuropathology for a woman, but also for the passion of psychology. A few weeks later, however, he took the opportunity to resume some laboratory research in collaboration with Dr. Von Darkschewitsch. Cf. S. Freud, Report on my Studies in Paris and Berlin Carried Out with the Assistance of a Travelling Bursary Granted from the University Jubilee Fund (October, 1885 — end of March, 1886), (1956*a* [1886]), *S.E.*, vol. I, pp. 3-15. E. Jones, *Sigmund Freud, Life and Work*, *o.c.*, pp. 231-232.
4. Jones, who quotes the entire letter, mentions that Freud was somewhat ashamed of his pronunciation of French. Cf. E. Jones, *Sigmund Freud, Life and Work*, *o.c.*, pp. 228-230. After having consulted the French edition of Charcot's work, it appears to be a direct allusion to the lectures given by Charcot in 1885 on 'hysterical mutism' or 'hysterical aphasia'. Cf. J.-M. Charcot, *Clinical Lectures on the Diseases of the Nervous System*, *o.c.*, pp. 360-373. I will later discuss at greater length the theme of aphasia.

5. According to Jones, Freud had already started translating while still in Paris. Cf. E. Jones, *Sigmund Freud, Life and Work*, *o.c.*, p. 203.
6. It is said that Charcot memorised his lectures in order to achieve a greater effect.
7. S. Freud, Some Points for a Comparative Study of Organic and Hysterical Motor Paralysis, (1893*c*), *S.E.*, vol. I, p. 171.
8. E. Roudinesco, *La bataille de cent ans. Histoire de la psychanalyse en France*, Paris, du Seuil, 1986, vol. I, p. 38. See also S. Bernfeld and S.C. Bernfeld, *Bausteine der Freud-Biographik*, Frankfurt am Main, Suhrkamp, 1988, 288 pp; G. Van de Vijver and F. Geerardyn, Over het statuut van het *Ontwerp* als psychoanalytische tekst, Introduction to: S. Freud, *Ontwerp van een natuurwetenschappelijke psychologie*, (1950*c*), Ghent, Idesça, Pegasosreeks no. 8, 1992, pp. ix-xx; F. Geerardyn, Voorbij biografie en vaderanalyse. Siegfried Bernfelds Freud, *Rondzendbrief uit het Freudiaanse Veld*, 1992, no. 50, pp. 14-21. Later we will see that, in his study on aphasia, Freud severely criticised the generalising claims of localisation. For an excellent examination of the history of localisation, I wish to direct the reader to E. Clarck and K. Dewhurst's book, *Die Funktionen des Gehirns, Lokalisationstheorien von der Antike bis zur Gegenwart*, München, Heinz Moos Verlag, 1973, 157 pp.
9. J.-M. Charcot, *Clinical Lectures on the Diseases of the Nervous System*, *o.c.*, pp. 7-8.
10. *Ibid.*, p. 8, Charcot's emphasis.
11. This is a view which Freud confirms in his publication on this subject. S. Freud, Some Points for a Comparative Study of Organic and Hysterical Motor Paralysis, *o.c.*, pp. 160-172.
12. Since 1854 a similar arrangement had already taken place in Bicêtre. It was, however, prompted by a different motive. It was argued that research suffered when different disorders were mixed together. In order successfully to study the syndrome and the evolution of the disorder it was necessary to group them together according to type. The ward in question here was placed under Charcot's authority on account of his seniority. Cf. E. Trillat, *Histoire de l'hystérie*, Paris, Edition Seghers, 1986, pp. 130-132. See also K. Libbrecht, *Hysterical Psychosis, A Historical Survey*, New Brunswick and London, Transaction, 1995, pp. 38-66.
13. "Charcot va faire entrer l'hystérie dans le rang. Elle faisait figure jusqu'ici d'un être morbide, fantasque et indiscipliné, un être insaisissable, aux apparitions multiples et trompeuses. Comment s'y prendre pour réduire l'indocile? Comment l'obliger à obéir à des règles précises, à entrer dans le lit de Procuste, à obéir à des règles de bonne conduite? Il suffit d'appliquer à l'hystérie la méthode anatomo-clinique qui avait donné des résultats éclatants dans l'exploration des maladies neurologiques." [Charcot is going to bring hysteria in line. It had so far generally been thought of as a morbid state, whimsical and undisciplined, an elusive state of multifarious and deceptive appearances. How was one to set about to tame the unruly? How was one to force it to obey precise rules, to enter the Procrustean bed, to obey rules of good conduct? One only needs to apply to hysteria the anatomo-clinical method which had given excellent results in the study of neurological diseases.] E. Trillat, *Histoire de l'hystérie*, *o.c.*, p. 136.
14. *Ibid.*, p. 132.

15. E. Jones, *Sigmund Freud, Life and Work, o.c.*, p. 249.

16. Gambetta probably served as a mediator for Charcot. Cf. E. Trillat, *Histoire de l'hystérie, o.c.*, p. 129. The creation of the new Chair meant the recognition of neurology as an independent discipline, which, at that time, as far as I can understand from Charcot's plea, was certainly no mean feat: "One is sure to be asked, for example, whether the official consecration of one more speciality is an event that is both desirable and legitimate; and whether, if such a path were once marked out, the unity of our science might not be imperilled thereby. To this it can be briefly replied, that in the science of medicine in the present day, analysis is becoming more and more penetrating, and multiplies without ceasing the number of facts; and inasmuch as our faculties of assimilation and our power of work develop *pari passu*, no one could seriously pretend to embrace and to fathom the whole science at a time. Specialisation has therefore become an inevitable necessity. One must accept it because it cannot be averted. Still it is important to place a limit on the indiscriminate cutting up of science and the barren isolation of specialities, so as not to go to the other extreme, which would certainly be deplorable." J.-M. Charcot, *Clinical Lectures on the Diseases of the Nervous System, o.c.*, pp. 5-6. [Translator's note: I assume that the underlined verb in the quote should be understood as 'claim' instead of 'pretend'].

17. The irony of fate is that precisely this movement will lead to psychology.

18. Both expressions come from J.-M. Charcot, *Clinical Lectures on the Diseases of the Nervous System, o.c.*, p. 1 and p. 4.

19. *Ibid.*, p. 5. See also Freud, Report on my Studies in Paris and Berlin Carried Out with the Assistance of a Travelling Bursary Granted from the University Jubilee Fund (October, 1885 — end of March, 1886), *o.c.*, p. 7.

20. "Several factors had contributed to this choice. In the first place, there was the certainty of finding collected together at the Salpêtrière a large assemblage of clinical material such as exists in Vienna only dispersed in various departments and therefore not easily accessible." Cf. Freud, Report on my Studies in Paris and Berlin Carried Out with the Assistance of a Travelling Bursary Granted from the University Jubilee Fund (October, 1885 — end of March, 1886), *o.c.*, p. 5.

21. J.-M. Charcot, *Clinical Lectures on the Diseases of the Nervous System, o.c.*, p. 4, Charcot's emphasis. [Translator's note: In Charcot's original text there were sixty beds (forty for women and twenty for men)].

22. An extrapyramidal syndrome characterised by sudden, involuntary and uncoordinated movements. There is a distinction between Chorea magna, characterised by constantly recurring convulsive movements and Chorea minor or sancti viti that primarily affects girls between the age of 6 and 13.

23. *Ibid.*, p. 12. It is Freud who will eventually solve the riddle of the Sphinx.

24. Cf. E. Roudinesco, *La bataille de cent ans. Histoire de la psychanalyse en France, o.c.*, p. 48: "Sous cette catégorie, on range des affections mentales auxquelles on attribue une origine organique précise; on les nomme 'fonctionnelles', c'est-à-dire sans inflammation ni lésion de l'organe où la douleur apparaît. Elles sont donc tenues pour des maladies nerveuses. [We can place those mental affections which can be attributed

to a precise organic origin under this heading; they are called 'functional', as they appear without any organic inflammation or lesion at the point where the pain is felt. They are therefore considered to be diseases of the nervous system]. A second attempt at explaining this appeared at the end of the nineteenth century. This explanation stressed the hereditary factor and was propounded by Charcot, amongst other scholars. As the aforementioned case descriptions indicate, the interest in the genealogy of the patient primarily focused on whether people suffering from nervousness, alcoholism or melancholy were present in the lineage of the patient in question. In 1885 microbiology began a revolution that literally transformed the field of medical science and that placed Charcot in a position to disseminate two seemingly opposed truths: hysteria is either a hereditarily transmittable nervous disease ("vérité pastorienne") or hysteria is not to be considered as a simulation, as deceit, but as an autonomous, functional nervous disease which exhibits no lesion. *Ibid.*, p. 26.

25. The problem with hysteria is that, even though it results from a 'functional or dynamic lesion', it could not, in the eyes of neurologists, be explained in terms of the anatomy of the nervous system. Charcot showed that the topography of hysterical symptoms remained deaf to neuro-anatomic laws.

26. These two stages are also known as 'clonism'. Cf. K. Libbrecht, *Hysterische waan. Symptoom of structuur?*, Ghent, Idesça, Pegasosreeks no. 3, 1989, p. 70. The apparent purposeless and ungraspable nature of hysterical manifestations will constitute a central theme in Freud's *Project.* Cf. S. Freud, Project for a Scientific Psychology, *o.c.*, pp. 347-349.

27. J.-M. Charcot, *Clinical Lectures on the Diseases of the Nervous System*, *o.c.*, p. 13. This description of a hysterical attack can already be located in 1881 in Charcot's introduction to the elementary work on the "grande hystérie" by P. Richer.

28. *Ibid.*, p. 13. Cf. Also K. Libbrecht, *Hysterical Psychosis, A Historical Survey*, *o.c.*, p. 41; E. Roudinesco, *La bataille de cent ans. Histoire de la psychanalyse en France*, *o.c.*, p. 36.

29. Roudinesco, on the other hand, mentions, in an allusion to Pontalis, the utter lack of 'psychical space' at the Salpêtrière. Whether this lack of space was effectively true is questionable, for Charcot not only led Freud on the track of psychology, but one of his students (Pierre Janet) also followed the same route. E. Roudinesco, *La bataille de cent ans. Histoire de la psychanalyse en France*, *o.c.*, p. 44; J.B. Pontalis, Le séjour de Freud à Paris, *Nouvelle Revue de Psychanalyse*, 1973, no. 8, p. 238.

30. E. Trillat, *Histoire de l'hystérie*, *o.c.*, p. 136.

31. *Ibid.*, p. 133.

32. This passage comes from E. Trillat, *Histoire de l'hystérie*, *o.c.*, p. 133. The last sentence seems to have had deplorable consequences. American surgeons, taking it too literally, started to remove the ovaries, convinced that the cause of the disease could thereby be obliterated. Ten years later Charcot rebutted the validity of these claims: "This is the horror of destruction: I have never propounded such folly ... I have never proclaimed that hysteria was caused by the ovarium ... This colleague from New York who accuses me of such ghastly excesses should have read my works instead of insisting that I should have said nothing." J.-M. Charcot, *The Tuesday Lessons 1887-*

1888, cited in E. Trillat, *Histoire de l'hystérie*, *o.c.*, p. 134. This sinister episode immediately calls to mind some passages in L. Israël's book, *L'hystérique, le sexe et le médecin*, Paris, Masson, 253 pp. Such practices still occur today. Recently, for instance, I heard of a slightly nervous female medical student whose "twisting and moving ovaries" were surgically put back in the right place.

33. "In his study of hysteria Charcot started out from the most fully developed cases, which he regarded as the perfect types of the disease. He began by reducing the connection of the neurosis with the genital system to its correct proportions by demonstrating the unsuspected frequency of cases of male hysteria and especially traumatic hysteria." Cf. Freud, Report on my Studies in Paris and Berlin Carried Out with the Assistance of a Travelling Bursary Granted from the University Jubilee fund (October, 1885 — end of March, 1886), *o.c.*, p. 11.
34. Cf. E. Jones, *Sigmund Freud, Life and Work*, *o.c.*, p. 273.
35. E. Roudinesco, *La bataille de cent ans. Histoire de la psychanalyse en France*, *o.c.*, p. 32.
36. As we will see, Charcot later attempted to develop an interpretation of the functional lesion, which, one could argue, goes in the direction of constructing a theory.
37. One could make the same observation about numerous other authors, including Breuer and Möbius. As clinicians they recognised the importance of sexuality. But they did not know what to do with anything that went beyond the phenomenology that surfaced from their case studies. Asking why there was an incapacity, is another question, but often not being *able* to do something is a case of not *wanting* to do it. Sulloway is right to point out that Freud was not the first to have recognised the important role played by sexuality ("Anerkennung"). But he mistakes the mere observation of Eros for a theorisation of it. Cf. F.J. Sulloway, *Freud, Biologist of the Mind*, London, Burnett Books, 1979, pp. 78-89.
38. E. Trillat, *Histoire de l'hystérie*, *o.c.*, pp. 147-153.
39. J.-M. Charcot, *Clinical Lectures on the Diseases of the Nervous System*, *o.c.*, p. 99.
40. That is to say, a less pronounced intermediate form.
41. The loss of sensitivity on one side.
42. I also quote the original text because of the delicate nature of this passage: "Mais chez lui, dans quelques cas au moins, l'irritation du testicule, retenu dans l'anneau, le pression du testicule, provoque ou arrête l'attaque." J.-M . Charcot, *Leçons sur les maladies du système nerveux, Faites à la Salpêtrière*, (1887), Paris, A. Delhaye et E. Lecrosnie, p. 116. I do not know what to make of the 'anneau' ['ring'] mentioned in the original text. Another passage from Charcot's book lifts any remaining doubts about the empirical mind of the Master: "The only hysterogenic zone discovered in Gui. is situated in the testicles and the course of the right spermatic cord reaching to the groin of the right side. The skin of the scrotum on this side is very sensitive, and when it is firmly pinched, exactly the same effects are produced as when one presses on the testicle itself or on the cord, that is to say, the development, or, on the other hand, the arrest of an attack." J.-M. Charcot, *Clinical Lectures on the Diseases of the Nervous System*, *o.c.*, p. 239. Charcot, however, did not attach any therapeutic implications to these findings. He further mentions several publications on the subject

of male hysteria: "This subject, male hysteria, is one of those which have been specially investigated by physicians of late years. Thus, one is able to count not less than five inaugural dissertations on this special subject presented to the Faculty of Paris between 1875 and 1880. Briquet in his excellent work has stated that for every twenty hysterical women, one man is met with, at least in Paris, affected with the same malady. This figure I confess appears to me to be a trifle too large. M. Klein, the author of one of these theses, to which I have already alluded, and which was written under the supervision of M. Ollier, has been able to collect from different authors seventy-seven cases of male hysteria, to which he has added three other personal observations, bringing the number up to the respectable total of eighty cases. Hence one is bound at least to conclude that hysteria in men is not such a very rare affection as is generally supposed." *Ibid.*, *o.c.*, p. 98. [Translator's note: In Charcot's original text the supervisor is called M. Ollivier]. From these case studies, Charcot propounds another difference between male and female hysteria: "Another fact is shown in the same work; namely, that when it occurs in men, hysteria is very often hereditary. This circumstance occurred twenty-three times out of thirty. It is generally maternal heredity, and similar heredity; thus it frequently happens that hysteria in the mother begets hysteria in the son." *Ibid.*, p. 99.

43. *Ibid.*, pp. 100-101.

44. E. Trillat, *Histoire de l'hystérie*, *o.c.*, p. 149. Trillat simply qualified these case studies, along with the complementary theoretical deductions, as historical. From my reading, which was aimed at discovering a psyche, or possibly a psychology, and its potential influence on Freud, this assessment seems slightly exaggerated. The case discussions and the experimental research were in any case not the first of their kind. It is impossible to determine from the publication the precise date of the lectures about this patient. Apart from the title, only the year 1886 is mentioned. One also learns from the text that the patient's traumatic accident took place on 21 October 1885, but that he was not directed to Charcot until 25 March 1886. What we do know is that Freud did not attend these lectures, as he had already returned to Vienna at that time. The account of these was made available by Babinski and Berbèz and was included in the appendix entitled 'Deux nouveaux cas de paralysie hystéro-traumatique chez l'homme'. However, I do not know whether they appeared in Freud's translation. Cf. J.-M. Charcot, *Clinical Lectures on the Diseases of the Nervous System*, *o.c.*, pp. 374-395. On the other hand, it is true that the text alludes on numerous occasions to lectures XX, XXI and XXII of the same volume. These lectures, given in May 1885, deal with 'Hysterical Brachial Monoplegia in the Male, of Traumatic Origin — Hystero-Traumatic Monoplegia'. *Ibid.*, pp. 261-316. From these lectures we understand that Charcot showed the similarity between traumatic diseases of the nervous system and hysteria with the help of hypnosis, in as early as May 1885: "We have been able, then, to obtain artificially in our hypnotised patient by means of suggestion, a perfect imitation of the monoplegia caused in our two patients by a process apparently very different, the action of traumatism." *Ibid.*, p. 302. One can find plenty of other identical psychological considerations corroborating this. I will therefore discuss the case Le Log., a more carefully written and substantiated analysis of this.

45. *Ibid.*, pp. 374-375, Charcot's emphasis.
46. Here hysterical mutism refers to the impossibility of speaking because of a hysterical paralysis of the larynx. I will deal with this theme in the chapter on aphasia.
47. *Ibid.*, p. 382.
48. *Ibid.*, pp. 382-383.
49. *Ibid.*, p. 383.
50. *Ibid.*, p. 384, Charcot's emphasis.
51. This is reminiscent of Freud, who wrote in his monograph on aphasia that the localisation of the psychical element of the idea in the nervous cell was nothing more than an elliptic description. Cf. S. Freud, *On Aphasia, A Critical Study*, (1891*b*), New York, International University Press, 1953, p. 55.
52. *Ibid.*, pp. 307-308.
53. *Ibid.*, pp. 308-309, my emphasis.
54. *Ibid.*, pp. 309-310, my emphasis.
55. The lecture referred to is lecture XVII, 'Isolation in the Treatment of Hysteria', *Ibid.*, pp. 205-219.
56. This was a rather ancient prescription which he, curiously enough, did *not* act in accordance with at the Salpêtrière. Had he complied with it, then the clinical entity of hysteria might have been disclosed by Charcot himself as being determined by 'psychical contagion'.
57. *Ibid.*, pp. 77-83.
58. *Ibid.*, p. 212.
59. *Ibid.*, p. 214, Charcot's emphasis.
60. For a psychoanalytical interpretation of the 'traitement moral', I refer the reader to P. Verhaeghe, *Klinische psychodiagnostiek vanuit de discourstheorie*, Ghent, Idesça, Pegasosreeks no. 5, pp. 81-95.
61. I would like to direct the reader to Freud's critical annotation added to the commemorative text in honour of Charcot: "Charcot's concern with hypnotic phenomena in hysterical patients led to very great advances in this important field of hitherto neglected and despite facts, for the weight of his name put an end once and for all to any doubt about the reality of hypnotic manifestations. But the exclusively nosographical approach adopted at the school of the Salpêtrière was not suitable for a purely psychological subject. The restriction of the study of hypnosis to hysterical patients, the differentiation between major and minor hypnotism, the hypothesis of three stages of 'major hypnosis', and their characterisation by somatic phenomena — all this sank in the estimation of Charcot's contemporaries when Liébault's pupil, Bernheim, set about constructing the theory of hypnotism on a more comprehensive psychological foundation and making suggestion the central point of hypnosis." S. Freud, Charcot, (1893*f*), *S.E.*, vol. III, pp. 22-23.
62. S. Freud, Report on my Studies in Paris and Berlin Carried Out with the Assistance of a Travelling Bursary Granted from the University Jubilee Fund (October, 1885 — end of March, 1886), *o.c.*, pp. 5-15.
63. I would like to make an observation about Meynert's reception of Freud. Meynert was openly hostile to Freud who, in spite of his training as an 'exact' neuro-

pathologist, dared to concern himself with hypnosis. In view of the fact that the "eindringlich" teachings (Freud's qualification) were part of Charcot's demonstrations, which precisely made male hysteria observable by means of experimental research (hypnosis), it is fitting to take into consideration the condescending comments Meynert pronounced on the subject of hypnosis at a reading on the second of July 1886 for the 'Gesellschaft der Ärzte'. The most sober evaluation of Meynert's reaction is found in Quackelbeen's conjecture, in which he stressed that Freud's *transference* onto his new master, Charcot, provoked Meynert's *jealousy*. From my own reading of the *Lectures* it seems that in this transference bond there was also room for a corresponding *transference of knowledge*. "In Vienna we have repeatedly had occasion to realise that the intellectual significance of an academic teacher is not necessarily combined with a direct personal influence on younger men which leads to the creation of a large and important school. If Charcot was so much more fortunate in this respect we must put it down to the personal qualities of the man, to the magic that emanated from his looks and from his voice, to the kindly openness which characterised his manner as soon as his relation with someone had overcome the stage of initial strangeness, to the willingness with which he put everything at the disposal of his pupils, and to his life-long loyalty to them." Cf. S. Freud, Charcot, *o.c.*, p. 16; J. Quackelbeen, De mannelijke hysterie. Hoe mannelijk?, *Colleges grondige studie van een auteur en/of een nosologisch concept uit het klinisch verleden*, Academiejaar 1990-1991; J. Quackelbeen and K. Libbrecht, On the Early History Of Male Hysteria and Psychic Trauma, Charcot's Influence on Freudian Thought, *Journal of the History of Behavioural Sciences*, 1995, vol. 31, 4, pp. 370-384. Th. Meynert, Über Hypnotismus, *Wiener Medizinische Blätter*, 1888, no. 23, pp. 718-720; Th. Meynert, *Wiener Klinische Wochenschrift*, 1888, no. 22, pp. 451-453, no. 23, pp. 473-476 and no. 24, pp. 495-498.

64. S. Freud, Some Points for a Comparative Study of Organic and Hysterical Motor Paralysis, *o.c.*, p. 71. One can read elsewhere that, "He succeeded in proving, by an unbroken chain of argument, that these paralyses were the result of ideas which had dominated the patient's brain at moments of special disposition. In this way, the mechanism of a hysterical phenomenon was explained for the first time. This incomparably fine piece of clinical research was afterwards taken up by his own pupil, Pierre Janet, as well as by Breuer and others who developed from it a theory of neurosis (...)." S. Freud, Charcot, *o.c.*, p. 22.

65. *Ibid.*, p. 12.

66. S. Freud, Some Points for a Comparative Study of Organic and Hysterical Motor Paralysis, *o.c.*, pp. 160-172. Let us not forget that Charcot had asked Freud to find an explanation for hysterical paralysis by comparing it to organic paralysis. One learns from Freud's correspondence with Fließ that a first draft of this article was written in May 1888. Cf. S. Freud, *The Complete Letters of Sigmund Freud to Wilhelm Fließ 1887-1904*, *o.c.*, letter dated 28 May 1888, pp. 21-23.

67. The anatomy of the nervous system shows that the course of the motor conductive fibres consists of two parts: the first one runs from the periphery (nerves) to the spinal cord; the second one goes from the spinal cord to the cerebral cortex. The anatomical

differences between these two parts of the 'route' explain very clearly the different symptomatologies emerging from the first or second part respectively. An injury in the first part results in a paralysis responding to the point-by-point projection, while an injury in the cerebral cortex causes a generalised paralysis. Accordingly, Freud proposed a different appellation in his study on aphasia: respectively "paralysie de projection" and "paralysie de représentation". Cf. S. Freud, Some Points for a Comparative Study of Organic and Hysterical Motor Paralysis, *o.c.*, p. 161.

68. S. Freud, Project for a Scientific Psychology, *o.c.*, p. 333.

69. In the case of hysterical aphasia, for example, the patient realised that his/her mouth was completely sealed (motor aphasia), while he still understood what was said to him. When speaking about a cortical injury, one never finds a clear delineation of the sensitive or sensorial language functions. Even more striking is the phenomenon involving a hysterical patient becoming deaf and dumb in one language, but not in another.

70. This phenomenon is also valid for other hysterical manifestations such as anaesthesia and contractions. Also worth mentioning is the fact that the patient suffering from an organic form of aphasia still manages to produce a 'yes', a 'no' or a swear word, whereas the hysterical patient, also suffering from aphasia, can no longer utter a single word.

71. S. Freud, Some Points for a Comparative Study of Organic and Hysterical Motor Paralysis, *o.c.*, pp. 167-168.

72. *Ibid.*, p. 170. I will come back to Freud's interpretation in more detail in the chapter on aphasia. For the time being, I would simply like to point out that Freud deemed a thorough investigation into the 'language function' necessary before he actually could give his opinion on the difference between hysterical and organic paralysis. Freud is perfectly aware of the explanatory limits of neurology when asking the reader the permission to move on to psychological ground.

73. *Ibid.*, p. 170, Freud's emphasis.

74. See above, p. 36.

75. J.-M. Charcot, *Clinical Lectures on the Diseases of the Nervous System*, *o.c.*, p. 290. It is also worth comparing this to the description of the ego Freud introduces in his *Project*. Cf. S. Freud, Project for a Scientific Psychology, *o.c.*, p. 323.

76. S. Freud, Some Points for a Comparative Study of Organic and Hysterical Motor Paralysis, *o.c.*, p. 170; J. Breuer and S. Freud, On the Psychical Mechanism of Hysterical Phenomena: Preliminary Communication, (1893*a*) in: *Studies on Hysteria*, *o.c.*, pp. 1-18.

77. This subtle distinction, to which M. Dhondt draws our attention, leads to epistemological considerations about psychoanalysis. A similar replacement of the notion of 'force' by that of 'energy' constituted a revolution within physics. For, 'energy' presupposes a medium or a field via which energy is transferred. Freud's introduction of the concept of psychical energy is accordingly explained. Cf. J. Quackelbeen, *Zeven avonden met Jacques Lacan, Psychoanalytische commentaren bij 'élévision'*, *o.c.*, pp. 102-106. I will come back to this point in the second part of this book.

78. S. Freud, Charcot, *o.c.*, pp. 11-23. This is apparently the only published obituary on Charcot. Cf. E. Roudinesco, *La bataille de cent ans. Histoire de la psychanalyse en France*, *o.c.*, p. 71.
79. S. Freud, Charcot, *o.c.*, p. 20.
80. *Ibid.*, pp. 20-21.
81. Charcot did eventually set up a laboratory for his psychology student, P. Janet.

CHAPTER 2

Suggestive Therapeutics

1. S. Freud, *Group Psychology and the Analysis of the Ego*, (1921*c*), *S.E.*, vol. XVIII, p. 89.
2. Freud was to describe these group mechanisms some 30 years later. Cf. S. Freud, *Group Psychology and the Analysis of the Ego*, (1921*c*), *S.E.*, vol. XVIII, pp. 65-94.
3. In the eyes of Nassif, the introduction of hypnosis to the medical institution was as fundamental as the 1838 statutory recognition of 'madness' in France. This does not mean that the application of the technique was to be granted a long life. Rather, from then onwards what had been known as "traitement moral" ever since Pinel, was systematically made possible. J. Nassif, *Freud, L'inconscient*, Paris, Flammarion, 1992, p. 468.
4. H. Bernheim, *Suggestive Therapeutics, A Treatise on the Nature and Uses of Hypnotism*, (1887), Translated from the second and revised French Edition by Christian A. Herter, 11 ed., Putnam's Sons, New York/London, 1899, 420 pp; H. Bernheim, *Die Suggestion und ihre Heilwirkungen*, (1887), Autorisierte deutsche Ausgabe von Dr. Sigm. Freud, (1888), Tübingen, Diskord, 1985, 415 pp. In *An Autobiographical Study*, Freud erroneously reports that he started the translation after his visit to Bernheim in August 1889. Cf. S. Freud, *An Autobiographical Study*, (1925*d*), *S.E.*, vol. XX, pp. 1-70. Freud too translated the second revised edition of 1887.
5. S. Freud, Preface to the Translation of Bernheim's Suggestion, (1888-89), *S.E.*, vol. I, p. 75. See also Th. Meynert, Über Hypnotismus, *o.c.*, pp. 718-720.
6. Meynert adopted another hostile viewpoint. He contended that hypnosis was hazardous for the mental health of the subject of the experiment and added that it boiled down to "an experimentally produced psychosis". Freud tersely remarked that this assertion was not borne out by all those involved in the field and that only those unfamiliar with it reported on the hazards of hypnosis. Cf. S. Freud, Preface to the Translation of Bernheim's Suggestion, (1888-89), *S.E.*, vol. I, p. 76. See also Th. Meynert, Über hypnotische Erscheinungen, *o.c.*, no. 22, pp. 451-453, no. 23, pp. 473-476 and no. 24, pp. 495-498.
7. S. Freud, Preface to the Translation of Bernheim's Suggestion, (1888-89), *o.c.*, p. 75.
8. H. Bernheim, *Suggestive Therapeutics*, *o.c.*, p. vii. This triumphal report sharply contrasts with the results achieved by Freud in his praxis. This was partly the reason

for his visit to Bernheim in the summer of 1889, when he expected to improve his hypnotic technique. Because of his own experience with hypnosis, Freud was later to strongly oppose the notion of authority.

9. *Ibid.*, p. viii. In the *Project*, Freud pointed to the hallucinatory nature of dreams as being one of their essential characteristics. Cf. S. Freud, Project for a Scientific Psychology, *o.c.*, pp. 338-340.

10. One need not lose sleep over this knowledge. For experimental research has shown that suggestions are discarded when in conflict with the morality of the sleeper.

11. *Ibid.*, p. x.

12. *Ibid.*, p. x. Attention, judgement, reality testing, inhibition and facilitation are all terms which will reoccur in Freud's psychology for neurologists in order to explain psychological mechanisms. I will later come back at greater length to some of these terms. Let me point out for the time being, that Freud was confronted with an instance of borrowing concepts from other fields. Bernheim's facilitation ["Bahnung"] and inhibition ["Hemmung"] originate from the neurophysiological field of that time. See also Exner, *Entwurf zu einer physiologischen Erklärung der psychischen Erscheinungen*, Leipzig and Vienna, Franz Deuticke, 1894, pp. 69-82.

13. For a meticulous description of the various stages according to their characteristic phenomena see H. Bernheim, *Suggestive Therapeutics*, *o.c.*, pp. 5-8 (Liébault) and pp. 11-15 (Bernheim).

14. *Ibid.*, p. 15.

15. Needless to say Bernheim's accommodating conception helped Freud when he decided to give up his attempts to hypnotise his own patients. Cf. J. Breuer and S. Freud, *Studies on Hysteria*, *o.c.*, pp. 107-109.

16. S. Freud, *An Autobiographical Study*, *o.c.*, p. 21.

17. H. Bernheim, *Suggestive Therapeutics*, *o.c.*, pp. 1-2.

18. *Ibid.*, p. x.

19. Bernheim also discusses changes in sensibility, motility, suggestive catalepsy and automatic movements. *Ibid.*, pp. 21-31.

20. I will come back to this point in Part I, Chapter 3 which deals with the *Studies on Hysteria*.

21. A case in point is his use of the observations and writings of A. Bertrand, General Noiset, Dr. Liébault and Ch. Richet on post-hypnotic suggestion.

22. H. Bernheim, *Suggestive Therapeutics*, *o.c.*, p. 32.

23. Freud analyzed 'false connections' on various occasions in his work. In his *Studies on Hysteria* he associates them, amongst other things, with the 'compulsion to associate' characteristic of compulsive neurotics, and he considers them as one of the factors responsible for the formation of dreams. Cf. J. Breuer and S. Freud, *Studies on Hysteria*, *o.c.*, p. 67. In his *Project*, he puts this 'compulsion to associate' down to the psychical processes which are part of the dream and he interprets the hysterical 'proton pseudos' as a disruption of 'thought' caused by sexual affects. Cf. Project for a Scientific Psychology, *o.c.*, pp. 352-356. In *The Interpretation of Dreams*, Freud alludes to them in relation to the suppressed unconscious motives: "This explanation [of the beautiful butcher's wife] struck me as unconvincing. Inadequate reasons like

this usually conceal unconfessed motives. They remind one of Bernheim's hypnotized patients. When one of these carries out a post-hypnotic suggestion and is asked why he is acting in this way, instead of saying that he has no idea, he feels compelled to invent some obviously unsatisfactory reason." S. Freud, *The Interpretation of Dreams*, (1900*a*), *S.E.*, vol. IV, pp. 147-148. Incidentally, this is the only reference to Bernheim in *The Interpretation of Dreams*, despite the several interesting theses and observations concerning dreams in the latter's writings.

24. A few years previously, massages and electric baths had managed to slightly improve her condition. Freud therefore prescribed warm baths as she also suffered from symptoms such as sensations of cold and pains in the limbs. He also massaged her whole body twice a day. Cf. J. Breuer and S. Freud, *Studies on Hysteria*, *o.c.*, p. 50.

25. One can subsequently attribute the status of a resistance phenomenon to the false connection. Just like the lapsus linguae and the unwillingness to know, it emerges in the transference onto the physician or analyst. Cf. J. Lacan, *The Seminar, Book I, Freud's Papers on Technique, 1953-1954*, Edited by J.-A. Miller, Translated with Notes by John Forrester, Cambridge, Cambridge University Press, 1988, pp. 38-51.

26. H. Bernheim, *Suggestive Therapeutics*, *o.c.*, p. 36.

27. *Ibid.*, pp. 3-4.

28. *Ibid.*, pp. 187-188.

29. *Ibid.*, p. 212.

30. The notion that everyone displays a certain degree of suggestibility may very well be replaced by the idea that a certain quota of resistance is put up against suggestion.

31. *Ibid.*, p. 210.

32. Bernheim repeatedly uses this term to designate hypnotism, since he was convinced that both phenomena were identical.

33. *Ibid.*, p. 291.

34. Cf. J. Breuer and S. Freud, *Studies on Hysteria*, *o.c.*, pp. 109-111.

35. H. Bernheim, *Suggestive Therapeutics*, *o.c.*, p. 291.

36. This partially explains why Freud advocated Charcot's view in the foreword he wrote to Bernheim's book. As we have seen in Charcot's *Clinical Lectures*, the notion of 'auto-suggestion' (which he defined as an idea highly charged with 'force' on account of its isolation from other cerebral activities) still offers the possibility of making a connection between the trauma and the effective idea.

37. One of Bernheim's tricks for indirectly imposing the 'suggestive' idea consists in impressing a new personality onto the patient: "One of my patients, a good somnambulist, had an unconquerable distaste for meat. I had in vain suggested that she would eat it with pleasure; she absolutely refused to accept the suggestion, she did not even wish to taste meat during her sleep. I made her change her personality; she was no longer herself; and then she ate the meat with the greatest appetite." *Ibid.*, p. 210.

38. Charcot, like Bernheim, had very little interest in his patient's life history. However, his 'excessively intense idea' clearly shows more similarities with that of Freud as developed in the *Project*. Cf. also the 'counter will' ["Gegenwillen"] of hysterical patients in S. Freud, A Case of Successful Treatment by Hypnotism — With Some

Remarks on the Origin of Hysterical Symptoms through 'Counter Will', (1892-93), *S.E.*, vol. I, pp. 115-128. I will come back to this question later on in this chapter.

39. H. Bernheim, *Suggestive Therapeutics*, *o.c.*, pp. 57-58. Indeed, this question caused much ink to flow. There was a real controversy, at one stage, between those advocating a strict legal control of the application of hypnosis which would be the prerogative of the medical profession and those who realised that no-one would ever suggest murders. Joseph Delboeuf from Liege, for one, experimentally proved that the somnambulic state could not eliminate the critical faculty. An effect, such as the one described in Bernheim's demonstration, can be explained by the fact that the complete absorption in the suggested role is merely an appearance. For the hypnotised patient senses the experimental nature of the situation. Bernheim also shared this view. Cf. F. Duyckaerts, Sigmund Freud: lecteur de Joseph Delboeuf, *Frénésie, Histoire, Psychiatrie, Psychanalyse*, 1989, II, n° 8, p. 74. One more observation on the link between crime and hypnosis: history proved Delboeuf right in the case of the hypnosis of individuals, but history equally speaks of the possibility of obliterating the critical faculty — which would pave the way to crime — when an entire nation succumbs to a hypnotic influencing.
40. H. Bernheim, *Suggestive Therapeutics*, *o.c.*, pp. 59-60.
41. *Ibid.*, p. 65.
42. *Ibid.*, pp. 66.
43. *Ibid.*, pp. 67-69.
44. The fifth chapter of Bernheim's book deals with the topic of suggestion in a waking state. *Ibid.*, pp. 78-86. The fact that hypnosis is not a prerequisite for psychical treatment will have a considerable incidence on Freud's emancipation from Breuer's notion of the hypnoid state.
45. *Ibid.*, p. 125.
46. *Ibid.*, p. 133.
47. In a footnote to his translation Freud attributes this finding to Flechsig.
48. *Ibid.*, p. 129.
49. *Ibid.*, p. 129.
50. *Ibid.*, p. 130.
51. *Ibid.*, p. 131.
52. S. Freud, Project for a Scientific Psychology, *o.c.*, pp. 327-337.
53. H. Bernheim, *Suggestive Therapeutics*, *o.c.*, p. 131.
54. Bernheim admits that such a description amounts to no more than a formula and adds: "I do not pretend to advance a theory". *Ibid.*, p. 139.
55. Bernheim attributed both notions to Brown-Séquard: "The organism possesses dynamic mechanisms, by the aid of which control or activity may be suddenly suspended. This is what Brown-Séquard calls *inhibition*. The control or activity may on the contrary be re-enforced, and Brown-Séquard calls this *dynamogeny*." *Ibid.*, p. 138.
56. Term used by Brown-Séquard.
57. Delboeuf, for one, did not believe in the inevitable loss of memory of what happened during hypnosis, and devised experiments in order to prove this. Together with

Charles Féré he managed to demonstrate that memory remains intact. Cf. F. Duyckaerts, Sigmund Freud: lecteur de Joseph Delboeuf, *o.c.*, p. 73.

58. H. Bernheim, *Suggestive Therapeutics*, *o.c.*, p. 147.

59. Bernheim writes: "I do not say unconscious memories, evidently", but does not justify this choice. *Ibid.*, p. 145.

60. J. Breuer and S. Freud, *Studies on Hysteria*, *o.c.*, pp. 109-111.

61. Breuer postulates two extreme states in the central nervous system: dreamless sleep and the conscious waking state. The essential difference between these two states is "[...] that in sleep the paths of connection and conduction in the brain are not traversable by excitations of the psychical elements (cortical cells?), whereas in waking life they are completely so traversable. [...] The existence of these two different conditions of the paths of conduction can, it seems, only be made intelligible if we suppose that in waking life those paths are in a state of tonic excitation (what Exner calls 'intercellular tetanus'), that this intracerebral excitation is what determines their conductive capability, and the diminution and disappearance of that excitation is what sets up the state of sleep." *Ibid.*, p. 193.

62. As is commonly known, it was his treatment of Anna O. that led him to this procedure. Cf. F. Geerardyn, The Princeps Case of Psychoanalysis: Breuer's Anna O. Revisited, *Journal of the Centre for Freudian Analysis and Research*, 1994, 4, pp. 54-70.

63. As I pointed out earlier, the first part of the book as well as Freud's foreword appeared in August 1888. The second part was not translated by Freud. In a brief afterword, written in January 1889, Freud thanked Dr. Otto von Springer who provided all the translations of the case histories. Cf. H. Bernheim, *Die Suggestion und Ihre Heilwirkung*, *o.c.*, p. 415. [Lacks in an English translation]

64. H. Bernheim, *Suggestive Therapeutics*, *o.c.*, p. 197.

65. *Ibid.*, pp. 289-291.

66. In this context 'transference' refers to the transition of a symptom from one half of the body to the other.

67. *Ibid.*, p. 213.

68. For instance: "became ill after the funeral of a sister", "hysterical attack following a dispute with a sister", "hysterical attack on learning of the death of her mother and the occurrence of a second attack at the cemetery", "occurrence of a generalised paraplegia (paralysis) on the occasion of her first menstruation at the age of eighteen".

69. Cf. the reference to therapy according to Delboeuf in J. Breuer and S. Freud, On the Psychical Mechanism of Hysterical Phenomena: Preliminary Communication, *o.c.*, in: J. Breuer and S. Freud, *Studies on Hysteria*, *o.c.*, p. 7. In *The Interpretation of Dreams* Freud refers to: J. Delboeuf, *Le sommeil et les rêves*, Paris, 1885; H. Maudsley, *Physiology and Pathology of Mind*, London, 1868; L.F.A. Maury, Nouvelles observations sur les analogies des phénomènes du rêve et de l'aliénation mentale, *Annales médico-psychologiques*, 1853, no. 5, p. 404; L.F.A. Maury, *Le sommeil et les rêves*, Paris, 1878.

70. There are some doubts about the dates of the case history of Emmy von N. In his own text, Freud reports that the treatment started on 1 May 1889. Strachey, however, notes

the inconsistency of the date mentioned by Freud and estimates that 1 May 1888 is more probably the correct date. The noticeable influence of Bernheim's book in the daily notes encourages one to opt for Strachey's version. One finds additional evidence in Freud's letter to Fließ dated the 28 May 1888. In this letter — written while a female patient of his, whose name is not mentioned, was under hypnosis — he refers to both his translation and an article on hysteria published in Villaret's *Handwörterbuch*. This article alludes to Breuer's psycho-cathartic method for the very first time and corresponds with Freud's first application of it. Cf. S. Freud, *The Complete Letters of Sigmund Freud to Wilhelm Fließ 1887-1904*, *o.c.*, pp. 21-22. S. Freud, Hysteria, (1888*b*), *S.E.*, vol. I, pp. 53-57.

71. S. Freud, Remembering, Repeating and Working-Through, (1914*g*), *S.E.*, vol. XII, p. 154.
72. S. Freud, Preface to the Translation of Bernheims *Suggestion*, (1888-89), *S.E.*, vol. I, p. 77.
73. J.-M. Charcot, *Clinical Lectures on the Diseases of the Nervous System*, *o.c.*, p. 290. Charcot refers here to his own study entitled *Essai d'une distinction nosographique des divers états nerveux compris sous le nom d'hypnotisme*, Note communiquée à l'Académie des Sciences, 1883.
74. J.-M. Charcot, *Clinical Lectures on the Diseases of the Nervous System*, *o.c.*, p. 290.
75. *Ibid.*, p. 290.
76. *Ibid.*, p. 292.
77. H. Bernheim, *Suggestive Therapeutics*, *o.c.*, pp. 88-91.
78. S. Freud, Preface to the Translation of Bernheim's *Suggestion*, *o.c.*, p. 78.
79. *Ibid.*, p. 78.
80. *Ibid.*, p. 79.
81. *Ibid.*, p. 82.
82. *Ibid.*, p. 83. Compare this with Charcot's formulation. See above, p. 37.
83. *Ibid.*, p. 83.
84. *Ibid.*, pp. 83-84.
85. It is worth mentioning that the foreword of the second edition of the translation (1896) was substantially shorter and that it thus left out the discussion just touched upon. He only deals with the necessity for a psychology, i.e., a psychological explanation of suggestion.
86. *Ibid.*, pp. 82-83.
87. Be it or not in collaboration with Josef Breuer whose formulation of the psychical "Spaltung" resembles Charcot's psychological indication of the functional lesion. It also implies that Freud makes room for Breuer's theory of hypnoid states.
88. *Ibid.*, p. 84. Freud reiterated this position in a critical footnote to Bernheim's work in which the latter ascribed the function of memory (depending on the degree of consciousness) to various parts of the nervous system. "Moreover, that which the mind has lost track of, spinal automatism may resume. The artist no longer remembers all the phrases of a musical composition. His recollection has become defective; he is incapable of playing the piece through, in consequence of his mental confusion. The spinal memory, if I may use the expression, supplements the cerebral memory. The

fingers frequently recover the difficult arrangements of stops and movements on the key-board, and accomplish them precisely, even when these movements assimilated, so to speak, by the spinal cord, have become a mechanical operation, owing to their frequent repetition." Upon which Freud commented: "It appears to me unjustifiable, and unnecessary, to assume that an executive act changes its localization in the nervous system if it is begun consciously and continued later unconsciously. It is, on the contrary, probable that the portion of the brain concerned can operate with a varying quota of attention (or consciousness)." Cf. H. Bernheim, *Suggestive Therapeutics*, *o.c.*, p. 127. For Freud's comment see S. Freud, Preface to the Translation of Bernheim's *Suggestion*, *o.c.*, pp. 84-85, footnote 1.

89. Which paraphrases in a way the rather disturbing expression "the unconscious is the *primary* question of psychology", a question which introduced me to psychoanalysis. J. Quackelbeen, *Colleges principes en methodes van de psychologische raadpleging*, Academic Year 1981-1982, University of Ghent.

CHAPTER 3

Studies on Hysteria

1. J. Breuer and S. Freud, *Studies on Hysteria*, *o.c.*; Sigmund Freud, Project for a Scientific Psychology, *o.c.*
2. Jones in particular propounds this view. He accounts for the 'exactness' of the *Project* by arguing that Freud wanted to accommodate Fließ who was strongly leaning towards physiology. Cf. E. Jones, *Sigmund Freud, Life and Work*, *o.c.*, p. 329; J. Buelens, *Sigmund Freud, Kind van zijn tijd*, Meppel, Boom, 1971, p. 186.
3. I would like to mention one exception, I.F. Knight's article 'Freud's "Project": a theory for *Studies on Hysteria*, *Journal of the History of the Behavioural Sciences*, 1984, pp. 340-358.
4. Buelens advocates a totally different viewpoint. He argues that it is impossible to make out the respective importance of both authors. He explicitly departs from the assumption that the theoretical chapter is the product of an intense collaboration between Freud and Breuer. Cf. J. Buelens, *Sigmund Freud, Kind van zijn tijd*, *o.c.*, pp. 120-124.
5. Freud retrospectively stressed these two aspects in the *Studies*. Cf. S. Freud, On the History of the Psycho-Analytic Movement, (1914*d*), *S.E.*, vol. XIV, pp. 11-13; S. Freud, *An Autobiographical Study*, *o.c.*, pp. 23-26. This statement is invariably weakened in the secondary literature by references to Breuer's theoretical chapter in which he does allude to defence and sexuality as being two important elements partaking in the aetiology of hysteria.
6. S. Freud, *The Complete Letters of Sigmund Freud to Wilhelm Fließ 1887-1904*, *o.c.*, letter dated 28 June, 1892, p. 31.
7. *Ibid.*, letter dated 20 April, 1895, p. 125.

8. A. Hirschmüller, *The life and work of Josef Breuer, Physiology and Psychoanalysis*, (1978), New York and London, New York University Press, 1989, p. 96.
9. Freud must have been very inspired by Breuer's story, for he is said to have reported it to Charcot who, for his part, did not seem to be overly impressed. E. Jones, *Sigmund Freud, Life and Work*, *o.c.*, p. 248.
10. Jones and Hirschmüller, amongst others, report different reasons for the delayed publication of the *Studies*. Jones maintains that when Freud drew Breuer's attention to the problems of hysteria — in as early as 1888 or 1889 — he met with great resistance on the part of Breuer. Breuer's reluctance may be linked with the complications at the end of Anna O.'s treatment. Hirschmüller, who is obviously more sympathetic to Breuer, argues that, apart from medical discretion, Breuer wanted to make sure that Anna O.'s treatment had been completed successfully — which was not the case before 1890. A second possibility to which Hirschmüller alludes has to do with the method employed by Freud. Breuer is said not to have agreed with the combination of the cathartic method and direct hypnotic suggestion. Cf. E. Jones, *Sigmund Freud, Life and Work*, *o.c.*, p. 275; A. Hirschmüller, *The Life and Work of Josef Breuer, Physiology and Psychoanalysis*, *o.c.*, pp. 152-153.
11. This is what Breuer exclaimed upon terminating the treatment. Cf. K. Levin, *Freud's Early Psychology of the Neuroses, A Historical Perspective*, Hassocks, The Harvester Press, 1978, p. 84; P.F. Cranefield, Josef Breuer's Evaluation of His Contribution to Psychoanalysis, *International Journal of Psychoanalysis*, 1958, vol. 39, pp. 319-322.
12. S. Freud, Psychical (or Mental) Treatment, (1905*b*), *S.E.*, vol. VII, pp. 281-302. For a long time it was thought that this article was written in 1905. Indeed, it was published in *Die Gesundheit*, a popular book about medicine. The content of this article also casts a doubt on the date of its origin, even though one was surprised that in as late as 1905 Freud dedicated an entire article exclusively to hypnosis. Even on a cursory reading of other works from that same year such as *Three Essays on Sexuality* and the case history of Dora, this view appears outdated. As far as Freud's starting point is concerned, even today it is conducive to thought about what psychotherapy essentially should be. Freud's treatment of the technique of hypnosis is undoubtedly the most well known to us.
13. *Ibid.*, p. 283. In the writings of Frederik van Eeden dating from the same period, I found a similar description of psychotherapy as being a treatment using tools which have a direct impact on the psyche: "Under the term psychotherapy I include all cures which attempt to eradicate the disease through psychical means or via the intervention of psychical functions." Cf. F, van Eeden, Het beginsel der psychotherapie, (1894), in: *Frederik van Eeden, Een bloemlezing uit zijn studies*, Katwijk, Servire, 1982, p. 84.
14. Let me draw your attention to Freud's translation of Charcot's *Lectures*, in which one finds an almost identical phrasing. Cf. above pp. 25-26.
15. S. Freud, Psychical (or Mental) Treatment, *o.c.*, pp. 285-286.
16. *Ibid.*, p. 286.
17. As a matter of fact, the conception of neuroses as functional disorders concealed the lack of anatomical knowledge of the nervous system.

18. *Ibid.*, p. 288.
19. *Ibid.*, p. 288. The psychical mechanism of attention is introduced here for the first time in Freud's work. It refers to the use of a psychical process in order to influence the body. Later, this mechanism will principally denote the act of focusing one's attention on a psychical element, such as an idea. In this respect, this mechanism lies at the very basis of the rule of free association. I will deal more extensively with this notion in the second part of this book.
20. *Ibid.*, p. 291.
21. Five years later, in the *Studies*, Freud was to refer to this human liking ("Zuneigung") aroused in the patient by the doctor by using the term transference. He also recognised its function as being one of resistance. I will come back to this point in section 3.5.
22. *Ibid.*, p. 293.
23. *Ibid.*, p. 295.
24. *Ibid.*, p. 296.
25. *Ibid.*, pp. 300-301.
26. Cf. P. Verhaeghe, *Klinische psychodiagnostiek vanuit de discourstheorie. Impasses en antwoorden*, *o.c.*, pp. 81-95.
27. H. Bernheim, *Suggestive Therapeutics*, *o.c.*, p. 138.
28. J. Breuer and S. Freud, *Studies on Hysteria*, *o.c.* pp. 21-47.
29. I would like to make the following observation. The spontaneously occurring auto-hypnosis may not be as spontaneous as Breuer claims. Let us not forget that Breuer was very well versed in the literature on hypnotism and that he also experimented with hypnosis for a certain time. Cf. A. Hirschmüller, *The Life and Work of Josef Breuer, Physiology and Psychoanalysis*, *o.c.*, pp. 91-95. This would imply that Anna O.'s "total unsuggestibility" was only an appearance. For didn't Bernheim also argue that hypnosis itself is purely determined by suggestion?
30. On the relationship between Anna O. and her father, the reader merely learns that she used to nurse him during his illness. The relationship she had with her mother, brothers and sisters is never alluded to. Is this a matter of discretion, didactic intention or misjudgement? In any case, he completely overlooked her transference. Cf. J. Lacan, *Le Séminaire, Livre VIII, Le Transfert, (1960-1961)*, Paris, du Seuil, 1991, pp. 16-17; F. Geerardyn, The Princeps Case of Psychoanalysis: Breuer's Anna O. Revisited, *Journal of the Centre for Freudian Analysis and Research*, 1994, 4, pp. 54-70.
31. Concluded in December 1892.
32. It is fairly obvious that Breuer and Freud allude to the 'Charcotian' traumatic hysteria, that is to say to cases involving a recent physical trauma that is easily demarcated, such as the cases of "railway spine" or "railway brain". Let me add that Charcot was also quick to recognise the role of physical impressions in psychical traumas. Cf. above, Chapter 1.
33. In medical terms this appellation was originally used to describe autonomous diseases which were thus not caused by any other diseases.
34. J. Breuer and S. Freud, *Studies on Hysteria*, *o.c.* p. 6.
35. *Ibid.*, p. 6.

36. *Ibid.*, p. 68.
37. S. Freud, On the Psychical Mechanism of Hysterical Phenomena: a Lecture, (1893*h*), *S.E.*, vol. III, pp. 27-39. The date of this is between the publication of the two parts of the 'Preliminary Communication'. Freud's lecture is, furthermore, written in a more linear fashion.
38. Unlike in the 'Preliminary Communication', Freud in his lecture departs from Charcot and his demonstrations whereas 'Preliminary Communication' opens on the case description of Anna O.
39. Cf. chapter 1.
40. S. Freud, On the Psychical Mechanism of Hysterical Phenomena: a lecture, *o.c.*, p. 34.
41. J. Breuer and S. Freud, *Studies on Hysteria, o.c.* p. 185.
42. Freud will claim the opposite: in the *Studies* hysteria does not exist. See also S. Freud, Preface and Footnotes to Charcot's *Tuesday Lectures (1892-94)*, (1892-94), *S.E.*, vol. I, pp. 137-143.
43. Even today, this is the viewpoint of many authors who speak of affects or emotions. Cf. N. Frijda, *The Emotions*, Cambridge, Cambridge University Press, 1986, 544 pp.
44. For the significance of Breuer's physiological work, I refer the reader to A. Hirschmüller, *The Life and Work of Josef Breuer, Physiology and Psychoanalysis, o.c.*, pp. 51-86.
45. J. Breuer and S. Freud, *Studies on Hysteria, o.c.*, p. 188.
46. F. Geerardyn, Paul Julius Möbius: een gemiste ontmoeting met de psychologie?, *Rondzendbrief uit het Freudiaanse Veld*, 1993, nr. 53, pp. 3-12.
47. J. Breuer and S. Freud, *Studies on Hysteria, o.c.*, p. 191. There is a reference to Oppenheim's notion of "the instability of the molecules" in a footnote to this statement.
48. Let me remind you that Bernheim, in his book on suggestion, advocates the conception of the dream as the "Normalvorbild" of the somnambulistic state. Freud too had been interested in this topic for quite some time. This interest stemmed from both the literature on hypnosis as well as from his clinic.
49. In other terms, sensory stimuli do not become conscious perceptions.
50. J. Breuer and S. Freud, *Studies on Hysteria, o.c.*, p. 193.
51. *Ibid.*, pp. 193-194.
52. *Ibid.*, p. 197. As the citation intimates, Breuer attributes the postulate of this tendency to Freud. One indeed finds a first formulation of this law on the psychical mechanism of hysterical phenomena in Freud's 'Lecture' (and not in the 'Preliminary Communication'). He writes that "If a person experiences a psychical impression, something in his nervous system which we will for the moment call the sum of excitation is increased. Now in every individual there exists a tendency to diminish this sum of excitation once more, in order to preserve his health. The increase of the sum of excitation takes place along sensory paths, and its diminution along motor ones." Cf. S. Freud, On the Psychical Mechanism of Hysterical Phenomena: a Lecture, *o.c.*, p. 36. The same principle can be found in the *Project* under the appellation of the

"principle of inertia" (of neurones). Cf. S. Freud, Project for a Scientific Psychology, *o.c.*, p. 296.

53. Breuer also indicates that the comparison with an electrical lighting system is still applicable. For if the optimal tension is exceeded in the network of lines of conduction, the functioning of it could be impaired because the electric light filaments could, for instance, burn through. *Ibid.* p. 198.
54. *Ibid.*, p. 199.
55. *Ibid.*, p. 200.
56. *Ibid.*, p. 200.
57. *Ibid.*, p. 200.
58. *Ibid.*, p. 203. This formulation echoes that of Oppenheim and von Strümpell. Cf. H. Oppenheim, Thatsächliches und Hypothetisches über das Wesen der Hysterie, *Berliner klinische Wochenschrift*, 1890, vol. 27; A. von Strümpell, *Über die Entstehung und die Heilung von Krankheiten durch Vorstellungen*, Erlangen, 1844. Such "an abnormal expression of the emotions" is found in the conversion symptom. Strümpell's name is often mentioned in this context as one of the pioneers in the field of psychosomatics.
59. J. Breuer and S. Freud, *Studies on Hysteria, o.c.*, p. 204. Breuer distinguishes between four different forms of dispositions: the innate disposition, the pubertal disposition (which is characterised by a prolonged state of excitation), one which is due to a state of exhaustion (in the case of illnesses or under-nourishment), and one which originates from a local illness.
60. *Ibid.*, p. 205.
61. *Ibid.*, p. 213.
62. *Ibid.*, p. 209.
63. The difference and the analogy between both phenomena was already touched upon in the 'Preliminary Communication'. Cf. J. Breuer and S. Freud, On the Psychical Mechanism of Hysterical Phenomena, *o.c.*, p. 5. See also S. Freud, The Psychical Mechanism of Hysterical Phenomena: a Lecture, *o.c.*, pp. 28-29; S. Freud, Observation of a Severe Case of Hemi-Anaesthesia in a Hysterical Male, (1886*d*), *S.E.*, vol. I, pp. 25-31; J. Quackelbeen and K. Libbrecht, On the Early History Of Male Hysteria and Psychic Trauma, Charcot's Influence on Freudian Thought, *o.c.*, pp. 370-384.
64. J. Breuer and S. Freud, *Studies on Hysteria, o.c.*, p. 210.
65. *Ibid.*, p. 214. S. Freud, The Neuro-Psychosis of Defence (An Attempt at a Psychological Theory of Acquired Hysteria, of Many Phobias and Obsessions and of Certain Hallucinatory Psychoses), (1894*a*), *S.E.*, vol. III, pp. 44-61.
66. J. Breuer and S. Freud, *Studies on Hysteria, o.c.*, p. 214, Breuer's emphasis.
67. P.J. Möbius, Über Astasie-Abasie, (1890), *Neurologische Beiträge*, vol. 1, p. 17, cited by J. Breuer and S. Freud, *Studies on Hysteria, o.c.*, p. 215. As we have seen in the discussion of the 'Preliminary Communication', the dissociation of the psyche can be caused by a trauma or can be the result of an innate disposition that precedes the trauma. Möbius's formulation echoes that of Herbart, who speaks of a fight between various ideas, the strongest of which becomes conscious.
68. *Ibid.*, p. 216.

69. *Ibid.*, p. 218.
70. *Ibid.*, p. 218.
71. *Ibid.*, pp. 222-223.
72. One also finds this explanation in S. Freud, The Neuro-Psychosis of Defence (An Attempt at a Psychological Theory of Acquired Hysteria, of Many Phobias and Obsessions and of Certain Hallucinatory Psychoses), *o.c.*, pp. 58-61.
73. J. Breuer and S. Freud, *Studies on Hysteria*, *o.c.*, p. 224.
74. *Ibid.*, p. 227.
75. *Ibid.*, pp. 227-228.
76. Freud had already voiced an opposition to this. See above, Chapter 2, p. 73 and n. 88.
77. *Ibid.*, p. 229.
78. *Ibid.*, p. 232. This is recurrently emphasised by Freud in his case histories published in the *Studies*.
79. Cf. K. Libbrecht, Mystici, hysterici en hun verhouding tot de Andere, *Rondzendbrief uit het Freudiaanse Veld*, 1991, No. 47, pp. 41-50.
80. J. Breuer and S. Freud, *Studies on Hysteria*, *o.c.*, p. 233.
81. Breuer encountered a combination of both in Anna O.: her 'day-dreaming' or 'private theatre' and the affective attention she devoted to her father.
82. *Ibid.*, pp. 235-236.
83. *Ibid.*, p. 240.
84. *Ibid.*, p. 241.
85. *Ibid.*, p. 243.
86. *Ibid.*, p. 244.
87. *Ibid.*, pp. 245-246.
88. Breuer alludes to Freud's discovery that the coitus interruptus and ejaculatio praecox cause anxiety neurosis. S. Freud, On the Grounds for Detaching a Particular Syndrome from Neurasthenia under the Description 'Anxiety Neurosis', (1895 [1894]), *S.E.*, vol. III, pp. 90-115. I will return at greater length to this point in the second part of this book.
89. Four documents concerning a case Freud treated during that period were recently included in the Nachtragsband to the *Gesammelte Werke*. Cf. S. Freud, Anamnese 'Nina R.', (1978*a* [1891]), *G.W.*, Nachtragsband, pp. 313-315; S. Freud, Krankengeschichte 'Nina R.', (1978*b* [1893]), *G.W.*, Nachtragsband, pp. 316-319; S. Freud, Brief an Robert Binswanger vom 7. jan. 1894, (1978*c* [1894]), *G.W.*, Nachtragsband, p. 321; J. Breuer, Bericht über 'Nina R.', (1978 [1893]), *G.W.*, Nachtragsband, p. 320. It is important to keep in mind the fact that the case histories reflect an evolution in the therapeutic technique and the theoretical viewpoints they give rise to. Chronologically speaking, the chapter on psychotherapy was the last to be written and it conveys the views which Freud held in 1895. One can deduce from his correspondence with Fließ that he was still busy writing it in March 1895. Cf. S. Freud, *The Complete Letters of Sigmund Freud to Wilhelm Fließ 1887-1904*, *o.c.*, letters dated 4, 8 and 13 March 1895, pp. 113-121.
90. S.n., Wegwerktekst, *Rondzendbrief uit het Freudiaanse Veld*, 1991, nr. 46, pp. 46-47. For a psychoanalytical viewpoint concerning the cure and the therapeutic effects

consult J. Quackelbeen, *Zeven avonden met Jacques Lacan, Psychoanalytische commentaren bij 'Télévision', o.c.*, pp. 50-53.

91. A cogent argument in favour of this view, as well as a bibliography on this subject can be found in H. Van Hoorde, Inleiding tot de vergadering van het 'Gezelschap voor psychoanalyse en psychotherapie' te Gent in het Flanders Hotel op 30 september 1990, *Rondzendbrief uit het Freudiaanse Veld*, 1991, no. 46, pp. 15-19.

92. J. Breuer and S. Freud, On the Psychical Mechanism of Hysterical Phenomena: Preliminary Communication, *o.c.*, pp. 1-19.

93. As such, this view is diametrically opposed to Breuer's conception in which the suggestibility of the hysterical patient is explained by the "splitting" of the mind.

94. None of the cases described by Freud exhibit this characteristic, even though he genuinely attempted to model his treatment of Emmy von N. on the morning and evening sessions Breuer was wont to hold.

95. J. Breuer and S. Freud, *Studies on Hysteria, o.c.*, p. 256.

96. The minimalist option, as advocated by Breuer, prescribes the application of the hypno-cathartic method for the treatment of hysterical symptoms. If there is already a proclivity to focus on the symptom in the *Studies on Hysteria*, it must be accredited to Breuer and not to Freud.

97. *Ibid.*, pp. 256-257.

98. The evolution of Freud's conception of the "Aktualneurosen" can be followed in his correspondence with Fließ. It seems indeed that for a relatively long time Freud was convinced of the existence of neuroses in which no psychical mechanism played a part. The examination of the "Aktualneurosen" gave him a good understanding of the importance of sexuality, also in the case of neuroses where psychical mechanisms did not come into play. I will come back to this point in the second part of the present book.

99. *Ibid.*, p. 259.

100. *Ibid.*, pp. 260-261. This statement by Freud throws a different light on the question alluded to earlier, namely the delayed publication of the *Studies on Hysteria*. For Freud suggests that he experienced no difficulty in procuring the necessary quantity of clinical material. Freud only seems to have carried out the agreement he had initially made with Breuer (June 1892). According to this agreement only pure cases of hysteria were to be covered in the book. In March 1895, i.e. the period during which he was working on his chapter on psychotherapy, he had reached a radically different viewpoint. His agreement with Breuer appeared to be untenable, for he now believed that pure cases of hysteria do not exist. The discrepancy between the declared intentions and the final result backs up the thesis that Freud, unlike Breuer, had effectively progressed in the course of the elaboration of the *Studies*.

101. In his case history Breuer observes that the sexual element was particularly undeveloped: "She had never been in love; and in all the enormous number of hallucinations which occurred during her illness that element of mental life never emerged." Cf. *Ibid.*, p. 22. Freud later revised his judgement and argued that Breuer was not enough of a Faust to be in a position effectively to inaugurate psychotherapy, precisely because he recoiled from facing the demon that inhabits hysteria. This demon is not

the actual physiologically based splitting of the mind, as Breuer contended in his theoretical chapter, but rather Eros as it surfaces through the transference process. Cf. S. Freud, *Letters of Sigmund Freud 1873-1939, o.c.*, letter to Stephan Zweig, dated 2 June 1932, pp. 427-428; J. Lacan, *Le Séminaire, Livre VIII, Le Transfert, o.c.*, pp. 16-17; F. Geerardyn, The Princeps Case of Psychoanalysis: Breuer's Anna O. Revisited, *Journal of the Centre for Freudian Analysis and Research*, 1994, 4, pp. 54-70.

102. J. Breuer and S. Freud, *Studies on Hysteria, o.c.*, p. 260. As we have seen in the chapter devoted to Freud's translation of Bernheim's book, he commenced the treatment of Emmy von N. in May 1888. The following dates were found for the remaining case studies: August 1890 (Căcilie M.); autumn 1892 (Elisabeth von R.); end 1892 (Lucy R.); 1893 (Nina R.); August 1893 (Katharina).

103. J. Breuer and S. Freud, *Studies on Hysteria, o.c.*, p. 265, my emphasis.

104. Let us not be mistaken by the 'level of intelligence' Freud mentions. He qualifies his assertion by writing that any trace of feebleness of mind renders the application of the method more difficult. *Ibid.*, p. 265. For an indication concerning possible YAVIS-conceptions, I refer the reader to J. Quackelbeen, *Zeven avonden met Jacques Lacan, Psychoanalytische commentaren bij 'Télévision', o.c.*, pp. 77-98.

105. J. Breuer and S. Freud, *Studies on Hysteria, o.c.*, pp. 265-266.

106. Cf. S. Freud, Address Delivered in the Goethe House at Frankfurt, (1930*e*), *S.E.*, vol. XXI, pp. 208-212.

107. The Oedipus complex is mentioned for the very first time in a letter to Fließ dated October 15, 1897. Cf. S. Freud, *The Complete Letters of Sigmumd Freud to Wilhelm Fließ 1887-1904, o.c.*, pp. 270-273.

108. J. Breuer and S. Freud, *Studies on Hysteria, o.c.*, p. 107.

109. *Ibid.*, p. 108.

110. One cannot refer to Lucy R.'s case as being symptomatic of Freud's orientation towards the hysterical conversion symptom. A more attentive reading shows that the therapy also touched on her general state of sadness rooted in her relationship with her mother and reinforced by her disappointing love affair. The therapy also involved a certain degree of mourning and a victory over the moral cowardice which is characteristic of melancholy.

111. I will return to this essential aspect of not only psychotherapy but also psychoanalysis in the conclusion to this chapter.

112. *Ibid.*, p. 268. It was Lacan who was later to reassign a central place to the passion of the unwillingness to know which he set side by side with Eros and Thanatos.

113. *Ibid.*, p. 268, Freud's emphasis.

114. Reducing the notion of resistance or defence to the temporal frame and the study of electricity which was flourishing at the time, seems to trivialise Freud's clinic in a harrowing manner. Which contemporary psychotherapist has not experienced the endless repetition of the neurotic 'mock fighting'? This can take on epic proportions, since it sometimes goes as far as visiting therapists of different schools of thought in order to provoke such fights.

115. *Ibid.*, p. 278.

116. *Ibid.*, p. 279.
117. *Ibid.*, p. 279.
118. *Ibid.*, p. 279. Freud observes an indication of a successful defence in this "Verneinung" or negation. The fact that the reemergence of pathogenic ideas into consciousness appears to be so insignificant, leads one to deduce, concerning the defence process, that an intense idea can be weakened by depleting it of its affect.
119. Let me point out that in Freud's later theory, there will be room made for the "splitting" of the mind. This notion appears at the very end of Freud's work. Cf. S. Freud, Splitting of the Ego in the Process of Defence, (1940*e* [1938]), *S.E.*, vol. XXIII, pp. 271-278. The use of this concept is also found in the work of other neurologists. I will only mention Möbius's excellent pathography of Goethe in which the notion of the splitting of the mind enables the author to account for Goethe's melancholic mood and the split of his psychical life. Cf. P.J. Möbius, *Goethe*, (1909), I. Theil, Leipzig, Johann Ambrosius Verlag, pp. 189-190. Lacan was eventually to fall back on the splitting of the mind in his attempt to construct a theory on the constitution of the subject. Cf. J. Lacan, *Le Séminaire X, L'angoisse, (1962-1963)*, unpublished. Yet Breuer's theoretical chapter does not seem to refer to this meaning. In the chapter in question, the "splitting" of the mind is explained in physiological terms, which implicitly subjects psychology to a stalemate. The clinical entity of the syndrome of hysteria as conceptualised by Breuer, acquires the characteristics of what is described in contemporary psychiatry as 'endogenous depression', i.e. an organically determined depression. On a practical level, making such a diagnosis often results in the abandonment of the patient's therapy to the 'psycho'-pharmacopoeia.
120. J. Breuer and S. Freud, *Studies on Hysteria*, *o.c.*, p. 284.
121. Bernheim's book offers no definite answer as to the duration of the hypnotic effect on 'non-hysterical' patients. Most case discussions make mention of a rapid success during the patient's stay at the clinic.
122. *Ibid.*, pp. 285-286. Freud remains very courteous towards Breuer. Further on, he unambiguously states that one of the major resistances against psychotherapy lies in the transference involving the psychotherapist. It is precisely this transference that Breuer totally misunderstands.
123. A closer analysis of the third form of hysteria (retention hysteria) also leads one to designate defence as the primary mechanism giving rise to all forms of hysteria. *Ibid.*, p. 286.
124. This conclusion is based on a paper presented to a postgraduate course on clinical psychology and psychotherapy (option: Freudian-Lacanian psychoanalysis), on 12 February 1992, 'On Psychoanalysis and Psychotherapy'.
125. J. Breuer and S. Freud, On the Psychical Mechanism of Hysterical Phenomena: Preliminary Communication, *Studies on Hysteria*, *o.c.*, p. 3.
126. *Ibid.*, p. 268.
127. *Ibid.*, p. 291. I should like to draw your attention to the fact that in the case studies the *interpretation* and *construction* already fulfil the same function, namely to support the patient's speech.
128. J. Breuer and S. Freud, *Studies on Hysteria*, *o.c.*, p. 299, my emphasis.

129. This passage brings to mind the text written in 1925, on 'Negation', in which Freud propounds a similar approach. Cf. S. Freud, Negation, (1925*h*), *S.E.*, vol. XIX, pp. 233-239.
130. J. Breuer and S. Freud, *Studies on Hysteria*, *o.c.*, p. 300, my emphasis.
131. This means that the finality of psychotherapy rests in pronouncing judgements enabling a distancing from an alienation ("this I have been") and the possibility of assuming a desire ("this I will have been").
132. *Ibid.*, p. 282.
133. This is the most obvious message to be derived from Apuleius's fairy tale. For more information see S. Freud, The Theme of the Three Caskets, (1913*f*), *S.E.*, vol. XII, pp. 289-301; J. Lacan, *Le Séminaire, Livre VIII, Le Transfert*, *o.c.*, pp. 261-275.
134. J. Strachey, Editors's Introduction to the *Studies on Hysteria*, *o.c.*, p. xviii, my emphasis.
135. J. Breuer and S. Freud, *Studies on Hysteria*, *o.c.*, p. 265, my emphasis.
136. *Ibid.*, p. 301.
137. *Ibid.*, p. 304.
138. This then is my definition of clinical psychology. I thence imply that clinical psychology is too important to be left entirely in the hands of non-analysts. Psychoanalytical theory may be distinguished from psychology by either those in favour of it or those who oppose it, yet to me it *also* is and remains a clinical psychology.

CHAPTER 4

On Aphasia

1. J. Lacan, *The Seminar, Book III, The Psychoses 1955-1956*, Edited by J.-A. Miller, Translated with notes by Russell Grigg, London, Routledge, 1993, p. 243.
2. J. Breuer and S. Freud, *Studies on Hysteria*, *o.c.*, p. 302.
3. S. Freud, *On Aphasia, A Critical Study*, (1891*b*), New York, International University Press, 1978, xv + 105 pp.
4. E. Kris, Introduction to the first edition of S. Freud, *Aus den Anfängen der Psychoanalyse 1887-1902, Briefe an Wilhelm Fließ*, (1950*c*), Frankfurt am Main, Fischer, p. 23, note 2.
5. For a more elaborate assessment and an evaluation of the place Freud's monograph occupies within the field of neurology, I should like direct the reader to E. Stengel's introduction to the English translation. Cf. S. Freud, *On Aphasia, A Critical Study*, (1891*b*), New York, International University Press, 1978, xv + 105 pp. Cf. also: I. Rosenfield, *The Invention of Memory: A New View of the Brain*, New York, Basic Books, 1988; M. Solms, and M. Saling, *A Moment of Transition, Two Neuroscientific Articles by Sigmund Freud*, London, Karnac Books, 1990, 164 pp.
6. "Monsieur le Professeur, fasciné depuis deux mois de votre parole, immensément intéressé par le sujet que vous traitez en maître, il m'est venu de m'offrir à vous pour la traduction en allemand du tôme troisième de vos 'Leçons', si toutefois vous désirez

un traducteur et si vous consentez à vous valoir de mon oeuvre. Quant à ma capacité pour cette entreprise, il faut dire que je n'ai que l'aphasie motrice du français mais non l'aphasie sensorielle, j'ai donné la preuve de mon style allemand par ma traduction d'un volume d'étude par John Stuart Mill" S. Freud's letter addressed to Charcot, dating from the period of his stay in Paris, cited in E. Jones, *Sigmund Freud, Life and Work*, *o.c.*, vol. I, p. 229.

7. J.-M. Charcot, *Clinical Lectures on the Diseases of the Nervous System*, *o.c.*, pp. 360-373; M. Cartez, On Hysterical Mutism (From Prof. Charcot's lectures, by M. Cartez.) in *Ibid.*, pp. 411-433.
8. In a footnote at the end of this lecture it is mentioned that the patient under examination was so impressed by what he had heard and seen that the following morning, shortly after waking, he suddenly regained his speech. Cf. *Ibid.*, p. 372, n. 1.
9. J.-M. Charcot, *Clinical Lectures on the Diseases of the Nervous System*, *o.c.*, p. 360.
10. *Ibid.*, pp. 360-361.
11. *Ibid.*, pp. 361-362. Charcot alludes to his own lectures of December 1885.
12. *Ibid.*, pp. 363-364.
13. *Ibid.*, pp. 364-365.
14. *Ibid.*, pp. 366-367.
15. *Ibid.*, pp. 368-369.
16. *Ibid.*, pp. 369-370.
17. *Ibid.*, p. 373.
18. *Ibid.*, pp. 413-418.
19. This is the diagnosis of the doctor in attendance. However, earlier on I pointed out that in Charcot's view the hysterical paralysis of the muscles of the larynx could not account for complete mutism.
20. *Ibid.*, p. 421.
21. S. Freud, Some Points for a Comparative Study of Organic and Hysterical Motor Paralysis, *o.c.*, pp. 160-172.
22. P. Broca, *Sur le siège de la faculté du langage articulé avec deux observations d'aphémie (perte de la parole)*, Paris, 1861.
23. C. Wernicke, *Der aphasische Symptomencomplex*, Breslau, 1874.
24. E. Stengel, Introduction, in: S. Freud, *On Aphasia, A Critical Study*, *o.c.*, p. x.
25. Jones in particular praises this and other aspects of Freud's work: "It is the first authentic glimpse we get of the Freud of years later. It has the close reasoning, the lucidity, the persuasive and thought-provoking argumentation, the candid discussion of objections, and the remarkable capacity for ordering his material, that became so characteristic of his writings. Freud, now thirty-five years old, is no longer the modest student, but an experienced neurologist who can speak in a confident tone to his seniors as his equals, and any criticism of their doctrines, however devastating, is expressed in a polite and matter-of-fact manner." Cf. E. Jones, *Sigmund Freud, Life and Work*, *o.c.*, p. 234.
26. Paraphasia.
27. S. Freud, *On Aphasia, A Critical Study*, *o.c.*, p. 4.
28. *Ibid.*, p. 11.

29. Wernicke later adopted the schema of his student.
30. *Ibid.*, p. 6.
31. *Ibid.*, pp. 9-10. Freud refers to Eisenlohr, a neurologist according to whom Lichtheim's schema could not be said to have more than a didactic value.
32. For the notion of the point-by-point projection or representation presupposes nerve fibres ascending to the cortex for every point in the periphery of the body. However, Freud contended that "(...) if the way in which the periphery is reflected in the spinal cord is called a 'projection', its counterpart in the cerebral cortex might suitably be called a 'representation'." *Ibid.*, p. 51.
33. *Ibid.*, p. 53.
34. *Ibid.*, p. 3.
35. Freud adds in a footnote that "Hughlings Jackson has most emphatically warned against such a confusion of the physical with the psychical in the study of speech: 'In all of our studies of diseases of the nervous system we must be on our guard against the fallacy that what are physical states in lower centres fine away into psychical states in higher centres, that for example vibrations of sensory nerves become sensations, or that somehow or another an idea produces a movement.'" *Ibid.*, pp. 54-56.
36. *Ibid.* pp. 62-63.
37. This corresponds to the case which, according to Wernicke and Lichtheim, resulted from the interruption of the conduction pathways.
38. *Ibid.*, p. 87.
39. *Ibid.*, p. 13.
40. Freud reserves his judgement on the connection between the words involved in paraphasia: "If we suppose the pathway for spontaneous speech to go via the sensory centre A, the speech disorder resulting from a lesion of that centre naturally assumes particular interest for us. Indeed we have the impression that Wernicke and Lichtheim have not done full justice to it by calling it "paraphasia". By paraphasia we are to understand a speech disorder in which the appropriate word is replaced by a less appropriate one, which, however, still retains a certain relationship to the correct word. Following the philosopher Delbrück we may describe these relations as follows: In paraphasia words of a similar content, or linked by frequent association, are used in place of one another, e.g., "pen" instead of "pencil", "Potsdam" instead of "Berlin". Furthermore, words of a similar sound are mistakenly used for each other, such as "Butter" for "Mutter" or "Campher" for "Pamphlet"; and finally, if the patient makes mistakes in articulation (literal paraphasia), single letters are replaced by others. It is tempting to differentiate between various types of paraphasia according to the part of the speech apparatus at which the mistake took place. One also speaks of paraphasia when two intended words are fused into one malformation, such as "Vutter" for "Mutter" or "Vater"; by common consent circumlocutions by which a specific noun is replaced by a very general one ("Dings", "machine", "chose") or by a verb, have also been regarded as paraphasia." *Ibid.*, pp. 21-22.
41. This also holds for his two articles on the same subject, namely S. Freud, Aphasia, (1888*c*), an article published anonymously in: A. Villaret, *Handwörterbuch der gesammten Medizin*, Stuttgart, Ferdinand Enke Verlag, 1888-1891 and S. Freud,

Aphasia, (1893*i*), a publication recently rediscovered, in: A. Bum and M.T. Schnirer, *Diagnostisches Lexikon für praktische Ärzte*, Wien, 1893, vol. 1.

42. J. Buelens, *Sigmund Freud, Kind van zijn tijd, o.c.*, p. 83.
43. S. Freud, Some Points for a Comparative Study of Organic and Hysterical Motor Paralysis, *o.c.*, p. 160.
44. In this paper, which was originally published in French, Freud does indeed use the verb "simuler", which in the present case does not refer to conscious simulation, but rather to the similarities between the hysterical symptomatology and certain organic disorders.
45. S. Freud, Some Points for a Comparative Study of Organic and Hysterical Motor Paralysis, *o.c.*, p. 167-168. Let me draw your attention to Freud's devastating criticism, in this paragraph, of diagrams similar to those of Wernicke and Lichtheim. Although they are not capable of explaining the symptomatology of organic aphasias, paradoxically enough, they seem to account for the well delineated symptomatology of hysterical diseases.
46. *Ibid.*, p. 169, Freud's emphasis.
47. *Ibid.*, p. 169.
48. *Ibid.*, p. 170, my emphasis.
49. *Ibid.*, p. 170.
50. *Ibid.*, pp. 170-171.
51. S. Freud, *On Aphasia, A Critical Study*, *o.c.*, p. 77.
52. *Ibid.*, pp. 77-78.
53. A. Stephan, *Sinn als Bedeutung, Bedeutungstheoretische Untersuchungen zur Psychoanalyse Sigmund Freuds*, Berlin, Walter de Gruyter, 1989, pp. 85-92.
54. S. Freud, *Fragment Of An Analysis Of A Case Of Hysteria*, (1905*e* [1901]), *S.E.*, vol. VII, pp. 40-41.
55. Whereas in the aforementioned cases of aphasia we were dealing with the mechanisms of circumvention and circumscription, in this case we are dealing with a "*ver*taling" [Dutch for 'translation' or 'putting into words'].
56. The volume in question is part of the first edition of the collected works of Mill prepared under the auspices of Theodor Gomperz. Freud took over from the deceased Eduard Wessel. Cf. A. Weinberg, Theodor Gomperz and John Stuart Mill, *Travaux de droit, d'économie, de sociologie et de sciences politiques*, 1963, n° 16, 63 pp.
57. It was in Stricker's lab that Koller carried out his conclusive experiments on the anaesthetic properties of cocaine. This Viennese physician fully embraced what later became known as 'psychological semantics'. The fundamental similarities between Freud, Mill and Stricker forms the object of A. Stephan, *Sinn als Bedeutung, Bedeutungstheoretische Untersuchungen zur Psychoanalyse Sigmund Freuds, o.c.*, pp. 85-87.
58. E. Tugendhat, *Vorlesungen zur Einführung in die sprachanalytische Philosophie*, Frankfurt, 1976, p. 356. Cited in A. Stephan, *Sinn als Bedeutung, Bedeutungstheoretische Untersuchungen zur Psychoanalyse Sigmund Freuds, o.c.*, p. 86.
59. *Ibid.*, p. 88.
60. G. Frege, On Sense and Reference, (1892), in *Translations of the Philosophical Writings of Gottlob Frege* (Edited by P. Geach and M. Black), Oxford, Basil Black-

well, 1966, p. 59; G. Van de Vijver and J. Van Dormael, Lectures *Logica en Taalwetenschap*, University of Ghent, Academic year 1990-1991.

61. L. Binswanger, Freud et la constitution de la psychiatrie clinique, (1936), in *Discours, parcours et Freud*, Paris, Gallimard, 1970, p. 190.

62. This is also apparent from the fact that the publishers of the *Standard Edition* appended this schema to Freud's 1915 article on the unconscious. Cf. S. Freud, The Unconscious, (1915*e*), *S.E.*, vol. XIV, pp. 209-215.

63. S. Freud, *The Complete Letters of Sigmund Freud to Wilhelm Fließ 1887-1904*, *o.c.*, letter dated from May 21, 1894, pp. 73-75.

PART II

FREUD'S *PROJECT FOR A SCIENTIFIC PSYCHOLOGY*

INTRODUCTION

1. J. Breuer, letter to Wilhelm Fließ dated 5 July 1895, in A. Hirschmüller, *The Life and Work of Joseph Breuer, Physiology and Psychoanalysis*, *o.c.*, p. 315. Cf. also the letter dated 13 July 1895 in S. Freud, *The Complete Letters of Sigmund Freud to Wilhelm Fließ 1887-1904*, *o.c.*, pp. 133-134 and note 1.

2. S. Freud, Project for a Scientific Psychology, *o.c.*, p. 295.

3. J. Quackelbeen, *Zeven avonden met Jacques Lacan, Psychoanalytische commentaren by 'Télévision'*, *o.c.*, pp. 99-128.

4. S. Exner, *Entwurf zu einer physiologischen Erklärung der psychischen Erscheinungen*, *o.c.* This work, written by Freud's senior colleague, is often described in the secondary literature as one of the "similar experiments" alluded to in the opening paragraph. This means that one simply refers to this work to qualify Freud's *Project* as a physiological text. But this, however, is never demonstrated.

5. J. Quackelbeen, *Zeven avonden met Jacques Lacan, Psychoanalytische commentaren by 'Télévision'*, *o.c.*, p. 20.

6. E. Jones, *Sigmund Freud, Life and Work*, *o.c.*, see in particular pp. 415-433. This position is also adopted by S. Marcus, Introductory Essay, (1977), in Freud, *The Origins of Psychoanalysis, Letters to Wilhelm Fließ*, 1950*c*, New York, Basis Books, p. xi.

7. F.J. Sulloway, *Freud Biologist of the Mind, Beyond the Psychoanalytic Legend*, *o.c.*, pp. 101-131.

8. A. Hirshmüller, *The Life and Work of Josef Breuer, Physiology and Psychoanalysis*, *o.c.*, p. 164; S. Marcus, Introductory Essay, *o.c.*, p. xiii; E. Kris, Introduction, (1954), in S. Freud, *The Origins of Psychoanalysis, Letters to Wilhelm Fließ*, *o.c.*, pp. 25-27; A. Grünbaum, *The Foundations of Psychoanalysis, A Philosophical Critique*, Berkeley, Los Angeles and London, University of California Press, 1984, pp. 3-5.

9. K. Levin, *Freud's Early Psychology of the Neuroses, A Historical Perspective*, Brighton, Harvester Press, 1978, pp. 152-183.

10. Which on account of the undisputed link between *Project* and Freud's subsequent theories, is even extended by some authors so as to include the status of psychoanalysis in general. Cf. J. Buelens, *Sigmund Freud, Kind van zijn tijd, o.c.*, p. 107.

CHAPTER 1

The concept of quantity

1. *Ibid.*, draft C, dated Easter 1893, p. 45.
2. From an entirely different angle, a similar sort of unease sometimes issues forth from the SAMCDA circle — the Société d'Assistance Mutuelle Contre le Discours Analytique, or better known as "this famous coalition of analysts who are opposed to their own discourse". Here questions about the Lacanian view on the concepts of psychical energy, the affect and the drives are brought up with a degree of concern, for in spite of his "retour à Freud" there hovers a sense that Lacan neglected these issues in favour of the "verbalism and intellectualism", implied in Lacan's thesis: "the unconscious is structured like a language". Cf. J. Quackelbeen, *Zeven avonden met Jacques Lacan, Psychoanalytische commentaren by 'Télévision', o.c.*, p. 90 and p. 101.
3. "It was his last seminar in Sainte-Anne. The SAMCDA then forbad trainee analysts to follow these teachings." *Ibid.*, p. 119.
4. *Ibid.*, p. 105.
5. J. Buelens, *Sigmund Freud, kind van zijn tijd, o.c.*
6. *Ibid.*, p. 97.
7. *Ibid.*, p. 96. It is frequently assumed that Freud borrowed this term from Jackson. This assumption is fairly understandable since, as we have seen in the chapter devoted his study on aphasia, Freud himself referred to Jackson. Buelens, however, traced the notion back to Spencer and not to Jackson.
8. Cf. S. Freud, Hysterie und Hysteroepilepsie, *o.c.*, pp. 69-92.
9. J. Buelens, *Sigmund Freud, Kind van zijn tijd, o.c.*, p. 107.
10. *Ibid.*, p. 124. Buelens starts off from the assumption that there was no theoretical discordance at all between Breuer and Freud, at least not prior to spring 1896, the time of the separation between both authors of the *Studies*. This separation is said to coincide with the more passionate relation that Freud enjoyed with Fließ, who appeared to be more suitable as an interlocutor on the subject of the new sexual conception.
11. For Buelens the *Studies* is a book about hysteria and not, as it was for Freud, a book about the fundamentally hysterical speech as it manifests itself in the "psychical treatment". By deferring to a later date the idea that all neuroses have a sexual aetiology, the differences in opinion between Breuer and Freud do not *seem* to be relevant at the time of the publication of the *Studies*.
12. Russelman offers an excellent discussion of the place and function of the concept of energy in the various scientific disciplines such as: natural sciences, physiology and psychology. Cf. G.H.E. Russelman, *Van James Watt to Sigmund Freud, De opkomst*

van het stuwmodel van de zelfexpressie, Deventer, Van Loghum Slaterus, 1983, 413 pp. Russelman distinguishes four different groups with regard to the appellation psychical energy. 1. Psychical energy as a *metaphorical concept,* in which case the physiological basis is irrelevant. The use of the concept of the libido by psychoanalysts is accordingly purely to be conceived of as an expedient. 2. Psychical energy as a form of *physical energy*, as is expressed in the writings of Carpenter and Griesinger. 3. Psychical energy as a *psychical concomitant* of nervous energy. This view was also held by Spencer, who distinguished between two parallel levels, i.e. the psychical and the physical-physiological. Fechner also adhered to this interpretation. He opined that the psychical and the physical were two sides of the same coin. However, since human understanding is not able to grasp this unity in its entirety, science has no other option than to differentiate between psychical and physical processes, and to view them as running in *parallel* with one another. Such a conception does away with the theory of interaction. To Fechner, these processes could be explained on a physical plane, using the notion of physical causality, while at the same time (and independently of any physical factor), these processes be could also explained in purely psychical terms by the notion of psychical causality. 4. Psychical energy as a form of *physical-chemical energy* which is available for psychical activity. On this subject Russelman refers to Meynert and Freud, amongst others. *Ibid.*, pp. 134-141. Russelman's subdivision is praiseworthy, yet one realises that it becomes extremely difficult to allocate a place to Freud within the boundaries of this framework, since his developing viewpoints can be classified under each one of these categories when taking his entire oeuvre into consideration. This is evidently of no significance. But when one confines oneself to Freud's early writings, difficulties concerning their interpretation also arise; if one is so willing, they can be made to fit into any slot.

13. Cited in J. Buelens, *Sigmund Freud, Kind van zijn tijd, o.c.*, p. 139.
14. *Ibid.*, p. 146.
15. *Ibid.*, p. 107.
16. Indeed, physics too "since Galilee was based on experiments with ideas", as A. Koyré demonstrated. Cf. J. Quackelbeen, *Zeven avonden met Jacques Lacan, Psychoanalytische commentaren bij 'Télévision', o.c.*, p. 104.
17. S. Freud, Project for a Scientific Psychology, *o.c.*, p. 295.
18. S. Freud, *The Complete Letters of Sigmund Freud to Wilhelm Fließ 1887-1904, o.c.*, p. 129.
19. S. Freud, Project for a Scientific Psychology, *o.c.*, pp. 295-296.
20. I allude to these facts from the understanding that 'facts' only emerge in the discourse.
21. I must also draw the reader's attention to the unmistakable logic concealed in Freud's works: clinical observation takes precedence and the theoretical development only takes place at a subsequent stage. Besides, Freud used the appellation 'psychoanalysis' to refer to three distinct aspects: 1. a therapeutic instrument; 2. an instrument employed to probe the human psyche; 3. a theory. Cf. S. Freud, Two Encyclopedia Articles, (1923*a* [1922]), *S.E.*, vol. XVIII, p. 236.

22. J. Lacan, *The Seminar, Book XI, The Four Fundamental Concepts of Psychoanalysis 1964*, Edited by J.-A. Miller, Translated by A. Sheridan, Harmondsworth, Penguin Books, 1991, 290 pp.
23. In the *Studies on Hysteria* Breuer argues that the "old 'reflex theory'" should not be completely rejected as an explanatory model for some symptoms which form part of the clinical picture of hysteria. Cf. J. Breuer and S. Freud, *Studies on Hysteria, o.c.*, p. 242. At times Freud mentions his theory in his correspondence with Fließ. For instance, he criticises the view of Peyer (1893), who contended that reflex neurosis results from minor anatomical changes in the genitals, instead of changes in the nervous system. Cf. S. Freud, *The Complete Letters of Sigmund Freud to Wilhelm Fließ 1887-1904, o.c.*, Draft C 30 May 1893, p. 45.
24. S. Freud, Hysteria, *o.c.*, p. 50.
25. Cf. S. Freud, Preface and Footnotes to the Translation of Charcot's *Leçons du mardi à la Salpétrière (1887-1888)*, *S.E.*, vol. I, pp. 133-143; S. Freud, Charcot, *o.c.*, pp. 11-23; S. Freud, The Neuro-Psychoses of Defence, *o.c.*, p. 47; S. Freud, Heredity and the Aetiology of the Neuroses, *S.E.*, vol. III, p. 143 f.
26. S. Freud, The Neuro-Psychoses of Defence, *o.c.*, pp. 47-48.
27. *Ibid.*, pp. 48-49.
28. *Ibid.*, p. 49. Freud argues that this conversion may either be total or partial. In the *Studies on Hysteria*, however, it appeared that pure conversion hysteria only exists in theory. Alongside the symptoms that the patients manifest, the mood or affective state of his female patients must always also be taken into account. Consider for example the feelings of melancholy and anxiety in respectively Lucy R. and Emmy von N.
29. S. Freud, The Neuro-Psychoses of Defence, *o.c.*, p. 52.
30. *Ibid.*, p. 52. This point was also confirmed for obsessions less than a year later in S. Freud, Obsessions and Phobias: their Psychical Mechanisms and their Aetiology, *o.c.*, pp. 74-83.
31. Freud, The Neuro-Psychoses of Defence, *o.c.*, p. 52-53.
32. *Ibid.*, p. 53. The word Freud uses here to qualify his patients' reaction is "Einwendung" (objection) and not "Verneinung" (negation).
33. *Ibid.*, p. 53.
34. *Ibid.*, pp. 60-61.
35. S. Freud , *The Complete Letters of Sigmund Freud to Wilhelm Fließ 1887-1904, o.c.*, letter dated 24 November 1887, p. 15. Commenting on a case, Freud mentions the characteristic of "hypochondriacal alteration" in order to distinguish between neurasthenic and organic diseases. The term "Aktualneurose" appears for the first time in his published works in 1898. Cf. S. Freud, Sexuality in the Aetiology of the Neuroses", (1898*a*), *S.E.*, vol. III, p. 279. The first case that Freud informs Fließ of is that of Frau A. who suffers from neurasthenia. Cf. S. Freud, *The Complete Letters of Sigmund Freud to Wilhelm Fließ 1887-1904, o.c.*, letters dated 24 November and 28 December 1887, and 4 February and 28 May 1888, pp. 15-21.
36. In Draft C2, which contains comments on one of Fließ's texts, Freud formulates his views as follows: "Our view [which is to say his and Fließ'] is of the purport that this factor [the abusis sexualis] is the specific etiology of the neurosis, either in the sense

that it suffices in order to make the healthy nervous system change into a neurasthenic one, or in other cases that it constitutes the indispensable condition under which other causes of illness may bring about neurasthenia (...)." Fließ adopted this proposal in his publication. Cf. W. Fließ, Die nasale Reflexneurose, (1893), in *Verhandlungen des Kongresses für innere Medizin*, 12. Kongress, p. 391 and next; S. Freud, *The Complete Letters of Sigmund Freud to Wilhelm Fließ 1887-1904*, *o.c.*, p. 38.

37. For the moment, Freud does not discard the possibility of the existence of hereditary neurasthenia.

38. *Ibid.*, pp. 40-41.

39. Such an anxiety neurosis then takes on three forms: a chronic state of anxiety, an attack of anxiety and periodic mild depression. The third form, unlike melancholy, is always connected with a seemingly rational psychic trauma. The first two forms often occur together as the attack of anxiety is always accompanied by chronic symptoms of anxiety such as: "(1). anxiety relating to the body — hypochondria; (2) anxiety relating to the functioning of the body — agoraphobia, claustrophobia, giddiness at heights; (3) anxiety relating to decisions and memory (therefore one's own fantasies, psychic functioning) with respect to folie de doute, obsessive brooding etc.." *Ibid.*, pp. 42-43.

40. *Ibid.*, p. 44. In the *Studies*, Freud observed that the psycho-cathartic method was of no use in cases of "Aktualneurosen", i.e. in cases of neurasthenia and anxiety neuroses. J. Breuer and S. Freud, *Studies on Hysteria*, *o.c.*, p. 261.

41. A short while later Freud wrote that he could undertake this research alone since he was confronted with numerous cases of neurasthenia in his practice and that having access to the required material presented no problem to him. Cf. S. Freud, *The Complete Letters of Sigmund Freud to Wilhelm Fließ 1887-1904*, *o.c.*, letter dated 10 July 1893, p. 50. This large scale research project was ultimately not carried out by Freud himself, but by Felix Gattel. Cf. *Ibid.*, letter dated 3 April 1898, pp. 306-307.

42. This ultimately led to the publication of an article. Cf. S. Freud, On the Grounds for Detaching a Particular Syndrome from Neurasthenia under the Description 'Anxiety Neurosis', *o.c.*

43. Years later Freud defined this phenomenon with greater accuracy: "Negation is a way of taking cognisance of what is repressed; indeed it is already a lifting of the repression, though not, of course, an acceptance of what is repressed." Cf. S. Freud, On Negation, (1925*h*), *o.c.*, pp. 235-236.

44. S. Freud, *The Complete Letters of Sigmund Freud to Wilhelm Fließ 1887-1904*, *o.c.*, letter dated 6 October 1893, p. 57.

45. *Ibid.*, letter dated 30 May 1893, p. 48.

46. *Ibid.*, letter dated 30 May 1893, p. 49. Freud's emphasis.

47. J. Breuer and S. Freud, *Studies on Hysteria*, *o.c.*, pp. 125-134, Freud described his encounter with 'Katharina' in his letter dated 20 August 1893, which he wrote in the holiday resort of Reichenau. Cf. S. Freud, *The Complete Letters of Sigmund Freud to Wilhelm Fließ 1887-1904*, *o.c.*, p. 53. For the sake of completeness, I should like to add that this letter was discovered by the publisher of the unabridged edition of the correspondence found in Freud's desk. It is thus not certain whether Fließ ever

received this letter. In the letter, Freud confirms that Katharina was in fact abused by her father and not her uncle; a fact which he had added in a footnote to the case in 1924. According to my own reading and interpretation of Freud, the 'theory of seduction' is of no significance at all. In my view, this entire question seems hopelessly overblown, in the sense that the importance that Freud attached to the hypothesis of seduction is unduly exaggerated. The excessive importance attributed to this 'theory' serves almost as a ploy to criticise Freud's abandonment of it at a later stage — which incidentally is the attitude adopted by the aforementioned publisher. In my opinion, Freud only used this hypothesis in a schematic manner. The most important element in this letter is the *date*, which makes it possible to precisely locate the period of Katharina's treatment, not within Freud's line of reasoning about the hypothesis on seduction, but instead — as I will attempt to demonstrate — within the realm of his ambition to constitute a comprehensive theory of neuroses underlain by the hypothesis of quantity. For a more detailed analysis of Freud's 'theory of seduction' see P. Verhaeghe, *Does the Woman Exist ?, From Freud's Hysteric to Lacan's Feminine*, Translated by M. Du Ry, London, Rebus Press, 1996, 269 pp.; K. Van Dycke, "Facts and Figures" versus "Alice in Wonderland", De controverse over de verleidingstheorie, naar aanleiding van J.M. Masson, *Rondzendbrief uit het Freudiaanse Veld*, 1986, nr. 22, pp. 23-37; K. Libbrecht, Enkele opmerkingen over het statuut van het trauma en het concept van de psychische realiteit, *Rondzendbrief uit het Freudiaanse Veld*, 1992, nr. 50, pp. 33-37; J.F. Masson, *The Assault on Truth, Freud's Suppression of the Seduction Theory*, Farrar, Straus and Giroux, New York, 1984.

48. J. Breuer and S. Freud, *Studies on Hysteria*, *o.c.*, p. 125.
49. S. Freud, Constructions in Analysis, (1937*d*), *S.E.*, vol. XXIII, pp. 255-269.
50. I will return to this aspect later when dealing with the scope of Freud's psychology of judgement and its direct roots in the clinic.
51. J. Breuer and S. Freud, *Studies on Hysteria*, *o.c.*, pp. 125-134. What I perceive in this dialogue to be of the nature of a judgement is stressed.
52. In German, "anschauen" denotes the incapacity to part with something. On the other hand, the enunciation or the judgement "it looks at me" implies a first distancing.
53. One could of course object that the judgement I have stressed is passed by Freud and not by Katharina. Yet one cannot deny that all the components of this construction were brought forward by her and that she simply failed to put them coherently into words and this after all is what psychical treatment is about. Freud mentions later on that a construction of this kind should not be considered as final.
54. S. Freud, *The Complete Letters of Sigmund Freud to Wilhelm Fließ 1887-1904*, *o.c.*, letter dated 21 May 1894, p. 73.
55. *Ibid.*, letter dated 27 November 1893, p. 61.
56. Cf. Draft E in which he wrote the following: "Now, at first I followed various false tracks. I thought that the anxiety from which the patients suffer should be looked on as a continuation of the anxiety felt during the sexual act — that is to say, that it actually was a hysterical symptom. Indeed, the connections between anxiety neuroses and hysteria are obvious enough. Two things might give rise to the feeling of anxiety

in coitus interruptus: in the woman, a fear of becoming pregnant; in the man worry that his [preventive] device might fail. I then convinced myself from various cases that anxiety neurosis also appeared where there was no question of these factors, where it was basically of no importance to these people whether they had a baby. Thus the anxiety of anxiety neurosis was not a continued, recollected, hysterical one. A second extremely important point became established for me from the following observation: anxiety neurosis affects women who are anaesthetic in coitus just as much as sensitive ones. This is most peculiar, but it can only mean that the source of the anxiety is not to be looked for in the psychic sphere. It must accordingly lie in the physical sphere: it is a physical factor in sexual life that produces anxiety." *Ibid.*, p. 78.

57. See Draft D, dating from the same period, which contains a detailed plan 'On the Aetiology and Theory of the Major Neuroses'. *Ibid.*, pp. 76-78. If one takes a close look at the evolution of Freud's line of reasoning, one is compelled to regard this draft, which is little more than a table of contents, as a prefiguration of Freud's *Project.* I pointed out earlier that a comparable ambition transpires in the *Studies on Hysteria*, at any rate in the parts that were written by Freud.

58. *Ibid.*, letter dated 21 May 1894, p. 74.

59. *Ibid.*, letter dated 21 May 1894, p. 75.

60. Freud discerned: 1. anxiety in *virginal people* as the result of sexual observations, information or suspicions of sexual life; 2. anxiety in *intentionally abstinent people* for whom everything sexual is abhorrent. These people convert their anxiety into phobias, compulsions and *folie de doute*; 3., anxiety of *necessarily abstinent* people such as women who are neglected by their husbands or who have impotent husbands.; 4. anxiety of women who experience *coitus interruptus* and the wives of men who suffer from ejaculatio praecox. These people do not obtain satisfaction by physical stimulation; 5. anxiety of men practising *coitus interruptus* and men who excite themselves in various ways but do not use their erection for coitus; 6. anxiety of men who *go beyond their desire or strength*, older people whose potency is decreasing, but who nevertheless forcibly bring about coitus; 7. anxiety of men who abstain at times, or rather young men who have married older women, by whom they are in fact disgusted, or *neurasthenics* who have been diverted from masturbation by intellectual occupations without making up for it by coitus ... Cf. *Ibid.*, p. 79.

61. Freud put a comparable mechanism forward for melancholy, but in the case of melancholy *psychical* sexual tension is converted in the affect of sadness. Cf. *Ibid.*, p. 81. In the *Studies* anxiety is seen as not allowing for further interpretation or "psychical discharge" and it is suggested that it should be conceived of as an accumulation of stimuli. Cf. J. Breuer and S. Freud, *Studies on Hysteria, o.c.*

62. S. Freud, *The Complete Letters of Sigmund Freud to Wilhelm Fließ 1887-1904, o.c.*, p. 80.

63. This is corroborated by Draft G, *Ibid.*, p. 101.

64. *Ibid.*, pp. 80-81.

65. *Ibid.*, p. 82.

66. *Ibid.*, p. 82. For this comparison see S. Freud, On the Grounds for Detaching a Particular Syndrome from Neurasthenia under the Description 'Anxiety Neurosis', *o.c.*, p. 112.
67. S. Freud, *The Complete Letters of Sigmund Freud to Wilhelm Fließ 1887-1904, o.c.*, Draft E, p. 82 and the letter dated 22 June 1894, p. 83.
68. *Ibid.*, Draft F, pp. 90-91 and letters dated 23 and 29 August 1894, pp. 91-97.
69. For a clinical illustration and interpretation based on the genesis of meaning see C. Scheulen, Menstruatieangsten, (translation G. Van de Vijver): *Rondzendbrief uit het Freudiaanse Veld*, 1989, nr. 36, pp. 31-34; G. Van de Vijver, Hoe sexuele betekenissen emergeren. Naar aanleiding van een vertaling, *Rondzendbrief uit het Freudiaanse Veld*, 1989, n° 36, pp. 35-38.
70. S. Freud, *The Complete Letters of Sigmund Freud to Wilhelm Fließ 1887-1904, o.c.*, p. 100.
71. S. Freud, *The Complete Letters of Sigmund Freud to Wilhelm Fließ 1887-1904, o.c.*, Draft G dated January 1895, pp. 98-105.
72. *Ibid.*, p. 99.
73. *Ibid.*, p. 99.
74. Cf. S. Freud, Mourning and Melancholia, (1917*e* [1915]), *S.E.*, vol. XIV, pp. 237-258.
75. S. Freud, *The Complete Letters of Sigmund Freud to Wilhelm Fließ 1887-1904, o.c.*, Draft H dated January 24, 1895, p. 107.
76. *Ibid.* p. 108.
77. *Ibid.*, pp. 108-109.
78. Here, judgement means more than the traditional "statement", it also denotes an appraisal, or even a condemnation.
79. *Ibid.*, p. 109.
80. I should like to draw your attention to the fact that to Freud not only the hysterical symptom but also the phenomenon of transference is considered as a syllogism or false connection.
81. *Ibid.*, pp. 109-110.
82. This draft also contains a chart in which he compares the mechanism of defence of paranoia to those of hysteria, obsessional neurosis, hallucinatory confusion and hysterical psychosis. *Ibid.* p. 111.
83. S. Freud, Analysis Terminable and Interminable, (1937*c*), *S.E.*, vol. XXIII, p. 225; J. W. von Goethe, *Faust*, Part I, Scene 6.
84. S. Freud, *The Complete Letters of Sigmund Freud to Wilhelm Fließ 1887-1904, o.c.*, letters dated 4 and 13 March 1895, pp. 113 and 119.
85. *Ibid.*, letter dated 27 April 1895, p. 127.
86. *Ibid.*, letter dated 25 May 1895, p. 129.
87. *Ibid.*, letter dated 25 May 1895, p. 129.
88. S. Freud, Project for a Scientific Psychology, *o.c.*, p. 347, Freud's emphasis.
89. In other words, the *excessively intense idea* is *not* the prerogative of hysteria. Rather, it forms the only possible point of departure for psychotherapy. In 1895, only the "Aktualneurosen" were seen as falling outside the scope of psychical treatment, for Freud believed that no ideas could be descried in their aetiology.

90. *Ibid.*, p. 348. Freud's emphasis.
91. *Ibid.*, p. 348. Freud's emphasis.
92. The "complicated psychic action" can only refer to either, the repression of *B* or the annihilation of this repression via *speech*, which may imply the abreaction through the judgement.
93. Yet again by means of repression or via the judgement.
94. *Ibid.*, pp. 348-349. Freud's emphasis.
95. *Ibid.*, p. 350. Freud's emphasis.
96. *Ibid.*, p. 350. Freud's emphasis.
97. *Ibid.*, p. 350. Freud's emphasis.
98. In his monumental work on emotions Frijda comes to the conclusion that: "(...) 'emotion' is, in fact, a substantive psychological category. There is a mechanism, or set of mechanisms, ensuring satisfaction. That is, there is a mechanism or set of mechanisms that compare stimuli to preference states of the organism and thus turn stimuli into rewards and punishments; it generates pleasure and pain." N. Frijda, *The Emotions*, Cambridge, Cambridge University Press, 1986, p. 473. In my view, this excerpt bears glad tidings, since the material gathered from a hundred years of experimental scientific research has proved sufficient to confirm a clinically observable law, i.e. the pleasure principle. However, this also raises the question as to how many centuries will be needed to check Freud's hypothesis of the death drive. That being said, Frijda's schematic representation of the emotion process, though enriching, is of no clinical use at all. Cf. *Ibid.*, p. 454.
99. S. Freud, Project for a Scientific Psychology, *o.c.*, pp. 351-353.
100. *Ibid.*, p. 352. Cf. also p. 353: "We know from clinical evidence that all this only occurs in the sexual sphere; so perhaps we shall have to explain the special psychical determinant from natural characteristics of sexuality."
101. *Ibid.*, p. 352.
102. *Ibid.*, pp. 353-356. Such cases, as we have seen, play an important part in the development of Freud's theory. Consider comparable cases which Freud refers to in his correspondence, as well as the case of Katharina. The importance of these cases lies in the fact that they led him to the notion of the "pure affect aetiology", from which the diagram of sexuality for the "Aktualneurosen" initially germinated.
103. My emphasis. One recognises in this statement a judgement denoting that she is coming to terms with a sexual desire. In addition, this desire manifests itself more vividly than what was suggested in the symbol formation as a substitute for the recollection of the offence: the German "Kleider" (clothes) also denotes — when pronounced excessively intense — the exclamation "leider!" (Alas!).
104. In his correspondence with Fließ (Draft B), Freud mentions a case of painful hypochondria that set in at puberty and which he could trace back to an assault that took place when the patient was eight. Freud classified this case in the third group of anxiety neuroses, that of the "periodic mild depression, an attack of anxiety lasting for weeks or months, which in contrast to melancholia proper, almost always has an apparently rational connection with a psychic trauma". This trauma, however, was merely the provoking cause. S. Freud, *The Complete Letters of Sigmund Freud to*

Wilhelm Fließ 1887-1904, *o.c.*, p. 43. I have not been able to trace whether this refers to Emma Eckstein. This reference does however demonstrate how dubious the distinction between "Aktualneurosen" and "Abwehr-Neuropsychosen" is.

105. S. Freud, Project for a Scientific Psychology, *o.c.*, p. 355. The term 'proton pseudos' is explained on page 352. n. 1.
106. This is an allusion to my interpretation of the *Studies* as being less concerned with hysteria as a clinical entity, than with *speech* whose hysterical nature is inevitably revealed in psychotherapy.
107. This point is in accordance with Freud's description, which can be found in the *Studies*, of the phenomenon of transference as false connection.
108. Cf. the description of "pre-sexual anxiety" and of "pure affect aetiology, still of a sexual nature".
109. This ambition was already visible in Draft D. It was in the meantime reinforced, not only from the observation that defence also plays a part in 'normal' life, but also from his interest in peripheral phenomena such as dreams.
110. *Ibid.*, p. 295.
111. *Ibid.*, p. 295. Elsewhere I raised a fundamental question about whether Freud's text should be qualified as being either neurological or psychological. F. Geerardyn, Freuds *Entwurf*: neurologie of psychologie?, in *Fragmenten uit de geschiedenis van de psychoanalyse, Een parcours onder overdracht*, University of Ghent, 1991, pp. 27-43.
112. Cf. above, pp. 151-152.
113. S. Freud, Project for a Scientific Psychology, *o.c.*, pp. 295-296.
114. *Ibid.*, p. 347.
115. *Ibid.*, p. 296.
116. For instance in terms such as "somatic conversion of excessive excitation" or "abreaction of excitation surplus".
117. *Ibid.*, p. 297.
118. Freud uses the term "specific action" to refer to the changes to be brought about in the external world. This term had already been used within the context of his schematic diagram of sexuality in which he employed the term "specific reaction", which for the coitus "brings the sexual object into a favourable position". S. Freud, *The Complete Letters of Sigmund Freud to Wilhelm Fließ 1887-1904*, *o.c.*, p. 101.
119. S. Freud, Project for a Scientific Psychology, *o.c.*, p. 297.
120. I have chosen to present the various systems in a different order from that featured in Freud's manuscript. In his text Freud introduces the systems in the following order: ϕ, ψ and ω. I designed these diagrams myself, since Freud did not provide any representation of the ϕ-ψ-ω apparatus. The diagrams are based on the text itself and are inspired by Freud's representation of the psychical apparatus in the seventh chapter of *The Interpretation of Dreams*.
121. In this connection cf. *ibid.*, pp. 305-306.
122. For example, one perceives these vibrations, which both in terms of quantity (*Q1-Q2*) as well as in terms of quality (*F1-F2*) in a relatively short period, as 'sounds'.
123. *Ibid.*, p. 307.

124. Freud does not use the term frequency but speaks of the "period" of the excitation. In the science of electricity, frequency is defined as the number of periods per second. He introduces the concept as follows: "I can see only one way out of the difficulty: a revision of our fundamental hypothesis about the passage of $Q\eta$. So far I have regarded it only in the transference of $Q\eta$ from one neurone to another. But it must have still another characteristic, of temporal nature; for the mechanics of the physicists have allowed this temporal characteristic to the other motions of masses in the external world as well. I speak of this as the period for short. Thus I shall assume that all the resistance of the contact-barriers applies only to the transference of *Q*, but that the period of the neuronal motion is transmitted without inhibition in all directions, as though it were a process of induction." *Ibid.*, p. 310. Freud's emphasis.

125. *Ibid.*, p. 299.

126. *Ibid.*, p. 300.

127. I am only alluding to the essential idea discussed in the first twenty pages of the manuscript. An accurate evaluation and localisation of the neurology upon which Freud relied remains necessary. Cf. K.H. Pribram, The Neuropsychology of Sigmund Freud, in: A.J. Bachrach (ed.), *Experimental Foundations of Clinical Psychology*, New York, 1962, chapter XIII, pp. 442-468; K.H. Pribram, Freud's Project: An Open, Biologically Based Model for Psychoanalysis, in: N.S. Greenfield and W.C. Lewis (eds.), *Psycho-Analysis and Current Biological Thought*, Madison and Milwaukee, 1965, pp. 81-92; K.H. Pribram and M.M. Gill, *Freud's Project Re-Assessed, Preface to Contemporary Cognitive Theory and Neuropsychology*, New York, Basic Books, 1976, 181 pp.

128. S. Freud, Project for a Scientific Psychology, *o.c.*, p. 298 and note 3.

129. This is an allusion to the works of the Belgian astro-physicist Gerard Bodifée, whose books clearly show the limits of such an explanation when one attempts to grasp the 'human factor'. He also takes a radically different course: that of metaphysics and religion, which at best may bring comfort, but offers no explanation. G. Bodifée, *Ruimte voor vrijheid*, Kapellen, Pelckmans, 1988, 236 pp.; G. Bodifée, *Het zichtbare en het denkbare*, Kapellen, Pelckmans, 1990, 160 pp.; G. Bodifée, *Het vreemde van de aarde*, Kapellen, Pelckmans, 1990, 181 pp.

130. S. Freud, Project for a Scientific Psychology, *o.c.*, p. 312. Freud's emphasis.

131. *Ibid.*, pp. 315-316. Freud's emphasis.

132. *Ibid.*, p. 317. In this passage quantity *Q* should obviously be interpreted as $Q\eta$, the endogenous excitation. In the *Project*, Freud does not expound on the relation between *will* and *drives* in the way it was traditionally done in the then-contemporary psychological theories. As far as I know, Freud never returns to this topic in his later works. A possible explanation for this may lie in the peculiar status of the drive as being halfway between the physical and the psychical. This renders the distinction between will (psychical) and instincts (physical), which was made in the aforementioned theories, superfluous.

133. *Ibid.*, p. 311.

134. Except, of course, in the case of anxiety as a pure, un-bound affect.

135. *Ibid.*, p. 317-321.

136. My discussion of the primary experience of satisfaction and pain is more narrative than Freud's, for he did not mention the fatherly slap nor the "Verpönung".
137. *Ibid.*, p. 331.
138. *Ibid.*, p. 318. Freud's emphasis.
139. Freud located system ψ in the cerebral cortex where he made a distinction between the pallium and the nucleus. Every neurone in the pallium is directly linked to a neurone in the nucleus.
140. Some of these points are reminiscent of the features described by Lacan in his theory of the mirror phase: the essential pre-maturity of the new-born child and its dependency on the attribution of meaning by the Other in order to become an adult.
141. Cf. the awakening of the affect aroused by a recollection, as I have discussed earlier on in the case of Katharina and Emma.
142. *Ibid.*, pp. 322-324.
143. *Ibid.* p. 322. Freud's emphasis.
144. Cf. the definition of unpleasure as the perception in ω of a strong increase of *Q*η in ψ, *ibid.*, p. 312.
145. Freud introduces the mechanism of attention in the following manner: "It is easy to now imagine how, with the help of a mechanism which draws the ego's attention to the imminent fresh cathexis of the hostile mnemic image, the ego can succeed in inhibiting the passage [of quantity] from a mnemic image to a release of unpleasure by a copious side-cathexis which can be strengthened according to need. Indeed, if we suppose that the original *Q*η release of unpleasure is taken up by the ego itself, we shall have in itself the source of the expenditure which is required by the inhibiting side-cathexis from the ego. In that case, the stronger the unpleasure, the stronger will be the primary defence." *Ibid.*, p. 324. Freud's emphasis.
146. In this connection, one should bear in mind that the ego is not just to be defined in terms of the primary experiences. For the ego is extended by each passage of quantity. This also shows that as far as the psyche is concerned, there can never be said to be an instance of totally identical repetition.
147. Freud's attribution of the pleasure principle to Fechner is mentioned in: S. Freud, Beyond the Pleasure Principle, (1920g), *S.E.*, vol. XVIII, pp. 8-10; Cf. G.T. Fechner, *Einige Ideen zur Schöpfungs- und Entwicklungsgeschichte der Organismen*, (1873), Tübingen, Edition Diskord, 1985, pp. 25-35 and pp. 88-95.
148. S. Freud, Project for a Scientific Psychology, *o.c.*, p. 331.

CHAPTER 2

The hypothesis of the neurone N

1. S. Freud, *The Complete Letters of Sigmund Freud to Wilhelm Fließ 1887-1904*, *o.c.*, letter dated from May 25, 1895, p. 129.
2. This description of the *Project* can be found in the correspondence with Fließ. Cf. S. Freud, *The Complete Letters of Sigmund Freud to Wilhelm Fließ 1887-1904*, *o.c.*,

letter dated 27 April 1895, pp. 127-128. By saying this, Freud did not mean to suggest that his text only became intelligible when actually resorting to a microscope, is something I was able to ascertain when I undertook an exploratory study of the "best head among neurologists", Paul Julius Möbius. His pathography of Goethe reveals him as, among other things, a particularly subtle clinician who attributed a central position to sexuality in his analysis of Man's inner life, even though he remained far removed from a strictly theoretical framework. Cf. P.J. Möbius, *Goethe*, *o.c.*; F. Geerardyn, Paul Julius Möbius: een gemiste ontmoeting met de psychologie?, *o.c.*.

3. S. Freud, Project for a Scientific Psychology, *o.c.*, p. 297-298.
4. *Ibid.*, p. 347.
5. More particularly in the system ψ. For a detailed discussion on this subject consult the paragraph about the genesis of hysterical compulsion. *Ibid.*, pp. 347-350.
6. *Ibid.*, p. 349.
7. J. Breuer and S. Freud, *Studies on Hysteria*, *o.c.*, pp. 295-297; S. Freud, The Neuro-Psychoses of Defence, *o.c.*, pp. 49-50.
8. J. Breuer and S. Freud, *Studies on Hysteria*, *o.c.*, p. 300. My emphasis.
9. This is an allusion to the discussion of the case of Katharina which aptly illustrates how the progression of the therapeutic conversation is marked out with judgements of this kind. The case of Lucy R. also points towards the same direction since only a *coming to terms in the judgement* with the initially repressed *desire* puts her in a position to make her mind up concerning this desire. The excessively intense ideas of "burnt pudding" and "cigar smoke" only vanished when they had been decoded as the "Ersatz" or substitutive formations for the misunderstood, yet burning desire.
10. J. Breuer and S. Freud, *Studies on Hysteria*, *o.c.*, p. 279.
11. S. Freud, *The Complete Letters of Sigmund Freud to Wilhelm Fließ 1887-1904*, *o.c.*, letter dated 25 May, 1895, p. 129, Freud's emphasis. W. Jerusalem, *Die Urtheilsfunction, Eine psychologische und erkenntniskritische Untersuchung*, Vienna and Leipzig, Wilhelm Braumüller, 1895, 269 pp.
12. My discussion of Jerusalem's book does not claim to be exhaustive. Assessing the scope of many of its aspects — such as the logical, epistemological, grammatical and philosophical features it encompasses — is far beyond the reach of the present analysis. Jerusalem undoubtedly belongs to the myriad of brilliant minds that were the product of the eastern European Jewish community which "at one time was able to fill twelve universities". S. Wiesenthal in an interview with Martin van Amerongen in *De Morgen*, dated 29 August 1992. Incidentally, Jerusalem's life bears some similarities with that of Freud. He was born on 11 October 1854 in a village of Bohemia. According to his father's wishes, he was to become a Talmudist. However, once he entered secondary school, his interest in mathematics, history and above all classical literature lead him to the university of Prague, where he studied classical philology. As a secondary school teacher he was in charge of the course in logic and psychology which tallied with his mounting interest in philosophy. In 1888, he published his *Lehrbuch der Psychologie*, which, in my view, can still be considered as a brilliant example of lucidity. At that time, he had already spent about three years as a teacher in Vienna where he was trying to obtain an appointment at the university.

On account of his *Lehrbuch*, his study on Laura Bridgman and other publications, he was appointed as "Privatdozent" by a jury, in 1890. One of the members of this jury was Théodor Gomperz. In 1891, he started working on his book on *Die Urtheils-function* which was published in 1895. Jerusalem himself was of the opinion that the polemic with Franz Brentano contained in it could partly be put down to the unexpected turn his university career had taken. The peak of his career was his essay on Kant written on the occasion of the official commemoration of the great philosopher organised by the Viennese university in 1904. For more details on Jerusalem and his work see, F. Kaltenbeck, Sigmund Freud et Wilhelm Jerusalem, *Ornicar?*, 1985, n° 32, pp. 111-113; W. Jerusalem, Mein curriculum vitae, in: *Gedanken und Denker*, Vienna, 1925, pp. 10-35. Apparently, in his own opinion *Urtheilsfunction* betokened a sort of catharsis, in the same way as Jakob Bernays interpreted Aristotle. Cf. N. van der Ben and J.M. Bremer, Catharsis, in: Aristotle, *Poetica*, (Dutch translation N. van der Ben and J.M. Bremer), Amsterdam, Athenaeum, 1988, pp. 177-193. In psychoanalytic literature little attention has hitherto been paid to Jerusalem's book. Apart from Kaltenbeck's above-mentioned article (1985), I have only found one other publication that devotes some attention to it: F. Sauvagnat, Le sujet du jugement: une réponse à la controverse de l'infaillibilité pontificale, *Cahiers de lectures freudiennes*, 1986, n° 10, pp. 43-53. Kaltenbeck (*o.c.*, p. 108) also mentions the study by the Freudian scholar I. Hermann, Das Ich und das Denken, *Imago*, 1929, XV, n° 1, pp. 89-110 and N° 3/4, pp. 325-348. Both Jones (1953) and Anzieu (1988) confine themselves to mentioning the name and title of the work. Assoun (1981) and Gay (1989) overlook this basic reference. E. Jones, *Sigmund Freud, Life and Work, o.c.*, p. 406; D. Anzieu, *L'auto-analyse de Freud et la découverte de la psychanalyse*, Paris, PUF, 1988, p. 532; P.-L. Assoun, *Introduction à l'épistémologie freudienne*, Paris, Payot, 1981; P. Gay, *Freud, A Life for Our Time*, New York, 1989. With the exception of the aforementioned letter to Fließ, Freud himself makes no further mention of Jerusalem. Yet it cannot be denied that this author provided him with the *inspiration* for an elemental point in the elaboration of his theory, i.e. the distinction between primary and secondary judgements, as described in the *Project*. He was later to go back to this distinction in his article on 'Negation'. S. Freud, Project for a Scientific Psychology, *o.c.*, pp. 332-335; S. Freud, 'Negation', *o.c.* I emphatically speak of *inspiration*, for in my description of the *Project*, I do not wish to lapse into the reasoning which I myself criticised from the outset and which consists in defining the Freudian epistemology in terms of the frames of reference he employed. Rather, Freud used some aspects of a pre-existing theory in function of his own object of study.

13. W. Jerusalem, *Die Urtheilsfunction, Eine psychologische und erkenntniskritische Untersuchung, o.c.*, p. 1.

14. *Ibid.*, p. 1.

15. This runs counter to the conception of John Stuart Mill who believed that the action involved in judgement was of a metaphysical nature. To back up his viewpoint Jerusalem invoked the works of Sigwart, Schuppe, Wundt and Erdmann among others. *Ibid.*, p. 2. It also becomes evident that Jerusalem's ultimate goal lies in the domain

of theoretical epistemology. This is to say that his psychological analysis of the act involved in judging is entirely bolstered by questions such as "how does one acquire knowledge?", "what is the status of knowledge?", "how does one come to believe in the independent existence of the external world?". By the same token, a question concerning the truth value or validity of the judgement comes into consideration, be it only in a psychological sense. Jerusalem makes a conjecture about what exactly one does when one considers a judgement to be true or false and how one arrives at this conclusion. His research was later to crystallise into a chapter on the epistemological meaning of the function of judgement and into remarks on the "Weltanschauung" as implied in his theory. However, this aspect is beyond the scope of the present discussion. *Ibid.*, pp. 222-267.

16. *Ibid.*, p. 2.
17. *Ibid.*, p. 3.
18. *Ibid.*, p. 4. This is one of the two main ideas Freud found in Jerusalem's work. The clinic of the excessively intense idea had long convinced Freud that the psyche was not commensurate with consciousness. In a letter to Fließ, Freud conveys this understanding in clinical terms: "(...) the internal perception cannot claim to be 'evidence'". This is an overt allusion to what he called, in the *Project*, the incomprehensible nature of the excessively intense idea. S. Freud, *The Complete Letters of Sigmund Freud to Wilhelm Fließ 1887-1904*, *o.c.*, p. 129; S. Freud, Project for a Scientific Psychology, *o.c.*, pp. 347-350. While this empirical observation impelled Freud to supply a device (the system ψ) which was supposed to be the seat of the psychical function of *memory*, the same observation led Jerusalem to postulate unconscious psychical processes. Jerusalem remarks that to describe the realm of the psychical, one often resorts to features presupposing an awareness of psychical phenomena, or even to actual psychical phenomena. On the other hand, one all too readily forgets that physical processes are only known to us as conscious contents, and that the way in which they reveal themselves to us therefore also contains psychical elements. Brentano, for one, does not manage to elude these two pitfalls when arguing that "psychical phenomena always entail a relation with an intentional object". For Brentano, this means that psychical processes are characterised by a relation between consciousness and the proposed conscious content. However, the critique Jerusalem levels at Brentano is that he describes the psychical with something psychical, i.e. with "the relation of consciousness". In addition, there unmistakably exists psychical processes, such as emotions, whose relation with an intentional object is not quite clear. *Relation* in this context refers to "die Stellungnahme des Bewusstseins zu einem Bewusstseinsinhalte", a meaning which, according to Jerusalem, is only found in the work of Brentano and his disciples. The *intentional object* does not deal with the transcendental or metaphysical cause of psychical processes, but only represents the proposed conscious content. W. Jerusalem, *Die Urtheilsfunction, Eine psychologische und erkenntniskritische Untersuchung*, *o.c.*, p. 5.
19. *Ibid.*, p. 6. W. Jerusalem, *Lehrbuch der Psychologie*, (1888), fifth edition, Vienna and Leipzig, 1912, 217 pp. Meynert also alludes to the conception of the psychical as an epiphenomenon of the physical.

20. W. Jerusalem, *Die Urtheilsfunction, Eine psychologische und erkenntniskritische Untersuchung, o.c.*, p. 7.
21. *Ibid.*, p. 8. It should be pointed out that this description does bear some similarity with Freud's typification of the ego. "In fact, however, with the hypothesis of 'wishful attraction' and of the inclination towards repression we have already touched on a state of ψ which has not yet been discussed. For these two processes indicate that an organization has been formed in ψ whose presence interferes with passages [of quantity] which on the first occasion occurred in a particular way [i.e. accompanied by satisfaction or pain]. This organization is called the 'ego'. It can easily be depicted if we consider that the regularly repeated reception of endogenous *Qή* in certain neurones (of the nucleus) and the facilitating effect proceeding thence will produce a group of neurones which is constantly cathected and thus corresponds to the vehicle of the store required by the secondary function. Thus the ego is to be defined as the totality of the ψ cathexes, at the given time, in which a permanent component is distinguished from a changing one. It is easy to see that the facilitations between ψ neurones are a part of the ego's possessions, as representing possibilities, if the ego is altered, for determining its extent in the next few moments." S. Freud, Project for a Scientific Psychology, *o.c.*, pp. 322-323.
22. W. Jerusalem, *Die Urtheilsfunction, Eine psychologische und erkenntniskritische Untersuchung, o.c.*, p. 7.
23. However, in the *Project* Freud has no problem ascribing a substratum to the psychical processes in order "(...) to represent psychical processes as quantitatively determinate states of specifiable material particles (...) ". S. Freud, *Project for a Scientific Psychology, o.c.*, p. 295. I already explained this radically different point of departure in terms of the necessity to account, within clinical psychology, for the unmistakable quantitative element within the economy of psychical processes. This led Freud to situate the concept of the drive halfway between the physical and the psychical. This blatant distinction between the two theories gives us an important key to understanding the epistemology of the *Project.*
24. W. Jerusalem, *Die Urtheilsfunction, Eine psychologische und erkenntniskritische Untersuchung, o.c.*, p. 10.
25. *Ibid.*, p. 10.
26. *Ibid.*, p. 12.
27. The reference to the hypnotic phenomena is not gratuitous. In a footnote to the German edition Ernst Kris asserts that Jerusalem was familiar with the writings of Charcot, Bernheim and Richet. However, he does not give the source of his information. S. Freud, *Briefe an Wilhelm Fließ 1887-1904*, (1985*c* [1887-1904]), Ungekürzte Ausgabe, Frankfurt am Main, Fisher Verlag, 1986, p. 131, n° 3.
28. W. Jerusalem, *Die Urtheilsfunction, Eine psychologische und erkenntniskritische Untersuchung, o.c.*, pp. 12-13.
29. Again, this is not the case according to Brentano. He and his disciples maintained that judgements make up a basic class of psychical phenomena, and that judging is a primary process which cannot be broken down to a more simple form. In the act of judging, Brentano believes that there is a very special relation between consciousness

and the represented object that can only be made comprehensible by referring to the inner perception. He called this connection "anerkennen" (to acknowledge) or "verwerfen" (to reject). For Brentano, judging represents an elementary process that has to be distinguished from the ideational act (representation) and from phenomena of the inner life such as love and hate. *Ibid.*, pp. 13-14.

30. *Ibid.*, p. 19.
31. The soul of the child and the mind of the primitive were also soon to become important sources of knowledge to Freud in the construction and verification of his theory. A further similarity between the two scholars was already apparent from the way in which Jerusalem made use of existing literature.
32. *Ibid.*, p. 19.
33. *Ibid.*, p. 19.
34. *Ibid.*, pp. 19-20. My emphasis.
35. Both Jerusalem and Freud distinguish a primal or pre-linguistic judgement.
36. S. Freud, *The Complete Letters of Sigmund Freud to Wilhelm Fließ 1887-1904, o.c.*, letter dated 25 May 1895, p. 129.
37. S. Freud, *Project for a Scientific Psychology*, *o.c.*, p. 334.
38. *Ibid.*, p. 334.
39. W. Jerusalem, *Die Urtheilsfunction, Eine psychologische und erkenntniskritische Untersuchung*, *o.c.*, pp. 20-21.
40. S. Freud, Project for a Scientific Psychology, *o.c.*, p. 302, pp. 321-327, pp. 360-371, and others.
41. A comparison between Jerusalem's language theory and that of Lacan falls outside of the scope of this book. Jerusalem does however demonstrate that a theory of judgement implies a language theory, which to us constitutes an additional argument for reading of the *Project* as a response to the clinic of the excessively intense idea.
42. *Ibid.*, p. 26.
43. *Ibid.*, p. 29.
44. G. Van de Vijver directs our attention to Frege's triad which in linguistics led to the distinction between concept, signifier and signified.
45. *Ibid.*, p. 31.
46. *Ibid.*, p. 33.
47. *Ibid.*, p. 78.
48. *Ibid.*, p. 79.
49. *Ibid.*, p. 80.
50. *Ibid.*, p. 82.
51. From a philosophical perspective, the question raised here relates to the origin of man's general conception of causality, a question which Jerusalem proposed to answer by referring to the conceptions of matter held by Hume, Kant and the neo-Kantians, to name but a few. Cf., *ibid.*, pp. 227-235 and pp. 253-254. Another volume in which this epistemological question is dealt with is: S. Stricker, *Studien über die Bewegungsvorstellungen*, Vienna, Wilhelm Braumüller, 1882, 72 pp.
52. S. Freud, Project for a Scientific Psychology, *o.c.*, p. 328.

53. W. Jerusalem, *Die Urtheilsfunction, Eine psychologische und erkenntniskritische Untersuchung, o.c.*, p. 86.
54. *Ibid.*, p. 89.
55. *Ibid.*, p. 89-90.
56. In the *Project*, Freud seems to echo Jerusalem's view when he speaks of the unpleasure that is experienced in the event of logical errors: "During a passage of thought, whether it is cognitive, testing, or practical thought, all kinds of events may occur which deserve to be described. Thought may lead to unpleasure or to contradiction." S. Freud, Project for a Scientific Psychology, *o.c.*, p. 380.
57. W. Jerusalem, *Die Urtheilsfunction, Eine psychologische und erkenntniskritische Untersuchung, o.c.*, pp. 92-93.
58. *Ibid.*, p. 94. To Leibniz, apperception consists in "consciousness or the reflective knowledge of the inner condition" that constitutes perception. In his *Critique of Pure Reason*, paragraph 16, Kant defines this concept as the "motion in which an idea is linked to the self-consciousness (empirical apperception). The pure or transcendental apperception is the self-consciousness, the 'I think'." Herbart speaks of the "fusion of an idea or a series of ideas with an earlier kindred idea". Cf. A. Lalande, *Vocabulaire technique et critique de la philosophie*, Paris, PUF, 1976, pp. 66-68.
59. S. Freud, Project for a Scientific Psychology, *o.c.*, pp. 321-324.
60. W. Jerusalem, *Die Urtheilsfunction, Eine psychologische und erkenntniskritische Untersuchung, o.c.*, pp. 97-98.
61. S. Freud, *Project for a Scientific Psychology*, *o.c.*, p. 318.
62. W. Jerusalem, *Die Urtheilsfunction, Eine psychologische und erkenntniskritische Untersuchung, o.c.*, pp. 99-100.
63. *Ibid.*, pp. 99-100.
64. *Ibid.*, p. 102.
65. *Ibid.*, pp. 102-103.
66. *Ibid.*, p. 104-105.
67. *Ibid.*, p. 250. I should like to point out that "biologically serviceable" in Jerusalem's work carries the same meaning as in Freud's *Project*, i.e. that which supports the preservation of the individual and the species.
68. S. Freud, Project for a Scientific Psychology, *o.c.*, p. 334. Freud's emphasis.
69. The function of the attribution of meaning by the other was recently stressed in the 'erverted' schema of homeostasis which is implied in the *Project*. J. Quackelbeen, *De psychoanalytische kliniek en het lichaam*, lecture given in Ghent on 24 April, 1991.
70. For this paragraph, I drew on a paper I published on this subject. F. Geerardyn, De betekenis van het aandachtsmechanisme in het *Entwurf*, *Rondzendbrief uit het Freudiaanse Veld*, 1991, nr.. 48, pp. 31-39.
71. Cf. S. Freud, Negation, (1925*h*), *o.c.*, pp. 233-239.
72. S. Freud, Project for a Scientific Psychology, *o.c.*, p. 324.
73. *Ibid.*, pp. 359.
74. In his later writings Freud seldom went back to the mechanism of attention so explicitly. Nowhere else does one find such an elaborate theoretical passage on psychical reality or the interconnection between the idea and the affect. As far as I

know, this cannot be found in any treatises offering a theoretical explanation for the therapeutic efficiency of speech or in the sparse sections devoted to the mechanism of sublimation. Yet a thorough examination of the mechanism of attention in conjunction with these very topics may be illuminating.

75. This obviously does not refer to a massive release of unpleasure, bur rather a feeling of unease.

76. Another aspect of Jerusalem's conception becomes apparent once again. To him the most important feature of the act of judging lies in its isolating character, i.e. the effect of mastering produced by the judgement. This feature evidently remains not only valid but also important within the talking cure, whose purpose could be described as enabling one to come to terms with a sexual desire in the judgement. However, this goal presupposes a sustained effort governed by the rule of free association. While for Jerusalem inner associations are called to a halt by judgement, Freud departs from the clinical observation that judging (verbal associations) is discontinued by the mechanism of *defence*. In the cure, judgement is necessary for carrying through the process of free association.

77. With regard to the possibility of reconstructing an entire dream, one could raise the objection that one only rarely can spontaneously reach satisfactory results in a single session, as Freud himself over-enthusiastically reports. Normally, association on the basis of one element from a dream leads to other paths than that of the recollection of the entire content of a manifest dream. However, the same pre-condition of attention and naming also applies for these other paths. The analytic setting is neither suited nor sufficient for a full recollection of a forgotten manifest dream, because it does not *per se* intend such reconstructions, and as a result it is unable to mobilise the required amount of attention. The reconstruction and analysis of dreams such as demonstrated by Freud in *The Interpretation of Dreams*, does indeed require a particularly demanding effort of attention.

78. I should like to add that suspended attention and the interpretation of a manifest dream are most efficiently directed towards certain categories of signifiers, such as proper names and nouns.

79. *Ibid.*, p. 323.

80. *Ibid.*, p. 325.

81. *Ibid.*, p. 325.

82. Except when this mnemic image is abundantly cathected, lending it an hallucinatory force. As a rule this is prevented by means of the side-cathexis of primary psychical processes.

83. At this point, Freud introduces his metapsychology of judgement. Cf. S. Freud, Project for a Scientific Psychology, *o.c.*, pp. 327-335.

84. *Ibid.*, p. 365. The connection between "ψ neurones with neurones which serve sound-presentations" echoes Freud's theory on the origin of meaning as being determined by the association between the word-presentation and object-presentation. Cf. the discussion of *On Aphasia*.

85. I should like to direct the attention of those who wish to ascertain the relevance of the *Project* for Freud's later works to the footnotes provided by the Editor of the

Standard Edition. These footnotes virtually permeate Freud's entire oeuvre. I should also like to mention an excellent study which painstakingly mapped out these references, namely G. Endrass, *Zur Geschichte und Systematik von Qualität in Freuds Metapsychology*, *o.c.*

86. J. Quackelbeen, Lectures *Principes en methoden van de psychologische raadpleging*, academic year 1981-1982. Every year, this is indirectly corroborated by the effect produced by the classes devoted to the subject of the unconscious. The curriculum of the students is invariably determined by a judgement relative to the unconscious, once they have become acquainted with the "nuisance".

87. It is thence decidedly not the case that these two discoveries are exclusively to be attributed to Freud's self-analysis. In addition, one should not lose sight of the fact that at the time he was writing the *Project*, he already had five children between the ages of two and eight, which must have been of significance to a subtle observer such as Freud.

CONCLUSION

1. J. Lacan, *The Seminar, Book IX, The Four Fundamental Concepts of Psychoanalysis 1964*, Edited by J.-A. Miller, Translated by A. Sheridan, Harmondsworth, Penguin Books, 1991, p. 263.

BIBLIOGRAPHY

ARISTOTLE, *Poetics*, in *The Complete Works of Aristotle, The Revised Oxford Translation*, vol. II, Edited by J. Barnes, Princeton, Princeton University Press, 1984, pp. 2316-2340; *Poetica*, (335-323), Dutch Translation by N. van der Ben and J.M. Bremer, Amsterdam, Athenaeum, 1988, 215 pp.

ANZIEU, D., *L'auto-analyse de Freud et la découverte de la psychanalyse*, Paris, PUF, 1988, 554 pp.

ASSOUN, P.-L., *Introduction à l'épistémologie freudienne*, Paris, Payot, 1981, 223 pp.

BERNFELD, S., Freuds früheste Theorien und die Helmholtz-Schule, (1944), in: Bernfeld, S. and Bernfeld, S.C., *Bausteine der Freud-Biographik*, Frankfurt am Main, Suhrkamp, 1988, pp. 54-77.

BERNFELD, S. and BERNFELD, S.C., *Bausteine der Freud-Biographik*, Frankfurt am Main, Suhrkamp, 1988, 288 pp.

BERNHEIM, H., *Suggestive Therapeutics, A Treatise on the Nature and Uses of Hypnotism*, (1887), Translated from the second and revised French Edition by Christian A. Herter, 11 ed., Putnam's Sons, New York/London, 1899, 420 pp.; *Die Suggestion und ihre Heilwirkung*, (1888), Autorisierte deutsche Ausgabe von Dr. Sigm. Freud, Tübingen, Diskord, 1985, 415 pp.

BILLIET, L., Freuds topografische voorstellingen, *Rondzendbrief uit het Freudiaanse Veld*, 1982, nrs. 9/10, 1982, pp. 15-22.

BINSWANGER, L., Freud et la constitution de la psychiatrie clinique, (1936), in *Discours, parcours et Freud*, Paris, Gallimard, 1970, 360 pp.

BODIFÉE, G., *Ruimte voor vrijheid*, Kapellen, Pelckmans, 1988, 236 pp.

BODIFÉE, G., *Het zichtbare en het denkbare*, Kapellen, Pelckmans, 1990, 160 pp.

BODIFÉE, G., *Het vreemde van de aarde*, Kapellen, Pelckmans, 1990, 181 pp.

BREUER, J., Bericht über 'Nina R.', (1978 [1893]), *G.W.*, Nachtragsband, p. 320.

BREUER, J. and FREUD, S., (1893*a*), On the Psychical Mechanism of Hysterical Phenomena: Preliminary Communication, *S.E.*, vol. II, pp. 1-17.

BREUER, J. and FREUD, S., (1895*d*), *Studies on Hysteria*, S.E., vol. II, pp. 1-305.

BROCA, P., *Sur le siège de la faculté du langage articulé avec deux observations d'aphémie (perte de la parole)*, Paris, 1861.

BUELENS, J., *Sigmund Freud, Kind van zijn tijd*, Meppel, Boom, 1971, 334 pp.

BUM, A. and SCHNIRER, M.T., *Diagnostisches Lexikon für praktische Ärzte*, Wien, 1893, Bd. 1.

CARTAZ, M., Du mutisme hystérique, d'après les leçons de M. Charcot, (1887), in: *Charcot, J.-M., Leçons sur les maladies du système nerveux, Faites à la Salpêtrière*, Paris, A. Delahaye et E. Lecrosnie, 1887, pp. 481-506.

CHARCOT, J.-M., *Essai d'une distinction nosographique des divers états nerveux compris sous le nom d'hypnotisme*, Note communiquée à l'Académie des Sciences, 1883.

CHARCOT, J.-M., *Clinical Lectures on the Diseases of the Nervous System*, (1887), English translation by T. Savill, London, Routledge, 1991, 433 pp.; *Leçons sur les maladies du système nerveux, Faites à la Salpêtrière*, Paris, A. Delahaye et E. Lecrosnie, 1887, 518 pp.

CLARKE, E. and DEWHURST, K., *Die Funktionen des Gehirns, Lokalisationstheorien von der Antike bis zur Gegenwart*, München, Heinz Moos Verlag, 1973, 157 pp.

CRANEFIELD, P.F., Josef Breuer's Evaluation of His Contribution to Psychoanalysis, *International Journal of Psychoanalysis*, 1958, vol. 39, pp. 319-322.

DARWIN, C., *The Expression of the Emotions in Man and Animals*, (1872), Chicago, The University of Chicago Press, 1970.

DELBOEUF, J., *Le sommeil et les rêves*, Paris, 1885.

DU BOIS-REYMOND, E., *Jugendbriefe von Emil du Bois-Reymond an Edoard Hallmann*, (1918), Berlin, D. Reimer.

DECLERCQ, F., Het verlangen om te weten dient de passie der onwetendheid, *Rondzendbrief uit het Freudiaanse Veld*, 1991, nr. 47, pp. 51-66.

DUYCKAERTS, F., Sigmund Freud: lecteur de Joseph Delboeuf, *Frénésie, Histoire, Psychiatrie, Psychanalyse*, 1989, II, nr. 8, pp. 1-88.

ENDRASS, G., *Zur Geschichte und Systematik von Qualität und Quantität in Freuds Metapsychologie*, Dissertation zur Erlangung der Würde eines Dokters der Philosophie, Basel, Clausthal-Zellerfeld, 1975, 359 pp.

EVANS, D., *An Introductory Dictionary of Lacanian Psychoanalysis*, London, Routledge, 1996, 239 pp.

EXNER, S., *Entwurf zu einer physiologischen Erklärung der psychischen Erscheinungen*, Leipzig and Vienna, Franz Deuticke, 1894, pp. 380 pp.

FECHNER, G.T., *Einige Ideen zur Schöpfungs- und Entwicklungsgeschichte der Organismen*, (1873), Tübingen, Edition Diskord, 1985, 108 pp.

FLIESS, W., Die nasale Reflexneurose, (1893), in: *Verhandlungen des Kongresses für innere Medizin*, 12. Kongreß, pp. 391 e.v.

FREGE, G., On Sense and Reference, in *Translations of the Philosophical Writings of Gottlob Frege*, Edited by P. Geach and M. Black, Oxford, Basil Blackwell, 1966, pp. 56-78; Über Sinn und Bedeutung, (1892), *Zeitschrift für Philosophie und philosophische Kritiek*, nr. 100, pp. 25-50.

FREUD, S., Observations of a Severe Case of Hemianaesthesia in a Hysterical Male, (1886*d*), *S.E.*, vol. I, pp. 23-31.
FREUD, S., Hysteria, (1888*b3*), *S.E.*, vol. I, pp. 37-57.
FREUD, S., Hystero-Epilepsy, (1888*b4*), *S.E.*, vol. I, pp. 58-59.
FREUD, S., Preface to the Translation of Bernheims *Suggestion*, (1888-89), *S.E.*, vol. I, pp. 71-87.
FREUD, S., Psychical (or Mental) Treatment, (1890*a*), *S.E.*, vol. VII, pp. 281-302.
FREUD, S., *On Aphasia, A Critical Study*, (1891*b*), New York, International University Press, 1953, xv + 105 pp.
FREUD, S., A case of Successful Treatment by Hypnotism — With Some Remarks on the Origin of Hysterical Symptoms through 'Counter Will', (1892-93*a*), *S.E.*, vol. I, pp. 115-128.
FREUD, S., Preface and Footnotes to the Translation of Charcot's *Tuesday Lectures*, (1892-4*a*), *S.E.*, vol. I, pp. 129-143.
FREUD, S., Some Points for a Comparative Study of Organic & Hysterical Motor Paralyses, (1893*c*), *S.E.*, vol. I, pp. 155-172.
FREUD, S., Charcot, (1893*f*), *S.E.*, vol. III, pp. 25-39.
FREUD, S., On the Psychical Mechanism of Hysterical Phenomena: a Lecture, (1893*h*), *S.E.*, vol. III, pp. 25-39.
FREUD, S., The Neuro-Psychosis of Defence (An Attempt at a Psychological Theory of Acquired Hysteria, of Many Phobias and Obsessions and of Certain Hallucinatory Psychoses), (1894*a*), *S.E.*, vol. III, pp. 41-61.
FREUD, S., On the Grounds for Detaching a Particular Syndrome from Neurasthenia under the Description 'Anxiety Neurosis', (1895*b* [1894]), *S.E.*, vol. III, pp. 85-115.
FREUD, S., Obsessions and Phobias, (1895*c* [1894]), *S.E.*, vol. III, pp. 69-82.
FREUD, S., Über Hysterie, zwei zeitgenössische Berichte über einen dreiteiligen Vortrag, gehalten am 14., 21., und 28 Oktober 1895, im Wiener medizinischen Doktorenkollegium, (1895*g*), *G.W.*, Nachtragsband, pp. 328-351.
FREUD, S., Heredity and the Aetiology of the Neuroses, (1896*a*), *S.E.*, vol. III, pp. 141-156.
FREUD, S., *The Interpretation of Dreams*, (1900*a*), *S.E.*, vol. IV-V, pp. 1-621.
FREUD, S., *Fragment of an Analysis of a Case of Hysteria*, (1905*e* [1901]), *S.E.*, VII, pp. 1-122.
FREUD, S., The Theme of the Three Caskets, (1913*f*), *S.E.*, vol. XII, pp. 289-301.
FREUD, S., On the History of the Psycho-Analytic Movement, (1914*d*), *S.E.*, vol. XIV, pp. 1-66.
FREUD, S., Remembering, Repeating and Working-Through, (1914*g*), *S.E.*, vol. XII, pp. 145-156.
FREUD, S., The Unconscious, (1915*e*), *S.E.*, vol. XIV, pp. 159-215.
FREUD, S., *Beyond the Pleasure Principle*, (1920*g*), *S.E.*, vol. XVIII, pp. 1-64.
FREUD, S., *Group Psychology and the Analysis of the Ego*, (1921*c*), *S.E.*, vol. XVIII, pp. 65-143.
FREUD, S., Two Encyclopedia Articles: a) Psycho-Analysis; b) Libido Theory, (1923*a* [1922]), *S.E.*, vol. XVIII, pp. 235-259.
FREUD, S., *An Autobiographical Study*, (1925*d*), *S.E.*, vol. XX, pp. 1-70.
FREUD, S., Negation, (1925*h*), *S.E.*, vol. XIX, pp. 233-239.

FREUD, S., Address Delivered in the Goethe House at Frankfurt, (1930*e*), *S.E.*, vol. XXI, pp. 206-212.

FREUD, S., Analysis Terminable and Interminable, (1937*c*), *S.E.*, vol. XXIII, pp. 209-253.

FREUD, S., Constructions in Analysis, (1937*d*), *S.E.*, vol. XXIII, pp. 255-269.

FREUD, S., Splitting of the Ego in the Process of Defence, (1940*e* [1938]), *S.E.*, vol. XXIII, pp. 271-278.

FREUD, S., Project for a Scientific Psychology, (1950*c*), *S.E.*, vol. I, pp. 281-397; Ontwerp van een natuurwetenschappelijke psychologie, (1950*c*), Translated into Dutch by G. Van de Vijver and F. Geerardyn, Ghent, Idesça, Pegasosreeks nr. 8, 1992, xxx + 81 pp.

FREUD, S., Report on my Studies in Paris and Berlin, (1956*a* [1886]), *S.E.*, vol. I, pp. 1-15.

FREUD, S., *Letters of Sigmund Freud 1873-1939*, (1960*a*), English Translation by T. and J. Stern, London, The Hogarth Press, 1961.

FREUD, S., Anamnese 'Nina R.', (1978*a* [1891]), *G.W.*, Nachtragsband, pp. 313-315.

FREUD, S., Krankengeschichte 'Nina R.', (1978*b* [1893]), *G.W.*, Nachtragsband, pp. 316-319.

FREUD, S., Brief an Robert Binswanger vom 7 jan. 1894, (1978*c* [1894]), *G.W.*, Nachtragsband, p. 321.

FREUD, S., *The Complete Letters of Sigmund Freud to Wilhelm Fließ 1887-1904* (1985*c* [1887-1904]), English translation by J.M. Masson, Cambridge, Massachusetts and London, The Belknap Press of Harvard University Press, 1985, pp. 505.

FRIJDA, N., *The Emotions*, Cambridge, Cambridge University Press, 1986, 544 pp.

GAY, P., *Freud, A Life for Our Times*, New York, Norton, 1988.

GEERARDYN, F., The Princeps Case of Psychoanalysis: Breuer's Anna O. Revisited, *Journal of the Centre for Freudian Analysis and Research*, 1994, 4, pp. 54-70.

GEERARDYN, F., Eerste tijd van de psychoanalyse of de tijd van de verzoeking. Over de ver-concepten I, *Rondzendbrief uit het Freudiaanse Veld*, 1989, nr. 36, pp. 51-65.

GEERARDYN, F., Van de verzoeking naar de verhouding. Over de ver-concepten II, *Rondzendbrief uit het Freudiaanse Veld*, 1989, nr. 37, pp. 3-15.

GEERARDYN, F., 'Le moment de conclure': gods wegen zijn doorgrondelijk. Over de ver-concepten III, in: *Fragmenten uit de geschiedenis van de psychoanalyse. Een parcours onder overdracht*, Rijksuniversiteit Ghent, 1991, pp. 3-13.

GEERARDYN, F., Freuds *Entwurf*: neurologie of psychologie?, in: *Fragmenten uit de geschiedenis van de psychoanalyse, Een parcours onder overdracht*, Universiteit Ghent, 1991, pp. 27-43.

GEERARDYN, F., De betekenis van het aandachtsmechanisme in het *Entwurf*, *Rondzendbrief uit het Freudiaanse Veld*, 1991, nr. 48, pp. 31-39.

GEERARDYN, F., Voorbij biografie en vaderanalyse. Siegfried Bernfelds Freud, *Rondzendbrief uit het Freudiaanse Veld*, 1992, nr. 50, pp. 14-21.

GEERARDYN, F., Paul Julius Möbius: een gemiste ontmoeting met de psychologie?, *Rondzendbrief uit het Freudiaanse Veld*, 1993, nr. 56, pp. 3-12.

GOETHE, von J.W., *Faust*, Translated by John Anster, London, Harrap, 1985, 256 pp.

GRÜNBAUM, A., *The Foundations of Psychoanalysis, A Philosophical Critique*, Berkeley, Los Angeles and Londen, University of California Press, 1984, pp. 3-5.

HERMANN, I., Das Ich und das Denken, *Imago*, 1929, XV, nr. 1, pp. 89-110 and nr. 3/4, pp. 325-348.

HIRSCHMÜLLER, A., *The life and work of Josef Breuer, Physiology and Psychoanalysis*, (1978), New York and Londen, New York University Press, 1989, 514 pp.

HYPPOLITE, J., Commentaire parlé sur la "Verneinung" de Freud, in: Lacan, J., *Ecrits*, Paris, du Seuil, 1966, pp. 879-887.

ISRAËL, L., *L'hystérique, le sexe et le médecin*, Paris, Masson, 253 pp.

JERUSALEM, W., *Die Urtheilsfunction, Eine psychologische und erkenntniskritische Untersuchung*, Vienna and Leipzig, Wilhelm Braumüller, 1895, 269 pp.

JERUSALEM, W., *Lehrbuch der Psychologie*, (1888), 5th ed., Vienna and Leipzig, 1912, 217 pp.

JERUSALEM, W., Mein curriculum vitae, in: *Gedanken und Denker*, Vienna, 1925, pp. 10-35.

JONES, E., *Sigmund Freud, Life and Work*, (1953), Londen, The Hogarth Press, vol. I, 1972, 454 pp.

JONCKHEERE, L., Freud met of zonder, *Rondzendbrief uit het Freudiaanse Veld*, 1988, nr. 29, pp. 55-56.

KALTENBECK, F., Sigmund Freud et Wilhelm Jerusalem, *Ornicar?*, 1985, nr. 32, pp. 87-113.

KNIGHT, I.F., Freud's "Project": a theory for *Studies on hysteria*, *Journal of the History of the Behavioural Sciences*, 1984, nr. 4, pp. 340-358.

KRIS, E., Introduction, (1954), in: S. Freud, *The Origins of Psychoanalysis, Letters to Wilhelm Fließ*, (1950c), New York, Basic Books, pp. 3-47.

LACAN, J., Le mythe individuel du névrosé ou Poésie et Vérité dans la névrose, (1953), in *Ornicar ?, revue du Champ freudien*, 1979, nr. 17/18, pp. 289-307.

LACAN, J., *The Seminar, Book I, Freud's Papers on Technique, 1953-1954*, Edited by J.-A. Miller, Translated with Notes by John Forrester, Cambridge, Cambridge University Press, 1988, 314 pp.

LACAN, J., *The Seminar, Book III, The Psychoses, 1955-1956*, Edited by J.-A. Miller, Translated with Notes by Russell Grigg, New York, Norton, 1993, 341 pp.

LACAN, J., Introduction au commentaire de Jean Hyppolite sur la "Verneinung" de Freud, (1956), *Ecrits*, Paris, du Seuil, 1966, pp. 369-380.

LACAN, J., Réponse au commentaire de Jean Hyppolite sur la "Verneinung" de Freud, (1956), *Ecrits*, Paris, du Seuil, 1966, pp. 381-399.

LACAN, J., *The Seminar, Book VII, The Ethics of Psychoanalysis, (1959-1960)*, Edited by J.-A. Miller, Translated with notes by Dennis Porter, London, Routledge, 1992, 342 pp.

LACAN, J., *Le Séminaire, Livre VIII, Le Transfert*, (1960-1961), Paris, du Seuil, 1991, 460 pp.

LACAN, J., *Le Séminaire, Livre X, L'angoisse*, (1962-1963), unpublished.

LACAN, J., *The Seminar, Book XI, The Four Fundamental Concepts of Psychoanalysis 1964*, Edited by J.-A. Miller, Translated by A. Sheridan, Harmondsworth, Penguin Books, 1991, 290 pp.

LALANDE, A., *Vocabulaire technique et critique de la philosophie*, Paris, PUF, 1976.

LEVIN, K., *Freud's Early Psychology of the Neuroses, A Historical Perspective*, Brighton, Harvester Press, 1978, 314 pp.

LIBBRECHT, K., *Hysterische waan. Symptoom of structuur?*, Ghent, Idesça, Pegasosreeks nr. 3, 1989, 175 pp.

LIBBRECHT, K., Mystici, hysterici en hun verhouding tot de Andere, *Rondzendbrief uit het Freudiaanse Veld*, 1991, nr. 47, pp. 41-50.

LIBBRECHT, K., *Hysterical Psychosis: A Historical Survey*, New Jersey, Transaction, 1994.
LIBBRECHT, K., Enkele opmerkingen over het statuut van het trauma en het concept van de psychische realiteit, *Rondzendbrief uit het Freudiaanse Veld*, 1992, nr. 50, pp. 33-37.
LORRÉ, D., De epistemologische coupure van Freud en de pedagogiek, 1987, nr. 26, pp. 1987, pp. 45-53.
MANNONI, O., 'L'analyse originelle', *Clefs pour l'imaginaire*, Paris, du Seuil, 1969, 319 pp.
MARCUS, S., Introductory Essay, (1977), in: FREUD, S., *The Origins of Psychoanalysis, Letters to Wilhelm Fließ*, (1950c), New York, Basis Books, p. vii-xix.
MASSON, J.M., *The Assault on Truth, Freud's Suppression of the Seduction Theory*, Farrar, Straus and Giroux, New York, 1984.
MAUDSLEY, H., *Physiology and Pathology of mind*, Londen, 1868.
MAURY, L.F.A., Nouvelles observations sur les analogies des phénomènes du rêve et de l'aliénation mentale, *Annales médico-psychologiques*, 1853, nr. 5.
MAURY, L.F.A., *Le sommeil et les rêves*, Paris, 1878.
MEYNERT, Th., Über hypnotische Erscheinungen, *Wiener klinische Wochenschrift*, 1888, nr. 22, pp. 451-453, nr. 23, pp. 473-476 en nr. 24, pp. 495-498.
MEYNERT, Th., Über Hypnotismus, *Wiener Medizinische Blätter*, 1888, nr. 23, pp. 718-720.
MÖBIUS, P.J., *Goethe*, (1909), I. Theil, Leipzig, Johann Ambrosius Verlag, 188 pp.
MCLAUGHLIN, C., *Corpus Linguistics, Collocation and Translation Studies*, M.A. Dissertation, Dublin City University, 1996.
NASSIF, J., *Freud, L'inconscient*, Paris, Flammarion, 1992, 637 pp.
NUNBERG, H. and FEDERN, E. (eds.), *Protokolle der Wiener Psychoanalytischen Vereinigung, Band I 1906-1906*, Frankfurt am Main, Fischer, 385 pp.
PLATTEAU, W., Een referentiekader voor de gevalsstudies van Freud, *Psychoanalytische Perspektieven*, 1982, nr. 2, pp. 11-183.
PRIBRAM, K.H., The Neuropsychology of Sigmund Freud, in: Bachrach, A.J. (ed.), *Experimental Foundations of Clinical Psychology*, New York, 1962, Chapter XIII, pp. 442-468.
PRIBRAM, K.H., Freud's Project: An Open, Biologically Based Model for Psychoanalysis, in: Greenfield, N.S. and Lewis, W.C. (eds.), *Psycho-analysis and Current Biological Thought*, Madison, Milwaukee, 1965, pp. 81-92.
PRIBRAM, K.H. and GILL, M.M., *Freud's Project Re-Assessed. Preface to Contemporary Cognitive Theory and Neuropsychology*, New York, Basic Books, 1976, 181 pp.
QUACKELBEEN, J., *Colleges principes en methodes van de psychologische raadpleging*, Academiejaar 1981-1982, Ghent, University of Ghent.
QUACKELBEEN, J., Een problematisch herlezen van de gevalsstudies van Freud, *Psychoanalytische Perspektieven*, 1982, nr. 2., pp. 5-9.
QUACKELBEEN, J., Bij een proefvertaling van "Science et vérité" van J. Lacan, *Rondzendbrief uit het Freudiaanse Veld*, 1982, nr. 7., p. 32.
QUACKELBEEN, J., Welke plaats verleent Lacan aan de psychische energie, het affect en de drift?, *Rondzendbrief uit het Freudiaanse Veld*, 1984, nr. 13, pp. 5-26.
QUACKELBEEN, J. (ed.), *Psychoanalyse en klinische psychiatrie: Een geschiedenis van eigenheid of verbondenheid?*, Ghent, Idesça, Pegasosreeks nr. 2, 1987, 164 pp.
QUACKELBEEN, J., De Freudiaanse epistemologische coupure en haar effecten voor de pedagogiek, *Rondzendbrief uit het Freudiaanse veld*, 1987, nr. 26, pp. 3-22.

QUACKELBEEN, J., *De 'mannelijke' hysterie. Hoe mannelijk?*, Colleges Grondige studie van een auteur en/of een nosologisch concept uit het klinisch verleden, Academiejaar 1990-1991, Ghent, University of Ghent.

QUACKELBEEN, J., *Zeven avonden met Jacques Lacan, Psychoanalytische commentaren bij 'Télévision'*, Ghent, Academia Press, 1991, 230 pp.

QUACKELBEEN, J., *De psychoanalytische kliniek en het lichaam*, uiteenzetting in het kader van de panelavond over het lichaam op 24 april 1991, University of Ghent.

QUACKELBEEN, J. and LIBBRECHT, K., On the Early History Of Male Hysteria and Psychic Trauma, *Charcot's Influence on Freudian Thought, Journal of the History of Behavioural Sciences*, 1995, vol. 31, 4, pp. 370-384.

ROSENFIELD, I., *The Invention of Memory: A New View of the Brain*, New York, Basic Books, 1988.

ROUDINESCO, E., *La bataille de cent ans. Histoire de la psychanalyse en France*, vol. I, Paris, du Seuil, 1986, 490 pp.

RUSSELMAN, G.H.E., *Van James Watt tot Sigmund Freud, De opkomst van het stuwmodel van de zelfexpressie*, Deventer, Van Loghum Slaterus, 1983, 413 pp.

SAUVAGNAT, F., Le sujet du jugement: une réponse à la controverse de l'infaillibilité pontificale, *Cahiers de lectures freudiennes*, 1986, nr. 10, pp. 43-53.

SCHEULEN, C., Menstruatieangsten (Dutch translation by G. Van de Vijver), *Rondzendbrief uit het Freudiaanse Veld*, 1989, nr. 36, pp. 31-34.

S.N., Wegwerktekst, *Rondzendbrief uit het Freudiaanse Veld*, 1991, nr. 46, pp. 46-47.

SOLMS, M. and SALING, M., *A Moment of Transition, Two Neuroscientific Articles by Sigmund Freud*, London, Karnac Books, 1990, 164 pp.

STENGEL, E., Introduction, in: S. Freud, *On Aphasia, A Critical Study*, (1891*b*), New York, International University Press, 1953, xv + 105 pp. pp.

STEPHAN, A., *Sinn als Bedeutung, Bedeutungstheoretische Untersuchungen zur Psychoanalyse Sigmund Freuds*, Berlin, Walter de Gruyter, 1989, 174 pp.

STRACHEY, J., Editor's Introduction to the *Studies on Hysteria*, in: Freud, S., *S.E.*, vol. II, pp. ix-xviii.

STRICKER, S., *Studien über die Bewegungsvorstellungen*, Wenen, Wilhelm Braumüller, 1882, 72 pp.

SULLOWAY, F.J., *Freud, Biologist of the Mind*, Londen, Burnett Books, 1979, 612 pp.

SZAFRAN, W., Voorwoord bij: S. Freud, Ontwerp van een natuurwetenschappelijke psychologie, (1950*c*), Ghent, Idesça, Pegasosreeks nr. 8, 1992, pp. vii-viii.

TRILLAT, E., *Histoire de l'hystérie*, Paris, Editions Seghers, 1986, 282 pp.

VAN CAMP, I., Freuds model van het psychisme: een vraag naar wetenschappelijke waarde en interne consistentie, *Rondzendbrief uit het Freudiaanse Veld*, 1988, nr. 29, pp. 61-77.

VANDAMME, F., *Spraak- en taalontwikkeling en stoornissen*, Ghent, Communication and Cognition, 1986, 144 p.

VAN DER BEN, N. and BREMER, J.M., Katharsis, in: Aristoteles, *Poetica*, (335-323), Dutch Translation by N. van der Ben and J.M. Bremer, Amsterdam, Athenaeum, 1988, pp. 177-193.

VAN DE VIJVER, G., Het ontstaan van betekenis: argumenten voor een schematisme van de struktuur, *Rondzendbrief uit het Freudiaanse Veld*, 1986, nr. 4, pp. 27-43.

VAN DE VIJVER, G., Morfogenese en betekenis: een pleidooi voor het onmogelijke?, *Psychoanalytische Perspektieven*, 1987, nr. 11, pp. 267-270.

VAN DE VIJVER, G., Terugblik op een interview, *Psychoanalytische Perspektieven*, 1988, nr. 12, pp. 141-142.

VAN DE VIJVER, G., Tussen een fenomenaal en een noumenaal onbewuste — vragen naar de constitutie van het object van de psychoanalyse. Een interview met Jean Petitot, *Psychoanalytische Perspektieven*, 1988, nr. 12, pp. 143-156.

VAN DE VIJVER, G., Hoe seksuele betekenissen emergeren. Naar aanleiding van een vertaling, *Rondzendbrief uit het Freudiaanse Veld*, 1989, nr. 36, pp. 35-38.

VAN DE VIJVER, G., De receptie van wetenschappelijk-epistemologische werken in de psychoanalyse. Naar aanleiding van 'Entre le temps et l'Eternité', *Rondzendbrief uit het Freudiaanse Veld*, 1989, nr. 38, pp. 33-37.

VAN DE VIJVER, G., *Van cybernetica naar connectionisme, Een epistemologische studie van doelgerichtheid*, Ghent, Academia Press, 1991, 375 pp.

VAN DE VIJVER, G., Freud, Husserl en de cognitieve wetenschappen, *Rondzendbrief uit het Freudiaanse Veld*, 1991, nr. 48, pp. 3-30.

VAN DE VIJVER, G. and GEERARDYN, F., Over het statuut van het *Ontwerp* als psychoanalytische tekst. Inleiding, in: Freud, S., Ontwerp van een natuurwetenschappelijke psychologie, (1950*c*), Ghent, Idesça, Pegasosreeks nr. 8, 1992, pp. ix-xxx.

VAN DE VIJVER, G. and VAN DORMAEL, J., Colleges *Logica en Taalwetenschap*, Academiejaar 1990-1991, University of Ghent.

VAN DYCKE, K., "Facts and Figures" versus "Alice in Wonderland". De controverse over de verleidingstheorie, naar aanleiding van J.M. Masson, *Rondzendbrief uit het Freudiaanse Veld*, 1986, nr. 22, pp. 23-37.

VAN EEDEN, F., Het beginsel der psychotherapie, (1894), in: *Frederik van Eeden, Een bloemlezing uit zijn studies*, Katwijk, Servire, 1982, 288 pp.

VAN HOORDE, H., De driften, *Rondzendbrief uit het Freudiaanse Veld*, 1990, nr. 43, pp. 7-31.

VAN HOORDE, H., Inleiding tot de vergadering van het 'Gezelschap voor psychoanalyse en psychotherapie' te Gent in het Flanders Hotel op 30 september 1990, *Rondzendbrief uit het Freudiaanse Veld*, 1991, nr. 46, pp. 15-19.

VAN HOORDE, H., *Psychiatrie en psychoanalyse, Scheiding van tafel en bank?*, Ghent, Idesça, Pegasosreeks nr. 9, 1992, 193 pp.

VERHAEGHE, P., Toelichtende nota bij de vertaling van een weinig gekende, vroege tekst van S. Freud, *Psychoanalytische Perspektieven*, 1984, nr. 6, pp. 19-21.

VERHAEGHE, P., De metafoor van de energie: een metonymie, *Psychoanalytische Perspektieven*, nr. 6., 1984, pp. 155-156.

VERHAEGHE, P., *Does the Woman Exist ?, From Freud's Hysteric to Lacan's Feminine*, Translated by M. Du Ry, London, Rebus Press, 1996, 269 pp.

VERHAEGHE, P., Van psychotherapie naar psychoanalyse: ethiek en aporie, *Rondzendbrief uit het Freudiaanse Veld*, 1987, nr. 27, pp. 3-17.

VERHAEGHE, P., Determinisme en causaliteit in de psychoanalyse: tuche en automaton, *Rondzendbrief uit het Freudiaanse Veld*, 1989, nr. 35, pp. 15-30.

VERHAEGHE, P., *Klinische psychodiagnostiek vanuit de discourstheorie*, Ghent, Idesça, Pegasosreeks nr. 5, 1991, 211 pp.

VILLARET, A., *Handwörterbuch der gesammten Medizin*, Stuttgart, Ferdinand Enke Verlag, 1888-1891.

VON STRÜMPELL, A., *Über die Entstehung und die Heilung von Krankheiten durch Vorstellungen*, Erlangen, 1844.

WEINBERG, A., Theodor Gomperz and John Stuart Mill, *Travaux de droit, d'économie, de sociologie et de sciences politiques*, 1963, nr. 16, 63 pp.

WERNICKE, C., *Der aphasische Symptomencomplex*, Breslau, 1874.

WIESENTHAL, S., Interview met Martin van Amerongen in *De Morgen* van 29 augustus 1992.

INDEX